# THE

# GREAT AMERICAN

# QUOTE BOOK

### compiled by

### Jim  Duriga

**First Edition**

ISBN 1-889991-50-3

Published by Seneca-Secor Books, P.O. Box 3062, Bakersfield, California, 93385.

## ABOUT THE COVER:

The cover design and layout is by Jim Duriga.  To the best of our knowledge, all photos used on the cover are in the public domain and/or freely distributable.  Should you have any concerns about a photo used, please contact us at jduriga@seneca-secor.com and we will resolve the issue immediately.

# DISCLAIMERS AND NOTIFICATIONS

It is my sincere belief that all the quotations within this book are in the public domain or freely available and thus allowed under appropriate laws of fair use. I have tried in all cases to give proper identification of the person to whom the quote is attributed.

Quotes are difficult, because often the person being quoted is merely the person who made the saying famous, not the person who originated it; I have tried to cross-check sources where possible. There is a second problem with quotes - often in the case of politicians and actors, the person who came up with the quotation is an uncredited script or speech writer, while the politician or actor who voiced the line gets the creedit for the quote.

If anyone should have a concern, please contact me at jduriga@seneca-secor.com and I will attempt to resolve the concerns immediately.

Thanks,

Jim Duriga

# ABOUT THE AUTHOR

Jim Duriga's poetry and articles have appeared in many collections and magazines over the years, including Army In Europe magazine, Atlantis Magazine, the **Of The I Sing** poetry anthology, the **Poetry-Coast To Coast** Anthology, and others. In addition, his 'crudely drawn but highly philosophical' Leroy cartoons have appeared in a variety of college and other newspapers and magazines over the last 40 years. His own books include poetry collections, cartoon collections, books about Kern County, California, books about the Monkees, books about Star Trek, and 'Alternate Universe' books about George Armstrong Custer. For several years in the mid-90s, Jim edited a nationwide Commodore Amiga Newsletter called **AMIGAMERICA**.

Jim Holds a BA in English from Mount Union College (Alliance, Ohio), a MA degree in English from California State University (Bakersfield, California), and an honorary PhD in Religion. In addition to being an Army Vietnam-era veteran, Jim is an ordained minister who doesn't preach.

While his work has been published by a variety of venues, he also owns and operates **Seneca-Secor Books**, a regional press in Bakersfield California. **Seneca** has made a continuing effort to publish books by new authors and little-known authors. The firm has also released several poetry and Sci-Fi anthologies in an effort to help authors gain exposure. The proceeds from several Seneca-Secor books (including **Trekkies, Trekkers, and Red Shirts** and **No Graceful Aging**) are being donated various charities.

Jim has been referred to the 'Knower of All Things Star Trek' by the **GreaseTrek** Website, and has received a variety of favorable reviews for his books online.

Jim's company, **Seneca-Secor Books** has been publishing books since the early 1970s and maintains worldwide distribution and a presence on the Internet through such sites as *Amazon.com, Barnes And Noble.com*, and *Borders.com*. Jim's books can be found and purchased the world over.

# FORWARD

We live in polarized times in which no one listens - political parties have become more important than the country's business, religious leaders call names with no thought of communicating, and music (which used to bring us all together) now serves to pull us apart. Perhaps if we can remember how much we have in common, rather than the things which divide us, we can begin to put our bickering aside.

I have included quotes from a variety of religious leaders, atheists, scientists, politicians, authors, comedians, writers, artists, comedians, and others.  All the presidents are included as are most of America's best and brightest.

If you read these quotes, you'll notice that we are all more alike than different. We all want America to succeed, regardless of where in the political or religious spectrum we happen to be. You may just realize  that we have more in common than we have things which divide us.

At this point, I would like to include two quotes not found elsewhere in the book which have influenced my own life;

The first is a line from the **Bret Maverick Theme Song** written by
Ed Bruce, Glenn Ray and Patsy Bruce and sung by James Garner and Ed Bruce.

*My ole pappy always told me your fate is in your hand*
*Stand pat or draw, it's yours to choose*
*Luck don't have a thing to do with how you play the game*
*Maverick didn't come here to lose.*

The other one is another song lyric, written by Fran Powers and sung by Dennis Weaver in the 1970s; the song is called **No Name**;

*Its not who you are - its what you do with what you have.*

I think both these remind us that how we act, treat others  and react is always more important than the things which might happen to us.  I think you'll find that many of the quotes in this book (including by people you thought you hated) touch a nerve or carry the same message.

Jim

# TABLE OF CONTENTS

# TABLE OF CONTENTS (Continued)

# TABLE OF CONTENTS (Continued)

# TABLE OF CONTENTS (Continued)

# TABLE OF CONTENTS (Continued)

# TABLE OF CONTENTS (Continued)

# TABLE OF CONTENTS (Continued)

## TABLE OF CONTENTS (Continued)

# EDWARD ABBEY (Author, 1927-1989)

You can't study the darkness by flooding it with light.

Grown men do not need leaders.

Society is like a stew. If you don't stir it up every once in a
while then a layer of scum floats to the top.

Growth for the sake of growth is the ideology of the cancer cell.

Power is always dangerous. Power attracts the worst and corrupts
the best.

Our 'neoconservatives' are neither new nor conservative, but old as
Bablyon and evil as Hell.

May your trails be crooked, winding, lonesome, dangerous, leading
to the most amazing view. May your mountains rise into and
above the clouds.

The missionaries go forth to Christianize the savages - as if the savages
weren't dangerous enough already.

Love implies anger. The man who is angered by nothing cares about nothing.

If the end does not justify the means - what can?

There is science, logic, reason; there is thought verified by experience. And
then there is California.

That which today calls itself science gives us more and more information,
and indigestible glut of information, and less and less understanding.

The idea of wilderness needs no defense, it only needs defenders.

The tragedy of modern war is that the young men die fighting each
other - instead of their real enemies back home in the capitals.

What is the purpose of the giant sequoia tree? The purpose of the
giant sequoia tree is to provide shade for the tiny titmouse.

When a man's best friend is his dog, that dog has a problem.

Wilderness is not a luxury but a necessity of the human spirit.

A patriot must always be ready to defend his country against his government.

A drink a day keeps the shrink away.

Abolition of a woman's right to abortion, when and if she wants.  It amounts
to compulsory maternity: a form of rape by the State.

Anarchism is founded on the observation that since few men are wise
enough to rule themselves, even fewer are wise enough to rule others.

Belief in the supernatural reflects a failure of the imagination.

Civilization is a youth with a molotov cocktail in his hand.
Culture is the Soviet tank or L.A. cop that guns him down.

Climbing K2 or floating the Grand Canyon in an inner tube; there
are some things one would rather have done than do.

For myself I hold no preferences among flowers, so long as they are wild,
free, spontaneous. Bricks to all greenhouses! Black thumb and
cutworm to the potted plant!

One man alone can be pretty dumb sometimes, but for real bona fide
stupidity, there ain't nothin' can beat teamwork.

Our culture runs on coffee and gasoline, the first often tasting
like the second.

Say what you like about my bloody murderous government but
don't insult me poor bleedin' country.

Taxation: how the sheep are shorn.

## ABIGAIL ADAMS (First Lady, 1744-1818)

Learning is not attained by chance, it must be sought for with
ardor and diligence.

Great necessities call out great virtues.

We have too many high-sounding words, and too few actions that
correspond with them

A little of what you call frippery is very necessary towards
looking like the rest of the world.

Arbitrary power is like most other things which are very hard,
very liable to be broken.

Do not put such unlimited power into the hands of husbands.
Remember all men would be tyrants if they could.

I am more and more convinced that man is a dangerous creature and
that  power, whether vested in many or a few, is ever
grasping, and like the grave, cries, 'Give, give.'

I begin to think, that a calm is not desirable in any situation
in life. Man was made for action and for bustle too, I believe.

I've always felt that a person's intelligence is directly
reflected by the number of conflicting points of view he can entertain
simultaneously on the same topic.

If we mean to have heroes, statesmen and philosophers, we should
have learned women.

Well, knowledge is a fine thing, and mother Eve thought so; but she
smarted so severely for hers, that most of her daughters
have been afraid of it since.

Wisdom and penetration are the fruit of experience, not the
lessons of  retirement and leisure. Great necessities call
out great virtues

## ANSEL ADAMS (Photographer 1902-1984)

It is horrifying that we have to fight our own government to save the environment.

A good photograph is knowing where to stand.

Simply look with perceptive eyes at the world about you, and trust to your own
reactions and convictions. Ask yourself: "Does this subject move me to
feel, think and dream? Can I visualize a print - my own personal statement of
what I feel and want to convey - from the subject before me?

When words become unclear, I shall focus with photographs. When images
become inadequate, I shall be content with silence.

Yosemite Valley, to me, is always a sunrise, a glitter of green and golden wonder
in a vast edifice of stone and space.

A great photograph is one that fully expresses what one feels, in the deepest
sense, about what is being photographed.

A photograph is usually looked at - seldom looked into.

A true photograph need not be explained, nor can it be contained in words.

Dodging and burning are steps to take care of mistakes God made in
establishing tonal relationships.

You don't make a photograph just with a camera. You bring to the act of
photography all the pictures you have seen, the books you have read,
the music you have heard, the people you have loved

I found that while the camera does not express the soul, perhaps a photograph can!

In wisdom gathered over time I have found that every experience
is a form of exploration.

It is my intention to present - through the medium of photography - intuitive
observations of the natural world which may have meaning to the spectators.

Landscape photography is the supreme test of the photographer - and often the
supreme disappointment.

Millions of men have lived to fight, build palaces and boundaries, shape destinies and
societies; but the compelling force of all times has been the force of originality
and creation profoundly affecting the roots of human spirit.

Myths and creeds are heroic struggles to comprehend the truth in the world.

No man has the right to dictate what other men should perceive, create or
produce, but all should be encouraged to reveal themselves, their perceptions
and emotions, and to build confidence in the creative spirit.

Not everybody trusts paintings but people believe photographs.

Photography is more than a medium for factual communication of
ideas. It is a creative art.

Photography, as a powerful medium of expression and communications, offers
an infinite variety of perception, interpretation and execution.

Some photographers take reality... and impose the domination of their own
thought and spirit. Others come before reality more tenderly and a
photograph to them is an instrument of love and revelation.

Sometimes I do get to places just when God's ready to
have somebody click the shutter.

The negative is comparable to the composer's score and the print to
its performance. Each performance differs in subtle ways.

The only things in my life that compatibly exists with this grand universe
are the creative works of the human spirit.

There are always two people in every picture: the photographer
and the viewer.

There are no rules for good photographs, there are only good photographs.

There are worlds of experience beyond the world of the aggressive man, beyond
history, and beyond science. The moods and qualities of nature and the
revelations of great art are equally difficult to define; we can grasp
them only in the depths of our perceptive spirit.

There is nothing worse than a sharp image of a fuzzy concept.

These people live again in print as intensely as when their images were captured
on old dry plates of sixty years ago... I am walking in their alleys,
standing in their rooms and sheds and workshops, looking in and out of
their windows. Any they in turn seem to be aware of me.

To photograph truthfully and effectively is to see beneath the surfaces and record
the qualities of nature and humanity which live or are latent in all things.

Twelve significant photographs in any one year is a good crop.

We must remember that a photograph can hold just as much as we put into it,
and no one has ever approached the full possibilities of the medium.

When I'm ready to make a photograph, I think I quite obviously see in my minds
eye something that is not literally there in the true meaning of the word.
I'm interested in something which is built up from within, rather than just
extracted from without.

You don't take a photograph, you make it.

## JOHN ADAMS (President, 1735-1826)

A desire to be observed, considered, esteemed, praised, beloved, and admired by his fellows is one of the earliest as well as the keenest dispositions discovered in the heart of man.

Democracy... while it lasts is more bloody than either aristocracy or monarchy. Remember, democracy never lasts long. It soon wastes, exhausts, and murders itself. There is never a democracy that did not commit suicide.

Facts are stubborn things; and whatever may be our wishes, our inclinations, or the dictates of our passions, they cannot alter the state of facts and evidence.

Fear is the foundation of most governments.

Genius is sorrow's child.

Great is the guilt of an unnecessary war.

A government of laws, and not of men.

Liberty, according to my metaphysics is a self-determining power in an intellectual agent. It implies thought and choice and power.

Old minds are like old horses; you must exercise them if you wish to keep them in working order.

Power always thinks it has a great soul and vast views beyond the comprehension of the weak.

Power always thinks... that it is doing God's service when it is violating all his laws.

Property is surely a right of mankind as real as liberty.

Remember, democracy never lasts long. It soon wastes, exhausts, and murders itself. There never was a democracy yet that did not commit suicide.

The Declaration of Independence I always considered as a theatrical show. Jefferson ran away with all the stage effect of that... and all the glory of it.

The essence of a free government consists in an effectual control of rivalries.

The fundamental law of the militia is, that it be created, directed and commanded by the laws, and ever for the support of the laws.

The happiness of society is the end of government.

The Hebrews have done more to civilize men than any other nation. If I were an atheist, and believed blind eternal fate, I should still believe that fate had ordained the Jews to be the most essential instrument for civilizing the nations.

The right of a nation to kill a tyrant in case of necessity can no more be doubted than to hang a robber, or kill a flea.

There are two educations. One should teach us how to make a living and the other how to live.

There is danger from all men. The only maxim of a free government ought to be to trust no man living with power to endanger the public liberty.

When people talk of the freedom of writing, speaking or thinking I cannot choose but laugh. No such thing ever existed. No such thing now exists; but I hope it will exist. But it must be hundreds of years after you and I shall write and speak no more.

While all other sciences have advanced, that of government is at a standstill - little better understood, little better practiced now than three or four thousand years ago.

Abuse of words has been the great instrument of sophistry and chicanery,
of party, faction, and division of society.

All the perplexities, confusion and distress in America arise, not from defects
in their Constitution or Confederation, not from want of honor or virtue,
so much as from the downright ignorance of the nature of coin, credit
and circulation.

As much as I converse with sages and heroes, they have very little of my
love and admiration. I long for rural and domestic scene, for the
warbling of birds and the prattling of my children.

Because power corrupts, society's demands for moral authority and character
increase as the importance of the position increases.

## JOHN QUINCY ADAMS (President 1767-1848)

All men profess honesty as long as they can. To believe all men honest would be
folly. To believe none so is something worse.

Always vote for principle, though you may vote alone, and you may cherish the
sweetest reflection that your vote is never lost.

America does not go abroad in search of monsters to destroy.

Courage and perseverance have a magical talisman, before which difficulties
disappear and obstacles vanish into air.

If your actions inspire others to dream more, learn more, do more and become more,
you are a leader.

Nip the shoots of arbitrary power in the bud, is the only maxim which can ever
preserve the liberties of any people.

Patience and perseverance have a magical effect before which difficulties disappear
and obstacles vanish.

Posterity: you will never know how much it has cost my generation to preserve your
freedom. I hope you will make good use of it

## ALAN ALDA (Actor 1936 - )

Begin challenging your own assumptions. Your assumptions are your windows on the
world. Scrub them off every once in awhile, or the light won't come in.

Be fair with others, but then keep after them until they're fair with you.

Be brave enough to live life creatively. The creative place where no one else has ever
been.

Be as smart as you can, but remember that it is always better to be wise
than to be smart.

I found I wasn't asking good enough questions because I assumed I knew
something. I would box them into a corner with a badly formed question, and
they didn't know how to get out of it. Now, I let them take me
through it step by step, and I listen.

I wouldn't live in California. All that sun makes you sterile.

I'm an angry person, angrier than most people would imagine, I get flashes of anger.
What works for me is working out when it's useful to use that anger.

I'm in the real world, some people try to steal from me, and I stop them, frequently,
take them to court. I love a good lawsuit. It's fun.

I'm most at home on the stage. I was carried onstage for the first time
when I was six months old.

I've been nominated twice before as actor in a leading part. Now I'm nominated as
actor in a supporting part. If I don't win, I'll just wait until I'm nominated for
being in the theater during the show. Do they have one like that?

I've never tried to manipulate my image.

If I can't get the girl, at least give me more money.

It isn't necessary to be rich and famous to be happy. It's only necessary to be rich.

It's really clear to me that you can't hang onto something longer than its time. Ideas lose certain freshness, ideas have a shelf life, and sometimes they have to be replaced by other ideas.

It's too bad I'm not as wonderful a person as people say I am, because the world could use a few people like that.

Laugh at yourself, but don't ever  aim your doubt at yourself. Be bold. When you embark for strange places, don't leave any of yourself safely on shore. Have the nerve to go into unexplored territory.

My mother didn't try to stab my father until I was six, but she must have shown signs of oddness before that.

Never Have Your Dog Stuffed is really advice to myself, a reminder to myself not to avoid change or uncertainty, but to go with it, to surf into change.

No man or woman of the humblest sort can really be strong, gentle and good, without the world being better for it, without somebody being helped and comforted by the very existence of that goodness.

When people are laughing, they're generally not killing one another.

You can't get there by bus, only by hard work and risk and by not quite  knowing what you're doing. What you'll discover will be wonderful. What you'll discover will be yourself. You have to leave the city of your comfort and go into the wilderness of your intuition. What you'll discover will be wonderful. What you'll discover is yourself.

## MORTIMER ALDER (Philosopher, 1902-2001)

Not to engage in the pursuit of ideas is to live like ants instead of like men.

In the case of good books, the point is not to see how many of them you can get through, but how many can get through to you.

One of the embarrassing problems for the early nineteenth-century champions of the Christian faith was that not one of the first six Presidents of the United States was an orthodox Christian.

The philosopher ought never to try to avoid the duty of making up his mind.

The purpose of learning is growth, and our minds, unlike our bodies, can continue growing as we continue to live.

If you never ask yourself any questions about the meaning of a passage, you cannot expect the book to give you any insight you do not already possess

Ask others about themselves, at the same time, be on guard not to talk too much about yourself.

Freedom is the emancipation from the arbitrary rule of other men.

Friendship is a very taxing and arduous form of leisure activity.

I wonder if most people ever ask themselves why love is connected with reproduction. And if they do ask themselves about this, I wonder what answer they give.

Love can be unselfish, in the sense of being benevolent and generous, without being selfless.

Love consists in giving without getting in return; in giving what is not owed, what is not due the other. That's why true love is never based, as associations for utility or pleasure are, on a fair exchange.

Love wishes to perpetuate itself. Love wishes for immortality.

Love without conversation is impossible.

Men value things in three ways: as useful, as pleasant or sources of pleasure, and as excellent, or as intrinsically admirable or honorable.

The telephone book is full of facts, but it doesn't contain a single idea.
The ultimate end of education is happiness or a good human life, a life enriched
by the possession of every kind of good, by the enjoyment
of every type of satisfaction.

## ETHAN ALLEN (American Revolutionary/Patriot, 1738-1789)

Those who invalidate reason ought seriously to consider whether they argue
against reason or without reason; if with reason, then they establish the
principle that they are laboring to dethrone: but if they argue without
reason (which, in order to be consistent with themselves
they must do), they are out of reach of rational conviction, nor do
they deserve a rational argument.
In those parts of the world where learning and science have prevailed, miracles have
ceased; but in those parts of it as are barbarous and ignorant, miracles are
still in vogue.
I have generally been denominated a Deist, the reality of which I never disputed,
being conscious I am no Christian, except mere infant baptism makes me
one; and as to being a Deist, I know not strictly speaking, whether I am
one or not.
There is not any thing, which has contributed so much to delude mankind in religious
matters, as mistaken apprehensions concerning supernatural inspiration or
revelation; not considering that all true religion originates
from reason, and can not otherwise be understood, but by the exercise
and improvement of it.

## STEVE ALLEN (Talk Show Host, 1921-2000)

The fundamentalist believer is mostly a weird intellectual who often lacks real faith
altogether. As a self-appointed attorney for God, who is in no need of
attorneys, he very easily turns out to be more godless than the agnostic
and the unbeliever. At all events, he seems deaf to poetry.
Humor is a social lubricant that helps us get over some of the bad spots.
I used to be a heavy gambler. But now I just make mental bets. That's how I
lost my mind.
If the Old Testament were a reliable guide in the matter of capital punishment,
half the people in the United States would have to be killed tomorrow.
If there is a God, the phrase that must disgust him is - holy war.
In a rational society we would want our presidents to be teachers. In
our actual society we insist they be cheerleaders.
One of the nice things about problems is that a good many of them do
not exist except in our imaginations.
Ours is a government of checks and balances. The Mafia and crooked
businessmen make out checks, and the politicians and other
compromised officials improve their bank balances.
Totalitarianism is patriotism institutionalized.

## WOODY ALLEN (Actor, Producer, 1935 -)

The chief problem about death, incidentally, is the fear that there may be
no afterlife -- a depressing thought, particularly for those who have
bothered to shave. Also, there is the fear that there is an afterlife
but no one will know where it's being held.
I do occasionally envy the person who is religious naturally, without being
brainwashed into it or suckered into it by all the organized hustles.

If only God would give me some clear sign! Like making a large deposit in
        my name at a Swiss bank.
Not only is there no God, but try getting a plumber on weekends.
How can I believe in God when just last week I got my tongue caught in the
        roller of an electric typewriter?
If it turns out that there is a God, I don't think that he's evil. But the worst
        that you can say about him is that basically he's an underachiever.
To YOU I'm an atheist; to God, I'm the Loyal Opposition.
In real life, [Diane]Keaton believes in God. But she also believes that the
        radio works because there are tiny people inside it.
I don't want to achieve immortality through my work ... I want to achieve
        it through not dying.

## POUL ANDERSON (Author, 1926-2001)

I have yet to see any problem, however complicated, which, when looked
        at in the right way did not become still more complicated.
We live with our archetypes, but can we live in them?
If we knew exactly what to expect throughout the Solar System, we would
        have no reason to explore it.
When facts are insufficient, theorizing is ridiculous at best, misleading
        at worst.

## RICHARD DEAN ANDERSON (Actor, 1950 -)

Dogs are my favorite people.
I can't tell you anything about what happens after the cameras go off,
        mostly because I'm usually unconscious  by then.

## MAYA ANGELOU (Poet, 1928 -)

Nothing will work unless you do.
Making a living is not the same thing as making a life.
There is no greater agony than bearing an untold story inside you.
There is nothing so pitiful as a young cynic because he has gone from
        knowing nothing to believing nothing.
Life loves the liver of it.
All great achievements require time.
The idea is to write it so that people hear it and it slides through the brain
        and goes straight to the heart.
Some critics will write 'Maya  Angelou  is a natural writer' - which is right after being
        a natural heart surgeon.
There's a world of difference between truth and facts. Facts can obscure the truth.
The ache for home lives in all of us, the safe place where we can go as we are
        and not be questioned.
If you don't like something, change it. If you can't change it, change your attitude.
If you find it in your heart to care for somebody else, you will have succeeded.
If you have only one smile in you give it to the people you love.
Any book that helps a child to form a habit of reading, to make reading one of
        his deep and continuing needs, is good for him.
As far as I knew white women were never lonely, except in books. White men adored
        them, Black men desired them and Black women worked for them.
My mother said I must always be intolerant of ignorance but understanding of
        illiteracy. That some people, unable to go to school, were more educated
        and more intelligent than college professors.

At fifteen life had taught me undeniably that surrender, in its place, was as
    honorable as resistance, especially if one had no choice.
All men are prepared to accomplish the incredible if their ideals are threatened.
Bitterness is like cancer. It eats upon the host. But anger is like
    fire. It burns it all clean.
Children's talent to endure stems from their ignorance of alternatives.
Courage is the most important of all the virtues, because without courage you
    can't practice any other virtue consistently. You can practice any virtue
    erratically, but nothing consistently without courage.
Effective action is always unjust.
For Africa to me... is more than a glamorous fact. It is a historical truth. No man can
    know where he is going unless he knows exactly where he has been
    and exactly how he arrived at his present place.
History, despite its wrenching pain, cannot be unlived, but if faced with courage,
    need not be lived again.
How important it is for us to recognize and celebrate our heroes and she-roes!
If one is lucky, a solitary fantasy can totally transform one million realities.
If we lose love and self respect for each other, this is how we finally die.
It is time for parents to teach young people early on that in diversity there is
    beauty and there is strength.
Life loves to be taken by the lapel and told: "I'm with you kid. Let's go."
Love is like a virus. It can happen to anybody at any time.
Love recognizes no barriers. It jumps hurdles, leaps fences, penetrates walls to arrive
    at it destination full of hope.
Most plain girls are virtuous because of the scarcity of opportunity to be otherwise.
Music was my refuge. I could crawl into the space between the notes and curl
    my back to loneliness.
My great hope is to laugh as much as I cry; to get my work done and try to
    love somebody and have the courage to accept the love in return.
My life has been one great big joke, a dance that's walked a song that's spoke,
    I laugh so hard I almost choke when I think about myself.
One isn't necessarily born with courage, but one is born with potential. Without
    courage, we cannot practice any other virtue with consistency. We can't
    be kind, true, merciful, generous, or honest.
Perhaps travel cannot prevent bigotry, but by demonstrating that all peoples
    cry, laugh, eat, worry, and die, it can introduce the idea that if we try
    and understand each other, we may even become friends.
Prejudice is a burden that confuses the past, threatens the future and renders
    the present inaccessible.
We may encounter many defeats but we must not be defeated.
I believe that every person is born with talent.
I believe we are still so innocent. The species are still so innocent that a person
    who is apt to be murdered believes that the murderer, just before he
    puts the final wrench on his throat, will have enough compassion to give
    him one sweet cup of water.
I have found that among its other benefits, giving liberates the soul of the giver.
The fact that the adult American Negro female emerges a formidable character is
    often met with amazement, distaste and even belligerence. It is seldom
    accepted as an inevitable outcome of the struggle won by survivors, and
    deserves respect if not enthusiastic acceptance.
The need for change bulldozed a road down the center of my mind.
I long, as does every human being, to be at home wherever I find myself.

The sadness of the women's movement is that they don't allow the necessity of love. See, I don't personally trust any revolution where love is not allowed.

There is a very fine line between loving life and being greedy for it

We allow our ignorance to prevail upon us and make us think we can survive alone, alone in patches, alone in groups, alone in races, even alone in genders.

When someone shows you who they are, believe them the first time.

While I know myself as a creation of God, I am also obligated to realize and remember that everyone else and everything else are also God's creation.

While the rest of the world has been improving technology, Ghana has been improving the quality of man's humanity to man.

Self-pity in its early stages is as snug as a feather mattress. Only when it hardens does it become uncomfortable.

Words mean more than what is set down on paper. It takes the human voice to infuse them with deeper meaning.

I love to see a young girl go out and grab the world by the lapels. Life's a bitch. You've got to go out and kick ass.

I've learned that people will forget what you said, people will forget what you did, but people will never forget how you made them feel.

I've learned that you shouldn't go through life with a catcher's mitt on both hands; you need to be able to throw something back.

## NATALIE ANGIER (Author, Journalist, Atheist, 1958 - )

Scientists have discovered that the small brave act of cooperating with another person, of choosing trust over cynicism, generosity over selfishness, makes the brain light up with quiet joy.

When I sent out a casual and nonscientific poll of my own to a wide cast of acquaintances, friends and colleagues, I was surprised, but not really, to learn that maybe 60 percent claimed a belief in a God of some sort, including people I would have bet were unregenerate skeptics. Others just shrugged. They don't think about this stuff. It doesn't matter to them. They can't know, they won't beat themselves up trying to know and for that matter they don't care if their kids believe or not.

. . . the current climate of religiosity can be stifling to nonbelievers, and it helps now and then to cry foul. For one thing, some of the numbers surrounding the deep religiousness of America, and the rarity of nonbelief, should be held to the fire of skepticism, as should sweeping  statistics of any sort. Yes, Americans are comparatively more religious than Europeans, but while the vast majority of them may say generically that they believe in God, when asked what their religion is, a sizable fraction, 11 percent, report "no religion," a figure that has more than doubled since the early 1970's and that amounts to about 26 million people.

Whatever else I might have thought of [President George W] Bush's call, with its assumption that prayer is some sort of miracle Vicks VapoRub for the national charley horse, it's clear that his hands were reaching for any hands but mine.

As [The Nation columnist Katha] Pollitt points out, when one starts looking beneath the surface of things and adding together the out-front atheists with the indifferent nonbelievers, you end up with a much larger group of people than Jews, Muslims, Buddhists and Unitarians put together.

You have your opinion, I have mine, and it takes all kinds of nuts and dips to make a party, right?

Among the more irritating consequences of our flagrantly religious society is the special dispensation that mainstream religions receive. We all may talk about religion as a powerful social force, but unlike other similarly powerful institutions, religion is not to be questioned, criticized or mocked.

Giving a girl the impression that girlhood is an extended bounce on Barney's knee is like prepping a young gazelle for life on the Serengeti by dipping it in cream.

## WALTER ANNENBERG (Businessman, 1908-2002)

Accomplish something every day of your life.

Live rich, die poor; never make the mistake of doing it the other way round.

Adversity tests us from time to time and it is inevitable that this testing continues during life.

All I ever seek from good deeds is a measure of respect.

Carter's done a lot more good since he's been out of the White House than when he was in it.

Don't worry about it. Babe Ruth struck out on occasion, too.

Everybody around the world wants to send their kids to our universities. But nobody wants to send their kids here to public school.

Few things are as essential as education.

God grant you the strength to fight off the temptations of surrender.

I cannot compromise or inhibit my independence.

I didn't feel the Depression at all. I always had a pocketful of money.

I didn't want to be greedy. It's a mark of bad character and I always believed that pigs go the slaughterhouse.

I have very little respect for Nancy Reagan. There is something about her that is very petty.

I shall participate, I shall contribute, and in so doing, I will be the gainer.

I thought Nixon was getting ganged up on, but when I heard the tapes, I was shocked and terribly saddened.

I'd heard he was good, and what the hell sense does it make not to hire somebody because of their color?

In the world today, a young lady who does not have a college education just is not educated.

It is not easy to find something that will intrigue and bind your interest and enthusiasm. This you must seek for yourself.

It is unsound for an independent editor to be a financial contributor to any cause which would cause any type of special pleading.

Many activities and team play participation will give you a training that will prove invaluable later on in life.

## SUSAN B ANTHONY (Suffragist, 1820 -1906)

The religious persecution of the ages has been done under what was claimed to be the command of God.

I distrust those people who know so well what God wants them to do because I notice it always coincides with their own desires.

To no form of religion is woman indebted for one impulse of freedom.

What you should say to outsiders is that a Christian has neither more nor less rights in our Association than an atheist. When our platform becomes too narrow for people of all creeds and of no creeds, I myself shall not stand upon it.

No man is good enough to govern any woman without her consent.

Cautious, careful people, always casting about to preserve their
reputations... can never effect a reform

I always distrust people who know so much about what God wants them to
do to their fellows.

## LOUIS ARMSTRONG (Musician, 1901-1971)

All music is folk music. I ain't never heard a horse sing a song.

If you have to ask what jazz is, you'll never know.

Musicians don't retire; they stop when there's no more music in them.

The memory of things gone is important to a jazz musician.

There are some people that if they don't know, you can't tell them.

There is two kinds of music, the good, and the bad. I play the good kind.

We all do 'do, re, mi,' but you have got to find the other notes yourself.

What we play is life.

## NEIL ARMSTRONG (Astronaut, 1930 - 2012)

Geologists have a saying - rocks remember.

I believe every human has a finite number of heartbeats. I don't intend to waste any
of mine.

I fully expected that, by the end of the century, we would have achieved
substantially more than we actually did.

I guess we all like to be recognized not for one piece of fireworks, but for the ledger
of our daily work.

I think we're going to the moon because it's in the nature of the human being to face
challenges. It's by the nature of his deep inner soul... we're required to do
these things just as salmon swim upstream.

Mystery creates wonder and wonder is the basis of man's desire to understand.

Pilots take no special joy in walking. Pilots like flying.

Research is creating new knowledge.

Science has not yet mastered prophecy. We predict too much for the next year
and yet far too little for the next 10.

## CHESTER A. ARTHUR (President, 1830 - 1886)

I may be president of the United States, but my private life is nobody's
damned business.

Men may die, but the fabrics of free institutions remains unshaken.

The extravagant expenditure of public money is an evil not to be measured
by the value of that money to the people who are taxed for it.

## ISAAC ASIMOV (Scientist, Author, 1920-1992)

Creationists make it sound as though a 'theory' is something you dreamt up after
being drunk all night.

Never let your sense of morals get in the way of doing what's right.

I don't believe in an afterlife, so I don't have to spend my whole life fearing hell, or
fearing heaven even more. For whatever the tortures of hell, I think the
boredom of heaven would be even worse.

...anger is the common substitute for logic among those who have no evidence for
what they desperately want to believe.

Naturally since the Sumerians didn't know what caused the flood any more than
we do, they blamed the gods. (That's the advantage of religion. You're
never short an explanation for anything.)

Humanity has the stars in its future, and that future is too important to be lost
     under the burden of juvenile folly and ignorant superstition.

Life is pleasant. Death is peaceful. It's the transition that's troublesome.

To surrender to ignorance and call it God has always been premature, and it
     remains premature today.

...if I were not an atheist, I would believe in a God who would choose to save people
     on the basis of the totality of their lives and not the pattern of their words. I
     think he would prefer an honest and righteous atheist to a TV preacher
     whose every word is God, God, God, and whose every deed is foul, foul, foul.

No sensible decision can be made any longer without taking into account not only
     the world as it is, but the world as it will be.

Part of the inhumanity of the computer is that, once it is competently
     programmed and working smoothly, it is completely honest.

People who think they know everything are a great annoyance to
     those of us who do.

Science fiction writers foresee the inevitable, and although problems and
     catastrophes may be inevitable, solutions are not.

Self-education is, I firmly believe, the only kind of education there is.

Writing, to me, is simply thinking through my fingers

Suppose that we are wise enough to learn and know - and yet not wise enough to
     control our learning and knowledge, so that we use it to destroy ourselves?
     Even if that is so, knowledge remains better than ignorance.

As it happens, Josephus, who mentions John the Baptist, does not mention Jesus.
     There is, to be sure, a paragraph in his history of the Jews which is devoted
     to Jesus, but it interrupts the flow of the discourse and seems suspiciously
     like an afterthought. Scholars generally believe this to have been an
     insertion by some early Christian editor who, scandalized that Joesphus
     should talk of the period without mentioning the Messiah, felt the
     insertion to be a pious act.

The most exciting phrase to hear in science, the one that heralds new
     discoveries, is not 'Eureka!' but 'That's funny...'

The saddest aspect of life right now is that science gathers knowledge
     faster than society gathers wisdom.

The fundamentalists deny that evolution has taken place; they deny that the
     earth and the universe as a whole are more than a few thousand years
     old, and so on. There is ample scientific evidence that the fundamentalists
     are wrong in these matters, and that their notions of cosmogony
     have about as much basis in fact as the Tooth Fairy has.

I certainly don't believe in the mythologies of our society, in heaven and hell, in God
     and angels, in Satan and demons. I've thought of myself as an ´atheist,´ but
     that simply described what I didn't believe in, not what I did. Gradually,
     though, I became aware there was a movement called ´humanism,´ which
     used that name because, to put it most simply, humanists believe that
     human beings produced the progressive advance of human society and also
     the ills that plague it. They believe that if the ills are to be alleviated, it is
     humanity that will have to do the job. They disbelieve in the influence of the
     supernatural on either the good or the bad of society.

The true delight is in the finding out rather than in the knowing.

There is a single light of science, and to brighten it anywhere is to brighten it
     everywhere.

To insult someone we call him "bestial." For deliberate cruelty and nature, "human"
     might be the greater insult.

It pays to be obvious, especially if you have a reputation for subtlety.

Violence is the last refuge of the incompetent.

When I read about the way in which library funds are being cut and cut, I can only think that American society has found one more way to destroy itself.

The bible must be seen in a cultural context. It didn't just happen. These stories are retreads. But, tell a Christian that -- No, No! What makes it doubly sad is that they hardly know the book, much less its origins.

A subtle thought that is in error may yet give rise to fruitful inquiry that can establish truths of great value.

To surrender to ignorance and call it God has always been premature, and it remains premature today.

All sorts of computer errors are now turning up. You'd be surprised to know the number of doctors who claim they are treating pregnant men.

And above all things, never think that you're not good enough yourself. A man should never think that. My belief is that in life people will take you at your own reckoning.

From my close observation of writers... they fall into two groups: 1) those who bleed copiously and visibly at any bad review, and 2) those who bleed copiously and secretly at any bad review.

I am not a speed reader. I am a speed understander.

I do not fear computers. I fear the lack of them.

I don't believe in personal immortality; the only way I expect to have some version of such a thing is through my books.

I write for the same reason I breathe - because if I didn't, I would die.

If knowledge can create problems, it is not through ignorance that we can solve them.

If my doctor told me I had only six minutes to live, I wouldn't brood. I'd type a little faster.

Individual science fiction stories may seem as trivial as ever to the blinder critics and philosophers of today - but the core of science fiction, its essence has become crucial to our salvation if we are to be saved at all.

It is change, continuing change, inevitable change, that is the dominant factor in society today. No sensible decision can be made any longer without taking into account not only the world as it is, but the world as it will be.

It is not only the living who are killed in war.

## JOHN ASTIN (Actor, 1930 - )

We are running ourselves into a damaged earth. But I am optimistic. I believe that we can change; we must change. As a human race, we are very young and quite primitive. The sooner we learn the greatness of humanity the better off we will all be.

I love to play for audiences that are simply made of people rather than so-called special people.

I think people really want to be happy

My background is basically scientific math. My Dad was a physicist, so I have it in my blood somewhere. Scientific method is very important to me. I think anything that contradicts it is probably not true.

My work is to reach people with ideas, hopes, dreams, encouragement, insight, and revelation. That's what an actor wants to do.

People are smarter than you might think.

**CHIEF AUPUMUT [Mohican, 1700s]**

When it comes time to die, be not like those whose hearts are filled with the fear of death, so when their time comes they weep and pray for a little more time to live their lives over again in a different way. Sing your death song, and die like a hero going home.

**BILL AYERS (Educator, 1944 -)**

You need to find a way to live your life, that it doesn't make a mockery of your values.

Your kids require you most of all to love them for who they are, not to spend your whole time trying to correct them.

I breathed the air of deliverance through books, and through books I leapt over the walls of confinement...

**LAUREN BACALL (Actor, 1924 -)**

A man's illness is his private territory and, no matter how much he loves you and how close you are, you stay an outsider. You are healthy.

Find me a man who's interesting enough to have dinner with and I'll be happy.

I am essentially a loner.

I am not a has-been. I am a will be.

I figure if I have my health, can pay the rent and I have my friends, I call it 'content.'

I think your whole life shows in your face and you should be proud of that.

I used to tremble from nerves so badly that the only way I could hold my head steady was to lower my chin practically to my chest and look up at Bogie. That was the beginning of The Look.

I wish Frank Sinatra would just shut up and sing.

Imagination is the highest kite one can fly.

In Hollywood, an equitable divorce settlement means each party getting fifty percent of publicity.

It's inappropriate and vulgar and absolutely unacceptable to use your private life to sell anything commercially.

Stardom isn't a profession; it's an accident.

They're guys who want to screw around all the time, which interests me not at all. God knows we've done that, been there, and we don't want to do that any more.

When you talk about a great actor, you're not talking about Tom Cruise.

Looking at yourself in a mirror isn't exactly a study of life.

You can't start worrying about what's going to happen. You get spastic enough worrying about what's happening now.

**JIM BACKUS (Actor. 1913-1989)**

Many a man owes his success to his first wife and his second wife to his success.

**MICHAEL BADNARIK (Politican, 1954 - )**

I find it very offensive when the government tells me what I can and cannot watch. Censor yourself.

The government never does anything successfully.

If we really want liberty - if we really want liberty - then we need to go out and get it, we need to take it, because nobody is going to give it to us. And we need to do it now.

The first lines of defense against criminals are the victims themselves.

I am opposed to any individual taxes until we eliminate all of the unconstitutional
agencies, and I suspect we wouldn't need a tax after that.

Gun bans disarm victims, putting them at the mercy of murderers or
terrorists who think nothing of breaking the gun laws.

When the state or federal government control the education of all of
our children, they have the dangerous and illegitimate monopoly
to control and influence the thought process of our citizens.

On average, drug prisoners spend more time in federal prison than rapists,
who often get out on early release because of the overcrowding in
prison caused by the Drug War.

Gun control means being able to hit your target. If I have a 'hot button' issue,
this is definitely it. Don't even think about taking my guns. My rights
are not negotiable, and I am totally unwilling to compromise when it
comes to the Second Amendment.

I just want everyone to know that 20,000 gun laws in the United States
are unconstitutional. They infringe on your right to protect your life,
the lives of your loved ones, and your property.

The question is: how bad do things have to get before you will do something
about it? Where is your line in the sand? If you don't enforce the
constitutional limitations on your government very soon, you are
likely to find out what World War III will be like.

War doesn't need more participants. It needs fewer participants.

Communities don't have rights. Only individuals in the community have rights.

Drug prohibition has caused gang warfare and other violent crimes by
raising the prices of drugs so much that vicious criminals enter the
market to make astronomical profits, and addicts rob and steal to
get money to pay the inflated prices for their drugs.

Government is necessary for our survival. We need government in order
to survive. The Founding Fathers created a special place for
government. It is called the Constitution.

## JOAN BAEZ (Folk Singer, 1941 - )

Action is the antidote to despair.

Hypothetical questions get hypothetical answers.

I've never had a humble opinion. If you've got an opinion, why be
humble about it?

If it's natural to kill, how come men have to go into training to learn how?

Instead of getting hard ourselves and trying to compete, women should try and give
their best qualities to men - bring them softness, teach them how to cry.

It seems to me that those songs that have been any good, I have nothing much
to do with the writing of them. The words have just crawled down my
sleeve and come out on the page.

Nonviolence is a flop. The only bigger flop is violence.

That's all nonviolence is - organized love.

The easiest kind of relationship for me is with ten thousand people. The
hardest is with one.

The only thing that's been a worse flop than the organization of non-violence
has been the organization of violence.

You don't get to choose how you are going to die or when. You can only
decide how you're going to live.

You may not know it, but at the far end of despair, there is a white clearing
where one is almost happy.

**F. LEE BAILEY (Lawyer, 1933 - )**

    Can any of you seriously say the Bill of Rights could get through Congress
            today? It wouldn't even get out of committee.
    I use the rules to frustrate the law. But I didn't set up the ground rules

**PEARL BAILEY (Actor, 1918-1990)**

    Everybody wants to do something to help, but nobody wants to be first.
    No one can figure out your worth but you.
    What the world really needs is more love and less paper work.
    A crown, if it hurts us, is not worth wearing.
    You never find yourself until you face the truth.
    We look into mirrors but we only see the effects of our times on us -
            not our effects on others.
    To talk to someone who does not listen is enough to tense the devil.
    Sometimes I would almost rather have people take away years of my
            life than take away a moment.
    A man without ambition is dead. A man with ambition but no love is dead. A man
            with ambition and love for his blessings here on earth is ever so alive.
    Hungry people cannot be good at learning or producing anything,
            except perhaps violence.
    I never really look for anything. What God throws my way comes. I wake up in
            the morning and whichever way God turns my feet, I go.
    Never, never rest contented with any circle of ideas, but always be
            certain that a wider one is still possible.
    People see God every day, they just don't recognize him.
    The first and worst of all frauds is to cheat one's self. All sin is easy after that.
    The sweetest joy, the wildest woe is love. What the world really needs
            is more love and less paperwork.
    There are two kinds of talent, man-made talent and God-given talent.
            With man-made talent you have to work very hard. With
            God-given talent, you just touch it up once in a while.
    There is a way to look at the past. Don't hide from it. It will not catch
            you if you don't repeat it.
    There's a period of life when we swallow a knowledge of ourselves and
            it becomes either good or sour inside.
    When you're young, the silliest notions seem the greatest achievements.
    You cannot belong to anyone else, until you belong to yourself.
    You must change in order to survive.

**ELLA BAKER (Activist, 1903-1986)**

    One of the things that has to be faced is the process of waiting to change
            the system, how much we have got to do to find out who we are,
            where we have come from and where we are going.
    Strong people don't need strong leaders.
    Give light and people will find the way.

**JIM BAKKER (Evangelist, 1940 - )**

It's not listed in the Bible, but my spiritual gift, my specific calling from
    God, is to be a television talk-show host.

The box got bigger, the outside, the buildings. And all that we were doing.
    I had to raise about $1 million every two days just to stay alive.

When you put your total faith in God, no matter what happens, to a person who's a
    true believer, if you die, you know you're going to heaven to be with God.

Why should I apologize because God throws in crystal chandeliers,
    mahogany floors, and the best construction in the world?

You can't fake it when you're alone with God, you know.

You know, I try not to look back, because looking forward is so much
    better than looking backward.

And God knows I needed to be forgiven. So I had to forgive everybody. And
    then God - as I read in the word, you're supposed to pray for your
    enemies. Try that one on.

God's forgiveness is the only thing. And, well, I take full responsibility for
    the adultery. It was my fault and, you know, no matter what went on,
    the man has to take responsibility; and I do.

I feel like God has forgiven me of so much, that I will forgive everyone
    who has hurt us.

I think - there's always going to be a percentage of people who maybe aren't
    as good as others.

Most of you are so young you don't know who I am, and that's good.

My dream became bigger and bigger. And the box got bigger than the
    message, than the Gospel.

Oh, I was never a businessman. I was a visionary, a dreamer.

So you can't lose serving God, and that all things work together for good.

They've all been through bad things. So bad things happen to people.
    They happen to all the great men of God.

When I first went to prison, I was even questioning where, God, where are you?

**TAMMY FAYE BAKKER (Evangelist, 1942-2007)**

You can educate yourself right out of a relationship with God.

I always say shopping is cheaper than a psychiatrist.

I shop, therefore I am.

I wake up every morning and I wish I were dead, and so does Jim.

You don't have to be dowdy to be a Christian.

**SCOTT BAKULA  (Actor, 1954 - )**

I am very much against weapons in space. And I wish we could be spearheading
    that program to come to some kind of international agreement so that
    doesn't happen. That is my only - fear - in further space exploration like
    always, we hope it doesn't get abused.

I've always been a big fan of time travel, and I'm very into the notion
    that some day we'll be able to do it. Beam me up!

Ideally, people find mates with whom they can express both their
    masculine and feminine sides.

On the whole, show business is a hard business in which to be married.

The great thing  about show business is that there's no mandatory
    retirement  age.

## JAMES MARK BALDWIN (Philosopher, 1861-1934)
Heredity provides for the modification of its own machinery.

## LUCILLE BALL  (Comedian, Actress, 1911-1989)
Ability  is of little account without opportunity.

How I Love Lucy was born? We decided that instead of divorce lawyers
profiting from our mistakes, we'd profit from them.

I am a real ham. I love an audience. I  work better with an audience. I  am
dead, in fact, without one.

I have an everyday religion that works for me. Love yourself first, and
everything else falls into line.

I regret the passing of the studio system. I was very appreciative of it
because I had no talent.

I think knowing what you cannot do is more important than knowing
what you can.

I'd rather regret the things I've done than regret the things I haven't done.

I'm happy that I have brought  laughter  because I have been shown by
many the value of it in so many lives, in so many ways.

I'm not funny. What I am is brave.

If you want something done, ask a busy person to do it. The more things
you do, the more you can do.

In life, all good things come hard, but wisdom is the hardest to come by.

It's a helluva start, being  able to recognize what makes you happy.

Love yourself first and everything else falls into line. You really have to
love yourself to get anything done in this world.

Luck? I don't know anything  about  luck. I've never banked on it and I'm
afraid of  people who  do. Luck to me is something else: Hard work -
and realizing what  is opportunity and what  isn't.

Once in his life, every man is entitled to fall madly in love with a gorgeous redhead.

One of the things I learned the hard  way was that  it  doesn' t pay to get
discouraged. Keeping busy and making optimism a way of life can restore
your faith in yourself.

The more things you do, the more you can do.

The secret of staying young is to live honestly, eat slowly, and lie
about your  age.

Women's Lib? Oh, I'm afraid it doesn't interest me one bit. I've been
so liberated it hurts.

You see much more of your children once they leave home.

## GEORGE BANCROFT (Historian, 1899-1891)
In nine times out of ten, the slanderous tongue belongs to
a disappointed person.

The prejudices of ignorance are more easily removed than the prejudices
of interest; the first are all blindly adopted, the second willfully preferred.

The public is wiser than the wisest critic.

Beauty is but the sensible image of the Infinite. Like truth and
justice it lives within us; like virtue and the moral law it
is a companion of the soul.

By common consent gray hairs are a crown of glory; the only object
of respect that can never excite envy.

Avarice is the vice of declining years.

Conscience is the mirror of our souls, which represents the errors
of our lives in their full shape.

Dishonesty is so grasping it would deceive God himself, were it possible.

If reason is a universal faculty, the decision of the common mind
is the nearest criterion of truth.

The best government rests on the people, and not on the few, on persons
and not on property, on the free development of public opinion
and not on authority.

The exact measure of the progress of civilization is the degree in which
the intelligence of the common mind has prevailed over wealth
and brute force.

The fears of one class of men are not the measure of the rights of another.

Truth is not exciting enough to those who depend on the characters
and lives of their neighbors for all their amusement.

Where the people possess no authority, their rights obtain no respect.

## TYRA BANKS (Model, 1973 - )

A smart model is a good model.

Black women have always been these vixens, these animalistic erotic women.
Why can't we just be the sexy American girl next

I don't go to the cool, trendy restaurants. I go to either the holes in the wall
or the super-fancy restaurants where there are no cool people.

I have so many goals.

I haven't seen the Eiffel Tower, Notre Dame, the Louvre. I haven't seen
anything. I don't really care.

I want to be like the athletes who seem stuck in time. When you see them
at 50, you say they probably can still run like a champ.

I'm competitive with myself. I always try to push past my own borders.

My mom never taught me to be waiting for some prince on a white horse
to swipe me off my feet.

The runway symbolizes something in society that's very intimidating to women.

When I am full, I stop eating.

## JOHN PERRY BARLOW (Author, 1947 - )

Relying on the government to protect your privacy is like asking a peeping
tom to install your window blinds.

. . . groundless hope, like unconditional love, is the only kind worth having.

Everyone seems to be playing well within the boundaries of his usual rule set.
I have yet to hear anyone say something that seemed likely to
mitigate the idiocy of this age.

I don't know that I believe in the supernatural, but I do believe in miracles,
and our time together was filled with the events of magical unlikelihood.

I look forward to the day when I can be Republican again. . . . I'm just
waiting until one party or the other actually gets a moral compass
and a backbone.

I personally think intellectual property is an oxymoron. Physical objects have
a completely different natural economy than intellectual goods. It's a
tricky thing to try to own something that remains in your possession
even after you give it to many others.

I'm still strongly opposed to antismoking laws, strongly opposed to any law
        that regulates personal behavior.
If all ideas have to be bought, then you have an intellectually regressive system
        that will assure you have a highly knowledgeable elite and an ignorant mass.
In Cyberspace, the First Amendment is a local ordinance.
Most libertarians are worried about government but not worried about
        business. I think we need to be worrying about business in exactly the
        same way we are worrying about government.
The Internet treats censorship as a malfunction and routes around it.
The one thing that I know government is good for is countervailing against
        monopoly. It's not great at that either, but it's the only force I know
        that is fairly reliable.

## LIONEL BARRYMORE (Actor, 1858-1954)
Half the people in Hollywood are dying to be discovered and the other half
        are afraid they will be.
Hollywood is tied hand and foot to the demands for artificiality of the masses
        all over the world.
I can remember when nobody believed an actor and didn't care what he believed.
I've got a lot of ham in me.
This is the age of insincerity. The movies had the misfortune to come along
        in the twentieth century, and because they appeal to the masses there
        can be no sincerity in them.

## ROY BEAN (Judge, 1825-1903)
You have been tried by twelve good men and true, not of your peers
        but as high above you as heaven is of hell, and they have .
Gentlemen, I find the law very explicit on murdering your fellow
        man, but there's nothing here about killing a Chinaman.
        Case dismissed.
Hang 'em first, try 'em later.
I know the law... I am it's greatest transgressor.

## SAUL BELLOW (Author, 1914-2005)
A fool can throw a stone in a pond that 100 wise men can not get out.
When we ask for advice, we are usually looking for an accomplice.
A good novel is worth more then the best scientific study.
A great deal of intelligence can be invested in ignorance when the need
        for illusion is deep.
A novel is balanced between a few true impressions and the multitude
        of false ones that make up most of what we call life.
A man is only as good as what he loves.
People can lose their lives in libraries. They ought to be warned.
Psychoanalysis pretends to investigate the Unconscious. The Unconscious
        by definition is what you are not conscious of. But the Analysts
        already know what's in it - they should, because they put it all in beforehand.
She was what we used to call a suicide blonde - dyed by her own hand.
There are evils that have the ability to survive identification and go on
        forever... money, for instance, or war.

There is an immense, painful longing for a broader, more flexible,
        fuller, more coherent, more comprehensive account of
        what we human beings are, who we are and what
        this life is for.
We are always looking for the book it is necessary to read next.
What is art but a way of seeing?
Whoever wants to reach a distant goal must take small steps.
With a novelist, like a surgeon, you have to get a feeling that you've
        fallen into good hands - someone from whom you can accept
        the anesthetic with confidence.
You never have to change anything you got up in the
        middle of the night to write.
All a writer has to do to get a woman is to say he's a
        writer. It's an aphrodisiac.
Any artist should be grateful for a naive grace which puts
        him beyond the need to reason elaborately.
Conquered people tend to be witty.
Everybody knows there is no fineness or accuracy of
        suppression; if you hold down one thing, you hold
        down the adjoining.
Everybody needs his memories. They keep the wolf of
        insignificance from the door.
Goodness is achieved not in a vacuum, but in the
        company of other men, attended by love.
Happiness can only be found if you can free yourself
        of all other distractions.
I'm glad I haven't lived in vain.
I've never turned over a fig leaf yet that didn't have a
        price tag on the other side.
If women are expected to do the same work as men, we
        must teach them the same things.
In expressing love we belong among the undeveloped countries.
No realistic, sane person goes around Chicago without protection.

## JACK BENNY (Comedian, 1894-1974)

Age is strictly a case of mind over matter. If you don't
        mind, it doesn't matter.
Gags die, humor doesn't.
Give me golf clubs, fresh air and a beautiful partner,
        and you can keep the clubs
        and the fresh air.
Hors D'oeuvre: A ham sandwich cut into forty pieces.
I don't deserve this award, but I have arthritis
        and I don't deserve that either.
Modesty is my best quality.
A scout troop consists of twelve little kids
        dressed like schmucks following a big schmuck
        dressed like a kid.

## DAVE BERRY (Journalist, Comedian, 1947 - )

Gravity is a contributing factor in nearly 73 percent of all accidents ] involving falling objects.

Although golf was originally restricted to wealthy, overweight Protestants, today it's open to anybody who owns hideous clothing.

Bill Gates is a very rich man today... and do you want to know why? The answer is one word: versions.

Camping is nature's way of promoting the motel  business.

What may seem depressing or even tragic to one person may seem like an absolute scream to another person, especially if he has had between four and seven beers.

You can only be young once. But you can always be immature.

Your modern teenager is not about to listen to advice from an old person, defined as a person who remembers when there was no Velcro.

American consumers have no problem with carcinogens, but they will not purchase any product, including floor wax, that has fat in it.

Fishing is boring, unless you catch an actual fish, and then it is disgusting.

For me, the worst part of playing golf, by far, has always been hitting the ball.

Auto racing is boring except when a car is going at least 172 miles per hour upside down.

Big business never pays a nickel in taxes, according to Ralph Nader, who represents a big consumer organization that never pays a nickel in taxes.

The only kind of seafood I trust is the fish stick, a totally featureless fish that doesn't have eyeballs or fins.

The problem with winter sports is that - follow me closely here - they generally take place in winter.

The problem with writing about religion is that you run the risk of offending sincerely religious people, and then they come after you with machetes

The real threat to whales is whaling, which has endangered many whale species.

The simple truth is that balding African-American men look cool when they shave their heads, whereas balding white men look like giant thumbs.

Never under any circumstances take a sleeping pill and a laxative on the same night.

Newspaper readership is declining like crazy. In fact, there's a good chance that nobody is reading my column.

Nobody cares if you can't dance well. Just get up and dance.

Not all chemicals are bad. Without chemicals such as hydrogen and oxygen, for example, there would be no way to make water, a vital ingredient in beer.

Once again, we come to the Holiday Season, a deeply religious time that each of us observes, in his own way, by going to the mall of his choice.

People who want to share their religious views with you almost never want you to share yours with them.

Scientists now believe that the primary biological function of breasts is to make males stupid.

Sharks are as tough as those football fans who take their shirts off during games in Chicago in January, only more intelligent.

Skiers view snowboarders as a menace; snowboarders view skiers as Elmer Fudd.

Skiing combines outdoor fun with knocking down trees with your face.

Snowboarding is an activity that is very popular with people who do not feel that regular skiing is lethal enough.

The Democrats [as opposed to Republicans] seem to be basically nicer
        people, but they have demonstrated time and again that they have
        the management skills of celery.
As a child, I was more afraid of tetanus shots than, for example, Dracula.
The four building blocks of the universe are fire, water, gravel and vinyl.
The information encoded in your DNA determines your unique biological
        characteristics, such as sex, eye color, age and Social Security number.
The Internet is the most important single development in the history of human
        communication since the invention of call waiting.
The Internet: transforming society and shaping the future through chat.
The leading cause of death among fashion models is falling through street grates.
The major parties could conduct live human sacrifices on their podiums
        during prime time, and I doubt that anybody would notice.
The nuclear generator of brain sludge is television.
The one thing that unites all human beings, regardless of age, gender, religion
        or ethnic background, is that we all believe we are above-average drivers.
The ultimate camping trip was the Lewis and Clark expedition.
The word user is the word used by the computer professional
        when they mean idiot.
The world is full of strange phenomena that cannot be explained by the laws
        of logic or science. Dennis Rodman is only one example.
There is a breed of fashion models who weigh no more than an abridged dictionary.
Thus the metric system did not really catch on in the States, unless you count the
        increasing  popularity of the nine-millimeter bullet.
To an adolescent, there is nothing in the world more embarrassing than a parent.
To better understand why you need a personal computer, let's take a look at the
        pathetic mess you call your life.
Violence and smut are of course everywhere on the airwaves. You cannot turn
        on your television without seeing them, although sometimes you have
        to hunt around.
We believe that electricity exists, because the electric company keeps sending us
        bills for it, but we cannot figure out how it travels inside wires.
We idolized the Beatles, except for those of us who idolized the Rolling
        Stones, who in those days still had many of their original teeth.
We journalists make it a point to know very little about an extremely wide
        variety of topics; this is how we stay objective.
The Sixties are now considered a historical period, just like the Roman Empire.
We operate under a jury system in this country, and as much as we complain
        about it, we have to admit that we know of no better system, except
        possibly flipping a coin.
We'll try to cooperate fully with the IRS, because, as citizens, we
        feel a strong patriotic duty not to go to jail.
What I look forward to is continued immaturity followed by death.
Dogs feel very strongly that they should  always go with you in the car, in case
        the need should arise for them to bark violently at nothing right in your ear.
Don't you wish you had a job like mine? All you have to do is think up a certain
        number of words! Plus, you can repeat words! And they don't even
        have to be true!
Eating rice cakes is like chewing on a foam coffee cup, only less filling.
'Escargot' is French for 'fat crawling bag of phlegm'.

Eugene is located in western Oregon, approximately 278 billion miles from anything.

Geographically, Ireland is a medium-sized rural island that is slowly but
steadily being consumed by sheep.

Guys are simple.. women are not simple and they always assume that men
must be just as complicated as they are, only way more mysterious.
The whole point is guys are not thinking much. They are just what they
appear to be. Tragically.

Have you noticed that whatever sport you're trying to learn, some earnest
person is always telling you to keep your knees bent?

Hobbies of any kind are boring except to people who have the same hobby. This
is also true of religion, although you will not find me saying so in print.

I am not the only person who uses his computer mainly for the purpose of
diddling with his computer.

I believe that we parents must encourage our children to become educated,
so they can get into a good college that we cannot afford.

I have been a gigantic Rolling Stones fan since approximately the
Spanish-American War.

I realize that I'm generalizing here, but as is often the case when I
generalize, I don't care.

I want a pit crew... I hate the procedure I currently have to go through
when I have car problems.

I would not know how I am supposed to feel about many stories if not for the
fact that the TV news personalities make sad faces for sad stories and
happy faces for happy stories.

If God had wanted us to be concerned for the plight of the toads, he
would have made them cute and furry.

If you had to identify, in one word, the reason why the human race has not
achieved, and never will achieve, its full potential, that word would be
'meetings.'

If you were to open up a baby's head - and I am not for a moment suggesting
that you should - you would find nothing but an enormous drool gland.

In 1765, Parliament passed the Stamp Act, which, as any American high
school student can tell you, was an act that apparently had something
to do with stamps.

If you have a big enough dictionary, just about everything is a word.

In fact, when you get right down to it, almost every explanation Man came
up with for anything until about 1926 was stupid.

It always rains on tents. Rainstorms will travel thousands of miles, against
prevailing winds for the opportunity to rain on a tent.

It is a scientific fact that your body will not absorb cholesterol if you take it
from another person's plate.

It was Public Art, defined as art that is purchased by experts who are not
spending their own personal money.

Life is anything that dies when you stomp on it.

Magnetism, as you recall from physics class, is a powerful force that causes
certain items to be attracted to refrigerators.

My problem with chess was that all my pieces wanted to end the game as
soon as possible.

Never assume that the guy understands that you  and he have a relationship.

## BLACKHAWK (Sauk Indian Chief, 1767-1838)

Courage is not afraid to weep, and she is not afraid to pray, even when she is not sure who she is praying to.

How smooth must be the language of the whites, when they can make right look like wrong, and wrong like right.

If you treat a sick child like an adult and a sick adult like a child, everything usually works out pretty well.

## HUMPHREY BOGART (Actor, 1889-1957)

Things are never so bad they can't be made worse.

A hot dog at the game beats roast beef at the Ritz.

I made more lousy pictures than any actor in history.

The only point in making money is, you can tell some big shot where to go.

The only thing you owe the public is a good performance.

The problem with the world is that everyone is a few drinks behind.

You're not a star until they can spell your name in Karachi.

## DANIEL BOONE (Frontiersman, Explorer, 1734-1820)

All you need for happiness is a good gun, a good horse, and a good wife.

Curiosity is natural to the soul of man and interesting objects have a powerful influence on our affections.

Felicity, the companion of content, is rather found in our own breasts than in the enjoyment of external things; and I firmly believe it requires but a little philosophy to make a man happy in whatever state he is.

Let peace, descending from her native heaven, bid her olives spring amidst the joyful nations; and plenty, in league with commerce, scatter blessings from her copious hand!

May the same Almighty Goodness banish the accursed monster, war, from all lands, with her hated associates, rapine and insatiable ambition!

I wouldn't give a tinker's damn for a man who isn't sometimes afraid. Fear's the spice that makes it interesting to go ahead.

Curiosity is natural to the soul of man and interesting objects have a powerful influence on our affections.

I have never been lost, but I will admit to being confused for several weeks.

## GUTZON BORGLUM (Sculptor of Mount Rushmore, 1867-1941)

A monument's dimensions should be determined by the importance to civilization of the events commemorated...Let us place there, carved high, as close to heaven as we can, the words of our leaders, their faces, to show posterity what manner of men they were. Then breathe a prayer that these records will endure until the wind and the rain alone shall wear them away.

## SHMULEY BOTEACH (Rabbi, 1966 -)

None of us is born thinking we are ordinary. Feeling special is an essential part of the human birthright. If you don't think you are special, you won't seek to contribute your gift to the world.

Amid the many challenges facing the American family today, soulless capitalism,
    along with its destructive effect on men and women, is the biggest problem
    of all.
We have to look at our everyday struggles in a different light. We have to
    stop letting life get us down. We have to stop feeling defeated. We
    can instead see the struggles we face each day as challenges that
    establish our uniqueness.
Does a country with a 50-percent divorce rate deserve to call itself civilized?
It is not normal for a man to come home after a long day's work at the office
    and feel more comfortable watching TV than talking to his kids.
I actually truly believe now in leading a wholesome life which is low-key. think
    you can hardly point to a celebrity today who has a wholesome life.
Being with perfect people is like watching a movie when you already know the
    ending. You can't thrill to perfect people's victories because they don't
    involve real courage. Real courage means to be victorious over fear. If
    you were never afraid, were your actions courageous? No.
Righteous action is more important than righteous motivation. What matters is
    doing the right thing, not why we're doing it. Correct action is always
    superior to proper intention. Given enough time, the intention will follow.
    [But] actions change the world.
I don't believe in greatness, I believe in everyday decency, in humility
    and gratitude, and writing this book has I think made me into a
    better person.
I think we live with incredibly irrational fears these days from our kids being
    kidnaped to the fear of rejection to the fear of making mistakes.
This is a generation that is really detached from the core, human values
    that lead to dignity.
Sometimes it can seem that every corner of our media-drenched society is
    sending an unmistakable message to our children and us: shed your
    dignity, exploit yourself and others, and you'll be on the path to glory.
The reason why many Jews—I'm not among them—are fearful of Christianity
    is, they're tired of Christians saying that we're a bunch of Christ killers.
    They're tired of the lie that we killed Jesus.
In our current state of human development it remains unclear whether we
    will correct one of life's greatest tragedies, namely, the inability to
    appreciate a blessing until it is lost

## PAPPY BOYINGTON (Military, 1912-1988)
Flying is hours and hours of boredom sprinkled with
    a few seconds of sheer terror.

## RAY BRADBURY (Author, 1920 - 2012 )
Americans are far more remarkable than we give ourselves credit for. We've
    been so busy damning ourselves for years. We've done it all, and
    yet we don't take credit for it.
Don't think. Thinking is the enemy of creativity. It's self-conscious, and anything
    self-conscious is lousy. You can't try to do things. You simply must do things.
Every morning I jump out of bed and step on a landmine. The landmine is me. After
    the explosion, I spent the rest of the day putting the pieces together.
I don't try to describe the future. I try to prevent it.

I know you've heard it a thousand times before. But it's true - hard work
        pays off. If you want to be good, you have to practice, practice,
        practice. If you don't love something, then don't do it.
I spent three days a week for 10 years educating myself in the public library,
        and it's better than college. People should educate themselves - you can
        get a complete education for no money. At the end of 10 years, I had
        read every book in the library and I'd written a thousand stories.
If we listened to our intellect, we'd never have a love affair. We'd never have
        a friendship. We'd never go into business, because we'd be cynical. Well,
        that's nonsense. You've got to jump off cliffs all the time and build your
        wings on the way down.
If you don't like what you're doing, then don't do it.
If you dream the proper dreams, and share the myths with people, they will
        want to grow up to be like you.
If you enjoy living, it is not difficult to keep the sense of wonder.
Jump, and you will find out how to unfold your wings as you fall.
Living at risk is jumping off the cliff and building your wings on the way down.
Love is easy, and I love writing. You can't resist love. You get an idea,
        someone says something, and you're in love.
Love is the answer to everything. It's the only reason to do anything. If you
        don't write stories you love, you'll never make it. If you don't write
        stories that other people love, you'll never make it.
Love. Fall in love and stay in love. Write only what you love, and love what
        you write. The key word is love. You have to get up in the morning
        and write something you love, something to live for.
My stories run up and bite me on the leg - I respond by writing down
        everything that goes on during the bite. When I finish, the idea lets
        go and runs off.
Stuff your eyes with wonder, live as if you'd drop dead in ten seconds. See the
        world. It's more fantastic than any dream made or paid for in factories.
The best scientist is open to experience and begins with romance - the
        idea that anything is possible.
There are worse crimes than burning books. One of them is not reading them.
Touch a scientist and you touch a child
We are an impossibility in an impossible universe.
        We are anthill men upon an anthill world.
We are cups, constantly and quietly being filled. The trick is, knowing how
        to tip ourselves over and let the beautiful stuff out.
We are the miracle of force and matter making itself over into imagination
        and will. Incredible. The Life Force experimenting with forms. You
        for one. Me for another. The Universe has shouted itself alive. We
        are one of the shouts.
Without libraries what have we? We have no past and no future.
You can't try to do things; you simply must do them.
You don't have to burn books to destroy a culture. Just get people to stop
        reading them.
You fail only if you stop writing.
You must stay drunk on writing so reality cannot destroy you.
You've got to jump off cliffs and build your wings on the way down.

**MATTHEW BRADY (Photographer, 1822-1896)**
Results are uncertain even among the more experienced photographers.

**RICHARD BRAUTIGAN (Author, 1935-1984)**
All of us have a place in history. Mine is clouds.
I didn't know the full dimensions of forever, but I knew it was longer
than waiting for Christmas to come.
I don't want my daughter to be educated. I think women should just
be decorative.
I'll think about things for thirty or forty years before I'll write it.
I'm in a constant process of thinking about things.
It's strange how the simple things in life go on while we become
more difficult.
Probably the closest things to perfection are the huge absolutely empty
holes that astronomers have recently discovered in space. If there's
nothing there, how can anything go wrong?

**BERKE BREATHED (Cartoonist, 1957 - )**
Despite what they tell you, there are simply no moral absolutes in a complex world.
I will go to my grave in a state of abject endless fascination that we all have
the capacity to become emotionally involved with a personality that
doesn't exist.
Some of us find our lives abridged even before the paperback comes out.
I ignore Hallmark Holidays. And this comes from a guy who has sold a million
Opus greeting cards.
It's never too late to have a happy childhood.
Negative humor is forgotten immediately. It's the stuff that makes us feel
better about our lives that lives long. Much more satisfying. Enter
children's books.

**DAVID BRINKLEY (Journalist, News Anchorman, 1920-2003)**
A successful man is one who can lay a firm foundation with the bricks
others have thrown at him.
I'm not a very good advertisement for the American school system.
Numerous politicians have seized absolute power and muzzled the press.
Never in history has the press seized absolute power and
muzzled the politicians.
People have the illusion that all over the world, all the time, all kinds of
fantastic things are happening. When in fact, over
most of the world, most of the time, nothing is happening.
The one function that TV news performs very well is that when there
is no news we give it to you with the same emphasis as if it were.
The only way to do news on television is not to be terrified of it.
Washington, D.C. is a city filled with people who believe
they are important.

**TOM BROKAW (Journalist, Commentator, 1940 -)**
While attendance at traditional churches has been declining for
decades... the evangelical movement is growing, and it is
changing the way America worships.

If fishing is a religion, fly fishing is high church.

It's easy to make a buck. It's a lot tougher to make a difference.

You are educated. Your certification is in your degree. You may
think of it as the ticket to the good life. Let me ask
you to think of an alternative. Think of it as your ticket
to change the world.

David Brinkley was an icon of modern broadcast journalism, a
brilliant writer who could say in a few words what the
country needed to hear during times of crisis, tragedy
and triumph.

I think they are paying a lot more attention to news now, by the
way, in part because of national-security issues. A lot of
young people have friends or family in the military today.

I'm not going to sit on the porch of the old anchorman's home with
a drool cup.

It's all storytelling, you know. That's what journalism is all about.

Speaking generally, people who are drawn to journalism are
interested in what happens from the ground up less than
they are from the top down.

TV is a fickle business. I'm only good for the length of my contract.

## LOUISE BROOKS (Actor, 1906-1985)

I never gave away anything without wishing I had kept it; nor kept it
without wishing I had given it away.

When I went to Hollywood in 1927, the girls were wearing lumpy sweaters
and skirts . . . I was wearing sleek suits and half naked beaded gowns
and piles and piles of furs.

A well dressed woman, even though her purse is painfully empty, can
conquer the world.

Love is a publicity stunt, and making love - after the first curious
raptures - is only another petulant way to pass the time waiting
for the studio to call.

Most beautiful dumb girls think they are smart and get away with it,
because other people, on the whole, aren't much smarter.

Every actor has a natural animosity toward every other actor, present
or absent, living or dead.

The great art of films does not consist of descriptive movement of face
and body but in the movements of thought and soul transmitted
in a kind of intense isolation.

There is no other occupation in the world that so closely resembled
enslavement as the career of a film star.

In my dreams I am not crippled. In my dreams, I dance.

I have a gift for enraging people, but if I ever bore you it will be with a knife.

## MEL BROOKS(Comedian, Director, Actor, 1926 - )

Anybody can direct, but there are only eleven good writers.

You're always a little disappointing in person because you can't be the
edited essence of yourself.

If Shaw and Einstein couldn't beat death, what chance have
I got?  Practically none.

If you're quiet, you're not living. You've got to be noisy and
    colorful and lively.
Life literally abounds in comedy if you just look around you.
As long as the world is turning and spinning, we're gonna be dizzy and
    we're gonna make mistakes.
Bad taste is simply saying the truth before it should be said.
Every human being has hundreds of separate people living under his skin.
    The talent of a writer is his ability to give them their separate names,
    identities, personalities and have them relate to other characters
    living with him.
Everything we do in life is based on fear, especially love.
He who hesitates is poor.
Humor is just another defense against the universe.
I don't believe in this business of being behind, better to be in front.
I only direct in self-defense.
If God wanted us to fly, He would have given us tickets.
If presidents can't do it to their wives, they do it to their country.
Look, I don't want to wax philosophic, but I will say that if you're alive
    you've got to flap your arms and legs, you've got to jump around a l
    ot, for life is the very opposite of death, and therefore you must at
    very least think noisy and colorfully, or you're not alive.
Rhetoric does not get you anywhere, because Hitler and Mussolini are just
    as good at rhetoric. But if you can bring these people down with
    comedy, they stand no chance.
Tragedy is when I cut my finger. Comedy is when you fall into an open
    sewer and die.
We want to get people laughing; we don't want to offend anybody.

## JERRY BROWN (Governor of California, 1938 - )
Inaction may be the biggest form of action.
Multinational corporations do control. They control the politicians. They control
    the media. They control the pattern of consumption, entertainment,
    thinking. They're destroying the planet and laying the foundation for
    violent outbursts and racial division.
Prisons don't rehabilitate, they don't punish, they don't protect, so what the
    hell do they do?
The reason that everybody likes planning is that nobody has to do anything.
Too often I find that the volume of paper expands to fill the available briefcases.
We have to deal with where we are. We have to create cooperatives, we have
    to create intentional communities, we have to work for local
    cooperation where we are.
We have to restore power to the family, to the neighborhood, and the
    community with a non-market principle, a principle of equality, of
    charity, of let's-take-care-of-one-another. That's the creative challenge.
It's a crazy society now. It's the richest society ever and yet people are overworked.
    There's more unemployment, more crime, more confusion, more broken
    marriages. This is a breakdown. Every culture breaks
    down. Every society breaks down, whether it's Rome, Spain, the British
    Empire. The people in charge probably didn't get it until they had
    their heads chopped off.

We just stay out of the woods as much as possible, don't disturb the trees.
The less the damage, the less we tear up, the less it will look like
we've been there. That's what we want.
The government is becoming the family of last resort.

## LENNY BRUCE (Comedian, 1925-1966)

A lot of people say to me, 'Why did you kill Christ?' I dunno, it was
one of those parties, got out of hand, you know.
Communism is like one big phone company.
Every day people are straying away from the church and going back to God.
I hate small towns because once you've seen the cannon in the park there's
nothing else to do.
I won't say ours was a tough school, but we had our own coroner. We used
to write essays like: What I'm going to be if I grow up.
I'll die young, but it's like kissing God.
If Jesus had been killed twenty years ago, Catholic school children would
be wearing little electric chairs around their necks instead of crosses.
If you can take the hot lead enema, then you can cast the first stone.
In the Halls of Justice the only justice is in the halls.
Miami Beach is where neon goes to die.
The "what should be" never did exist, but people keep trying to live up to it.
There is no "what should be," there is only what is.
The liberals can understand everything but people who don't understand them.
The only honest art form is laughter, comedy. You can't fake it... try to
fake three laughs in an hour - ha ha ha ha ha - they'll take you
away, man. You can't.
There are never enough I Love You's.
When you're eight years old nothing is your business.

## JAMES BUCHANAN (President, 1791-1868)

I like the noise of democracy.
What is right and what is practicable are two different things.
The ballot box is the surest arbiter of disputes among free men.
The test of leadership is not to put greatness into humanity, but to elicit it,
for the greatness is already there.
To avoid entangling alliances has been a maxim of our policy ever since
the days of Washington, and its wisdom no one will attempt to dispute.
We have a fairly sizable Muslim community, a fairly sizable Jewish community
and a large Christian community, but they have remained fairly
isolated from each other.

## ART BUCHWALD (Journalist, Columnist, 1925-2007)

Whether it's the best of times or the worst of times, it's
the only time we've got,.
If you attack the establishment long enough and hard enough, they
will make you a member of it.
A bad liver is to a Frenchman what a nervous breakdown is to an American.
Everyone has had one and everyone wants to talk about it.
You can't make up anything anymore. The world itself is a satire. All
you're doing is recording it.

Have you ever seen a candidate talking to a rich person on television?
I always wanted to get into politics, but I was never light
        enough to make the team.
I worship the quicksand he walks in.
It's easier to find a traveling companion than to get rid of one.
Every time you think television has hit its lowest ebb, a new program comes
        along to make you wonder where you thought the ebb was
Tax reform is taking the taxes off things that have been taxed in the past and
        putting taxes on things that haven't been taxed before.
So far things are going my way. I am known in the hospice as The Man Who
        Wouldn't Die. I don't know if this is true or not, but I think some people,
        not many, are starting to wonder why I'm still around.
Television has a real problem. They have no page two.
We seem to be going through a period of nostalgia, and everyone seems
        to think yesterday was better than today. I don't think it was, and I
        would advise you not to wait ten years before admitting today was great.
        If you're hung up on nostalgia, pretend today is yesterday and just go
        out and have one hell of a time.
People are broad-minded. They'll accept the fact that a person can be an
        alcoholic, a dope fiend, a wife beater and even a newspaperman,
        but if a man doesn't drive, there's something wrong with him.
The buffalo isn't as dangerous as everyone makes him out to be. Statistics
        prove that in the United States more Americans are killed in automobile
        accidents than are killed by buffalo.
Just when you think there's nothing to write about, Nixon says, "I am not a crook."
        Jimmy Carter says, "I have lusted after women in my heart." President
        Reagan says, "I have just taken a urinalysis test, and I am not on dope."
The powder is mixed with water and tastes exactly like powder mixed
        with water.
This is a wonderful way to celebrate an 80th birthday... I wanted to be 65
        again, but they wouldn't let me - Homeland Security.

## WILLIAM F. BUCKLEY, JR. (Conservative Author, 1925-2008)
I profoundly believe it takes a lot of practice to become a moral slob.
I won't insult your intelligence by suggesting that you really believe what
        you just said.
All adventure is now reactionary.
Idealism is fine, but as it approaches reality, the costs become prohibitive.
A Conservative is a fellow who is standing athwart history yelling 'Stop!'
Back in the thirties we were told we must collectivize the nation because
        the people were so poor. Now we are told we must collectivize the
        nation because the people are so rich.
Even if one takes every reefer madness allegation of the prohibitionists at face
        value, marijuana prohibition has done far more harm to far more
        people than marijuana ever could.
I get satisfaction of three kinds. One is creating something, one is being paid
        for it and one is the feeling that I haven't just been sitting on my ass
        all afternoon.
I would like to electrocute everyone who uses the word "fair" in connection
        with income tax policies.

I would like to take you seriously, but to do so would affront your intelligence.

I'd rather entrust the government of the United States to the first 400 people listed in the Boston telephone directory than to the faculty of Harvard University.

It had all the earmarks of a CIA operation; the bomb killed everybody in the room except the intended target!

It is not a sign of arrogance for the king to rule. That is what he is there for.

Life can't be all bad when for ten dollars you can buy all the Beethoven sonatas and listen to them for ten years.

One can't doubt that the American objective in Iraq has failed - different plans have to be made. And the kernel here is the acknowledgment of defeat.

One must bear in mind that the expansion of federal activity is a form of eating for politicians.

Scientists are people who build the Brooklyn Bridge and then buy it.

Some of my instincts are reprehensible.

The best defense against usurpatory government is an assertive citizenry.

The majority of the senior class of Vassar does not desire my company and I must confess, having read specimens of their thought and sentiments, that I do not desire the company of the majority of the senior class of Vassar.

The more complicated and powerful the job, the more rudimentary the preparation for it.

There is an inverse relationship between reliance on the state and self-reliance.

Truth is a demure lady, much too ladylike to knock you on your head and drag you to her cave. She is there, but people must want her, and seek her out.

## JIMMY BUFFETT (Musician, 1946 -)

Elvis was the only man from Northeast Mississippi who could shake his hips and still be loved by rednecks, cops, and hippies.

Humor has bailed me out of more tight situations than I can think of. If you go with your instincts and keep your humor, creativity follows. With luck, success comes, too.

I hate to mention age, but I come from an era when we weren't consumed by technology and television.

I just want to live happily ever after, every now and then.

I sell escapism.

## CHARLES BUKOWSKI (Author, 1820-1994)

An intellectual says a simple thing in a hard way. An artist says a hard thing in a simple way.

Show me a man who lives alone and has a perpetually clean kitchen, and 8 times out of 9 I'll show you a man with detestable spiritual qualities.

Some people never go crazy, What truly horrible lives they must live.

We have wasted History like a bunch of drunks shooting dice back in the men's crapper of the local bar.

The difference between a democracy and a dictatorship is that in a democracy you vote first and take orders later; in a dictatorship you don't have to waste your time voting.

If you want to know who your friends are, get yourself a jail sentence.
To do a dull thing with style-now that's what I call art.
If you're losing your soul and you know it, then you've still got a
        soul left to lose.
You begin saving the world by saving one man at a time; all else is
        grandiose romanticism or politics.
It's possible to love a human being if you don't know them too well.
Joan of Arc had style. Jesus had style.
Never get out of bed before noon.
Humanity, you never had it to begin with.
Genius might be the ability to say a profound thing in a simple way.
Bad taste creates many more millionaires than good taste.
I don't like jail, they got the wrong kind of bars in there.
I would be married, but I'd have no wife, I would be married to a single life.
There will always be something to ruin our lives, it all depends on what or
        which finds us first. We are always ripe and ready to be taken.

## SANDRA BULLOCK (Actor, 1964 -)

Does age matter? Time doesn't matter.
Beginnings are usually scary and endings are usually sad, but it's the middle
        that counts. You have to remember this when you find yourself at
        the beginning.
After a while, you have no idea how old you are because you've lied so
        many times.
Everyone does things for love.
Everyone told me to pass on Speed because it was a 'bus movie.'
Falling in love-you should go with it, regardless of whether or not your
        heart gets smashed. You'll be a better person.
Free is the best. Anything free is good.
Great acting may be a turn-on, but it won't make me fantasize about the
        person for a week.
I don't like guys who will lie down and take it. I want someone who'll fight
        back. I like people who can argue well.
I have these big piano-playing hands. I feel like I should be picking potatoes.
I think every human being has a level of melancholy in life and in general.
I was a brownie for a day. My mom made me stop. She didn't want
        me to conform.
I'm a true believer in karma. You get what you give, whether it's bad or good.
I've done all my tricks. I'm tired of myself.
I love humor. I always will fall back on humor. That's something that I
        think you can't ever get enough of and, if it's done well, it's great.
        When it's bad, it's horrible.
I'm angry all the time, and I don't know why.

## LUTHER BURBANK (Environmentalist, 1849 - 1926)

It is well for people who think to change their minds occasionally in order
        to keep them clean. For those who do not think, it is best at least
        to rearrange their prejudices once in a while.
Less than fifteen per cent of the people do any original thinking on any subject.
        The greatest torture in the world for most people is to think.

Heredity is nothing but stored environment.
If we had paid no more attention to our plants than we have to our children,
    we would now be living in a jungle of weed.
Flowers always make people better, happier, and more helpful; they are
    sunshine, food and medicine for the soul.
I see humanity now as one vast plant, needing for its highest fulfillment
    only love, the natural blessings of the great outdoors, and intelligent
    crossing and selection.
If you violate Nature's laws you are your own prosecuting attorney, judge,
    jury, and hangman.
In the span of my own lifetime I observed such wondrous progress in plant
    evolution that I look forward optimistically to a healthy, happy world
    as soon as its children are taught the principles of simple and
    rational living.
Science is knowledge arranged and classified according to truth, facts, and
    the general laws of nature.
The scientist is a lover of truth for the very love of truth itself, wherever
    it may lead.
The secret of improved plant breeding, apart from scientific knowledge, is love.
We must return to nature and nature's god.

## CAROL BURNETT(Actor, 1933 - )

. . . nobody goes through life without a scar.
Comedy is tragedy plus time.
I don't have false teeth. Do you think I'd buy teeth like these?
I liked myself better when I wasn't me.
. . . it makes you feel good when you help others. I've been helped
by acts of kindness from strangers. That's why we're here, after all,
to help others.
Only I can change my life. No one can do it for me.
We don't stop going to school when we graduate.
When you have a dream, you've got to grab it and never let go.
Words, once they are printed, have a life of their own.
You have to go through the falling down in order to learn
    to walk. It helps to know that you can survive it.
    That's an education in itself.

## GEORGE BURNS (Comedian, 1896-1996)

The secret of a good sermon is to have a good beginning and a good
    ending, then having the two as close together as possible.
Happiness is having a large, loving, caring, close-knit family in another city.
Acting is all about honesty. If you can fake that, you've got it made.
Be quick to learn and wise to know.
If it's a good script I'll do it. And if it's a bad script, and they pay
    me enough, I'll do it.
If you ask what is the single most important key to longevity, I
    would have to say it is avoiding worry, stress and tension.
    And if you didn't ask me, I'd still have to say it.
If you live to be one hundred, you've got it made. Very few people die
    past that age.

It takes only one drink to get me drunk. The trouble is, I can't remember
        if it's the thirteenth or the fourteenth.
It's good to be here. At 98, it's good to be anywhere.
Retirement at sixty-five is ridiculous. When I was sixty-five I
        still had pimples.
At my age flowers scare me.
Sex at age 90 is like trying to shoot pool with a rope.
This is the sixth book I've written, which isn't bad for a guy
        who's only read two.
Too bad that all the people who know how to run the country are
        busy driving taxicabs and cutting hair.
When I was a boy the Dead Sea was only sick.
You can't help getting older, but you don't have to get old.
You know you're getting old when you stoop to tie your shoelaces
        and wonder what else you could do while you're down there.
Don't stay in bed, unless you can make money in bed.
Happiness? A good cigar, a good meal, a good cigar and a good
        woman - or a bad woman; it depends on how much happiness
        you can handle.
I can remember when the air was clean and sex was dirty.
I can't afford to die; I'd lose too much money.
I don't believe in dying. It's been done. I'm working on a new exit.
        Besides, I can't die now - I'm booked.
I look to the future because that's where I'm going to spend the rest of
        my life.
I smoke ten to fifteen cigars a day. At my age I have to hold on
        to something.
I spent a year in that town, one Sunday.
I would go out with women my age, but there are no women my age.
I'd rather be a failure at something I love than a success at
        something I hate.
I'm at the age now where just putting my cigar in its holder is a thrill.
I'm very pleased to be here. Let's face it, at my age I'm very pleased
        to be anywhere.

## EDGAR RICE BURROUGHS (Author, 1875-1950)

I write to escape; to escape poverty.
Anger and hate against one we love steels our hearts, but contempt
        or pity leaves us silent and ashamed.
Death, only, renders hope futile.
Imagination is but another name for super intelligence.
It never seems to occur to some people, that, like beauty, a sense
        of humor may sometimes be fatal.
Love is a strange master, and human nature is still stranger.
The more one listens to ordinary conversations the more apparent it
        becomes that the reasoning faculties of the brain take little part
        in the direction of the vocal organs.
Were there no desire there would be no virtue, and because one man
        desires what another does not, who shall say whether the child
        of his desire be Vice or Virtue?

## BARBARA BUSH (First Lady, 1925 - )

Believe in something larger than yourself... get involved in the big
        ideas of your time.

Bias has to be taught. If you hear your parents downgrading women or
        people of different backgrounds, why, you are going to do that.

Cherish your human connections - your relationships with friends
        and family.

Giving frees us from the familiar territory of our own needs by
        opening our mind to the unexplained worlds occupied by
        the needs of others.

I married the first man I ever kissed. When I tell this to my children,
        they just about throw up.

I think togetherness is a very important ingredient to family life.

I'm not a competitive person, and I think women like me because
        they don't think I'm competitive, just nice.

If human beings are perceived as potentials rather than problems, as
        possessing strengths instead of weaknesses, as unlimited rather
        that dull and unresponsive, then they thrive and grow to their
        capabilities.

Never lose sight of the fact that the most important yardstick of your
        success will be how you treat other people - your family, friends,
        and coworkers, and even strangers you meet along the way.

One thing I can say about George... he may not be able to keep a job,
        but he's not boring.

The winner of the hoop race will be the first to realize her dream, not
        society's dream, her own personal dream.

To us, family means putting your arms around each other and being there.

When you come to a roadblock, take a detour.

You don't just luck into things as much as you would like to think you
        do. You build step by step, whether it is friendships or opportunities.

You have to love your children unselfishly. That's hard. But it's the only way.

## GEORGE H. W. BUSH (President, Vice President, 1924 - )

I can tell you this: If I'm ever in a position to call the shots, I'm not going to
        rush to send somebody else's kids into a war.

I do not like broccoli. And I haven't liked it since I was a little kid and my
        mother made me eat it. And I'm President of the United States and
        I'm not going to eat any more broccoli.

I have opinions of my own, strong opinions, but I don't always agree
        with them.

I am not one who - who flamboyantly believes in throwing a lot of words
        around.

But let me tell you, this gender thing is history. You're looking at a guy
        who sat down with Margaret Thatcher across the table and talked
        about serious issues.

I think I'd be a better president  because I was in combat.

America is never wholly herself unless she is engaged in high moral
        principle. We as a people have such a purpose today. It is to make
        kinder the face of the nation and gentler the face of the world.

I'll be glad to reply to or dodge your questions, depending on what I think
        will help our election most.
I'm conservative, but I'm not a nut about it.
I'm going to be so much better a president for having been at the CIA
        that you're not going to believe it.
It's a very good question, very direct, and I'm not going to answer it.
It's no exaggeration to say that the undecideds could go one way or another.
Please don't ask me to do that which I've just said I'm not going to do,
        because you're burning up time. The meter is running through the
        sand on you, and I am now filibustering.
Read my lips: no new taxes.
We are a nation of communities... a brilliant diversity spread like stars, like a
        thousand points of light in a broad and peaceful sky.
We are not the sum of our possessions.
We don't want an America that is closed to the world. What we want is a
        world that is open to America.
What's wrong with being a boring kind of guy?
You cannot be President of the United States if you don't have faith.
        Remember Lincoln, going to his knees in times of trial in the Civil
        War and all that stuff.

## GEORGE W. BUSH (President, 1946 - )

Too many good docs are getting out of the business. Too many OB-GYNs
        aren't able to practice their love with women all across this country
You work three jobs? ... Uniquely American, isn't it? I mean, that is fantastic
        that you're doing that. [to a divorced mother of 3, Omaha, Nebraska,
        Feb. 4, 2005 ]
We spent a lot of time talking about Africa, as we should. Africa is a nation
        that suffers from incredible disease.
Rarely is the question asked: Is our children learning?
They misunderestimated me.
If this were a dictatorship, it'd be a heck of a lot easier, just so long as I'm
        the dictator
As yesterday's positive report card shows, childrens do learn when standards
        are high and results are measured
There's an old saying in Tennessee -- I know it's in Texas, probably in
        Tennessee -- that says, fool me once, shame on --shame on you.
        Fool me -- you can't get fooled again
I am here to make an announcement that this Thursday, ticket counters
        and airplanes will fly out of Ronald Reagan Airport.
After the chaos and carnage of September 11th, it is not enough to serve
        our enemies with legal papers.
Do you have blacks, too? [to Brazilian President Fernando Cardoso,
        Washington, D.C., Nov. 8, 2001]
America is a Nation with a mission - and that mission comes from our most
        basic beliefs. We have no desire to dominate, no ambitions of empire.
        Our aim is a democratic peace - a peace founded upon the dignity
        and rights of every man and woman.
America is the land of the second chance - and when the gates of the prison
        open, the path ahead should lead to a better life.

America will never seek a permission slip to defend the security of our people.
Tribal sovereignty means that; it's sovereign. I mean, you're a -- you've
      been given sovereignty, and you're viewed as a sovereign entity. And
      therefore the relationship between the federal government and tribes
      is one between sovereign entities.
I couldn't imagine somebody like Osama bin Laden understanding the joy
      of Hanukkah
Americans are rising to the tasks of history, and they expect the same of us.
And the cornerstone of my economic policies, when I first got elected, was
      cutting taxes on everybody on who paid taxes.
And what's interesting, and I don't think a lot of Americans understand this
      fact, is that, one, most new jobs are created by small businesses; two,
      most small businesses pay tax at the individual income tax, or many
      small businesses pay tax there.
Bring them on.
Do I think faith will be an important part of being a good president? Yes, I do.
I'm the commander -- see, I don't need to explain -- I do not need to explain
      why I say things. That's the interesting thing about being president
Every nation in every region now has a decision to make. Either you are with
      us, or you are with the terrorists.
Oh, no, we're not going to have any casualties.[discussing the Iraq war with
      Christian Coalition founder Pat Robertson in 2003, as quoted
      by Robertson]
Everywhere that freedom stirs, let tyrants fear.
I'll be long gone before some smart person ever figures out what
      happened inside this Oval Office
I know how hard it is for you to put food on your family
For diplomacy to be effective, words must be credible - and no one can
      now doubt the word of America.
Free nations are peaceful nations. Free nations don't attack each other. Free
      nations don't develop weapons of mass destruction.
I am mindful not only of preserving executive powers for myself, but for
      predecessors as well.
I believe a marriage is between a man and a woman.
I had to abandon free market principles in order to save the free market system.
I have a different vision of leadership. A leadership is someone who brings
      people together.
I have written a book. This will come as quite a shock to some. They didn't
      think I could read, much less write.
I have zero desire, just so you know, to be in the limelight. I don't think it's
      good for the country to have a former president criticize his
      successor. You're not going to see me giving my opinions in the public
      arena, until I start selling my book. I'm going to emerge then submerge.
I just want you to know that, when we talk about war, we're really talking
      about peace..
I think we ought to raise the age at which juveniles can have a gun.
Families is where our nation finds hope, where wings take dream
I think you can judge from somebody's actions a kind of a stability and sense
      of purpose perhaps created by strong religious roots. I mean, there's
      a certain patience, a certain discipline, I think, that religion helps
      you achieve.

I want to thank you for taking time out of your day to come and
        witness my hanging.
I will never relent in defending America - whatever it takes.
I would like to be remembered as a guy who had a set of priorities, and was
        willing to live by those priorities. In terms of accomplishments, my
        biggest accomplishment is that I kept the country safe amidst a
        real danger.
I'm hopeful. I know there is a lot of ambition in Washington, obviously. But I
        hope the ambitious realize that they are more likely to succeed with
        success as opposed to failure.
If you're sick and tired of the politics of cynicism and polls and principles,
        come and join this campaign.
It is clear our nation is reliant upon big foreign oil. More and more of our
        imports come from overseas.
It's clearly a budget. It's got a lot of numbers in it.
It's going to be the year of the sharp elbow and the quick tongue.
Leadership to me means duty, honor, country. It means character,
        and it means listening from time to time
Natural gas is hemispheric. I like to call it hemispheric in nature because
        it is a product that we can find in our neighborhoods.
No one was more shocked or angry than I was when we didn't find the
        weapons. I had a sickening feeling every time I thought
        about it. I still do.
This foreign policy stuff is a little frustrating
Now, there are some who would like to rewrite history - revisionist
        historians is what I like to call them.
One of my proudest moments is I didn't sell my soul for the sake
        of popularity.
Only a liberal senator from Massachusetts would say that a 49 percent
        increase in funding for education was not enough.
Our nation must come together to unite.
People make suggestions on what to say all the time. I'll give you an  example; I
        don't read what's handed to me. People say, 'Here, here's your speech, or
        here's an idea for a speech.' They're changed. Trust me.
I'm the decider, and I decide what is best. And what's best is for Don
        Rumsfeld to remain as the Secretary of Defense.
I know the human being and fish can coexist peacefully
Senator Kerry has been in Washington long enough to take both sides on
        just about every issue.
So, I'm lying on the couch and Laura walks in and I say, 'Free at last,'
        and she says 'You're free all right, you're free to do the dishes.'
        So I say, 'You're talking to the former president, baby,' and she
        said, 'consider this your new domestic policy agenda.'
Some folks look at me and see a certain swagger, which in Texas is
        called "walking."
This is an impressive crowd -- the haves and the have mores. Some
        people call you the elite -- I call you my base
The California crunch really is the result of not enough power-generating plants and
        then not enough power to power the power of generating plants.
The true history of my administration will be written 50 years from now,
        and you and I will not be around to see it.

To those of you who received honors, awards and distinctions, I say well done. And to the C students, I say you, too, can be president of the United States.
We don't believe in planners and deciders making the decisions on behalf of Americans.
See, in my line of work you got to keep repeating things over and over and over again for the truth to sink in, to kind of catapult the propaganda.
You can fool some of the people all the time, and those are the ones you want to concentrate on.
You can't put democracy and freedom back into a box.
You teach a child to read, and he or her will be able to pass a literacy test.

## LAURA BUSH (First Lady, 1946 - )

A love of books, of holding a book, turning its pages, looking at its pictures, and living its fascinating stories goes hand-in-hand with a love of learning.
Every child in American should have access to a well-stocked school library.
Libraries allow children to ask questions about the world and find the answers. And the wonderful thing is that once a child learns to use a library, the doors to learning are always open.
Maybe it is the media that has us divided.
No one likes to be criticized.
Politics is a people business. I like people.
The power of a book lies in its power to turn a solitary act into a shared vision. As long as we have books, we are not alone.
Though my plans at the moment are vague, I can assure you that I'll never run for the Senate in New York.
We can overcome evil with greater good.
Well, we've faced very difficult decisions and challenges in our country, every one of us have, as we - since September 11th, as we fought the war on terror, all of those decisions that the President had to make to put young men and women in harm's way.
You know, there are a lot of would-be governors of Texas sitting around today who never took the opportunity to get into a race when the time was right.
I like politics. I like traveling in the United States.
I think there are a lot of reasons to be critical of the media in America.
I would never do anything to undermine my husband's point of view.
In fact, I have the privilege of traveling around our country and meeting people all over the country who are making a huge difference in the lives of their neighbors and themselves. That's what I'm really fortunate to be able to do.
It's not easy to have the job of president. It's not easy to run for it. And it's not a job for the faint of heart.

## JAMES CAAN (Actor, 1940 - )

Actors have bodyguards and entourages not because anybody wants to hurt them - who would want to hurt an actor? - but because they want to get recognized. God forbid someone doesn't recognize them.
Anyone of my generation who tells you he hasn't 'done Brando' is lying.
I always thought of myself as some sort of athlete until I started playing golf a couple years ago.
I don't think silicone makes a girl good or bad.
I never rode a bull - I'm not that stupid.

I think we have to believe in things we don't see. That's really important for all of us, whether it's your religion or Santa Claus, or whatever. That's pretty much what it's about.

## NICOLAS CAGE (Actor, 1964 - )

I am not a demon. I am a lizard, a shark, a heat-seeking panther. I want to be Bob Denver on acid playing the accordion.

I think I jump around more when I'm alone.

I was always shocked when I went to the doctor's office and they did my X-ray and didn't find that I had eight more ribs than I should have or that my blood was the color green.

Passion is very important to me. If you stop enjoying things, you've got to look at it, because it can lead to all kinds of depressing scenarios.

Shock is still fun. I won't ever shut the door on it.

There's a fine line between the Method actor and the schizophrenic.

## AL CAPP (Cartoonist, 1909-1979)

There are certain books in the world which every searcher for truth must know: the Bible, the Critique of Pure Reason, the Origin of Species, and Karl Marx's Capital.

Any place that anyone can learn something useful from someone with e xperience is an educational institution.

My work is being destroyed almost as soon as it is printed. One day it is being read; the next day someone's wrapping fish in it.

Success is following the pattern of life one enjoys most.

Anyone who can walk to the welfare office can walk to work.

Today's younger generation is no worse than my own. We were just as ignorant and repulsive as they are, but nobody listened to us.

Abstract art: a product of the untalented sold by the unprincipled to the utterly bewildered.

The public is like a piano. You just have to know what keys to poke.

The secret of how to live without resentment or embarrassment in a world in which I was different from everyone else. was to be indifferent to that difference.

## GEORGE CARLIN (Comedian, 1937-2008)

Swimming is not a sport. Swimming is a way to keep from drowning. That's just common sense!

A house is just a place to keep your stuff while you go out and get more stuff.

I wanna live. I don't wanna die. That's the whole meaning of life: Not dying! I figured that shit out by myself in the third grade.

I used to be Irish Catholic. Now I'm an American — you know, you grow.

If the Cincinnati Reds were really the first major league baseball team, who did they play?

Honesty may be the best policy, but it's important to remember that apparently, by elimination, dishonesty is the second-best policy.

If it's true that our species is alone in the universe, then I'd have to say that the universe aimed rather low and settled for very little      .

No one knows what's next, but everybody does it.

The very existence of flamethrowers proves that sometime, somewhere, someone said to themselves, "You know, I want to set those people over there on fire, but I'm just not close enough to get the job done.

The reason I talk to myself is because I'm the only one whose answers I accept.

Just when I  discovered the meaning of life, they changed it.

Religion has convinced people that there's an invisible man...living in the sky, who watches everything you do every minute of every day. And the invisible man has a list of ten specific things he doesn't want you to do. And if you do any of these things, he will send you to a special place, of burning and fire and smoke and torture and anguish for you to live forever, and suffer and burn and scream until the end of time. But he loves you. He loves you and he needs money.

Weather forecast for tonight: Dark. Continued dark overnight, with widely scattered light by morning.

If it requires a uniform, it's a worthless endeavor.

If you live long enough, sooner or later everybody you know has cancer.

You know the good part about all those executions in Texas? Fewer Texans.

Soft rock music isn't rock, and it ain't music. It's just soft.

As soon as someone is identified as an unsung hero, he no longer is.

The IQ and the life expectancy of the average American recently passed each other in opposite directions.

I put a dollar in a change machine. Nothing changed.

By and large, language is a tool for concealing the truth.

Ever notice that anyone going slower than you is an idiot, but  anyone going faster is a maniac?

Isn't it a bit unnerving  that doctors call what they do "practice"?

I don't like to think of laws as rules you have to follow, but more as suggestions.

I think it's the duty of the comedian to find out where the line is drawn and cross it deliberately.

When you're born you get a ticket to the freak show. When you're born in America, you get a front-row seat.

I never joined the Boy Scouts. I don't trust any organization that has a handbook.

I would never want to be a member of a group whose symbol was a man nailed to two pieces of wood.

Catholic — which I was until I reached the age of reason.

Here's a bumper sticker I'd like to see: "We are the proud parents of a child who's self-esteem is sufficient that he doesn't need us promoting his minor scholastic achievements on the back of our car."

I love and treasure individuals as I meet them; I loathe and despise the groups they identify with and belong to.

Beethoven was so hard of hearing, he thought he was a painter.

God bless the homicidal maniacs. They make life worthwhile.

One great thing about getting old is that you can get out of all sorts of social obligations just by saying you're too tired.

What year did Jesus think it was?

Have you ever wondered why Republicans are so interested in encouraging people to volunteer in their communities? It's because volunteers work for no pay. Republicans have been trying to get people to work for no pay for a long time.

In America, anyone can become president. That's the problem.

Once you leave the womb, conservatives don't care about you until you reach military age. Then you're just what they're looking for. Conservatives want live babies so they can raise them to be dead soldiers.

"One thing leads to another"? Not always. Sometimes one thing leads to the
same thing. Ask an addict.
Don Ho can sign autographs 3.4 times faster than Efrem Zimbalist Jr.
No one who has had "Taps" played for them has ever been able to hear it.
Property is theft. Nobody "owns" anything. When you die, it all stays here.
The future will soon be a thing of the past..
The real reason that we can't have the Ten Commandments in a courthouse:
You cannot post "Thou shalt not steal," "Thou shalt not commit adultery,"
and "Thou shalt not lie" in a building full of lawyers, judges, and
politicians. It creates a hostile work environment.
Boxing is a more sophisticated form of hockey.
The only good thing ever to come out of religion was the music.
I think everyone should treat one another in a Christian manner. I will not,
however, be responsible for the consequences.
Bowling is not a sport because you have to rent the shoes.
"When Will Jesus Bring the Pork Chops?" This title offends all three
major religions, and even vegetarians!
Thou shalt keep thy religion to thyself.
Atheism is a non-prophet organization.
Cloud nine gets all the publicity, but cloud eight actually is cheaper, less
crowded, and has a better view.
Have you ever noticed that the lawyer always smiles more than the client?
I'm always relieved when someone is delivering a eulogy and I realize I'm
listening to it.
Just think, right now as you read this, some guy somewhere is gettin'
ready to hang himself.
The reason they call it the American Dream is because you have to be
asleep to believe it
If all our national holidays were observed on Wednesdays, we could
wind up with nine-day weekends.
"Meow" means "woof" in cat.
Most people with low self-esteem have earned it.
Most people work just hard enough not to get fired and get paid just
enough money not to quit.
"No comment" is a comment.
If a man smiles all the time, he's probably selling something that doesn't work.
Most of the time people feel okay. Probably it's because at the
moment they're not actually dying.
So far, this is the oldest I've been.
When you think about it, attention-deficit order makes a lot of sense. In
this country there isn't a lot worth paying attention to.
The Golden Gate Bridge should have a long bungee cord for people who
aren't quite ready to commit suicide but want to get in a little practice.
I think I am, therefore, I am. I think.
If the cops didn't see it, I didn't do it!
Hooray for  most things!
Capitalism tries for a delicate balance: It attempts to work things out so that
everyone gets just enough stuff to keep them from getting violent and
trying to take other people's stuff.
I don't have a fear of heights. I do, however, have a fear of falling from heights.
What was the best thing before sliced bread?

May the forces of evil become confused on the way to your house.

Life is a zero sum game.

I have as much authority as the Pope. I just don't have as many people
who believe it.

It isn't fair: the caterpillar does all the work, and the butterfly gets all the glory.

## DALE CARNEGIE (Writer, Speaker, 1888-1955)

Act enthusiastic and you will be enthusiastic.

Any fool can criticize, condemn, and complain - and most fools do.

Applause is a receipt, not a bill.

Are you bored with life? Then throw yourself into some work you believe in
with all your heart, live for it, die for it, and you will find happiness
that you had thought could never be yours.

Develop success from failures. Discouragement and failure are two of
the surest stepping stones to success.

Do the hard jobs first. The easy jobs will take care of themselves.

Do the thing you fear to do and keep on doing it... that is the quickest and
surest way ever yet discovered to conquer fear.

Don't be afraid to give your best to what seemingly are small jobs. Every time
you conquer  one it makes you that much stronger. If you do the little
jobs well, the big ones will tend to take care of themselves.

Each nation feels superior to other nations. That breeds patriotism - and wars.

Fear not those who argue but those who dodge.

Feeling sorry for yourself, and your present condition, is not only a waste of
energy but the worst habit you could possibly have.

First ask yourself: What is the worst that can happen? Then prepare to accept
it. Then proceed to improve on the worst.

Flaming enthusiasm, backed up by horse sense and persistence, is the quality
that most frequently makes for success.

Happiness doesn't depend on any external conditions, it is governed by our
mental attitude.

If only the people who worry about their liabilities would think about the
riches they do possess, they would stop worrying.

If you believe in what you are doing, then let nothing hold you up in your work.
Much of the best work of the world has been done against seeming
impossibilities. The thing is to get the work done.

If you can't sleep, then get up and do something instead of lying there
worrying. It's the worry that gets you, not the lack of sleep.

If you want to gather honey, don't kick over the beehive.

Inaction breeds doubt and fear. Action breeds confidence and courage. If you
want to conquer fear, do not sit home and think about it. Go out
and get busy.

Instead of worrying about what people say of you, why not spend time
trying to accomplish something they will admire.

It isn't what you have, or who you are, or where you are, or what you are
doing that makes you happy or unhappy. It is what you think about.

Men of age object too much, consult too long, adventure too little, repent too
soon, and seldom drive business home to the full period, but content
themselves with a mediocrity of success

Most of the important things in the world have been accomplished by people
who have kept on trying when there seemed to be no hope at all.

Most of us have far more courage than we ever dreamed we possessed.

One of the most tragic things I know about human nature is that all of us tend to put off living. We are all dreaming of some magical rose garden over the horizon instead of enjoying the roses that are blooming outside our windows today.

Only the prepared speaker deserves to be confident.

Our fatigue is often caused not by work, but by worry, frustration and resentment.

People rarely succeed unless they have fun in what they are doing.

Remember happiness doesn't depend upon who you are or what you have; it depends solely on what you think.

Speakers who talk about what life has taught them never fail to keep the attention of their listeners.

Success is getting what you want. Happiness is wanting what you get.

Take a chance! All life is a chance. The man who goes farthest is generally the one who is willing to do and dare.

Tell the audience what you're going to say, say it; then tell them what you've said.

The essence of all art is to have pleasure in giving pleasure.

The expression a woman wears on her face is far more important than the clothes she wears on her back.

The ideas I stand for are not mine. I borrowed them from Socrates. I swiped them from Chesterfield. I stole them from Jesus. And I put them in a book. If you don't like their rules, whose would you use?

The only way to get the best of an argument is to avoid it.

The person who goes farthest is generally the one who is willing to do and dare. The sure-thing boat never gets far from shore.

The person who seeks all their applause from outside has their happiness in another's keeping .

The royal road to a man's heart is to talk to him about the things he treasures most.

The successful man will profit from his mistakes and try again in a different way.

There are always three speeches, for every one you actually gave. The one you practiced, the one you gave, and the one you wish you gave.

There are four ways, and only four ways, in which we have contact with the world. We are evaluated and classified by these four contacts: what we do, how we look, what we say, and how we say it.

There is only one way... to get anybody to do anything. And that is by making the other person want to do it.

Those convinced against their will are of the same opinion still.

Today is life-the only life you are sure of. Make the most of today. Get interested in something. Shake yourself awake. Develop a hobby. Let the winds of enthusiasm sweep through you. Live today with gusto.

We all have possibilities we don't know about. We can do things we don't even dream we can do.

When dealing with people, remember you are not dealing with creatures of logic, but creatures of emotion.

When fate hands you a lemon, make lemonade.

You can conquer almost any fear if you will only make up your mind to do so. For remember, fear doesn't exist anywhere except in the mind.

You can make more friends in two months by becoming interested in other people than you can in two years by trying to get other people interested in you.

You never achieve success unless you like what you are doing.

## JOHNNY CARSON (Talk Show Host, 1925-2005)

The only thing money gives you is the freedom of not worrying about money.

My success just evolved from working hard at the business at hand each day.

People will pay more to be entertained than educated.

Married men live longer than single men. But married men are a lot more willing to die.

If life was fair, Elvis would be alive and all the impersonators would be dead.

If variety is the spice of life, marriage is the big can of leftover Spam.

Democracy means that anyone can grow up to be president, and anyone who doesn't grow up can be vice president.

Talent alone won't make you a success. Neither will being in the right place at the right time, unless you are ready. The most important question is: "Are you ready?"

For days after death hair and fingernails continue to grow, but phone calls taper off.

Happiness is your dentist telling you it won't hurt and then having him catch his hand in the drill.

I know a man who gave up smoking, drinking, sex, and rich food. He was healthy right up to the day he killed himself.

I was so naive as a kid I used to sneak behind the barn and do nothing.

If it weren't for Philo T. Farnsworth, inventor of television, we'd still be eating frozen radio dinners.

Mail your packages early so the post office can lose them in time for Christmas.

Never continue in a job you don't enjoy. If you're happy in what you're doing, you'll like yourself, you'll have inner peace. And if you have that, along with physical health, you will have had more success than you could possibly have imagined.

Never use a big word when a little filthy one will do.

New York is an exciting town where something is happening all the time, most unsolved.

## JIMMY CARTER (President, 1924 - )

Aggression unopposed becomes a contagious disease.

America did not invent human rights. In a very real sense human rights invented America.

For this generation, ours, life is nuclear survival, liberty is human rights, the pursuit of happiness is a planet whose resources are devoted to the physical and spiritual nourishment of its inhabitants.

Globalization, as defined by rich people like us, is a very nice thing... you are talking about the Internet, you are talking about cell phones, you are talking about computers. This doesn't affect two-thirds of the people of the world.

Government is a contrivance of human wisdom to provide for human wants. People have the right to expect that these wants will be provided for by this wisdom.

Human rights is the soul of our foreign policy, because human rights is the very soul of our sense of nationhood.

I hate to see complacency prevail in our lives when it's so directly contrary to the teaching of Christ.

I have often wanted to drown my troubles, but I can't get my wife to go swimming.

I look forward to these confrontations with the press to kind of balance up the nice and pleasant things that come to me as president.

I say to you quite frankly that the time for racial discrimination is over.

I think what's going on in Guantanamo Bay and other places is a disgrace to the U.S.A. I wouldn't say it's the cause of terrorism, but it has given impetus and excuses to potential terrorists to lash out at our country and justify their despicable acts.

I've looked on many women with lust. I've committed adultery in my heart many times. God knows I will do this and forgives me.

If you fear making  anyone mad, then you ultimately probe for the lowest common denominator of human achievement.

If you're totally illiterate and living on one dollar a day, the benefits of globalization never come to you.

In this outward and physical ceremony we attest once again to the inner and spiritual strength of our Nation. As my high school teacher, Miss Julia Coleman, used to say: 'We must adjust to changing times and still hold to unchanging principles.'

It is difficult for the common good to prevail against the intense concentration of those who have a special interest, especially if the decisions are made behind locked doors.

It is good to realize that if love and peace can prevail on earth, and if we can teach our children to honor nature's gifts, the joys and beauties of the outdoors will be here forever.

It's not necessary to fear the prospect of failure but to be determined not to fail.

Like music and art, love of nature is a common language that can transcend political or social boundaries.

My decision to register women confirms what is already obvious throughout our society-that women are now providing all types of skills in every profession. The military should be no exception.

New Yorkers love it when you spill your guts out there. Spill your guts at Wimbledon and they make you stop and clean it up.

People make a big fuss over you when you're President. But I'm very serious about doing everything I can to make sure that it doesn't go to my head.

Republicans are men of narrow vision, who are afraid of the future.

Testing oneself is best when done alone.

The awareness that health is dependent upon habits that we control makes us the first generation in history that to a large extent determines its own destiny.

The best way to enhance freedom in other lands is to demonstrate here that our democratic system is worthy of emulation.

The experience of democracy is like the experience of life itself-always changing, infinite in its variety, sometimes turbulent and all the more valuable for having been tested by adversity.

There should be an honest attempt at the reconciliation of differences before resorting to combat.

To deal with individual human needs at the everyday level can be noble sometimes.

Unless both sides win, no agreement can be permanent.

War may sometimes be a necessary evil. But no matter how necessary, it is always an evil, never a good. We will not learn how to live together in peace by killing each other's children.

We become not a melting pot but a beautiful mosaic. Different people, different beliefs, different yearnings, different hopes, different dreams.

We cannot be both the world's leading champion of peace and the world's leading supplier of the weapons of war.

We must adjust to changing times and still hold to unchanging principles.
We must make it clear that a platform of 'I hate gay men and women' is not
     a way to become president of the United States.
We should live our lives as though Christ were coming this afternoon.
We will not learn how to live together in peace by killing each other's children.
Whatever starts in California unfortunately has an inclination to spread.
You can do what you have to do, and sometimes you can do it even better
     than you think you can.

## ROSALYNN CARTER (First Lady, 1927 - )

A leader takes people where they want to go. A great leader takes
     people where they don't necessarily want to go, but ought to be.
Do what you can to show you care about other people, and you will make
     our world a better place.
Don't worry about polls, but if you do, don't admit it.
There is nothing more important than a good, safe, secure home.
You have to have confidence in your ability, and then be tough enough
     to follow through.
You must accept that you might fail; then, if you do your best and still don't
     win, at least you can be satisfied that you've tried. If you don't accept
     failure as a possibility, you don't set high goals, you don't branch out,
     you don't try - you don't take the risk.

## STEPHEN CARTER (Lawyer, 1954 - )

Teaching civility is an obligation of the family.
There are no black conservatives. Oh, there are neoconservatives with
     black skin, but they lack any claim to blackness other than the
     biological. They have forgotten their roots.
To be black and an intellectual in America is to live in a box. On the box
     is a label, not of my own choosing.
When you shoot someone who is fleeing, it's not self-defense. It's an execution.

## JOHNNY CASH (Singer, 1933-2002)

A person knows when it just seems right to them.  Listen to your heart.
How  well I have learned that there is no fence to sit on between heaven and
     hell. There is a deep, wide gulf, a chasm, and in that chasm is no
     place for any man.
I start a lot more songs than I finish, because I realize when I get into them,
     they're no good. I don't throw them away, I just put them away, store
     them, get them out of sight.
My father was a man of love. He always loved me to death. He worked hard in the
     fields, but my father never hit me. Never. I don't ever remember a really
     cross, unkind word from my father.
Success is having to worry about every damn thing in the world, except money.
You build on failure. You use it as a stepping stone. Close the door on the past.
     You don't try to forget the mistakes, but you don't dwell on it. You don't
     let it have any of your energy, or any of your time, or any of your space.
You've got to know your limitations. I don't know what your limitations are. I
     found out what mine were when I was twelve. I found out that there
     weren't too many limitations, if I did it my way.

## DICK CAVETT (Talk Show Host, 1936 - )

As long as people will accept crap, it will be financially profitable to dispense it.

If your parents never had children, chances are... neither will you.

It's a rare person who wants to hear what he doesn't want to hear.

Can you picture yourself at the age 60 doing what you do now?

Censorship feeds the dirty mind more than the four-letter word itself.

Show people tend to treat their finances like their dentistry. They assume
      the man handling it knows what he is doing.

There's so much comedy on television. Does that cause comedy in the streets?

To label me an intellectual is a misunderstanding of what that is.

## HARRY CHAPIN (Folk Singer, 1942-1981)

When in doubt do something.

I am a greedy, selfish bastard. I want the fact that I existed to mean something

When you're going nowhere, anywhere's a better place to be.

Good dreams don't come cheap, you've got to pay for them and If you just dream
      when you're asleep this is no way for them to come alive... to survive.

Our lives are to be used and thus to be lived as fully as possible, and truly it seems
      that we are never so alive as when we concern ourselves with other people.

## RAY CHARLES (Musician, 1930-2004)

Affluence separates people. Poverty knits 'em together. You got some
      sugar and I don't; I borrow some of yours. Next month you might
      not have any flour; well, I'll give you some of mine.

I did it to myself. It wasn't society... it wasn't a pusher, it wasn't being
      blind or being black or being poor. It was all my doing.

I don't know what would have happened to me if I hadn't been able to hear.

I never wanted to be famous. I only wanted to be great.

I was born with music inside me. Music was one of my parts. Like my ribs,
      my kidneys, my liver, my heart. Like my blood. It was a force
      already within me when I arrived on the scene. It was a necessity
      for me - like food or water.

Learning to read music in Braille and play by ear helped me develop a
      damn good memory.

Love is a special word, and I use it only when I mean it. You say the word
      too much and it becomes cheap.

Music's been around a long time, and there's going to be music long after
      Ray Charles is dead. I just want to make my mark, leave something
      musically good behind. If it's a big record, that's the frosting on the
      cake, but music's the main meal.

My music had roots which I'd dug up from my own childhood, musical roots
      buried in the darkest soil.

My version of "Georgia" became the state song of Georgia. That was a big
      thing for me, man. It really touched me. Here is a state that used to
      lynch people like me suddenly declaring my version of a song as its
      state song. That is touching.

The fact of the matter is, you don't give up what's natural. Anything I've
      fantasized about, I've done.

There are many spokes on the wheel of life. First, we're here to explore
      new possibilities.

There's nothing written in the Bible, Old or New testament, that says,
"If you believe in Me, you ain't going to have no troubles."
What is a soul? It's like electricity - we don't really know what it is, but it's
a force that can light a room.
What makes my approach special is that I do different things. I do jazz,
blues, country music and so forth. I do them all, like a good
utility man.

## CESAR CHAVEZ (Labor Activist, 1927-1993)

Preservation of one's own culture does not require contempt or disrespect
for other cultures.
Our language is the reflection of ourselves. A language is an exact reflection
of the character and growth of its speakers.
Students must have initiative; they should not be mere imitators. They
must learn to think and act for themselves - and be free.
There is no such thing as defeat in non-violence.
If you really want to make a friend, go to someone's house and eat with
him... the people who give you their food give you their heart.
From the depth of need and despair, people can work together, can organize
themselves to solve their own problems and fill their own needs
with dignity and strength.
In some cases non-violence requires more militancy than violence.
Real education should consist of drawing the goodness and the best out of our
own students. What better books can there be than the book of humanity?
The fight is never about grapes or lettuce. It is always about people.
There is no substitute for hard work, 23 or 24 hours a day. And there is no
substitute for patience and acceptance.
We cannot seek achievement for ourselves and forget about progress and
prosperity for our community... Our ambitions must be broad enough to
include the aspirations and needs of others, for their sakes and for our own.
We draw our strength from the very despair in which we have been forced to live.
We shall endure.
We need to help students and parents cherish and preserve the ethnic and cultural
diversity that nourishes and strengthens this community - and this nation.
Who gets the risks? The risks are given to the consumer, the unsuspecting
consumer and the poor work force. And who gets the benefits? The benefits
are only for the corporations, for the money makers.
You are never strong enough that you don't need help.

## STEVEN CHU (Scientist, 1948 - )

Education in my family was not merely emphasized, it was our raison d'etre.
I approached the bulk of my schoolwork as a chore rather than an intellectual
adventure.
My physics teacher, Thomas Miner was particularly gifted. To this day, I remember
how he introduced the subject of physics. He told us we were going to learn
how to deal with very simple questions such as how a body falls due to the
acceleration of gravity.

## GROVER CLEVELAND (President, 1837-1908)

A government for the people must depend for its success on the intelligence,
  the morality, the justice, and the interest of the people themselves.

A truly American sentiment recognizes the dignity of labor and the fact that
  honor lies in honest toil.

Communism is a hateful thing, and a menace to peace and organized government.

He mocks the people who proposes that the government shall protect the
  rich and that they in turn will care for the laboring poor.

Honor lies in honest toil.

I have considered the pension list of the republic a roll of honor..

I know there is a Supreme Being who rules the affairs of men and whose goodness
  and mercy have always followed the American people, and I know He will
  not turn from us now if we humbly and reverently seek His powerful aid.

I would rather the man who presents something for my consideration subject
  me to a zephyr of truth and a gentle breeze of responsibility rather than
  blow me down with a curtain of hot wind.

In the scheme of our national government, the presidency is preeminently
  the people's office.

It is better to be defeated standing for a high principle than to run by
  committing subterfuge.

Minds do not act together in public; they simply stick together; and
  when their private activities are resumed, they fly apart again.

No man has ever yet been hanged for breaking the spirit of a law.

Officeholders are the agents of the people, not their masters.

Party honesty is party expediency.

Public officers are the servants and agents of the people, to execute the
  laws which the people have made.

Sensible and responsible women do not want to vote. The relative positions to
  be assumed by man and woman in the working out of our civilization
  were assigned long ago by a higher intelligence than ours.

Some day I will be better remembered.

Sometimes I wake at night in the White House and rub my eyes and wonder
  if it is not all a dream.

The ship of democracy, which has weathered all storms, may sink
  through the mutiny of those on board.

The United States is not a nation to which peace is a necessity.

Though the people support the government; the government should not
  support the people.

## HILLARY CLINTON (First Lady, Senator, Secretary of State, 1947 -)

Probably my worst quality is that I get very passionate about what
  I think is right.

The American people are tired of liars and people who pretend to be
  something they're not.

In the Bible it says they asked Jesus how many times you should forgive, and he
  said 70 times 7. Well, I want you all to know that I'm keeping a chart.

Voting is the most precious right of every citizen, and we have a moral o
  bligation to ensure the integrity of our voting process.

You cannot have maternal health without reproductive health. And
  reproductive health includes contraception and family planning
  and access to legal, safe abortion.

As I speak to you today, government censors somewhere are working
furiously to erase my words from the records of history. But history
itself has already condemned these tactics.
Both the American people and nations that censor the Internet should understand
that our government is committed to helping promote Internet freedom.
Countries that will not tax their elite who expect us to come in and help
them serve their people are just not going to get the kind of help
from us that historically they may have.
Every president, if you watch what they look like when they come into
office, you can see their hair turn white because it's such a hard job.
We'll hold out our hand; they have to unclench their fist.
What we have to do... is to find a way to celebrate our diversity and debate
our differences without fracturing our communities.
Let's not leave an educational vacuum to be filled by religious extremists
who go to families who have no other option and offer meals,
housing and some form of education. If we are going to combat
extremism then we must educate those very same children.
No matter what you think about the Iraq war, there is one thing we can all
agree on for the next days - we have to salute the courage and bravery
of those who are risking their lives to vote and those brave Iraqi and
American soldiers fighting to protect their right to vote.
Often times when you face such an overwhelming challenge as global climate
change, it can be somewhat daunting - it's kind of like trying to lose
weight, which I know something about.
One day after laying a wreath at the tomb of Martin Luther King Jr.,
President Bush appoints a federal judge who has built his career
around dismantling Dr. King's legacy.
The American taxpayer should not be treated more shabbily than debtors
from other nations and we should be encouraging other nations to
help rebuild Iraq's economy.
The challenge is to practice politics as the art of making what appears to be
impossible, possible.
The challenges of change are always hard. It is important that we begin to
unpack those challenges that confront this nation and realize that we
each have a role that requires us to change and become more
responsible for shaping our own future.
There are 4 billion cell phones in use today. Many of them are in the hands of
market vendors, rickshaw drivers, and others who've historically
lacked access to education and opportunity. Information networks
have become a great leveler, and we should use them together to help
lift people out of poverty and give them a freedom from want.
There is a great deal of political pressure to only talk about abstinence, and to
deny support for condoms and education on using them. This policy
will lead to the unnecessary deaths of many people.
Today we voted as Democrats and Republicans. Tomorrow we begin
again as New Yorkers.
We don't have enough support for maternal leave and the kinds of things
that some of the European countries do. So we still make it hard on
women to go into the work force and feel that they can be good at
work but then doing the most important job, which is raising your
children in a responsible and positive way.

All of us have to recognize that we owe our children more than we
    have been giving them.
We have a close, unshakable bond between the United States and Israel,
    and between the American and Israeli people. We share common
    values and a commitment to a democratic future for the world, and
    we are both committed to a two-state solution. But that doesn't mean
    that we're going to agree.
Every nation has to either be with us, or against us. Those who harbor
    terrorists, or who finance them, are going to pay a price.
We must stop thinking of the individual and start thinking about what is
    best for society.
I also believe that we have an extraordinary opportunity for the United
    States and European Union to lead the world in developing and
    implementing new and more efficient technologies - smart
    electrical grids and electrical vehicles.
I believe in a zone of privacy.
I feel very lucky because of my parents and then my education, the
    opportunities that I've had, so I would like to continue working
    to improve lives for others.
I think that we have to be constantly asking ourselves, 'How do we calculate
    the risk?' And sometimes we don't calculate it correctly; we either
    overstate it or understate it.
I'm undaunted in my quest to amuse myself by constantly changing my hair.
If I want to knock a story off the front page, I just change my hairstyle.
In almost every profession - whether it's law or journalism, finance or
    medicine or academia or running a small business - people rely on
    confidential communications to do their jobs. We count on the space
    of trust that confidentiality provides. When someone breaches that
    trust, we are all worse off for it.
In too many instances, the march to globalization has also meant the
    marginalization of women and girls. And that must change.

## WILLIAM CLINTON (President, 1946 - )

Frankly, I'm fed up with politicians in Washington lecturing the rest of us about
    family values. Our families have values. But our government doesn't.
The best social program is a good job.
I believe I'm a better authority than anybody else in America on my own wife. I
    have never known a person with a stronger sense of right and wrong
    in my life ever.
People really don't care if politicians attack each other with untrue stories. They
    figure if you don't want to get hurt, you shouldn't have filed for office.
    They figure whatever happens to us, our lives will be better than theirs.
Keep your eyes on the prize and don't turn back."
Pessimism is an excuse for not trying and a guarantee to a personal failure
The economy has produced 6.1 million jobs since I became president, and if
    Michael Jordan comes back to the Bulls, it will be 6,100,001 jobs
Strength and wisdom are not opposing values.
The new rage is to say that the government is the cause of all our problems,
    and if only we had no government, we'd have no problems. I can tell you,
    that contradicts evidence, history, and common sense.

There is nothing wrong with America that cannot be cured with what
     is right in America.
I haven't eaten at a McDonald's since I became President.
I tried marijuana once. I did not inhale.
Sometimes I feel like a fire hydrant looking at a pack of dogs."
I Like this quote I dislike this quote"We need to help younger people recognize their
     own capacity to do good, and help them discover the rewards of generosity.
Today, many companies are reporting that their number one constraint on growth
     is the inability to hire workers with the necessary skills.
We must teach our children to resolve their conflicts with words, not weapons.
The future is not an inheritance, it is an opportunity and an obligation.
The price of doing the same old thing is far higher than the price of change.
Profound and powerful forces are shaking and remaking our world. And the
     urgent question of our time is whether we can make change our friend
     and not our enemy.
Well, first of all, I think that a lot of the voters who are voting for the tea party
     candidates have really good impulses. That is, they believe that for years
     and years and years, the people with wealth and power or government
     power have done well and ordinary people have not. That's true.
When I think about the world I would like to leave to my daughter and the
     grandchildren I hope to have, it is a world that moves away from unequal,
     unstable, unsustainable interdependence to integrated communities -
     locally, nationally and globally - that share the characteristics of all
     successful communities.
     America just works better when more people have a chance to live
     their dreams.
Success is not the measure of a man but a triumph over those who choose
     to hold him back.
Just as war is freedom's cost, disagreement is freedom's privilege.
I Like this quote I dislike this quote"Taxing less and spending more... it's fun
     in the short run, but it's a recipe for disaster
Globalization is not something we can hold off or turn off . . . it is the
     economic equivalent of a force of nature -- like wind or water
I do not believe we can repair the basic fabric of society until people who are
     willing to work have work. Work organizes life. It gives structure and
     discipline to life.
By lifting the weakest, poorest among us, we lift the rest of us as well
We need not just a new generation of leadership but a new gender of leadership
The purpose of politics is to give people tools to make the most of their lives.
Politics is not religion and we should govern on the basis of evidence, not theology
The road to tyranny, we must never forget, begins with the destruction of the truth
Character is a journey, not a destination
Sometimes when people are under stress, they hate to think, and it's the time
     when they most need to think
Big things are expected of us, and nothing big ever came of being small
I like that about the Republicans; the evidence does not faze them, they
     are not bothered at all by the facts
You don't have to wait till your party's in power to have an impact on life
     at home and around the world.
You can't blame your opponents for applying a strategy that beats your
     brains out with regularity.

The most important family policy, urban policy, labor policy, minority policy, and foreign policy America can have is an expanding entrepreneurial economy of high-wage, high-skilled jobs.

Americans long to be united. After 9/11, we all just wanted to be one nation. Not a single American on September the 12, 2001, cared who won the next presidential election.

For too long we've been told about "us" and "them." Each and every election we see a new slate of arguments and ads telling us that "they" are the problem, not "us." But there can be no "them" in America. There's only us.

Banning human cloning reflects our humanity. It is the right thing to do. Creating a child through this new method calls into question our most fundamental beliefs. It has the potential to threaten the sacred family bonds at the very core of our ideals and our society. At its worst, it could lead to misguided and malevolent attempts to select certain traits, even to create certain kind of children -- to make our children objects rather than cherished individuals.

Abortion should not only be safe and legal, it should be rare.

If you live long enough, you'll make mistakes. But if you learn from them, you'll be a better person.

I mean, you know, this idea that somebody we disagree with on economic or social policy or something we have to turn into some kind of ogre or demon, think, is a mistake . . . it's like telling the American people or half the American people that don't agree with you they're all fools. That's just not true.

I still believe in a place called Hope, a place called America.

We cannot build our own future without helping others to build theirs.

When we give what we can and give it with joy, we don't just renew the American tradition of giving, we also renew ourselves.

Being president is like running a cemetery: you've got a lot of people under you and nobody's listening

I'm someone who had a deep emotional attachment to 'Starsky and Hutch

There are always going to be people who want to be president, and some days I'd like to give it to them

I may not have been the greatest president, but I've had the most fun eight years.

## GEORGE CLOONEY (Actor, 1961 -)

I don't like to share my personal life... it wouldn't be personal if I shared it.

The only failure is not to try.

The problem is, we elected a manager and we need a leader. Let's face it: Bush is just dim.

We're picking on people we can beat.

I bought a piano once because I had the dream of playing As Time Goes By as some girl's leaning on it drinking a martini. Great image. But none of it worked out. I can't even play Chopsticks. But I've got a nice piano at my house!

I don't believe in happy endings, but I do believe in happy travels, because ultimately, you die at a very young age, or you live long enough to watch your friends die. It's a mean thing, life.

I don't care. Charlton Heston is the head of the National Rifle Association. He deserves whatever anyone says about him.

I'm a Method actor. I spent years training for the drinking and carousing I had to do in this film.

I'm certainly the last person to give advice on, well, anything.

I'm not smart enough and I don't know enough about what's going on.

I'm really white trash.

I'm the flavor of the month.

I've been lucky enough to do a few films that will last longer than an opening weekend and those films are the ones I'm proud of.

I grew up in the world of bad television, on my dad's sets and then as a young schmuck on dating shows and so on.

I just found out about 10 days ago that I must live 300 or 400 yards from Britney Spears... so now I have to move.

I love children and I get along with them great. It's just that I believe if you're going to be a parent, there has to be something inside you that says, 'I want a family.' I don't feel that sense of urgency.

I was in a bar and I said to a friend, 'You know, we've become those 40-year-old guys we used to look at and say, 'Isn't it sad?'

I was watching 'Up In The Air' and I thought, 'Jesus, who's the old gray-haired guy?' And it was me. I never wear makeup for movies and now it's starting to show.

I'd think,'In a relationship, we should never have his kind of fight.' Then, instead of figuring out how to make it work, I looked for a way to get out of it. The truth is, you shouldn't be married if you're that kind of person.

It's incredibly unfair. You don't see a lot of 60-year-old women with 20-year-old men onscreen.

People know everything about everybody now.

Run for office? No. I've slept with too many women, I've done too many drugs, and I've been to too many parties.

The government itself is running exactly like the Sopranos and they sit back and they make deals. And they say okay, 'I'm going do this: France, you're getting the pipelines.'

The hardest thing is trying not to correct everything on the Internet. It'd be night and day - wrong, wrong, wrong, wrong. So you just have to say, 'All right, I'll take it, bring it on.'

There is a strange pecking order among actors. Theater actors look down on film actors, who look down on TV actors. Thank God for reality shows, or we wouldn't have anybody to look down on.

When you're young you believe it when people tell you how good you are. And that's the danger, you inhale. Everyone will tell you you're a genius, which you are not, and if you understand that, you win.

You have only a short period of time in your life to make your mark, and I'm there now.

## BILL COBSY (Comedian, Actor, 1937 - )

I don't know the key to success, but the key to failure is trying to please everybody.

When you become senile, you won't know it.

Immortality is a long shot, I admit. But somebody has to be first.

The main goal of the future is to stop violence. The world is addicted to it.

The past is a ghost, the future a dream, and all we ever have is now.

Parents aren't interested in justice - they want QUIET!

There is hope for the future because God has a sense of humor and we are funny to God.

Through humor, you can soften some of the worst blows that life delivers. And once you find laughter, no matter how painful your situation might be, you can survive it.

Women don't want to hear what you think. Women want to hear what they
    think - in a deeper voice.
There is no labor a person does that is undignified; if they do it right.
You can turn painful situations around through laughter. If you can find
    humor in anything, even poverty, you can survive it.
You know the only people who are always sure about the proper way to raise
    children? Those who've never had any.
A word to the wise ain't  necessary - it's the stupid ones that need the advice.
People can be more forgiving than you can imagine. But you have to forgive
    yourself. Let go of what's bitter and move on.
Gray hair is God's graffiti
I  wasn't always black... there was this freckle, and it got bigger and bigger.
Always end the name of your child with a vowel, so that when you yell the
    name will carry.
Human beings are the only creatures on earth that allow their children to
    come back home.
Any man today who returns from work, sinks into a chair, and calls for
    his pipe is a man with an appetite for danger.
 As I have discovered by examining my past, I started out as a child.
    Coincidentally, so did my brother. My mother did not put all her eggs
    in one basket, so to speak: she gave me a younger brother named
    Russell, who taught me what was meant by "survival of the fittest."
Decide that you want it more than you are afraid of it.
Even though your kids will consistently do the exact opposite of what you're
    telling them to do, you have to keep loving them just as much.
Every closed eye is not sleeping, and every open eye is not seeing.
Fatherhood is pretending the present you love most is soap-on-a-rope.
Having a child is surely the most beautifully irrational act that two
    people in love can commit.
I am certainly not an authority on love because there are no authorities on
    love, just those who've had luck with it and those who haven't
I am proud to be an American. Because an American can eat anything on
    the face of this earth as long as he has two pieces of bread.
I guess the real reason that my wife and I had children is the same reason that
    Napoleon had for invading Russia: it seemed like a good idea at the time.
If the new American father feels bewildered and even defeated, let him take
    comfort from the fact that whatever he does in any fathering situation
    has a fifty percent chance of being right.
Let us now set forth one of the fundamental truths about marriage: the
    wife is in charge.
Like everyone else who makes the mistake of getting older, I begin
    each day with coffee and obituaries.
Men and women belong to different species and communications between
    them is still in its infancy.
My childhood should have taught me lessons for my own fatherhood, but it didn't
    because parenting can only be learned by people who have no children.
No matter how calmly you try to referee, parenting will eventually produce
    bizarre behavior, and I'm not talking about the kids. Their behavior
    is always normal.
Nothing I've ever done has given me more joys and rewards than
    being a father to my children.

Nothing separates the generations more than music. By the time a child is eight or nine, he has developed a passion for his own music that is even stronger than his passions for procrastination and weird clothes.

It isn't a matter of black is beautiful as much as it is white is not all that's beautiful.

Old is always fifteen years from now.

Poets have said that the reason to have children is to give yourself immortality. Immortality? Now that I have five children, my only hope is that they are all out of the house before I die.

Raising children is an incredibly hard and risky business in which no cumulative wisdom is gained: each generation repeats the mistakes the previous one made.

Sex education may be a good idea in the schools, but I don't believe the kids should be given homework.

That married couples can live together day after day is a miracle that the Vatican has overlooked.

The essence of childhood, of course, is play, which my friends and I did endlessly on streets that we reluctantly shared with traffic.

The heart of marriage is memories; and if the two of you happen to have the same ones and can savor your reruns, then your marriage is a gift from the gods

## BARRY COMMONER (Scientist, 1917 - )

If you can see the light at the end of the tunnel, you are looking the wrong way.

Earth Day 1970 was irrefutable evidence that the American people understood the environmental threat and wanted action to resolve it.

The first law of ecology is that everything is related to everything else

The modern assault on the environment began about 50 years ago, during and immediately after World War II.

The most meaningful engine of change, powerful enough to confront corporate power, may be not so much environmental quality, as the economic development and growth associated with the effort to improve it.

As the earth spins through space, a view from above the North Pole would encompass most of the wealth of the world - most of its food, productive machines, doctors, engineers and teachers. A view from the opposite pole would encompass most of the world's poor.

Environmental concern is now firmly embedded in public life: in education, medicine and law; in journalism, literature and art.

Environmental quality was drastically improved while economic activity grew by the simple expedient of removing lead from gasoline - which prevented it from entering the environment.

It reflects a prevailing myth that production technology is no more amenable to human judgment or social interests than the laws of thermodynamics, atomic structure or biological inheritance.

No action is without its side effects.

Nothing ever goes away.

The environmental crisis arises from a fundamental fault: our systems of production - in industry, agriculture, energy and transportation - essential as they are, make people sick and die.

The environmental crisis is a global problem, and only global action will resolve it.

When you fully understand the situation, it is worse than you think.

## CHARLES HORTON COOLEY (Sociologist, 1866-1928)

Unless a capacity for thinking be accompanied by a capacity for action,
a superior mind exists in torture.

Every general increase of freedom is accompanied by some degeneracy,
attributable to the same causes as the freedom.

Failure sometimes enlarges the spirit. You have to fall back upon
humanity and God.

Institutions - government, churches, industries, and the like - have properly
no other function than to contribute to human freedom; and in so far
as they fail, on the whole, to perform this function, they are wrong
and need reconstruction.

A man may lack everything but tact and conviction and still be a forcible
speaker; but without these nothing will avail... Fluency, grace, logical
order, and the like, are merely the decorative surface of oratory.

There is hardly any one so insignificant that he does not seem imposing
to some one at some time.

The mind is not a hermit's cell, but a place of hospitality and intercourse.

A talent somewhat above mediocrity, shrewd and not too sensitive, is
more likely to rise in the world than genius.

An artist cannot fail; it is a success to be one.

To have no heroes is to have no aspiration, to live on the momentum of the
past, to be thrown back upon routine, sensuality, and the narrow self.

There is no way to penetrate the surface of life but by attacking it
earnestly at a particular point.

There is nothing less to our credit than our neglect of the foreigner and
his children, unless it be the arrogance most of us betray when
we set out to "Americanize" him.

To cease to admire is a proof of deterioration.

To get away from one's working environment is, in a sense, to get
away from one's self; and this is often the chief advantage of
travel and change.

We are ashamed to seem evasive in the presence of a straightforward
man, cowardly in the presence of a brave one, gross in the eyes of
a refined one, and so on. We always imagine, and in imagining share,
the judgments of the other mind.

We have no higher life that is really apart from other people. It is by
imagining them that our personality is built up; to be without
the power of imagining them is to be a low-grade idiot.

When one ceases from conflict, whether because he has won, because he
has lost, or because he cares no more for the game, the virtue
passes out of him.

Between richer and poorer classes in a free country a mutually respecting
antagonism is much healthier than pity on the one hand and dependence
on the other, as is, perhaps, the next best thing to fraternal feeling.

Each man must have his I; it is more necessary to him than bread; and if
he does not find scope for it within the existing institutions he will
be likely to make trouble.

If we divine a discrepancy between a man's words and his character, the
whole impression of him becomes broken and painful; he revolts
the imagination by his lack of unity, and even the good in him is
hardly accepted.

One should never criticize his own work except in a fresh and
      hopeful mood. The self-criticism of a tired mind is suicide.

Our individual lives cannot, generally, be works of art unless the
      social order is also.

As social beings we live with our eyes upon our reflection, but have no
      assurance of the tranquillity of the waters in which we see it.

Prudence and compromise are necessary means, but every man should
      have an impudent end which he will not compromise.

So far as discipline is concerned, freedom means not its absence but the
      use of higher and more rational forms as contrasted with those that
      are lower or less rational.

The bashful are always aggressive at heart.

The general fact is that the most effective way of utilizing human energy is
      through an organized rivalry, which by specialization and social control
      is, at the same time, organized co-operation.

The idea that seeing life means going from place to place and doing a great
      variety of obvious things is an illusion natural to dull minds.

The imaginations which people have of one another are the solid facts
      of society.

The literature of the inner life is very largely a record of struggle with the
      inordinate passions of the social self.

## CALVIN COOLIDGE (President, 1872-1933)

I have never been hurt by what I have not said.

No person was ever honored for what he received. Honor has
      been the reward for what he gave.

Advertising is the life of trade.

Any man who does not like dogs and want them about
      does not deserve to be in the White House.

Four-fifths of all our troubles would disappear, if we would
      only sit down and keep still.

We cannot do everything at once, but we can do something at once.

Nothing in this world can take the place of persistence. Talent will not;
      nothing is more common than unsuccessful people with talent.
      Genius will not; unrewarded genius is almost a proverb. Education
      will not; the world is full of educated failures. Persistence and
      determination alone are omnipotent.

It takes a great man to be a good listener.

Collecting more taxes than is absolutely necessary is legalized robbery.

Heroism is not only in the man, but in the occasion.

I have found it advisable not to give too much heed to what people say
      when I am trying to accomplish something of consequence.
      Invariably they proclaim it can't be done. I deem that the very
      best time to make the effort.

When more and more people are thrown out of work, unemployment results.

When people are bewildered they tend to become credulous.

I sometimes wish that people would put a little more emphasis upon
      the observance of the law than they do upon its enforcement.

If I had permitted my failures, or what seemed to me at the time a lack
      of success, to discourage me I cannot see any way in which I
      would ever have made progress.

If you don't say anything, you won't be called on to repeat it.

If you see ten troubles coming down the road, you can be sure
that nine will run into the ditch before they reach you

After all, the chief business of the American people is business. They
are profoundly concerned with producing, buying, selling, investing
and prospering in the world.

You can't know too much, but you can say too much.

All growth depends upon activity. There is no development physically
or intellectually without effort, and effort means work.

Christmas is not a time nor a season, but a state of mind. To cherish
peace and goodwill, to be plenteous in mercy, is to have the
real spirit of Christmas.

Civilization and profit go hand in hand.

Don't expect to build up the weak by pulling down the strong.

Duty is not collective; it is personal.

Economy is the method by which we prepare today to afford the
improvements of tomorrow.

In the discharge of the duties of this office, there is one rule of action more
important than all others. It consists in never doing anything that
someone else can do for you.

Industry, thrift and self-control are not sought because they create wealth,
but because they create character.

It is only when men begin to worship that they begin to grow.

Knowledge comes, but wisdom lingers. It may not be difficult to store up
in the mind a vast quantity of face within a comparatively short time,
but the ability to form judgments requires the severe discipline of
hard work and the tempering heat of experience and maturity.

Little progress can be made by merely attempting to repress what is evil.
Our great hope lies in developing what is good.

Mass demand has been created almost entirely through the development
of advertising.

Men speak of natural rights, but I challenge any one to show where in nature
any rights existed or were recognized until there was established for
their declaration and protection a duly promulgated body of
corresponding laws.

No enterprise can exist for itself alone. It ministers to some great need, it
performs some great service, not for itself, but for others; or failing
therein, it ceases to be profitable and ceases to exist.

No man ever listened himself out of a job.

No nation ever had an army large enough to guarantee it against attack in
time of peace, or ensure it of victory in time of war.

One with the law is a majority.

Patriotism is easy to understand in America. It means looking out for
yourself by looking out for your country.

Perhaps one of the most important accomplishments of my administration
has been minding my own business.

Prosperity is only an instrument to be used, not a deity to be worshiped.

The business of America is business.

The government of the United States is a device for maintaining in
perpetuity the rights of the people, with the ultimate extinction
of all privileged classes.

The man who builds a factory builds a temple, that the man who works
there worships there, and to each is due, not scorn and blame,
but reverence and praise.
The nation which forgets its defenders will be itself forgotten.
The right thing to do never requires any subterfuge, it is always simple
and direct.
There is no dignity quite so impressive, and no one independence quite
so important, as living within your means.
There is no force so democratic as the force of an ideal.
They criticize me for harping on the obvious; if all the folks in the
United States would do the few simple things they know they
ought to do, most of our big problems would take care
of themselves.
Those who trust to chance must abide by the results of chance.
To live under the American Constitution is the greatest political privilege
that was ever accorded to the human race.
Ultimately property rights and personal rights are the same thing.
We do not need more intellectual power, we need more spiritual power.
We do not need more of the things that are seen, we need more
of the things that are unseen.
We draw our Presidents from the people. It is a wholesome thing for them
to return to the people. I came from them. I wish to be one of
them again.
We need more of the Office Desk and less of the Show Window in politics.
Let men in office substitute the midnight oil for the limelight.

## JAMES FENIMORE COOPER (Author, 1879-1851)

Ignorance and superstition ever bear a close and mathematical
relation to each other.
It is a besetting vice of democracies to substitute public opinion for law.
This is the usual form in which masses of men exhibit their tyranny.
If the newspapers are useful in overthrowing tyrants, it is only to
establish a tyranny of their own
Individuality is the aim of political liberty
The principal advantage of a democracy, is a general elevation
in the character of the people
The tendency of democracies is, in all things, to mediocrity.
Should we distrust the man because his manners are not our manners,
and that his skin is dark?
Principles . . . become modified in practice, by facts.
A refined simplicity is the characteristic of all high bred
deportment, in every country.
The affairs of life embrace a multitude of interests, and he who reasons
in any one of them, without consulting the rest, is a visionary
unsuited to control the business of the world.
The minority of a country is never known to agree, except in its efforts
to reduce and oppress the majority
On the human imagination events produce the effects of time. Thus, he
who has traveled far and seen much is apt to fancy that he has
lived long; and the history that most abounds in important
incidents soonest assumes the aspect of antiquity.

The press, like fire, is an excellent servant, but a terrible master.

Misfortune begets misfortune: life is a misfortune, for it may be the
means of enduring misfortune; and death is a misfortune, as it
abridges the enjoyments of life.

The sublimity connected with vastness is familiar to every eye.

[Political] Party leads to vicious, corrupt and unprofitable legislation,
for the sole purpose of defeating [Political] party.

The expanse of the ocean is seldom seen by the novice with indifference.

Slavery is no more sinful, by the Christian code, than it is sinful to wear
a whole coat, while another is in tatters, to eat a better meal than
a neighbor, or otherwise to enjoy ease and plenty, while our fellow
creatures are suffering and in want.

I know but little of the customs of war, and wish to know less.

Friendship that flows from the heart cannot be frozen by adversity,
as the water that flows from the spring cannot congeal in winter.

The disposition of all power is to abuses, nor does it at all mend the
matter that its possessors are a majority.

Equality, in a social sense, may be divided into that of condition, and
that of rights. Equality of condition is incompatible with civilization, and is
found only to exist in those communities that are but slightly removed
from the savage state. In practice, it can only mean a common misery.

They who have reasoned ignorantly, or who have aimed at effecting their
personal ends by flattering the popular feeling, have boldly affirmed
that "one man is as good as another;" a maxim that is true in neither
nature, revealed morals, nor political theory.

...no civilized society can long exist, with an active power in its bosom
that is stronger than the law."

Individuality is the aim of political liberty. By leaving the citizen as much
freedom of action and of being as comports with order and the rights
of  others, the institutions render him truly a freeman. He is left to
pursue his means of happiness in his own manner

In America, it is indispensable that every well wisher of true liberty should
understand that acts of tyranny can only proceed from the public.
The public, then, is to be watched, in this country, as, in other
countries kings and aristocrats are to be watched.

Systems are to be appreciated by their general effects, and not by
particular exceptions.

Candor is a proof of both a just frame of mind and of a good tone of
breeding. It is a quality that belongs equally to the honest ;man
and to the gentleman.

The minority of a country is never known to agree, except in its efforts
to reduce and oppress the majority.

All greatness of character is dependent on individuality. The man who has
no other existence than that which he partakes in common with all
around him, will never have any other than an existence of mediocrity.

It is a governing principle of nature, that the agency which can produce most good,
when perverted from its proper aim, is most productive of evil. It behooves
the well-intentioned, therefore, vigorously to watch the tendency of even
their most highly prized institutions, since that which was established in the
interests of the right, may so easily become the agent of the wrong.

## DAVY CROCKETT (Explorer, Congressman, Frontiersman, 1786-1836)

I have always supported measures and principles and not men.

Be always sure you are right - then go ahead.

Fame is like a shaved pig with a greased tail, and it is only after it has
slipped through the hands of some thousands, that some fellow, by
mere chance, holds on to it!

I have suffered my self to be politically sacrificed to save my country from ruin
and disgrace and if I am never a gain elected I will have the gratification
to know that I have done my duty.

I would rather be beaten, and be a man, than to be elected and be a
little puppy dog.

I would rather be politically dead than hypocritically immortalized.

If one man in the country could take all the money, what was the use of
passing any bills about it?

It was expected of me that I was to bow to the name of Andrew Jackson... even
at the expense of my conscience and judgement. such a thing was new
to me, and a total stranger to my principles.

Let your tongue speak what your heart thinks.

Look at my arms, you will find no party hand-cuff on them.

The enemy fought with savage fury, and met death with all its horrors,
without shrinking or complaining: not one asked to be spared, but
fought as long as they could stand or sit.

Throughout the day no time for memorandums now. Go ahead! Liberty
and independence forever.

We have the right as individuals to give away as much of our own money
as we please in charity; but as members of Congress we have no
right to appropriate a dollar of the public money.

We must not permit our respect for the dead or our sympathy for the living
to lead us into an act of injustice to the balance of the living.

You may all go to Hell, and I will go to Texas.

## WALTER CRONKITE (Newscaster, 1916-2009)

America's health care system is neither healthy, caring, nor a system.

The perils of duck hunting are great - especially for the duck.

There is no such thing as a little freedom. Either you are all free, or you are not free.

I am dumbfounded that there hasn't been a crackdown with the libel and slander
laws on some of these would-be writers and reporters on the Internet

In seeking truth you have to get both sides of a story.

Everything is being compressed into tiny tablets. You take a little pill
of news every day - 23 minutes - and that's supposed to be enough.

I can't imagine a person becoming a success who doesn't give this game
of life everything he's got.

I think it is absolutely essential in a democracy to have competition in the
media, a lot of competition, and we seem to be moving away from that.

I think somebody ought to do a survey as to how many great, important men
have quit to spend time with their families who spent any more time
with their family.

Objective journalism and an opinion column are about as similar as the
Bible and Playboy magazine.

Our job is only to hold up the mirror - to tell and show the public
what has happened.

The great sadness of my life is that I never achieved the hour newscast,
    which would not have been twice as good as the half-hour newscast,
    but many times as good.
We are not educated well enough to perform the necessary act of
    intelligently selecting our leaders.

## GEORGE CUSTER (Army Officer, Civil War Hero, 1839-1876)

I would be willing, yes glad, to see a battle every day during my life.
My purpose is to make my narrative as truthful as possible.
There are not enough Indians in the world to defeat the Seventh Cavalry.
You ask me if I will not be glad when the last battle is fought, so far as the
    country is concerned I, of course, must wish for peace, and will be glad
    when the war is ended, but if I answer for myself alone, I must say that
    I shall regret to see the war end.

## RODNEY DANGERFIELD (Actor, Comedian, 1921-2004)

I met the surgeon general - he offered me a cigarette.
I remember the time I was kidnaped and they sent a piece of my finger
    to my father. He said he wanted more proof.
A girl phoned me the other day and said... 'Come on over, there's  nobody
    home.' I went over. Nobody was home.
Acting deals with very delicate emotions. It is not putting up a mask. Each
    time an actor acts he does not hide; he exposes himself.
At twenty a man is full of fight and hope. He wants to reform the world. When
    he is seventy he still wants to reform the world, but he knows he can't.
I came from a real tough neighborhood. I put my hand in some cement
    and felt another hand.
I could tell my parents hated me. My bath toys were a toaster and a radio.
I get no respect. The way my luck is running, if I was a politician I would be honest.
I haven't spoken to my wife in years. I didn't want to interrupt her.
I told my dentist my teeth are going yellow. he told me to wear a brown tie.
I worked in a pet store and people would ask how big I would get.
It's tough to stay married. My wife kisses the dog on the lips, yet she
    won't drink from my glass.
Life is just a bowl of pits.
Men who do things without being told draw the most wages.
Most of the arguments to which I am party fall somewhat short of being
    impressive, knowing to the fact that neither I nor my opponent
    knows what we are talking about.
My father carries around the picture of the kid who came with his wallet.
My mother had morning sickness after I was born.
My wife and I were happy for 20 years. Then we met.
My wife is always trying to get rid of me. The other day she told me to
    put the garbage out. I said to her I already did. She told me to go
    and keep an eye on it.

## CLARENCE DARROW (Lawyer, 1857-1938)

As long as the world shall last there will be wrongs, and if no man
    objected and no man rebelled, those wrongs would last forever.
Calvin Coolidge was the greatest man who ever came out of Plymouth
    Corner, Vermont.

Chase after the truth like all hell and you'll free yourself, even though
        you never touch its coat tails.
Depressions may bring people closer to the church but so do funerals.
Even if you do learn to speak correct English, whom are you going to speak it to?
History repeats itself, and that's one of the things that's wrong with history.
I am a friend of the working man, and I would rather be his friend, than be one.
I am an agnostic; I do not pretend to know what many ignorant men are sure of.
I do not believe in God because I do not believe in Mother Goose.
I do not consider it an insult, but rather a compliment to be called an
        agnostic. I do not pretend to know where many ignorant men are
        sure - that is all that agnosticism means.
I don't like spinach, and I'm glad I don't, because if I liked it I'd eat
        it, and I just hate it.
I have never killed a man, but I have read many obituaries with great pleasure.
I have suffered from being misunderstood, but I would have suffered a hell
        of a lot more if I had been understood.
If a man is happy in America, it is considered he is doing something wrong.
If you lose the power to laugh, you lose the power to think.
In spite of all the yearnings of men, no one can produce a single fact or
        reason to support the belief in God and in personal immortality.
Just think of the tragedy of teaching children not to doubt.
Justice has nothing to do with what goes on in a courtroom; Justice is
        what comes out of a courtroom.
Laws should be like clothes. They should be made to fit the people they serve.
Lost causes are the only ones worth fighting for.
No other offense has ever been visited with such severe penalties as
        seeking to help the oppressed.
None meet life honestly and few heroically.
Some of you say religion makes people happy. So does laughing gas.
Someday I hope to write a book where the royalties will pay for the
        copies I give away.
The best that we can do is to be kindly and helpful toward our friends and
        fellow passengers who are clinging to the same speck of dirt while
        we are drifting side by side to our common doom.
The first half of our lives are ruined by our parents and the second
        half by our children.
The law does not pretend to punish everything that is dishonest. That
        would seriously interfere with business.
The only real lawyers are trial lawyers, and trial lawyers try cases to juries.
The origin of the absurd idea of immortal life is easy to discover; it is kept
        alive by hope and fear, by childish faith, and by cowardice.
The pursuit of truth will set you free; even if you never catch up with it.
The trouble with law is lawyers.
The world is made up for the most part of morons and natural tyrants, sure
        of themselves, strong in their own opinions, never doubting anything.
There is no such thing as justice - in or out of court.
To think is to differ.
True patriotism hates injustice in its own land more than anywhere else.
When I was a boy I was told that anybody could become President; I'm
        beginning to believe it.
Working people have a lot of bad habits, but the worst of these is work.

You can only be free if I am free.
You can only protect your liberties in this world by protecting the
        other man's freedom.

## JAMES DEAN (Actor, 1931-1955)

Dream as if you'll live forever. Live as if you'll die today.
Only the gentle are ever really strong.
The gratification comes in the doing, not in the results.
Being an actor is the loneliest thing in the world. You are all alone with
        your concentration and imagination, and that's all you have.
I also became close to nature, and am now able to appreciate the beauty
        with which this world is endowed.
If a man can bridge the gap between life and death, if he can live on
        after he's dead, then maybe he was a great man.
Studying cows, pigs and chickens can help an actor develop his character. There
        are a lot of things I learned from animals. One was that they couldn't
        hiss or boo me.
The only greatness for man is immortality.
There is no way to be truly great in this world. We are all impaled on
        the crook of conditioning.
To grasp the full significance of life is the actor's duty; to interpret it
        his problem; and to express it his dedication.
To me, acting is the most logical way for people's neuroses to manifest
        themselves, in this great need we all have to express ourselves.
To my way of thinking, an actor's course is set even before he's out of the cradle.
Trust and belief are two prime considerations. You must not allow yourself
        to be opinionated.
When an actor plays a scene exactly the way a director orders, it isn't acting. It's
        following instructions. Anyone with the physical qualifications can do that.

## JIMMY DEAN (Actor, Singer, Businessman, 1928 -)

You gotta try your luck at least once a day, because you could be going
        around lucky all day and not even know it.
Poverty was the greatest motivating factor in my life.
I can't change the direction of the wind, but I can adjust my sails
        to always reach my destination.
A lot of things I am, and a lot of things I am not. But I think I'm about as
        good an American as there is. I love this country. It's been very,
        very good to me. And it will be good to anybody if they are willing
        to give of themselves.
God is bigger than people think.
I made more money yesterday than I ever thought I'd make in an entire lifetime.
        But it's like somebody's going to take it all away from me and I'll be
        back in Texas, installing them damned irrigation wells. I didn't like that
        when I was sixteen. And I know I wouldn't like it when I'm eighty.
I used to help my granddaddy make sausage. He would mix it up in a cleaned-out
        washtub with his hands, no gloves. Man, if we did anything like
        that today, they would jack the jail up and throw us under it.
Love is an ice cream sundae, with all the marvelous coverings. Sex is
        the cherry on top.

## VINE DELORIA JR. (American Indian Activist, 1933-2005)

When asked by an anthropologist what the Indians called America before the white man came, an Indian said simply, 'Ours.'

Western civilization, unfortunately, does not link knowledge and morality but rather, it connects knowledge and power and makes them equivalent.

## JOHN DENVER (Musician, 1943-1997)

I believe that we are here for each other, not against each other. Everything comes from an understanding that you are a gift in my life - whoever you are, whatever our differences.

I think the biggest problem in the world is that we have a generation of young people, and maybe two, who don't think it's going to get any better.

I would so much like young people to have a sense of the gift that they are. Not many of them feel like that.

Peace is a conscious choice.

We don't teach kids how to feel, we don't give them the words to go by.

We must begin to make what I call "conscious choices," and to really recognize that we are the same. It's from that place in my heart that I write my songs.

Perhaps love is like a resting place, A shelter from the storm, It exists to give you comfort, It is there to keep you warm, And in those times of trouble, When you are most alone, The memory of love will bring you home.

I would make my job a work of art. I would like whatever it is that I'm doing - everyone's experience of me, everyone's interaction with me, everyone's discussion, conversation, relationship with me - [to be] an event within which they get to see who they are. I would make of my life a work of art.

There's an aspect of human nature in which we want to think we're better than somebody else. They're a different color. They speak a different language. They have a different name for the Creator. Whatever it is, that makes it okay for me to hate them, to try to get some of their land or some of their resources.

There's one piece of advice my dad gave me when he dropped me off at college. He said, "You've got the talent. You can sing and play guitar. That doesn't make you any better than anyone else."

We don't teach kids how to feel, we don't give them the words to go by.

There has never been a time on Earth like we see today. What we need are more ways to experience our interconnectedness - it is a precursor to deep love. So in this quickening light, with the dawn of each new day, let us look for love. Let us no longer struggle. Let us ever become who we most want to be. As we begin to be who we truly are, the world will be a better place.

## JOHNNY DEPP (Actor, 1963 - )

If there's any message to my work, it is ultimately that it's OK to be different, that it's good to be different, that we should question ourselves before we pass judgment on someone who looks different, behaves different, talks different, is a different color.

I pretty much try to stay in a constant state of confusion just because of the expression it leaves on my face.

The only creatures that are evolved enough to convey pure love are dogs and infants.

Am I a romantic? I've seen 'Wuthering Heights' ten times. I'm a romantic.

I was ecstatic they re-named 'French Fries' as 'Freedom Fries'. Grown men
and women in positions of power in the U.S. government showing
themselves as idiots.

The term 'serious actor' is kind of an oxymoron, isn't it? Like
'Republican party' or 'airplane food.'

As a teenager I was so insecure. I was the type of guy that never fitted in
because he never dared to choose. I was convinced I had absolutely
no talent at all. For nothing. And that thought took away all my
ambition too.

France, and the whole of Europe have a great culture and an amazing history.
Most important thing though is that people there know how to live! In
America they've forgotten all about it. I'm afraid that the American
culture is a disaster.

How many chances to you get to make a musical about a serial killer? The
minute Tim Burton approached me, I was in.

I am doing things that are true to me. The only thing I have a problem
with is being labeled.

I don't pretend to be captain weird. I just do what I do.

I may have a feather duster down my pants.

I think everybody's nuts.

I think the thing to do is enjoy the ride while you're on it.

I'm an old-fashioned guy... I want to be an old man with a beer belly
sitting on a porch, looking at a lake or something.

I'm not sure I'm adult yet.

I'm shy, paranoid, whatever word you want to use. I hate fame. I've done
everything I can to avoid it.

If you catch me saying 'I am a serious actor,' I beg you to slap me.

It's all kinds of these profound things crashing on you when your child arrives
into the world. It's like you've met your reason to live.

It's good to experience Hollywood in short bursts, I guess. Little snippets.
I don't think I can handle being here all the time, it's pretty nutty.

Life's pretty good, and why wouldn't it be? I'm a pirate, after all.

Me, I'm dishonest, and you can always trust a dishonest man to be
dishonest. Honestly, it's the honest ones you have to watch out for.

People say I make strange choices, but they're not strange for me. My
sickness is that I'm fascinated by human behavior, by what's
underneath the surface, by the worlds inside people.

The only gossip I'm interested in is things from the Weekly World News -
'Woman's bra bursts, 11 injured'. That kind of thing.

There are four questions of value in life... What is sacred? Of what is
the spirit made? What is worth living for, and what is worth dying
for? The answer to each is the same. Only love.

There are necessary evils. Money is an important thing in terms of
representing freedom in our world. And now I have a daughter
to think about. It's really the first time I've thought about the
future and what it could be.

There's a drive in me that won't allow me to do certain things that are easy.

Tomorrow it'll all be over, then I'll have to go back to selling pens again.

When kids hit one year old, it's like hanging out with a miniature drunk.
You have to hold onto them. They bump into things. They laugh
and cry. They urinate. They vomit.

With any part you play, there is a certain amount of yourself in it. There
       has to be, otherwise it's just not acting. It's lying.
You use your money to buy privacy because during most of your life
       you aren't allowed to be normal.

## EMILY DICKINSON (Poet, 1830-1886)

A word is dead when it is said, some say. I say it just begins to live that day.
A wounded deer leaps the highest.
After great pain, a formal feeling comes. The Nerves sit ceremonious, like tombs.
Beauty is not caused. It is.
Because I could not stop for death, He kindly stopped for me; The carriage
       held but just ourselves and immortality.
Behavior is what a man does, not what he thinks, feels, or believes.
Celebrity is the chastisement of merit and the punishment of talent.
Dogs are better than human beings because they know but do not tell.
Dwell in possibility.
Dying is a wild night and a new road.
Fame is a fickle food upon a shifting plate.
Find ecstasy in life; the mere sense of living is joy enough.
Finite to fail, but infinite to venture.
For love is immortality.
Forever is composed of nows.
Fortune befriends the bold.
He ate and drank the precious Words, his Spirit grew robust; He knew no
       more that he was poor, nor that his frame was Dust.
Hope is the thing with feathers that perches in the soul - and sings the
       tunes without the words - and never stops at all.
How strange that nature does not knock, and yet does not intrude!
I argue thee that love is life. And life hath immortality.
I do not like the man who squanders life for fame; give me the man
       who living makes a name.
I hope you love birds too. It is economical. It saves going to heaven.
I'm nobody, who are you?
If I can stop one heart from breaking, I shall not live in vain.
If I feel physically as if the top of my head were taken off, I know that is poetry.
If I read a book and it makes my whole body so cold no fire can ever warm
       me, I know that is poetry.
It is better to be the hammer than the anvil.
Love is anterior to life, posterior to death, initial of creation, and the
       exponent of breath.
Luck is not chance, it's toil; fortune's expensive smile is earned.
Morning without you is a dwindled dawn.
My friends are my estate.
Not knowing when the dawn will come I open every door.
Old age comes on suddenly, and not gradually as is thought.
Parting is all we know of heaven, and all we need of hell.
People need hard times and oppression to develop psychic muscles.
Saying nothing... sometimes says the most.
Success is counted sweetest by those who never succeed.
Tell the truth, but tell it slant.
That it will never come again is what makes life sweet.

The brain is wider than the sky.

The soul should always stand ajar, ready to welcome the ecstatic experience.

There is no Frigate like a book to take us lands away nor any coursers like
a page of prancing Poetry.

They might not need me; but they might. I'll let my head be just in sight; a
smile as small as mine might be precisely their necessity.

They say that God is everywhere, and yet we always think of Him as
somewhat of a recluse.

To live is so startling it leaves little time for anything else.

To make a prairie it takes a clover and one bee, One clover, and a
bee, And revery. The revery alone will do, If bees are few.

Truth is so rare that it is delightful to tell it.

Unable are the loved to die, for love is immortality.

Whenever a thing is done for the first time, it releases a little demon.

Where thou art, that is home.

## WALT DISNEY (Cartoonist, businessman, founder of Disneyland, 1901-1966)

The more you like yourself, the less you are like anyone else, which
makes you unique.

The way to get started is to quit talking and begin doing.

There is more treasure in books than in all the pirate's loot on
Treasure Island.

A man should never neglect his family for business.

All cartoon characters and fables must be exaggeration, caricatures.
It is the very nature of fantasy and fable.

There's nothing funnier than the human animal.

We allow no geniuses around our Studio.

We are not trying to entertain the critics. I'll take my chances with the public.

We keep moving forward, opening new doors, and doing new things,
because we're curious and curiosity keeps leading us down new paths.

When you believe in a thing, believe in it all the way, implicitly and unquestionable.

When you're curious, you find lots of interesting things to do.

Whenever I go on a ride, I'm always thinking of what's wrong with the
thing and how it can be improved.

You can't just let nature run wild.

You reach a point where you don't work for money.

All our dreams can come true, if we have the courage to pursue them.

All the adversity I've had in my life, all my troubles and obstacles, have
strengthened me... You may not realize it when it happens, but a
kick in the teeth may be the best thing in the world for you.

Animation can explain whatever the mind of man can conceive. This facility
makes it the most versatile and explicit means of communication yet
devised for quick mass appreciation.

Animation is different from other parts. Its language is the language
of caricature. Our most difficult job was to develop the cartoon's
unnatural but seemingly natural anatomy for humans and animals.

Animation offers a medium of story telling and visual entertainment
which can bring pleasure and information to people of
all ages everywhere in the world.

Crowded classrooms and half-day sessions are a tragic waste of our
greatest national resource - the minds of our children.

Disneyland will never be completed. It will continue to grow as long as there is imagination left in the world.

I always like to look on the optimistic side of life, but I am realistic enough to know that life is a complex matter.

I believe in being an innovator.

I do not like to repeat successes, I like to go on to other things.

I don't like formal gardens. I like wild nature. It's just the wilderness instinct in me, I guess.

I have been up against tough competition all my life. I wouldn't know how to get along without it.

I have no use for people who throw their weight around as celebrities, or for those who fawn over you just because you are famous.

I love Mickey Mouse more than any woman I have ever known.

I only hope that we don't lose sight of one thing - that it was all started by a mouse.

I started, actually, to make my first animated cartoon in 1920. Of course, they were very crude things then and I used sort of little puppet things.

I would rather entertain and hope that people learned something than educate people and hope they were entertained

If you can dream it, you can do it.

It's kind of fun to do the impossible.

Laughter is America's most important export.

Mickey Mouse is, to me, a symbol of independence. He was a means to an end.

Mickey Mouse popped out of my mind onto a drawing pad 20 years ago on a train ride from Manhattan to Hollywood at a time when business fortunes of my brother Roy and myself were at lowest ebb and disaster seemed right around the corner.

Movies can and do have tremendous influence in shaping young lives in the realm of entertainment towards the ideals and objectives of normal adulthood.

Of all of our inventions for mass communication, pictures still speak the most universally understood language.

Our heritage and ideals, our code and standards - the things we live by and teach our children - are preserved or diminished by how freely we exchange ideas and feelings.

## KIRK DOUGLAS (Actor, 1916 - )

Life is like a B-picture script! It is that corny. If I had my life story offered to me to film, I'd turn it down.

If you want to know about a man you can find out an awful lot by looking at who he married.

Love has more depth as you get older.

When you become a star, you don't change - everyone else does.

Why can't a woman be more like a dog, huh? So sweet, loving, attentive.

## FREDERICK DOUGLASS (Author, 1817-1895)

A little learning, indeed, may be a dangerous thing, but the want of learning is a calamity to any people.

A man's character always takes its hue, more or less, from the form
and color of things about him.
A battle lost or won is easily described, understood, and appreciated, but
the moral growth of a great nation requires reflection, as well as
observation, to appreciate it.
A gentleman will not insult me, and no man not a gentleman can insult me.
America is false to the past, false to the present, and solemnly binds
herself to be false to the future.
At a time like this, scorching irony, not convincing argument, is needed.
Find out just what any people will quietly submit to and you have the exact
measure of the injustice and wrong which will be imposed on them.
I didn't know I was a slave until I found out I couldn't do the things I wanted.
I prayed for twenty years but received no answer until I prayed with my legs.
I prefer to be true to myself, even at the hazard of incurring the ridicule of
others, rather than to be false, and to incur my own abhorrence.
If there is no struggle, there is no progress.
People might not get all they work for in this world, but they must
certainly work for all they get.
Power concedes nothing without a demand. It never did and it never will.
Slaves are generally expected to sing as well as to work.
The life of the nation is secure only while the nation is honest,
truthful, and virtuous.
The limits of tyrants are prescribed by the endurance of those whom they oppose.
The soul that is within me no man can degrade.
The thing worse than rebellion is the thing that causes rebellion.
The white man's happiness cannot be purchased by the black man's misery.
Those who profess to favor freedom, and yet depreciate agitation, are
men who want crops without plowing up the ground.
To suppress free speech is a double wrong. It violates the rights of
the hearer as well as those of the speaker.
We have to do with the past only as we can make it useful to the
present and the future.
What to the Slave is the 4th of July.
When men sow the wind it is rational to expect that they will reap the whirlwind.
Where justice is denied, where poverty is enforced, where ignorance prevails, and
where any one class is made to feel that society is an organized conspiracy
to oppress, rob and degrade them, neither persons nor property will be safe.
It is easier to build strong children than to repair broken men.
It is not light that we need, but fire; it is not the gentle shower, but
thunder. We need the storm, the whirlwind, and the earthquake.
Man's greatness consists in his ability to do and the proper application
of his powers to things needed to be done.
No man can put a chain about the ankle of his fellow man without at
last finding the other end fastened about his own neck.
One and God make a majority.

## JOHN FOSTER DULLES (Public Servant, 1888-1959)
The measure of success is not whether you have a tough problem to
deal with, but whether it is the same problem you had last year.
A man's accomplishments in life are the cumulative effect of his
attention to detail.

Of all tasks of government the most basic is to protect its citizens
against violence.
Mankind will never win lasting peace so long as men use their full
resources only in tasks of war. While we are yet at peace, let us
mobilize the potentialities, particularly the moral and spiritual
potentialities, which we usually reserve for war.
Once - many, many years ago - I thought I made a wrong decision.
Of course, it turned out that I had been right all along. But
I was wrong to have thought that I was wrong.
Our capacity to retaliate must be, and is, massive in order to deter
all forms of aggression.
The ability to get to the verge without getting into the war is the
necessary art. If you try to run away from it, if you are scared
to go to the brink, you are lost.
The world will never have lasting peace so long as men reserve for war
the finest human qualities. Peace, no less than war, requires
idealism and self-sacrifice and a righteous and dynamic faith.
There are plenty of problems in the world, many of them interconnected.
But there is no problem which compares with this central, universal
problem of saving the human race from extinction.

## BOB DYLAN (Musician, 1941 - )

There is nothing so stable as change.
People seldom do what they believe in. They do what is
convenient, then repent.
When you cease to exist, then who will you blame?
People today are still living off the table scraps of the sixties. They are
still being passed around - the music and the ideas.
A hero is someone who understands the responsibility that
comes with his freedom.
Chaos is a friend of mine.
Colleges are like old-age homes, except for the fact that
more people die in colleges.
A mistake is to commit a misunderstanding.
A poem is a naked person... Some people say that I am a poet.
A song is anything that can walk by itself.
All I can do is be me, whoever that is.
All the truth in the world adds up to one big lie.
All this talk about equality. The only thing people really have
in common is that they are all going to die.
Basically you have to suppress your own ambitions in
order to be who you need to be.
Being noticed can be a burden. Jesus got himself crucified because
he got himself noticed. So I disappear a lot.
Democracy don't rule the world, You'd better get that in
your head; This world is ruled by violence, But I guess
that's better left unsaid.
Don't matter how much money you got, there's only two kinds of people:
there's saved people and there's lost people.
I am against nature. I don't dig nature at all. I think nature
is very unnatural.

I think the truly natural things are dreams, which nature
        can't touch with decay.
I accept chaos, I'm not sure whether it accepts me.
I consider myself a poet first and a musician second. I live like
        a poet and I'll die like a poet.
I define nothing. Not beauty, not patriotism. I take each thing as it is,
        without prior rules about what it should be.
I don't think the human mind can comprehend the past and the future.
        They are both just illusions that can manipulate you into thinking
        there's some kind of change.
I like America, just as everybody else does. I love America, I
        gotta  say  that. But America will be judged.
I say there're no depressed words just depressed minds.
I'll let you be in my dreams if I can be in yours.
I'm speaking for all of us. I'm the spokesman for a generation.
If I wasn't Bob Dylan, I'd probably think that Bob Dylan has a lot of
        answers myself.
Just because you like my stuff doesn't mean I owe you anything.
Money doesn't talk, it swears.
No one is free, even the birds are chained to the sky.
Take care of all your memories. For you cannot relive them.
The radio makes hideous sounds.
This land is your land and this land is my land, sure, but the
        world is run  by those that never listen to music anyway.
To live outside the law, you must be honest.
Well, the future for me is already a thing of the past.
What's money? A man is a success if he gets up in the morning and
        goes to bed at night and in between does what he wants to do.
Yesterday's just a memory, tomorrow is never what it's supposed to be.
You learn from a conglomeration of the incredible past - whatever
        experience gotten in any way whatsoever.

## AMELIA EARHART (Pilot, Adventurer, 1898-1937)
Adventure is worthwhile in itself.
Better do a good deed near at home than go far away to burn incense.
Courage is the price that life exacts for granting peace.
Flying might not be all plain sailing, but the fun of it is worth the price.
I want to do it because I want to do it.
In soloing - as in other activities - it is far easier to start something
        than it is to finish it.
Never do things others can do and will do if there are things others
        cannot do or will not do.
Never interrupt someone doing what you said couldn't be done.
The more one does and sees and feels, the more one is able to do, and the
        more genuine may be one's appreciation of fundamental things
        like home, and love, and understanding companionship.
The most difficult thing is the decision to act, the rest is merely tenacity. The
        fears are paper tigers. You can do anything you decide to do. You can
        act to change and control your life; and the procedure , the process
        is its own reward.
The most effective way to do it, is to do it.

The woman who can create her own job is the woman who will win fame and fortune.

There are two kinds of stones, as everyone knows, one of which rolls.

There is so much that must be done in a civilized barbarism like war.

Women must pay for everything. They do get more glory than men for comparable feats, but, they also get more notoriety when they crash.

Women, like men, should try to do the impossible. And when they fail, their failure should be a challenge to others.

## CRYSTAL EASTMAN (Lawyer, 1881-1928)

A good deal of tyranny goes by the name of protection.

I am not interested in women just because they're women. I am interested, however, in seeing that they are no longer classed with children and minors.

I would not have a woman go to Congress merely because she is a woman.

If the feminist program goes to pieces on the arrival of the first baby, it's false and useless.

Indifference is harder to fight than hostility, and there is nothing that kills an agitation like having everybody admit that it is fundamentally right.

It is all right for the lion and the lamb to lie down together if they are both asleep, but if one of them begins to get active, it is dangerous.

It is not so much that women have a different point of view in politics as that they give a different emphasis. And this is vastly important, for politics is so largely a matter of emphasis.

The average man has a carefully cultivated ignorance about household matters - from what to do with the crumbs to the grocer's telephone number - a sort of cheerful inefficiency which protects him.

Until women learn to want economic independence, and until they work out a way to get this independence without denying themselves the joys of love and motherhood, it seems to me feminism has no roots.

## GEORGE EASTMAN (Inventor, Founder of Kodak, 1854-1932)

Light makes photography. Embrace light. Admire it. Love it. But above all, know light. Know it for all you are worth, and you will know the key to photography.

What we do during our working hours determines what we have; what we do in our leisure hours determines what we are.

## CLINT EASTWOOD (Actor, 1930 - )

I don't believe in pessimism. If something doesn't come up the way you want, forge ahead. If you think it's going to rain, it will.

I have a very strict gun control policy: if there's a gun around, I want to be in control of it.

I tried being reasonable, I didn't like it.

I've never met a genius. A genius to me is someone who does well at something he hates. Anybody can do well at something he loves - it's just a question of finding the subject.

If you want a guarantee, buy a toaster.

In school, I could hear the leaves rustle and go on a journey.

It takes tremendous discipline to control the influence, the power you have over other people's lives.

My old drama coach used to say, 'Don't just do something, stand
        there.' Gary Cooper wasn't afraid to do nothing.
Respect your efforts, respect yourself. Self-respect leads to self-discipline. When
        you have both firmly under your belt, that's real power.
Sometimes if you want to see a change for the better, you have to take
        things into your own hands.
The less secure a man is, the more likely he is to have extreme prejudice.
There's a lot of great movies that have won the Academy Award, and a lot
        of great movies that haven't. You just do the best you can.
There's only one way to have a happy marriage and as soon as I learn
        what it is I'll get married again.
They say marriages are made in Heaven. But so is thunder and lightning.
This film cost $31 million. With that kind of money I could have
        invaded some country.
We are like boxers, one never knows how much longer one has.
We boil at different degrees.

## BARBARA EDEN (Actor, 1934 - )

Work makes me feel productive, as though I'm contributing something. I
        like being productive and feeling productive.
I don't know what I am doing from one moment to the next. I like that not
        knowing because it's always a surprise. You don't know what's around
        the corner, you know what role am I going to play next and who am I
        going to be working with. It's like opening a present.
Every New Year's I resolve to have a better year than I had before.
I've never stopped working. If you're active, you can appreciate what you
        did in the past, you don't feel like it's gone.
If gentlemen prefer blondes then I'm a blonde that prefers gentlemen.

## THOMAS A. EDISON (Inventor, 1847-1931)

Opportunity is missed by most people because it is dressed in
        overalls and looks like work.
Show me a thoroughly satisfied man and I will show you a failure.
Religion is all bunk.
Results! Why, man, I have gotten a lot of results.
        I know several thousand things that won't work.
What you are will show in what you do.
I am proud of the fact that I never invented weapons to kill.
There is no expedient to which a man will not go to avoid the labor of thinking.
If we did all the things we are capable of, we would literally
        astound ourselves.
Many of life's failures are people who did not realize how close
        they were to success when they gave up.
Maturity is often more absurd than youth and very frequently is
        most unjust to youth.
Nearly every man who develops an idea works it up to the point
        where it looks impossible, and then he gets discouraged.
        That's not the place to become discouraged.
Non-violence leads to the highest ethics,
        which is the goal of all evolution. Until we stop
        harming all other living beings, we are still savages.

One might think that the money value of an invention constitutes
        its reward to the man who loves his work. But... I continue
        to find my greatest pleasure, and so my reward, in the work
        that precedes what the world calls success.
Our greatest weakness lies in giving up. The most certain way to
        succeed is always to try just one more time.
Restlessness is discontent and discontent is the first necessity of progress.
        Show me a thoroughly satisfied man and I will show you a failure.
The best thinking has been done in solitude. The worst has
        been done in turmoil.
The chief function of the body is to carry the brain around.
The three great essentials to achieve anything worth while are:
        Hard work, Stick-to-itiveness, and Common sense.
The value of an idea lies in the using of it.
There is far more opportunity than there is ability.
There's a way to do it better - find it.
To have a great idea, have a lot of them.
To invent, you need a good imagination and a pile of junk.
To my mind the old masters are not art; their value is in their scarcity.
Waste is worse than loss. The time is coming when every person who
        lays claim to ability will keep the question of waste before
        him constantly. The scope of thrift is limitless.
We don't know a millionth of one percent about anything.
What a man's mind can create, man's character can control.
When I have fully decided that a result is worth getting I go ahead of it
        and make trial after trial until it comes.
Your worth consists in what you are and not in what you have.
There is no substitute for hard work.
Anything that won't sell, I don't want to invent. Its sale is proof
        of utility, and utility is success.
Discontent is the first necessity of progress.
Everything comes to him who hustles while he waits.
Genius is one percent inspiration and ninety-nine percent perspiration.
Be courageous. I have seen many depressions in business. Always
        America has emerged from these stronger and more prosperous.
        Be brave as your fathers before you. Have faith! Go forward!
Being busy does not always mean real work. The object of all work is
        production or accomplishment and to either of these ends there
        must be forethought, system, planning, intelligence, and honest
        purpose, as well as perspiration. Seeming to do is not doing.
Great ideas originate in the muscles.
Hell, there are no rules here - we're trying to accomplish something.
I have friends in overalls whose friendship I would not swap for the
        favor of the kings of the world.
I know this world is ruled by infinite intelligence. Everything that
        surrounds us- everything that exists - proves that there are
        infinite laws behind it. There can be no denying this fact. It is
        mathematical in its precision.
I never did a day's work in my life. It was all fun.
I never did anything by accident, nor did any of my inventions
        come by accident; they came by work.

I start where the last man left off.
It is astonishing what an effort it seems to be for many people to put
        their brains definitely and systematically to work.
Just because something doesn't do what you planned it to do
        doesn't mean it's useless.

## ALBERT EINSTEIN (Scientist, 1879-1955)

My religion consists of a humble admiration of the illimitable superior spirit
        who reveals himself in the slight details we are able to perceive with
        our frail and feeble mind.
Yes, we have to divide up our time like that, between our politics and our
        equations. But to me our equations are far more important, for politics are
        only a matter of present concern. A mathematical equation stands forever.
The release of atom power has changed everything except our way of thinking...the
        solution to this problem lies in the heart of mankind. If only I had known, I
        should have become a watchmaker.
Any intelligent fool can make things bigger, more complex, and more
        violent. It takes a touch of genius -- and a lot of courage -- to move
        in the opposite direction.
Imagination is more important than knowledge.
Gravitation is not responsible for people falling in love.
Great spirits have always found violent opposition from mediocrities. The latter
        cannot understand it when a man does not thoughtlessly submit to
        hereditary prejudices but honestly and courageously uses his intelligence.
The most beautiful thing we can experience is the mysterious. It is the source of all
        true art and all science. He to whom this emotion is a stranger, who can no
        longer pause to wonder and stand rapt in awe, is as good as dead: his eyes
        are closed.
A man's ethical behavior should be based effectually on sympathy, education, and
        social ties; no religious basis is necessary. Man would indeeded be in a poor
        way if he had to be restrained by fear of punishment and hope of reward
        after death.
The further the spiritual evolution of mankind advances, the more certain it seems
        to me that the path to genuine religiosity does not lie through the fear of
        life, and the fear of death, and blind faith, but through striving after
        rational knowledge.
I want to know God's thoughts; the rest are details.
The hardest thing in the world to understand is the income tax.
Reality is merely an illusion, albeit a very persistent one.
In order to form an immaculate member of a flock of sheep one must, above all, be
        a sheep.
The fear of death is the most unjustified of all fears, for there's no risk of accident
        for someone who's dead.
Too many of us look upon Americans as dollar chasers. This is a cruel libel, even
        if it is reiterated thoughtlessly by the Americans themselves.
Heroism on command, senseless violence, and all the loathsome nonsense that goes
        by the name of patriotism -- how passionately I hate them!
No, this trick won't work...How on earth are you ever going to explain in terms of
        chemistry and physics so important a biological phenomenon as first love?
The only real valuable thing is intuition.
A person starts to live when he can live outside himself.

I am convinced that He (God) does not play dice.

God is subtle but he is not malicious.

If A is a success in life, then A equals x plus y plus z. Work is x; y is
    play; and z is keeping your mouth shut

Two things are infinite: the universe and human stupidity; and I'm not
    sure about the  universe.

As far as the laws of mathematics refer to reality, they are not certain, as
    far as they are certain, they do not refer to reality.

Whoever undertakes to set himself up as a judge of Truth and
    Knowledge is shipwrecked by the laughter of the gods.

I know not with what weapons World War III will be fought, but
    World War IV will be fought with sticks and stones.

Weakness of attitude becomes weakness of character.

I never think of the future. It comes soon enough.

The eternal mystery of the world is its comprehensibility.

Sometimes one pays most for the things one gets for nothing.

The most incomprehensible thing about the world is that it is comprehensible.

Science without religion is lame. Religion without science is blind.

Anyone who has never made a mistake has never tried anything new.

We can't solve problems by using the same kind of thinking we used when we
    created them.

Great spirits have often encountered violent opposition from weak minds.

Everything should be made as simple as possible, but not simpler.

Education is what remains after one has forgotten everything he learned in school.

Common sense is the collection of prejudices acquired by age eighteen.

Science is a wonderful thing if one does not have to earn one's living at it.

The secret to creativity is knowing how to hide your sources.

The only thing that interferes with my learning is my education.

God does not care about our mathematical difficulties. He integrates empirically.

The whole of science is nothing more than a refinement of everyday thinking.

Technological progress is like an axe in the hands of a pathological criminal.

Do not worry about your difficulties in Mathematics. I can assure you
    mine  are still greater.

...one of the strongest motives that lead men to art and science is escape from
    everyday life with its painful crudity and hopeless dreariness, from the fetters
    of one's own ever-shifting desires. A finely tempered nature longs to escape
    from the personal life into the world of objective perception and thought.

He who joyfully marches to music rank and file, has already earned my contempt.
    He has been given a large brain by mistake, since for him the spinal cord
    would surely suffice. This disgrace to civilization should be done away with at
    once. Heroism at command, how violently I hate all this, how despicable and
    ignoble war is; I would rather be torn to shreds than be a part of so base an
    action. It is my conviction that killing under the cloak of war is nothing but
    an act of murder.

A human being is a part of a whole, called by us 'universe,' a part limited in time
    and space. He experiences himself, his thoughts and feelings as something
    separated from the rest... a kind of optical delusion of his consciousness. This
    delusion is a kind of prison for us, restricting us to our personal desires and
    to affection for a few persons nearest to us. Our task must be to free
    ourselves from this prison by widening our  circle of compassion to embrace
    all living creatures and the whole of nature in its beauty.

Equations are more important to me, because politics is for the present, but an
    equation is something for eternity.
One had to cram all this stuff into one's mind for the examinations, whether one
    liked it or not. This coercion had such a deterring effect on me that, after I
    had passed the final examination, I found the consideration of any scientific
    problems distasteful to me for an entire year.
Peace cannot be kept by force. It can only be achieved by understanding.
The important thing is not to stop questioning. Curiosity has its
    own reason  for existing.

## DWIGHT D. EISENHOWER (President, Soldier,1890-1969)

There is no glory in battle worth the blood it costs.
History does not long entrust the care of freedom to the weak or the timid.
Don't join the book burners. Do not think you are going to conceal
    thoughts by concealing evidence that they ever existed.
Farming looks mighty easy when your plow is a pencil and you're
    a thousand miles from the corn field.
A people that values its privileges above its principles soon loses both.
May we never confuse honest dissent with disloyal subversion.
Few women, I fear, have had such reason as I have to think the long
    sad years of youth were worth living for the sake of middle age.
    We must guard against the acquisition of unwarranted influence,
    whether sought or unsought, by the military-industrial complex.
We seek peace, knowing that peace is the climate of freedom.
We will bankrupt ourselves in the vain search for absolute security.
Well, when you come down to it, I don't see that a reporter could
    do much to a president, do you?
What counts is not necessarily the size of the dog in the fight - it's
    the size of the fight in the dog.
Whatever America hopes to bring to pass in the world must first come
    to pass in the heart of America.
From behind the Iron Curtain, there are signs that tyranny is in trouble
    and reminders that its structure is as brittle as its surface is hard.
Here in America we are descended in blood and in spirit from
    revolutionists and rebels - men and women who dare to
    dissent from accepted doctrine. As their heirs, may we never
    confuse honest dissent with disloyal subversion.
When people speak to you about a preventive war, you tell them to go
    and fight it. After my experience, I have come to hate war.
If you want total security, go to prison. There you're fed, clothed,
    given medical care and so on. The only thing lacking... is freedom.
When you are in any contest, you should work as if there were - to the
    very last minute - a chance to lose it. This is battle, this is politics,
    this is anything.
When you put on a uniform, there are certain inhibitions that you accept.
'Worry' is a word that I don't allow myself to use.
You don't lead by hitting people over the head - that's assault, not leadership.
Motivation is the art of getting people to do what you want them to
    do because they want to do it.
Peace and justice are two sides of the same coin.
If a problem cannot be solved, enlarge it.

Pessimism never won any battle.

Things are more like they are now than they ever were before.

Plans are nothing; planning is everything.

Neither a wise man nor a brave man lies down on the tracks of history
       to wait for the train of the future to run over him.

No one should ever sit in this office over 70 years old, and that I know.

I despise people who go to the gutter on either the right or the left and
       hurl rocks at those in the center.

Oh, that lovely title, ex-president.

Only Americans can hurt America.

Unlike presidential administrations, problems rarely have terminal dates.

War settles nothing.

We are going to have peace even if we have to fight for it.

We are tired of aristocratic explanations in Harvard words.

Only our individual faith in freedom can keep us free.

Only strength can cooperate. Weakness can only beg.

Our forces saved the remnants of the Jewish people of Europe for a new
       life and a new hope in the reborn land of Israel. Along with all men
       of good will, I salute the young state and wish it well.

Our pleasures were simple - they included survival.

Our real problem, then, is not our strength today; it is rather the vital
       necessity of action today to ensure our strength tomorrow.

Politics is a profession; a serious, complicated and, in its true sense,
       a noble one.

Politics ought to be the part-time profession of every citizen who would
       protect the rights and privileges of free people and who would
       preserve what is good and fruitful in our national heritage.

Pull the string, and it will follow wherever you wish. Push it, and it will
       go nowhere at all.

Some people wanted champagne and caviar when they should have
       had beer and hot dogs.

The best morale exist when you never hear the word mentioned. When
       you hear a lot of talk about it, it's usually lousy.

I hate war as only a soldier who has lived it can, only as one who has
       seen its brutality, its futility, its stupidity.

I have found out in later years that we were very poor, but the glory of
       America is that we didn't know it then.

I have one yardstick by which I test every major problem - and that
       yardstick is: Is it good for America?

I like to believe that people in the long run are going to do more to
       promote peace than our governments. Indeed, I think that
       people want peace so much that one of these days governments
       had better get out of the way and let them have it.

I'm saving that rocker for the day when I feel as old as I really am.

If men can develop weapons that are so terrifying as to make the
       thought of global war include almost a sentence for suicide,
       you would think that man's intelligence and his comprehension...
       would include also his ability to find a peaceful solution.

If the United Nations once admits that international disputes can be
       settled by using force, then we will have destroyed the foundation
       of the organization and our best hope of establishing a world order.

In most communities it is illegal to cry "fire" in a crowded assembly.
Should it not be considered serious international misconduct to
manufacture a general war scare in an effort to achieve local
political aims?
In the councils of government, we must guard against the acquisition
of unwarranted influence, whether sought or unsought, by the
military-industrial complex. The potential for the disastrous rise
of misplaced power exists and will persist.
In the final choice a soldier's pack is not so heavy as a prisoner's chains.
It is far more important to be able to hit the target than it is to haggle
over who makes a weapon or who pulls a trigger.
An atheist is a man who watches a Notre Dame - Southern Methodist
University game and doesn't care who wins.
An intellectual is a man who takes more words than necessary to tell
more than he knows.
Ankles are nearly always neat and good-looking, but knees are
nearly always not.
Any man who wants to be president is either an egomaniac or crazy.
Disarmament, with mutual honor and confidence, is a
continuing imperative.
Every gun that is made, every warship launched, every rocket fired,
signifies in the final sense a theft from those who hunger and
are not fed, those who are cold and are not clothed.
How far you can go without destroying from within what you are
trying to defend from without?
Humility must always be the portion of any man who receives acclaim
earned in the blood of his followers and the sacrifices of his friends.
I can think of nothing more boring for the American people than to
have to sit in their living rooms for a whole half hour looking
at my face on their television screens.
I deplore the need or the use of troops anywhere to get American citizens
to obey the orders of constituted courts.
The clearest way to show what the rule of law means to us in everyday
life is to recall what has happened when there is no rule of law.
The free world must not prove itself worthy of its own past.
The history of free men is never really written by chance but by
choice; their choice!
The most terrible job in warfare is to be a second lieutenant leading a
platoon when you are on the battlefield.
The older I get the more wisdom I find in the ancient rule of taking
first things first. A process which often reduces the most
complex human problem to a manageable proportion.
The problem in defense is how far you can go without destroying from
within what you are trying to defend from without.
The purpose is clear. It is safety with solvency. The
country is entitled to both.
The spirit of man is more important than mere physical strength,
and the spiritual fiber of a nation than its wealth.
The supreme quality for leadership is unquestionably integrity.
Without it, no real success is possible, no matter whether it
is on a section gang, a football field, in an army, or in an office.

The world moves, and ideas that were once good are not always good.
There are a number of things wrong with Washington. One of them is
      that everyone is too far from home.
The sergeant is the Army.
There is no victory at bargain basement prices.
There is nothing wrong with America that faith, love of freedom,
      intelligence, and energy of her citizens cannot cure.
There's no tragedy in life like the death of a child. Things never get
      back to the way they were.
This desk of mine is one at which a man may die, but from which
      he cannot resign.
This world of ours... must avoid becoming a community of dreadful
fear and hate, and be, instead, a proud confederation of mutual trust
      and respect.
Though force can protect in emergency, only justice, fairness,
      consideration and cooperation can finally lead men to the dawn
      of eternal peace.
Together we must learn how to compose differences, not with arms,
      but with intellect and decent purpose.

## RALPH WALDO EMERSON (Poet, 1803-1882)

Shallow men believe in luck. Strong men believe in cause and effect.
The faith that stands on authority is not faith.
Reality is a sliding door.
Revolutions go not backward.
Science does not know its debt to imagination.
A chief event of life is the day in which we have encountered
      a mind that startled us.
Do not go where the path may lead, go instead where there
      is no path and leave a trail.
God screens us evermore from premature ideas.
Good men must not obey the laws too well.
Great geniuses have the shortest biographies.
Great hearts steadily send forth the secret forces that incessantly draw
      great events.
Great men are they who see that spiritual is stronger than any material
      force - that thoughts rule the world.
Great men or men of great gifts you shall easily find, but symmetrical men never.
Happy is the hearing man; unhappy the speaking man.
He who is not everyday conquering some fear has not learned the secret of life.
Hitch your wagon to a star.
I hate quotations. Tell me what you know.
I hate the giving of the hand unless the whole man accompanies it.
I have no hostility to nature, but a child's love to it. I expand and live in the
      warm day like corn and melons.
I have thought a sufficient measure of civilization is the influence of good women.
I like the silent church before the service begins, better than any preaching.
If a man can... make a better mousetrap, the world will make a beaten
      path to his door.
In the morning a man walks with his whole body; in the evening, only
      with his legs.

It is a fact often observed, that men have written good verses under the
    inspiration of passion, who cannot write well under other circumstances.
It is my desire, in the office of a Christian minister, to do nothing which I
    cannot do with my whole heart. Having said this, I have said all.
Men are what their mothers made them.
Men love to wonder, and that is the seed of science.
Men's actions are too strong for them. Show me a man who has acted, and
    who has not been the victim and slave of his action.
Society is always taken by surprise at any new example of common sense.
Some books leave us free and some books make us free.
The age of a woman doesn't mean a thing. The best tunes are played on the
    oldest fiddles.
The ancestor of every action is a thought.
The best effort of a fine person is felt after we have left their presence.
The civilized man has built a coach, but has lost the use of his feet.
The creation of a thousand forests is in one acorn.
The desire of gold is not for gold. It is for the means of freedom and benefit.
The earth laughs in flowers.
In skating over thin ice our safety is in our speed.
The end of the human race will be that it will eventually die of civilization.
The first wealth is health.
The fox has many tricks. The hedgehog has but one. But that is the best of all.
The greatest gift is a portion of thyself.
The greatest glory in living lies not in never falling, but in rising every time we fall.
The health of the eye seems to demand a horizon. We are never tired, so long as we
    can see far enough.
The highest revelation is that God is in every man.
The invariable mark of wisdom is to see the miraculous in the common.
The man of genius inspires us with a boundless confidence in our own powers.
The martyr cannot be dishonored. Every lash inflicted is a tongue of fame; every
    prison a more illustrious abode.
Money often costs too much.
Mysticism is the mistake of an accidental and individual symbol for
    an universal one.
Nature always wears the colors of the spirit.
Nature and books belong to the eyes that see them.
Nature hates calculators.
Nature is a mutable cloud which is always and never the same.
Never lose an opportunity of seeing anything beautiful, for beauty is God's
handwriting.
No change of circumstances can repair a defect of character.
No great man ever complains of want of opportunity.
No man ever prayed heartily without learning something.
Nobody can bring you peace but yourself.
Nothing astonishes men so much as common sense and plain dealing.
Nothing external to you has any power over you.
Nothing great was ever achieved without enthusiasm.
Nothing is at last sacred but the integrity of your own mind.
O Day of days when we can read! The reader and the book, either
    without the other is naught.
Once you make a decision, the universe conspires to make it happen.

It is not length of life, but depth of life.

It is one of the beautiful compensations in this life that no one can
        sincerely try to help another without helping himself.

It is one of the blessings of old friends that you can afford to be stupid with them.

It is said that the world is in a state of bankruptcy, that the world owes the
        world more than the world can pay.

It is the quality of the moment, not the number of days, or events, or of
        actors, that imports.

It was high counsel that I once heard given to a young person, 'always do
        what you are afraid to do.'

Judge of your natural character by what you do in your dreams.

Knowledge is knowing that we cannot know.

Let us be silent, that we may hear the whispers of the gods.

Life consists in what a man is thinking of all day.

Little minds have little worries, big minds have no time for worries.

Love of beauty is taste. The creation of beauty is art.

Make the most of yourself, for that is all there is of you.

Make yourself necessary to somebody.

Manners require time, and nothing is more vulgar than haste.

Men admire the man who can organize their wishes and thoughts in
        stone and wood and steel and brass.

If the stars should appear but one night every thousand years how
        man would marvel and stare.

If the tongue had not been framed for articulation, man would still
        be a beast in the forest.

If you would lift me up you must be on higher ground.

In art, the hand can never execute anything higher than the heart can imagine.

In every society some men are born to rule, and some to advise.

Do the thing we fear, and death of fear is certain.

Doing well is the result of doing good. That's what capitalism is all about.

Don't be too timid and squeamish about your actions. All life is an experiment.

Each age, it is found, must write its own books; or rather,
        each generation for the next succeeding.

Earth laughs in flowers.

Enthusiasm is the mother of effort, and without it nothing great was ever achieved.

Every actual State is corrupt. Good men must not obey laws too well

Every man supposes himself not to be fully understood or appreciated.

Every mind must make its choice between truth and repose. It cannot have both.

Every natural fact is a symbol of some spiritual fact.

Every sentence spoken by Napoleon, and every line of his writing, deserves
        reading, as it is the sense of France.

Every spirit makes its house, and we can give a shrewd guess from
        the house to the inhabitant.

Every wall is a door.

Everything in Nature contains all the powers of Nature. Everything
        is made of one hidden stuff.

Fate is nothing but the deeds committed in a prior state of existence.

Fear defeats more people than any other one thing in the world.

Fiction reveals truth that reality obscures

Flowers... are a proud assertion that a ray of beauty outvalues all
        the utilities of the world.

For every benefit you receive a tax is levied.

For every minute you remain angry, you give up sixty seconds of peace of mind.

For everything you have missed, you have gained something else, and for
everything you gain, you lose something else.

Fine manners need the support of fine manners in others.

Friendship, like the immortality of the soul, is too good to be believed.

Genius always finds itself a century too early.

Getting old is a fascination thing. The older you get, the older you want to get.

Give a boy address and accomplishments and you give him the mastery
of palaces and fortunes where he goes.

God enters by a private door into every individual.

Every artist was first an amateur.

Every book is a quotation; and every house is a quotation out of all
forests, and mines, and stone quarries; and every man is a
quotation from all his ancestors.

Every burned book enlightens the world.

Every experiment, by multitudes or by individuals, that has a
sensual and selfish aim, will fail.

Every fact is related on one side to sensation, and, on the other, to morals. The
game of thought is, on the appearance of one of these two sides, to
find the other: given the upper, to find the under side.

Every hero becomes a bore at last.

Every known fact in natural science was divined by the presentiment
of somebody, before it was actually verified.

Every man has his own courage, and is betrayed because he seeks
in himself the courage of other persons.

Every man I meet is in some way my superior.

Every man in his lifetime needs to thank his faults.

Every man is a consumer, and ought to be a producer. He is
by constitution expensive, and needs to be rich.

Every man is a quotation from all his ancestors.

A foolish consistency is the hobgoblin of little minds, adored by
little statesmen and philosophers and divines.

A friend may well be reckoned the masterpiece of nature.

A good indignation brings out all one's powers.

A great man is always willing to be little.

A great part of courage is the courage of having done the thing before.

A hero is no braver than an ordinary man, but he is brave
five minutes longer.

A man in debt is so far a slave.

A man is a god in ruins. When men are innocent, life shall be longer, and
shall pass into the immortal, as gently as we awake from dreams.

A man is a method, a progressive arrangement; a selecting principle,
gathering his like to him; wherever he goes.

A man is relieved and gay when he has put his heart into his work and done
his best; but what he has said or done otherwise shall give him no peace.

Always do what you are afraid to do.

America is another name for opportunity.

An ounce of action is worth a ton of theory.

As a cure for worrying, work is better than whiskey.

As long as a man stands in his own way, everything seems to be in his way.

As soon as there is life there is danger.
As we grow old, the beauty steals inward.
Bad times have a scientific value. These are occasions a good learner
    would not miss.
Beauty is an outward gift, which is seldom despised, except by those to
    whom it has been refused.
Beauty without expression is boring.
Beauty without grace is the hook without the bait.
Before we acquire great power we must acquire wisdom to use it well.
Build a better mousetrap and the world will beat a path to your door.
Can anything be so elegant as to have few wants, and to serve them one's self?
Cause and effect are two sides of one fact.
Character is higher than intellect. A great soul will be strong
    to live as well as think.
Children are all foreigners.
Common sense is genius dressed in its working clothes.
Curiosity is lying in wait for every secret.
Death comes to all, but great achievements build a monument
    which shall endure until the sun grows cold.
A man is the whole encyclopedia of facts.
A man is usually more careful of his money than he is of his principles.
A man is what he thinks about all day long.
The method of nature: who could ever analyze it?
The only way to have a friend is to be one.
Why need I volumes, if one word suffice?
Win as if you were used to it, lose as if you enjoyed it for a change.
Wisdom has its root in goodness, not goodness its root in wisdom.
With the past, I have nothing to do; nor with the future. I live now.
Words are also actions, and actions are a kind of words.
Write it on your heart that every day is the best day in the year.
You cannot do a kindness too soon, for you never know how soon it
    will be too late.
The real and lasting victories are those of peace, and not of war.
The reason why men do not obey us, is because they see the mud at the
    bottom of our eye.
The reason why the world lacks unity, and lies broken and in heaps, is,
    because man is disunited with himself.
The revelation of thought takes men out of servitude into freedom.
The reward of a thing well done is having done it.
The search after the great men is the dream of youth, and the most serious
    occupation of manhood.
The secret of ugliness consists not in irregularity, but in being uninteresting.
The sky is the daily bread of the eyes.
The sum of wisdom is that time is never lost that is devoted to work.
The value of a dollar is social, as it is created by society.
The value of a principle is the number of things it will explain.
The wave of evil washes all our institutions alike.
There is always safety in valor.
There is an optical illusion about every person we meet.
There is creative reading as well as creative writing.
There is more difference in the quality of our pleasures than in the amount.

There is no chance and anarchy in the universe. All is system and gradation.
    Every god is there sitting in his sphere.
There was never a child so lovely but his mother was glad to get him to sleep.
This time, like all times, is a very good one, if we but know what to do with it.
Though we travel the world over to find the beautiful, we must carry it
    with us or we find it not.
To be great is to be misunderstood.
To be yourself in a world that is constantly trying to make you
    something else is the greatest accomplishment.
To know even one life has breathed easier because you have lived. This
    is to have succeeded.
Trust men and they will be true to you; treat them greatly and they
    will show themselves great.
Trust your instinct to the end, though you can render no reason.
Truth is beautiful, without doubt; but so are lies.
We are a puny and fickle folk. Avarice, hesitation, and following are our diseases.
We are always getting ready to live but never living.
We are born believing. A man bears beliefs as a tree bears apples.
We are by nature observers, and thereby learners. That is our permanent state.
We are rich only through what we give, and poor only through what we refuse.
We are symbols, and inhabit symbols.
We are wiser than we know.
We do not yet possess ourselves, and we know at the same time
    that we are much more.
We find delight in the beauty and happiness of children that
    makes the heart too big for the body.
We gain the strength of the temptation we resist.
We must be our own before we can be another's.
We see God face to face every hour, and know the savor of Nature.
What is a weed? A plant whose virtues have never been discovered.
What lies behind you and what lies in front of you, pales in comparison
    to what lies inside of you.
What we seek we shall find; what we flee from flees from us.
What you are comes to you.
When nature has work to be done, she creates a genius to do it.
When we quarrel, how we wish we had been blameless.
Who hears me, who understands me, becomes mine, a possession for all time.
Who you are speaks so loudly I can't hear what you're saying
Truth is handsomer than the affectation of love. Your goodness must
    have some edge to it, else it is none.
Truth is the property of no individual but is the treasure of all men.
Unless you try to do something beyond what you have already
    mastered, you will never grow.
Use what language you will, you can never say anything but what you are.
We acquire the strength we have overcome.
The world is all gates, all opportunities, strings of tension waiting to be struck.
The years teach much which the days never know.
There are as many pillows of illusion as flakes in a snow-storm. We wake
    from one dream into another dream.
There are other measures of self-respect for a man, than the number
    of clean shirts he puts on every day.

There is a blessed necessity by which the interest of men is always driving
        them to the right; and, again, making all crime mean and ugly.
There is a tendency for things to right themselves.
We aim above the mark to hit the mark.
A man's growth is seen in the successive choirs of his friends.
Adopt the pace of nature: her secret is patience.
All diseases run into one, old age.
All I have seen teaches me to trust the creator for all I have not seen.
All life is an experiment. The more experiments you make the better.
One must be an inventor to read well. There is then creative reading
        as well as creative writing.
Our admiration of the antique is not admiration of the old, but of the natural.
Our best thoughts come from others.
Our chief want is someone who will inspire us to be what we know we could be.
Our faith comes in moments; our vice is habitual.
Our greatest glory is not in never failing, but in rising up every time we fail.
Passion rebuilds the world for the youth. It makes all things alive and significant.
Peace cannot be achieved through violence, it can only be
        attained through understanding.
People disparage knowing and the intellectual life, and urge
        doing. I am content with knowing, if only I could know.
People do not seem to realize that their opinion of the world is
        also a confession of character.
People only see what they are prepared to see.
People seem not to see that their opinion of the world is also
        a confession of character.
People that seem so glorious are all show; underneath they are like everyone else.
People with great gifts are easy to find, but symmetrical and balanced ones never.
Pictures must not be too picturesque.
Power and speed be hands and feet.

## JERRY FALWELL (Evangelist, 1933-2007)

Christians, like slaves and soldiers, ask no questions.
Textbooks  are Soviet  propaganda.
I am such a strong admirer and supporter of George W. Bush that if he suggested
        eliminating the income tax or doubling it, I would vote yes on first blush.
I don't think religious groups should be allowed to apply for federal funds to start
        new ministries they have not been doing before the funding was available.
The idea that religion and politics don't mix was invented by the Devil to keep
        Christians from running their own country.
The whole global warming thing is created to destroy America's free
        enterprise system and our economic  stability.
There's been a concerted effort to steal Christmas.
. . . I don't believe anyone begins a homosexual.
AIDS is not just God's punishment for homosexuals; it is God's punishment
        for the society that tolerates homosexuals.
. . .these Islamic fundamentalists, these radical terrorists, these Middle Eastern
        monsters are committed to destroying the Jewish nation, driving her
        into the Mediterranean, conquering the world.
Any sex outside of the marriage bond between a man and a woman
        is violating God's law.

God continues to lift the curtain and allow the enemies of America
        to give us probably what we deserve.
God created the family to provide the maximum love and support and
        morality and example that one can imagine.
God himself preserved the Bible, and brought it down through the ages.
I am a Christian.
I am saying pornography hurts anyone who reads it, garbage in, garbage out.
I believe that all of us are born heterosexual, physically created with a plumbing
        that's heterosexual, and created with the instincts and desires that are
        basically, fundamentally, heterosexual.
I believe that global warming is a myth. And so, therefore, I have no conscience
        problems at all and I'm going to buy a Suburban next time.
I believe that the people of Israel are the chosen people of God.
I believe with all my heart that the Bible is the infallible word of God.
I do not believe we can blame genetics for adultery, homosexuality, dishonesty
        and other character flaws.
I don't think I know a Scientologist except when I see one or two of their actors on
the Hollywood screen.
I think hell's a real place where real people spend a real eternity.
I think pornography is a scourge on society.
I think the Moslem faith teaches hate.
I truly cannot imagine men with men, women with women, doing what they were
        not physically created to do, without abnormal stress and misbehavior.
I work 6:00 a.m. to midnight, seven days a week.
I'm glad now, at age 66, that I never used alcohol or tobacco... I've
        buried a lot of friends who used tobacco or alcohol.
If I were doing something that the Bible condemns, I have two choices. I can
        straighten up my act, or I can somehow distort and twist and change
        the meaning of the Bible.
If I were president of the United States, I would include Moslems in my presidency.
If you're not a born-again Christian, you're a failure as a human being.
It is God's planet - and he's taking care of it. And I don't believe that
        anything we do will raise or lower the temperature one point.
My father was an agnostic.
Temptation has been here ever since the Garden of Eden.
The First Amendment is not without limits.
We will see a breakdown of the family and family values if we decide to approve
        same-sex marriage, and if we decide to establish homosexuality as an
        acceptable alternative lifestyle with all the benefits that go with equating it
        with the heterosexual lifestyle.
When you have a godly husband, a godly wife, children who respect their parents
        and who are loved by their parents, who provide for those children their
        physical and spiritual and material needs, lovingly, you have the ideal unit.

**LOUIS FARRAKHAN (Founder, Nation of Islam, 1933 - )**
        If we don't make earnest moves toward real solutions, then each day we move
                one day closer to revolution and anarchy in this country. This is the sad,
                and yet potentially joyous, state of America.
        Everything that I'm attempting to do is based on my understanding of the
                Honorable Elijah Muhammad and what he wanted for his people.

I think that rather than condemning Islam, Islam needs to be studied by
        those who are sincere.
The Jews don't like Farrakhan, so they call me Hitler. Well, that's a
        good name. Hitler was a very great man.
Without an advocate for the poor, without a new state of mind in
        America, the country lies on the brink of anarchy.
They should regard me as what I am. I am a spiritual leader and teacher

## WILLIAM FAULKNER (Author, 1897-1962)

A gentleman can live through anything.
A man's moral conscience is the curse he had to accept from the
        gods in order to gain from them the right to dream.
A mule will labor ten years willingly and patiently for you, for the
        privilege of kicking you once.
A writer must teach himself that the basest of all things is to be afraid.
All of us failed to match our dreams of perfection. So I rate us on the
        basis of our splendid failure to do the impossible.
An artist is a creature driven by demons. He doesn't know why they
        choose him  and he's usually too busy to wonder why.
Clocks slay time... time is dead as long as it is being clicked off by little
        wheels; only when the clock stops does time come to life.
Don't bother just to be better than your contemporaries or
        predecessors. Try to be better than yourself.
Everything goes by the board: honor, pride, decency to get the book written.
Facts and truth really don't have much to do with each other.
Given a choice between grief and nothing, I'd choose grief.
Hollywood is a place where a man can get stabbed in the back
        while climbing a ladder.
I decline to accept the end of man.
I feel like a wet seed wild in the hot blind earth.
I have found that the greatest help in meeting any problem is to know
        where you yourself stand. That is, to have in words what you believe
        and are acting from.
I never know what I think about something until I read what I've written on it.
I would say that music is the easiest means in which to express, but since
        words are my talent, I must try to express clumsily in words what
        the pure music would have done better.
I'm bad and I'm going to hell, and I don't care. I'd rather be in hell
        than anywhere where you are.
I'm inclined to think that a military background  wouldn't  hurt anyone
If a writer has to rob his mother, he will not hesitate: The "Ode on a
        Grecian Urn" is worth any number of old ladies.
If I were reincarnated, I'd want to come back a buzzard. Nothing hates him
        or envies him or wants him or needs him. He is never bothered or
        in danger, and he can eat anything.
It is my aim, and every effort bent, that the sum and history of my life, which
        in the same sentence is my obit and epitaph too, shall be them
        both: He made the books and he died.
It's a shame that the only thing a man can do for eight hours a day is work. He
        can't eat for eight hours; he can't drink for eight hours; he can't make
        love for eight hours. The only thing a man can do for eight hours is work.

Man performs and engenders so much more than he can or should have to
        bear. That's how he finds that he can bear anything.
Man will not merely endure; he will prevail.
Maybe the only thing worse than having to give gratitude constantly
        is having to accept it.
        If I had not existed, someone else would have written me,
        Hemingway, Dostoevski, all of us.
Memory believes before knowing remembers. Believes longer than
        recollects, longer than knowing even wonders.
Our tragedy is a general and universal physical fear so long sustained by now
        that we can even bear it... the basest of all things is to be afraid.
Perhaps they were right in putting love into books... Perhaps it could not live
        anywhere else.
Pointless... like giving  caviar to an elephant.
The aim of every artist is to arrest motion, which is life, by artificial means and
        hold it fixed so that a hundred years later, when a stranger looks at
        it, it moves again since it is life.
The artist doesn't have time to listen to the critics. The ones who want to be
        writers read the reviews, the ones who want to write don't have the
        time to read reviews.
The best job that was ever offered to me was to become a landlord in
        a brothel. In my opinion it's the perfect milieu for an artist to work in.
The end of wisdom is to dream high enough to lose the dream in the seeking of it.
The last sound on the worthless earth will be two human beings trying to
        launch a homemade spaceship and already quarreling about where
        they are going next.
The man who removes a mountain begins by carrying away small stones.
The past is never dead. It's not even past.
The salvation of the world is in man's suffering.
The scattered tea goes with the leaves and every day a sunset dies.
The tools I need for my work are paper, tobacco, food, and a little whiskey.
There is something about jumping a horse over a fence, something that makes you
        feel good. Perhaps it's the risk, the gamble. In any event it's a thing I need.
This is a free country. Folks have a right to send me letters, and I have a
        right not to read them.
To live anywhere in the world today and be against equality because of
        race or color is like living in Alaska and being against snow.
To understand the world, you must first understand a place like Mississippi.
Tomorrow night is nothing but one long sleepless wrestle with yesterday's
        omissions and regrets.
Unless you're ashamed of yourself now and then, you're not honest.
We have to start teaching ourselves not to be afraid.
Well, between Scotch and nothin', I suppose I'd take Scotch. It's the
        nearest thing to good moonshine I can find.
You should approach Joyce's Ulysses as the illiterate Baptist preacher
        approaches the Old Testament: with faith.

## WILLIAM FEATHER (Author, 1889-1981)
The wisdom of the wise and the experience of the ages is
        preserved into perpetuity by a nation's proverbs, fables,
        folk sayings and quotations.

Books open your mind, broaden your mind, and strengthen you as nothing else can.
Business is always interfering with pleasure - but it makes other pleasures possible.
Success seems to be largely a matter of hanging on after
       others have let go.
Setting a good example for your children takes all the fun
       out of middle age.
We always admire the other person more after we've tried to
       do his job.
If people really liked to work, we'd still be plowing the land
       with sticks and transporting goods on our backs.
When lying, be emphatic and indignant, thus behaving like
       your children.
The reward of energy, enterprise and thrift is taxes
Beware of the person who can't be bothered by details.
Most of us regard good luck as our right, and bad luck as
       a betrayal of that right.
If we do not discipline ourselves the world will do it for us.
If you're naturally kind, you attract a lot of people you don't like.
Early morning cheerfulness can be extremely obnoxious.
Every social injustice is not only cruel, but it is economic waste.
Few of us get anything without working for it.
Finishing a good book is like leaving a good friend.
Back of ninety-nine out of one-hundred assertions that a thing
       cannot be done is nothing, but the unwillingness to do it.
A budget tells us what we can't afford, but it doesn't keep us from buying it.
A man must not deny his manifest abilities, for that is to evade his obligations.
An idea isn't worth much until a man is found who has the energy
       and ability to make it work.
An invitation to a wedding invokes more trouble than a
       summons to a police court.
Any man who makes a speech more than six times a year is bound
       to repeat himself, not because he has little to say, but
       because he wants applause and the old stuff gets it.
The tragedy is that so many have ambition and so few have ability.
Wealth flows from energy and ideas.
When ordering lunch, the big executives are just as
       indecisive as the rest of us.
Women lie about their age; men lie about their income.
Many of our prayers were not answered, and for this
       we are now grateful.
Next to a sincere compliment, I think I like a well-deserved
       and honest rebuke.
No man is a failure who is enjoying life.
Not a tenth of us who are in business are doing as well as we
       could if we merely followed the principles that were
       known to our grandfathers.
One of the funny things about the stock market is
       that every time one person buys, another sells,
       and both think they are astute.
One of the indictments of civilizations is that happiness and
       intelligence are so rarely found in the same person.

One of the many things nobody ever tells you about middle age
      is that it's such a nice change from being young.
One way to get the most out of life is to look upon it as an adventure.
Plenty of people miss their share of happiness, not because
      they never found it, but because they didn't
      stop to enjoy it.
Some of us might find happiness if we quit struggling
      so desperately for it.
Some people are making such thorough preparation for rainy days
      that they aren't enjoying today's sunshine.
Something that has always puzzled me all my life is why, when
      I am in special need of help, the good deed is usually done
      by somebody on whom I have no claim.
Temporary success can be achieved in spite of lack
      of other fundamental qualities, but no advancements
      can be maintained without hard work.
That they may have a little peace, even the best dogs are
      compelled to snarl occasionally.
The best sermon is preached by the minister who
      has a sermon to preach and not by the man who
      has to preach a sermon.
The philosophy behind much advertising is based on the old
      observation that every man is really two men - the man
      he is and the man he wants to be.
The prizes go to those who meet emergencies successfully,
      and the way to meet emergencies is to do each daily
      task the best we can.
Concentrate on your job and you will forget your other troubles.
Don't let ambition get so far ahead that it loses sight of the job at hand.
He isn't a real boss until he has trained subordinates to shoulder most of his
      responsibilities.
Here is the secret of inspiration: Tell yourself that thousands and
      tens of thousands of people, not very intelligent and certainly
      no more intelligent than the rest of us, have mastered problems
      as difficult as those that now baffle you.

## W.C. FIELDS (Comedian, Actor, 1880-1946)

If at first you don't succeed, try again. Then quit. There's no
      use being a damn fool about it.
A rich man is nothing but a poor man with money.
A woman drove me to drink and I didn't even have the decency to thank her.
Abstaining is favorable both to the head and the pocket.
Ah, the patter of little feet around the house. There's nothing
      like having a midget for a butler.
All the men in my family were bearded, and most of the women.
Anyone who hates children and animals can't be all bad.
Children should neither be seen or heard from - ever again.
Don't worry about your heart, it will last you as long as you live.
Drown in a cold vat of whiskey? Death, where is thy sting?
Hell, I never vote for anybody, I always vote against.
Here lies W. C. Fields. I would rather be living in Philadelphia.

Horse sense is the thing a horse has which keeps it from betting on people.
I am an expert of electricity. My father occupied the chair of applied
electricity at the state prison.
I am free of all prejudices. I hate every one equally.
I cook with wine, sometimes I even add it to the food.
I drink therefore I am.
I like children - fried.
I like to keep a bottle of stimulant handy in case I see a snake, which I
also keep handy
I must have a drink of breakfast.
I never drink water because of the disgusting things that fish do in it.
I never drink water; that is the stuff that rusts pipes.
I never drink water. I'm afraid it will become habit-forming.
I never met a kid I liked.
I never worry about being driven to drink; I just worry about being driven home.
I once spent a year in Philadelphia, I think it was on a Sunday.
If I had to live my life over, I'd live over a saloon.
If there's a will, prosperity can't be far behind.
If you can't dazzle them with brilliance, baffle them with bull.
It ain't  what they call you, it's what you answer to.
It's morally wrong to allow a sucker to keep his money.
Last week, I went to Philadelphia, but it was closed
Marry an outdoors woman. Then if you throw her out into the yard on a
cold night, she can still survive.
Never cry over spilt milk, because it may have been poisoned.
Never give a sucker an even break.
Never try to impress a woman, because if you do she'll expect you to
keep up the standard for the rest of your life
No doubt exists that all women are crazy; it's only a question of degree.
Now don't say you can't swear off drinking; it's easy. I've done it a thousand times.
On the whole, I'd rather be in Philadelphia.
Once, during Prohibition, I was forced to live for days on
nothing but food and water.
Remember, a dead fish can float downstream, but it takes a
live one to swim upstream.
Set up another case bartender! The best thing for a case of
nerves is a case of Scotch.
Show me a great actor and I'll show you a lousy husband. Show me a
great actress, and you've seen the devil.
Sleep - the most beautiful experience in life - except drink.
Some things are better than sex, and some are worse, but there's
nothing exactly like it.
Some weasel took the cork out of my lunch.
Start every day off with a smile and get it over with.
The best cure for insomnia is to get a lot of sleep.
The clever cat eats cheese and breathes down rat holes with baited breath.
The cost of living has gone up another dollar a quart.
The laziest man I ever met put popcorn in his pancakes so they would
turn over by themselves.
The world is getting to be such a dangerous place, a man is lucky to
get out of it alive.

There are only two real ways to get ahead today - sell liquor or drink it.
There comes a time in the affairs of man when he must take the bull by
  the tail and face the situation.
When we have lost everything, including hope, life becomes a disgrace,
  and death a duty.
Women are like elephants. I like to look at 'em, but I wouldn't want to own one.
You can't trust water: Even a straight stick turns crooked in it.

## MILLARD FILLMORE (President, 1800-1874)

Nothing brings out the lower traits of human nature like office-seeking.
  Men of good character and impulses are betrayed by it into all
  sorts of meanness.
It is not strange... to mistake change for progress.
May God save the country, for it is evident that the people
  will not.
The man who can look upon a crisis without being willing to offer
  himself upon the altar of his country is not fit for public trust.
Liberty unregulated by law degenerates into anarchy, which soon
  becomes the most horrid of all despotism.
An honorable defeat is better than a dishonorable victory.
Nothing brings out the lower traits of human nature like
  office-seeking.  Men of good character and impulses are
  betrayed by it into all sorts of meanness.

## ELLA FITZGERALD (Singer, 1918-1996)

It isn't where you came from, its where you're going that counts.
I stole everything I ever heard, but mostly I stole from the horns.
Just don't give up trying to do what you really want to do. Where there is
  love and inspiration, I don't think you can go wrong.

## JANE FONDA (Actress, 1937 - )

We cannot always control our thoughts, but we can control our words, and repetition
  impresses the subconscious, and we are then master of the situation.
To be a revolutionary you have to be a human being. You have to care
  about people who have no power.
When you can't remember why you're hurt, that's when you're healed.
It's never too late - never too late to start over, never too late to be happy.
My mother killed herself when I was 12. I won't complete that
  relationship. But I can try to understand her.
If the career you have chosen has some unexpected inconvenience,
  console yourself by reflecting that no career is without them.

## MALCOLM FORBES (Publisher, 1917-1990)

Anyone who says businessmen deal in facts, not fiction, has never
  read old five-year projections.
People who never get carried away should be.
It's so much easier to suggest solutions when you don't know
  too much about the problem
The best vision is insight.
Diversity: the art of thinking independently together.
Victory is sweetest when you've known defeat.

Let your children go if you want to keep them.
If you expect nothing, you're apt to be surprised. You'll get it.
If you have a job without any aggravations, you don't have a job.
If you never budge, don't expect a push.
Never hire someone who knows less than you do about
        what he's hired to do.
The purpose of education is to replace an empty mind with an open one.
Thinking well to be wise: planning well, wiser: doing well
        wisest and best of all.
Pay your people the least possible and you'll get from them the same.
People who matter are most aware that everyone else does too.
Presence is more than just being there.
Success follows doing what you want to do. There is no
        other way to be successful.
The biggest mistake people make in life is not trying to make a
        living at doing what they most enjoy.
The more sympathy you give, the less you need.
Those who enjoy responsibility usually get it; those who merely like
        exercising authority usually lose it.
To measure the man, measure his heart.
Too many people overvalue what they are not
        and undervalue what they are.
When things are bad, we take comfort in the thought that they could
        always get worse. And when they are, we find hope in the
        thought that things are so bad they have to get better.
When what we are is what we want to be, that's happiness.
When you cease to dream you cease to live.
Being right half the time beats being half-right all the time.
By the time we've made it, we've had it.
Diamonds are nothing more than chunks of coal that stuck to their jobs.
Elected leaders who forget how they got there won't the next time.
Everybody has to be somebody to somebody to be anybody.
Failure is success if we learn from it.
Few businessmen are capable of being in politics, they don't
        understand the democratic process, they have neither the
        tolerance or the depth it takes. Democracy isn't a business.
If you don't know what to do with many of the papers piled on your
        desk, stick a dozen colleagues initials on them and pass them along.
When in doubt, route.
It is all one to me if a man comes from Sing Sing Prison or Harvard.
        We hire a man, not his history.
It's more fun to arrive a conclusion than to justify it.

## GERALD R. FORD (President, Vice-President, 1913-2006)

I am a Ford, not a Lincoln.
I had a lot of experience with people smarter than I am.
I know I am getting better at golf because I am hitting fewer spectators.
I love sports. Whenever I can, I always watch the Detroit Tigers on the radio.
I watch a lot of baseball on the radio.
I would hope that understanding and reconciliation are
        not limited to the 19th hole alone.

If Lincoln were alive today, he'd be turning over in his grave.

A government big enough to give you everything you want is a
government big enough to take from you everything you have.

For millions of men and women, the church has been the hospital for the
soul, the school for the mind and the safe depository for moral ideas.

History and experience tell us that moral progress comes not in comfortable
and complacent times, but out of trial and confusion.

I am acutely aware that you have not elected me as your President by your
ballots, so I ask you to confirm me with your prayers.

I have had a lot of adversaries in my political life, but no
enemies that I can remember.

In all my public and private acts as your president, I expect to follow my
instincts of openness and candor with full confidence that honesty
is always the best policy in the end.

It's the quality of the ordinary, the straight, the square, that accounts for
the great stability and success of our nation. It's a quality to be proud
of. But it's a quality that many people seem to have neglected.

My commitment to the security and future of Israel is based upon basic
morality as well as enlightened self-interest. Our role in supporting
Israel honors our own heritage.

Our constitution works. Our great republic is a government of laws, not of men.

Tell the truth, work hard, and come to dinner on time.

The political lesson of Watergate is this: Never again must America allow
an arrogant, elite guard of political adolescents to by-pass the
regular party organization and dictate the terms of a national election.

There are no adequate substitutes for father, mother, and children bound
together in a loving commitment to nurture and protect. No
government, no matter how well-intentioned, can take the place
of the family in the scheme of things.

Truth is the glue that holds government together.

When a man is asked to make a speech, the first thing he has
to decide is what to say.

## HENRY FORD (Industrialist, 1863-1947)

Anyone who stops learning is old, whether at twenty or eighty. Anyone who keeps
learning stays young. The greatest thing in life is to keep your mind young.

As we advance in life we learn the limits of our abilities.

Before everything else, getting ready is the secret of success.

Business is never so healthy as when, like a chicken, it must do a certain
amount of scratching around for what it gets.

Capital punishment is as fundamentally wrong as a cure for crime as
charity is wrong as a cure for poverty.

Coming together is a beginning; keeping together is progress; working
together is success.

Competition is the keen cutting edge of business, always shaving away at costs.

Don't find fault, find a remedy.

Enthusiasm is the yeast that makes your hopes shine to the stars.

Enthusiasm is the sparkle in your eyes, the swing in your gait. The grip of your
hand, the irresistible surge of will and energy to execute your ideas.

Even a mistake may turn out to be the one thing necessary to a
worthwhile achievement.

Exercise is bunk. If you are healthy, you don't need it: if you are sick
        you should not take it.
Failure is simply the opportunity to begin again, this time more intelligently.
History is more or less bunk.
I am looking for a lot of men who have an infinite capacity to not know
        what can't be done.
I believe God is managing affairs and that He doesn't need any advice from me.
        With God in charge, I believe everything will work out for the best
        in the end. So what is there to worry about.
I cannot discover that anyone knows enough to say definitely what
        is and what is not possible.
I do not believe a man can ever leave his business. He ought to think
        of it by day and dream of it by night.
If everyone is moving forward together, then success takes care of itself.
If money is your hope for independence you will never have it. The only real
        security that a man will have in this world is a reserve of knowledge,
        experience, and ability.
If there is any one secret of success, it lies in the ability to get the other
        person's point of view and see things from that person's angle as
        well as from your own.
If you think you can do a thing or think you can't do a thing, you're right.
It has been my observation that most people get ahead during the time
        that others waste.
It is not the employer who pays the wages. Employers only handle
        the money. It is the customer who pays the wages.
It is well enough that people of the nation do not understand our banking and
        monetary system, for if they did, I believe there would be a
        revolution before tomorrow morning.
Life is a series of experiences, each one of which makes us bigger, even though
        sometimes it is hard to realize this. For the world was built to develop
        character, and we must learn that the setbacks and grieves which
        we endure help us in our marching onward.
Most people spend more time and energy going around problems
        than in trying to solve them.
My best friend is the one who brings out the best in me.
Nothing is particularly hard if you divide it into small jobs.
Obstacles are those frightful things you see when you take your eyes off your goal.
One of the greatest discoveries a man makes, one of his great surprises, is
        to find he can do what he was afraid he couldn't do.
Quality means doing it right when no one is looking.
Speculation is only a word covering the making of money out of the
        manipulation of prices, instead of supplying goods and services.
The competitor to be feared is one who never bothers about you at all, but
        goes on making his own business better all the time
The highest use of capital is not to make more money, but to make money
        do more for the betterment of life.
The man who will use his skill and constructive imagination to see how much
        he can give for a dollar, instead of how little he can give for a
        dollar, is bound to succeed.
The only real security that a man can have in this world is a reserve
        of knowledge, experience and ability.

There are no big problems, there are just a lot of little problems
There is joy in work. There is no happiness except in the realization that
      we have accomplished something.
Money is like an arm or leg - use it or lose it.
There is no man living that can not do more than he thinks he can.
There is one rule for the industrialist and that is: Make the best quality of goods
      possible at the lowest cost possible, paying the highest wages possible.
Thinking is the hardest work there is, which is probably the reason
      why so few engage in it.
Time and money spent in helping men to do more for themselves is
      far better than mere giving.
We don't want tradition. We want to live in the present and the only history
      that is worth a tinker's dam is the history we make today.
Wealth, like happiness, is never attained when sought after directly. It
      comes as a by-product of providing a useful service.
What's right about America is that although we have a mess of problems, we
      have great capacity - intellect and resources - to do some thing about them.
Whatever you have, you must either use or lose.
When everything seems to be going against you, remember that the airplane
      takes off against the wind, not with it.
Whether you believe you can do a thing or not, you are right.
Whether you think that you can, or that you can't, you are usually right.
You can't build a reputation on what you are going to do.
You can't learn in school what the world is going to do next year.
You will find men who want to be carried on the shoulders of others, who think
      that the world owes them a living. They don't seem to see that we
      must all lift together and pull together.

## AL FRANKEN (Senator, Comedian, 1951 - )

When the president (G.W. Bush) during the campaign said he was against
      nation building, I didn't realize he meant our nation.
Mistakes are a part of being human. Appreciate your mistakes for what they are:
      precious life lessons that can only be learned the hard way. Unless it's a
      fatal mistake, which, at least, others can learn from.
The biases the media has are much bigger than conservative or liberal.
      They're about getting ratings, about making money, about doing
      stories that are easy to cover.
The point is that there is tremendous hypocrisy among the Christian right. And I
      think that Christian voters should start looking at global warming and
      extreme poverty as a religious issue that speaks to the culture of life.
. . . I think that being able to make people laugh and write a book that's funny
      makes the information go down a lot easier and it makes it a lot more fun
      to read, easier to understand, and often stronger. So there's all kinds of
      advantages to it.
. . . in the right-wing media, they do have a right-wing bias. And they also have
      an agenda. So their agenda is: we're an adjunct of the Republican Party,
      and we're going push that agenda every day, and, as you say, brand these
      stories that help further the right-wing cause.
If you hear, day after day, liberals are rooting against armed forces, that is
      eventually going to have an effect on soldiers and troops who are
      actually going to believe that and it's wrong. It's just wrong.

I also focus on Bush and his administration - who do a lot of lying - and how a
     right-wing media has allowed them to get away with a lot of stuff that,
     in a different media  environment, they probably wouldn't be able to
     get away with.
It's easier to put on slippers than to carpet the whole world.
It's the Power of the Almighty, the Splendor of Nature, and then you.
I do personal attacks only on people who specialize in personal attacks.
I once asked the most fabulous couple I know, Madonna and Guy Ritchie, how
     they kept things fresh despite having been married for almost seven
     months. 'It's a job, Al,' Guy told me. 'We work at it every day.'
The right wing has had a radio apparatus for years and years, so they've had
     minor leagues - they've had local rightwing guys who've become national
     rightwing guys, and who build slowly, and that's how it goes. We haven't
     had that. It isn't like we have a farm team.
The thing that interests me least about the radio business is the radio business.
     But I've had to learn a little bit about it. It's not rocket science: You get
     ratings, that's good.
To make the argument that the media has a left- or right-wing, or a liberal
     or a conservative bias, is like asking if the problem with Al-Qaeda is
     do they use too much oil in their hummus.
We need to be pro-science; we have to go back to science.
I think that there's a value to comedy in and of itself.
When you encounter seemingly good advice that contradicts other
     seemingly good advice, ignore them both.

## BEN  FRANKLIN (Publisher, Statesman, Founding Father, 1706-1790)
A countryman between two lawyers is like a fish between two cats.
A good conscience is a continual Christmas.
A great empire, like a great cake, is most easily diminished at the edges.
A house is not a home unless it contains food and fire for the mind as
     well as the body.
A learned blockhead is a greater blockhead than an ignorant one.
A life of leisure and a life of laziness are two things. There will be
     sleeping enough in the grave.
A man wrapped up in himself makes a very small bundle.
A penny saved is a penny earned.
A place for everything, everything in its place.
A small leak can sink a great ship.
Absence sharpens love, presence strengthens it.
Admiration is the daughter of ignorance.
All mankind is divided into three classes: those that are immovable,
     those that are movable, and those that move.
All wars are follies, very expensive and very mischievous ones.
All who think cannot but see there is a sanction like that of religion
     which binds us in partnership in the serious work of the world.
An investment in knowledge pays the best interest.
And whether you're an honest man, or whether you're a thief,
     depends on whose solicitor has given me my brief.
Anger is never without a reason, but seldom with a good one.
Any fool can criticize, condemn and complain and most fools do.
Applause waits on success.

As we must account for every idle word, so must we account for every idle silence.

At twenty years of age the will reigns; at thirty, the wit; and at forty, the judgment.

Be at war with your vices, at peace with your neighbors, and let every
new year find you a better man.

Be slow in choosing a friend, slower in changing.

Beauty and folly are old companions.

Being ignorant is not so much a shame, as being unwilling to learn.

Beware of little expenses. A small leak will sink a great ship.

Beware the hobby that eats.

Buy what thou hast no need of and ere long thou shalt sell thy necessities.

By failing to prepare, you are preparing to fail.

Certainty? In this world nothing is certain but death and taxes.

Content makes poor men rich; discontent makes rich men poor.

Creditors have better memories than debtors.

Diligence is the mother of good luck.

Distrust and caution are the parents of security.

Do good to your friends to keep them, to your enemies to win them.

Do not fear mistakes. You will know failure. Continue to reach out.

Do not squander time for that is the stuff life is made of.

Dost thou love life? Then do not squander time, for that is the stuff life is made of.

Each year one vicious habit  discarded, in time might  make the worst of us good.

Eat to please thyself, but dress to please others.

Either write something worth reading or do something worth writing.

Employ thy time well, if thou meanest to gain leisure.

Energy and persistence conquer  all things.

Even peace may be purchased at too high a price.

Experience is a dear teacher, but fools will learn at no other.

Experience keeps a dear school, but fools will learn in no other.

Fatigue is the best pillow.

For having lived long, I have experienced many instances of being obliged, by
better information or fuller consideration, to change opinions, even on
important subjects, which I once thought right but found to be otherwise.

Gain may be temporary and uncertain; but ever while you live, expense is constant
and certain: and it is easier to build two chimneys than to keep one in fuel.

Games lubricate the body and the mind.

Genius  without education is  like silver in the mine.

God helps those who help themselves.

God works wonders now and then; Behold a lawyer, an honest man.

Guests, like fish, begin to smell after three days.

Half a truth is often a great lie.

Having been poor is no shame, but being ashamed of it, is.

He does not possess wealth; it possesses him.

He that can have patience can have what he will.

He that composes himself is wiser than he that composes a book.

He that displays too often his wife and his wallet is in danger of having
both of them borrowed.

He that has done you a kindness will be more ready to do you
another, than he whom you yourself have obliged.

He that is good for making excuses is seldom good for anything else.

He that is of the opinion money will do everything may well be suspected
of doing everything for money.

He that lives upon hope will die fasting.

He that raises a large family does, indeed, while he lives to observe them,
      stand a broader mark for sorrow; but then he stands a broader
      mark for pleasure too.

He that rises late must trot all day.

He that speaks much, is much mistaken.

He that waits upon fortune, is never sure of a dinner.

He that won't be counseled can't be helped.

He that would live in peace and at ease must not speak all he knows or all he sees.

He that's secure is not safe.

He who falls in love with himself will have no rivals.

Hear reason, or she'll make you feel her.

Hide not your talents. They for use were made. What's a sundial in the shade?

Honesty is the best policy.

How few there are who have courage enough to own their faults, or resolution
      enough to mend them.

Human felicity is produced not as much by great pieces of good fortune that
      seldom happen as by little advantages that occur every day.

Hunger is the best pickle.

I conceive that the great part of the miseries of mankind are brought upon them by
      false estimates they have made of the value of things.

I didn't fail the test, I just found 100 ways to do it wrong.

I guess I don't so much mind being old, as I mind being fat and old.

I look upon death to be as necessary to our constitution as sleep. We shall rise
      refreshed in the morning.

I saw few die of hunger; of eating, a hundred thousand.

I should have no objection to go over the same life from its beginning to the
      end: requesting only the advantage authors have, of correcting in a
      second edition the faults of the first.

I wake up every morning at nine and grab for the morning paper. Then I look
      at the obituary page. If my name is not on it, I get up.

If a man could have half of his wishes, he would double his troubles.

If a man empties his purse into his head, no one can take it from him.

If all printers were determined not to print anything till they were sure
      it would offend nobody, there would be very little printed.

If passion drives you, let reason hold the reins.

If time be of all things the most precious, wasting time must
      be the greatest prodigality.

If you desire many things, many things will seem few.

If you know how to spend less than you get, you have the philosopher's stone.

If you would be loved, love, and be loveable.

If you would have a faithful servant, and one that you like, serve yourself.

If you would know the value of money, go and try to borrow some.

If you would not be forgotten as soon as you are dead, either write
      something worth reading or do things worth writing.

In general, mankind, since the improvement of cookery, eats
      twice as much as nature requires.

In the affairs of this world, men are saved not by faith, but by the want of it.

It is a grand mistake to think of being great without goodness and I
      pronounce it as certain that there was never a truly great man
      that was not at the same time truly virtuous.

It is easier to prevent bad habits than to break them.

It is much easier to suppress a first desire than to satisfy those that follow.

It is only when the rich are sick that they fully feel the impotence of wealth.

It is the eye of other people that ruin us. If I were blind I would want,
    neither fine clothes, fine houses or fine furniture.

It is the working man who is the happy man. It is the idle man who
    is the miserable man.

In this world nothing can be said to be certain, except death and taxes.

Industry [hard work] need not wish.

It takes many good deeds to build a good reputation, and only
    one bad one to lose it.

Keep your eyes wide open before marriage, half shut afterwards.

Laws too gentle are seldom obeyed; too severe, seldom executed.

Leisure is the time for doing something useful. This leisure the
    diligent person will obtain the lazy one never.

Life's Tragedy is that we get old to soon and wise too late.

Lost time is never found again.

Many a man thinks he is buying pleasure, when he is really selling himself to it.

Many foxes grow gray but few grow good.

Marriage is the most natural state of man, and... the state in
    which you will find solid happiness.

Mine is better than ours.

Money has never made man happy, nor will it, there is nothing in its nature
    to produce happiness. The more of it one has the more one wants.

Most people return small favors, acknowledge medium ones and repay
    greater ones - with ingratitude.

Necessity never made a good bargain.

Never confuse motion with action.

Never leave that till tomorrow which you can do today.

Never take a wife till thou hast a house (and a fire) to put her in.

No nation was ever ruined by trade.

Observe all men, thyself most.

One today is worth two tomorrows.

Our necessities never equal our wants.

Rather go to bed with out dinner than to rise in debt.

Rebellion against tyrants is obedience to God.

Remember not only to say the right thing in the right place, but far more
    difficult still, to leave unsaid the wrong thing at the tempting moment.

Remember that credit is money.

Savages we call them because their manners differ from ours.

She laughs at everything you say. Why? Because she has fine teeth.

Since thou are not sure of a minute, throw not away an hour.

Some people die at 25 and aren't buried until 75.

Speak ill of no man, but speak all the good you know of everybody.

Take time for all things: great haste makes great waste.

Tell me and I forget. Teach me and I remember. Involve me and I learn.

The absent are never without fault, nor the present without excuse.

The art of acting consists in keeping people from coughing.

The discontented man finds no easy chair.

The doors of wisdom are never shut.

The doorstep to the temple of wisdom is a knowledge of our own ignorance.

The eye of the master will do more work than both his hands.

The first mistake in public business is the going into it.

The strictest law sometimes becomes the severest injustice.

The U. S. Constitution doesn't guarantee happiness, only the pursuit
of it. You have to catch up with it yourself.

The use of money is all the advantage there is in having it.

The way to see by Faith is to shut the Eye of Reason.

The worst wheel of the cart makes the most noise.

There are three faithful friends - an old wife, an old dog, and ready money.

There are three things extremely hard: steel, a diamond, and to know one's self.

There are two ways of being happy: We must either diminish our wants or augment
our means - either may do - the result is the same and it is for each man to
decide for himself and to do that which happens to be easier.

There is no kind of dishonesty into which otherwise good people more
easily and frequently fall than that of defrauding the government.

There never was a truly great man that was not at the same time truly virtuous.

There was never a good war, or a bad peace.

They who can give up essential liberty to obtain a little temporary
safety deserve neither liberty nor safety.

Those disputing, contradicting, and confuting people are generally
unfortunate in their affairs. They get victory, sometimes, but they
never get good will, which would be of more use to them.

Those that won't be counseled can't be helped.

Those who govern, having much business on their hands, do not generally
like to take the trouble of considering and carrying into execution new
projects. The best public measures are therefore seldom adopted from
previous wisdom, but forced by the occasion.

Three can keep a secret, if two of them are dead.

Time is money.

To Follow by faith alone is to follow blindly.

To lengthen thy life, lessen thy meals.

To succeed, jump as quickly at opportunities as you do at conclusions.

Tomorrow, every Fault is to be amended; but that Tomorrow never comes.

Tricks and treachery are the practice of fools, that don't have
brains enough to be honest.

Trouble springs from idleness, and grievous toil from needless ease.

Wars are not paid for in wartime, the bill comes later.

We are all born ignorant, but one must work hard to remain stupid.

We must, indeed, all hang together or, most assuredly, we shall all hang separately.

Wealth is not his that has it, but his that enjoys it.

Well done is better than well said.

Whatever is begun in anger ends in shame.

When befriended, remember it; when you befriend, forget it.

When in doubt, don't.

When men and woman die, as poets sung, his heart's the last part
moves, her last, the tongue.

When will mankind be convinced and agree to settle their
difficulties by arbitration?

When you're finished changing, you're finished.

Where liberty is, there is my country.

Where sense is wanting, everything is wanting.

Where there's marriage without love, there will be love without marriage.
Who had deceived thee so often as thyself?.
Who is rich? He that rejoices in his portion.
Who is wise? He that learns from everyone. Who is powerful? He that governs
     his passions. Who is rich? He that is content. Who is that? Nobody.
Wine is constant proof that God loves us and loves to see us happy.
Wise  men don't need advice. Fools won't take it.
Without continual growth and progress, such words as
     improvement, achievement, and success have no meaning.
Words may show a man's wit but actions his meaning.
Work as if you were to live a hundred years. Pray as if you were to die tomorrow.
Write your  injuries  in dust, your benefits in marble.
You can bear your own faults, and why not a fault in your wife?
You may delay, but time will not.
Your  net worth to the world is usually determined by what remains  after
     your  bad habits are subtracted from your  good ones.

## ROBERT FROST (Poet, 1874-1963)

A bank is a place where they lend you an umbrella in fair weather
     and ask for it back when it begins to rain.
A civilized society is one which tolerates eccentricity to the point of doubtful sanity.
A diplomat is a man who always remembers a woman's birthday
     but.never remembers her age.
A jury consists of twelve persons chosen to decide who has the better lawyer.
A liberal is a man too broadminded to take his own side in a quarrel.
A mother takes twenty years to make a man of her boy, and another
     woman makes a fool of him in twenty minutes.
A person will sometimes devote all his life to the development of
     one part of his body - the wishbone.
A poem begins as a lump in the throat, a sense of wrong, a
     homesickness, a lovesickness.
A poem  begins in delight and ends in wisdom.
A poet  never takes notes. You never take notes in a love affair.
A successful lawsuit is the one  worn by a policeman.
Always fall in with what you're asked to accept. Take what is given, and
     make it over your way. My aim in life has always been to hold my
     own with whatever's going. Not against: with.
And were an epitaph to be my story I'd have a short one ready for my own. I would
     have written of me on my stone: I had a lover's quarrel with the world.
Being the boss anywhere is lonely. Being a female boss in a world of mostly
     men is especially so.
But I have promises to keep, and miles to go before I sleep, and miles to
     go before I sleep.
By working faithfully eight hours a day you may eventually get to be boss
     and work twelve hours a day.
College is a refuge from hasty judgment.
Don't ever take a fence down until you know why it was put up.
Education doesn't change life much. It just lifts trouble to a higher plane of regard.
Education is hanging around until you've caught on.
Education is the ability to listen to almost anything without losing your
     temper or your self-confidence.

Forgive me my nonsense, as I also forgive the nonsense of those that
        think they talk sense.
Forgive, O Lord, my little jokes on Thee, and I'll forgive Thy great
        big joke on me.
Freedom lies in being bold.
Half the world is composed of people who have something to say and can't,
        and the other half who have nothing to say and keep on saying it.
Happiness makes up in height for what it lacks in length.
Hell is a half-filled auditorium.
Home is the place where, when you have to go there, they have to take you in.
Humor is the most engaging cowardice.
I  alone of English writers have consciously set myself to make music
        out of what I may call the sound of sense.
I always entertain great hopes.
I am a writer of books in retrospect. I talk in order to understand; I
        teach in order to learn.
I had a lovers quarrel with the world.
I have never started a poem yet whose end I knew. Writing a poem is discovering.
I hold it to be the inalienable right of anybody to go to hell in his own way.
I never dared to be radical when young for fear it would make me
        conservative when old.
I often say of George Washington that he was one of the few in the whole
        history of the world who was not carried away by power.
I  would have written of me on my stone: I had a lover's quarrel with the world.
If one by one we counted people out For the least sin, it wouldn't take us long To
        get so we had no one left to live with. For to be social is to be forgiving.
If society fits you comfortably enough, you call it freedom.
If you don't know how great this country is, I know someone who does; Russia.
In three words I can sum up everything I've learned about life: it goes on.
It's a funny thing that when a man hasn't anything on earth to worry
        about, he goes off and gets married.
Let him that is without stone among you cast the first thing he can lay his hands on.
Love is an irresistible desire to be irresistibly desired.
Modern poets talk against business, poor things, but all of us write
        for money. Beginners are subjected to trial by market.
Most of the change we think we see in life is due to truths being in and out of favor.
My sorrow, when she's here with me, thinks these dark days of autumn rain are
        beautiful as days can be; she loves the bare, the withered tree; she walks
        the sodden pasture lane.
No memory of having starred atones for later disregard, or
        keeps the end from being hard.
No tears in the writer, no tears in the reader. No surprise in
        the writer, no surprise in the reader.
Nobody was ever meant, To remember or invent, What he did with every cent.
Nothing can make injustice just but mercy.
One aged man - one man - can't fill a house.
Poetry is a way of taking life by the throat.
Poetry is about the grief. Politics is about the grievance.
Poetry is when an emotion has found its thought and the thought has found words.
Poets are like baseball pitchers. Both have their moments. The
        intervals are the tough things.

Pressed into service means pressed out of shape.
Some say the world will end in fire, some say in ice.
Poetry is what gets lost in translation.
Space ails us moderns: we are sick with space.
Style is that which indicates how the writer takes himself and what he
          is saying. It is the mind skating circles around itself as it moves forward.
Take care to sell your horse before he dies. The art of life is passing losses on.
Talking is a hydrant in the yard and writing is a faucet upstairs in the house.
          Opening the first takes the pressure off the second.
The artist in me cries out for design.
The best things and best people rise out of their separateness; I'm against a
          homogenized society because I want the cream to rise.
The best way out is always through.
The brain is a wonderful organ; it starts working the moment you get up
          in the morning and does not stop until you get into the office
The chief reason for going to school is to get the impression fixed for life
          that there is a book side for everything.
The ear is the only true writer and the only true reader.
The father is always a Republican toward his son, and his
          mother's always a Democrat.
The figure a poem makes. It begins in delight and ends in wisdom... in a
          clarification of life - not necessarily a great clarification, such as sects
          and cults are founded on, but in a momentary stay against confusion.
The greatest thing in family life is to take a hint when a hint is intended -
          and not to take a hint when a hint isn't intended.
The middle of the road is where the white line is - and that's the
          worst place to drive.
The only certain freedom's in departure.
The reason why worry kills more people than work is that
          more people worry than work.
The strongest and most effective force in guaranteeing the long-term maintenance
          of power is not violence in all the forms deployed by the dominant to control
          the dominated, but consent in all the forms in which the dominated
          acquiesce in their own domination.
The world is full of willing people; some willing to work, the rest willing to let them.
The worst disease which can afflict executives in their work is not, as popularly
          supposed, alcoholism; it's egotism.
There are two kinds of teachers: the kind that fill you with so much quail
          shot that you can't move, and the kind that just gives you a little
          prod behind and you jump to the skies.
There never was any heart truly great and generous, that was not
          also tender and compassionate.
They would not find me changed from him they knew - only
          more sure of all I thought  was true.
Thinking isn't agreeing or disagreeing. That's voting.
To be social is to be forgiving.
Two roads diverged in a wood and I - I took the one less traveled
          by, and that has made all the difference.
Two such as you with such a master speed, cannot be parted nor be swept
          away, from one another once you are agreed, that life is only life
          forevermore, together wing to wing and oar to oar.

We dance round in a ring and suppose, but the secret sits in the middle and knows.
What we live by we die by.
To be a poet is a condition, not a profession.
Writing free verse is like playing tennis with the net down.
You can be a little ungrammatical if you come from the right part of the country.
You can be a rank insider as well as a rank outsider.
You can't get too much winter in the winter.
You don't have to deserve your mother's love. You have to deserve your father's.
You have freedom when you're easy in your harness.

## PAUL FUSSELL (Historian, 1944 - )

Americans are the only people in the world known to me whose status anxiety
prompts them to advertise their college and university affiliations in the
rear window of their automobiles.
I find nothing more depressing than optimism.
The more violent the body contact of the sports you watch, the
lower the class.
The worst thing about war was the sitting around and wondering what
you were doing morally.

## JOHN KENNETH GALBRAITH (Economist, Ambassador, 1908-2006)

A person buying ordinary products in a supermarket is in touch
with his deepest emotions.
All of the great leaders have had one characteristic in common: it was the
willingness to confront unequivocally the major anxiety of their people
in their time. This, and not much else, is the essence of leadership.
All successful revolutions are the kicking in of a rotten door.
By all but the pathologically romantic, it is now recognized that
this is not the age of the small man.
Economics is a subject profoundly conducive to cliche, resonant with boredom.
On few topics is an American audience so practiced in turning off its
ears and minds. And none can say that the response is ill advised.
Economics is extremely useful as a form of employment for economists.
Faced with the choice between changing one's mind and proving that there
is no need to do so, almost everyone gets busy on the proof.
Few can believe that suffering, especially by others, is in vain. Anything
that is disagreeable must surely have beneficial economic effects.
Few people at the beginning of the nineteenth century needed
an adman to tell them what they wanted.
Humor is richly rewarding to the person who employs it. It has some value in
gaining and holding attention, but it has no persuasive value at all.
If all else fails, immortality can always be assured by spectacular error.
If wrinkles must be written upon our brows, let them not be written upon the heart.
The spirit should never grow old.
In all life one should comfort the afflicted, but verily, also, one should afflict
the comfortable, and especially when they are comfortably, contentedly,
even happily wrong.
In any great organization it is far, far safer to be wrong with the
majority than to be right alone.
In economics, hope and faith coexist with great scientific pretension
and also a deep desire for respectability.

In economics, the majority is always wrong.

In the choice between changing ones mind and proving there's no need
        to do so, most people get busy on the proof.

In the United States, though power corrupts, the expectation of power paralyzes.

It has been the acknowledged right of every Marxist scholar to read into Marx the
        particular meaning that he himself prefers and to treat all others with .

It is a far, far better thing to have a firm anchor in nonsense than to
        put out on the troubled seas of thought.

It would be foolish to suggest that government is a good custodian of
        aesthetic goals. But, there is no alternative to the state.

Liberalism is, I think, resurgent. One reason is that more and more
        people are so painfully aware of the alternative.

Meetings are indispensable when you don't want to do anything.

Modesty is a vastly overrated virtue.

Money differs from an automobile or mistress in being equally important
        to those who have it and those who do not.

More die in the United States of too much food than of too little.

Much literary criticism comes from people for whom extreme specialization
        is a cover for either grave cerebral inadequacy or terminal laziness,
        the latter being a much cherished aspect of academic freedom.

Nothing is so admirable in politics as a short memory.

Of all classes the rich are the most noticed and the least studied.

One of the greatest pieces of economic wisdom is to know what you do not know.

People who are in a fortunate position always attribute virtue
        to what makes them so happy.

Politics is the art of choosing between the disastrous and the unpalatable.

Power is not something that can be assumed or discarded at will like underwear.

The commencement speech is not, I think, a wholly satisfactory
        manifestation of our culture.

The conspicuously wealthy turn up urging the character
        building values of the privation of the poor.

The conventional view serves to protect us from the painful job of thinking.

The enemy of the conventional wisdom is not ideas but the march of events.

The great dialectic in our time is not, as anciently and by some still supposed,
        between capital and labor; it is between economic enterprise and the state.

The Metropolis should have been aborted long before it
        became New York, London or Tokyo.

The modern conservative is engaged in one of man's oldest exercises
        in moral philosophy; that is, the search for a superior moral
        justification for selfishness.

The only function of economic forecasting is to make astrology look respectable.

The process by which banks create money is so simple that the mind is repelled.

The salary of the chief executive of a large corporation is not a market award for
        achievement. It is frequently in the nature of a warm personal
        gesture by the individual to himself.

There are few ironclad rules of diplomacy but to one there is no exception.
        When an official reports that talks were useful, it can safely be
        concluded that nothing was accomplished.

There are times in politics when you must be on the right side and lose.

There is certainly no absolute standard of beauty. That precisely
        is what makes its pursuit so interesting.

There is something wonderful in seeing a wrong-headed majority assailed by truth.
There's a certain part of the contented majority who love
    anybody who is worth a billion dollars.
Total physical and mental inertia are highly agreeable, much more so than we
        allow ourselves to imagine. A beach not only permits such inertia but
        enforces it, thus neatly eliminating all problems of guilt. It is now the
        only place in our overly active world that does.
Under capitalism, man exploits man. Under communism, it's just the opposite.
War remains the decisive human failure.
We all agree that pessimism is a mark of superior intellect.
We have escapist fiction, so why not escapist biography?
Wealth is not without its advantages and the case to the contrary,
        although it has often been made, has never proved widely persuasive.
Wealth, in even the most improbable cases, manages to convey
        the aspect of intelligence.
You will find that the State is the kind of organization which, though
        it does big things badly, does small things badly, too

## GALLAGHER (Comedian, 1946 - )
I saw a can that  said Pepsi Free and I said "That means it don't
        have Pepsi in it. That's a Coke."
What about 'Hog futures?'  I heard that. Hogs don't have no
        future. Bacon is not a career.
I want you to remember, behind every successful man is an amazed mother-in-law
There's a reason "Congress" begins with the word "con". Because "con" is the
        opposite of "pro", so "Congress" must be the opposite of "progress".
I wish there was a knob on the TV so you could turn up the intelligence. They got
        one marked "brightness" but it don't work, does it?"
Hey, what do you expect from a culture that drives on
        parkways and parks on driveways?
People like crowds. The bigger the crowd, the more people
        show up. Small crowd, hardly anybody shows up
What makes Teflon stick to the pan?
I like church though. Church was a reminder there was somethin' worse than school.
I found out why God made babies cute. It's so you don't kill them
If you water it and it dies, it's a plant. If you pull it out and it
        grows back, it's a weed.

## JAMES A. GARFIELD (President, 1831-1881)
The truth will set you free, but first it will make you miserable.
A brave man is a man who dares to look the Devil in the face
        and tell him he is a Devil.
If the power to do hard work is not a skill, it's the
        best possible substitute for it.
If you are not too large for the place you occupy, you are too small for it.
Justice and goodwill will outlast passion.
Man cannot live by bread alone; he must have peanut butter.
A law is not a law without coercion behind it.
A pound of pluck is worth a ton of luck.
All free governments are managed by the combined
        wisdom and folly of the people.

Few men in our history have ever obtained the Presidency
        by planning to obtain it.
He who controls the money supply of a nation controls the nation.
I am a poor hater.
I am trying to do two things: dare to be a radical and
        not a fool, which is a matter of no small difficulty.
I have had many troubles in my life, but the worst of them never came.
Poverty is uncomfortable; but nine times out of ten the best thing
        that can happen to a young man is to be tossed overboard
        and compelled to sink or swim.
Right reason is stronger than force.
Suicide is not a remedy.
Territory is but the body of a nation. The people who inhabit its hills
        and valleys are its soul, its spirit, its life.
The chief duty of government is to keep the peace and stand out
        of the sunshine of the people.
The civil service can never be placed on a satisfactory
        basis until it is regulated by law.
The President is the last person in the world to know
        what the people really want and think.
The sin of slavery is one of which it may be said that without
        the shedding of blood there is no remission.
There can be no permanent disfranchised peasantry in the United States.
Things don't turn up in this world until somebody turns them up.
I love to deal with doctrines and events. The contests of
        men about men I greatly dislike.
I mean to make myself a man, and if I succeed in that, I shall
        succeed in everything else.
Ideas are the great warriors of the world, and a war that has no idea
        behind it, is simply a brutality.
Ideas control the world.
If wrinkles must be written on our brows, let them not be written upon
        the heart. The spirit should never grow old.
Next in importance to freedom and justice is popular education, without
        which neither freedom nor justice can be permanently maintained.
Nobody but radicals have ever accomplished anything in a great crisis

## HOWARD GARDNER (Psychologist, 1943 -)

If I know you're very good in music, I can predict with just about
        zero accuracy whether you're going to be good or bad in
        other things
A lot of knowledge in any kind of an organization is what we call task knowledge.
        These are things that people who have been there a
        long time understand are important, but they may not know how
        to talk about them. It's often called the culture of the organization.
Stories are the single most powerful tool in a leader's toolkit.
. . . if storytelling is important, then your narrative ability, or your ability
        to put into words or use what someone else has put into words
        effectively, is important too.

## JAMES GARNER  (Actor, 1928 - )

Everybody wants blockbusters. I like to see a few pictures now and then that have
to do with people and have relationships, and that's what I want to do films
about. I don't want to see these sci-fi movies, and I don't want to do one of
those. I don't understand it.

I saw my wife at a pool, flipped over her, and 14 days later we were married.

When I started working, I didn't have a clue what I was doing, in that I was just
wandering around, hoping that I could succeed. Then after I got a little under
my belt, it took me about 25 years to feel like I knew what I was doing.

## JUDY GARLAND (Actor, Singer, 1922-1969)

Always be a first-rate version of yourself, instead of a second-rate
version of somebody else.

Behind every cloud is another cloud.

For it was not into my ear you whispered, but into my heart. It was not
my lips you kissed, but my soul.

How strange when an illusion dies. It's as though you've lost a child.

I can live without money, but I cannot live without love.

I think there's something peculiar about me that I haven't died. It
doesn't make sense but I refuse to die.

I try to bring the audience's own drama - tears and laughter they know
about - to them.

I was born at the age of twelve on an MGM lot.

I'm the original take-orders girl.

I've always taken 'The Wizard of Oz' very seriously, you know. I believe in the
idea of the rainbow. And I've spent my entire life trying to get over it.

I've never looked through a keyhole without finding someone was looking back.

If you have to be in a soap opera try not to get the worst role.

In the silence of night I have often wished for just a few words of love from
one man, rather than the applause of thousands of people.

It's lonely and cold on the top... lonely and cold.

There have been times when I have deliberately tried to take my
life... I think I must have been crying for some attention.

We cast away priceless time in dreams, born of imagination, fed upon
illusion, and put to death by reality.

## BILL GATES (Businessman, Creator of 'Windows,' 1955 - )

640K  ought to be enough for anybody.

As we look ahead into the next century, leaders will be those who empower others.

Be  nice to nerds. Chances are you'll end up working for one.

I really had a lot of dreams when I was a kid, and I think a great deal of
that grew out of the fact that I had a chance to read a lot.

If you can't make it good, at least make it look good.

If you think your teacher is tough, wait until you get a boss. He doesn't have tenure.

Intellectual property has the shelf life of a banana.

It's fine to celebrate success but it is more important to heed the lessons of failure.

Just in terms of allocation of time resources, religion is not very efficient. There's a
lot more I could be doing on a Sunday morning.

Life is not divided into semesters. You don't get summers off and very few
employers are interested in helping you find yourself.

Life is not fair; get used to it.

Like almost everyone who uses e-mail, I receive a ton of spam every day. Much
of it offers to help me get out of debt or get rich quick. It would be funny
if it weren't so exciting.

Microsoft is not about greed. It's about innovation and fairness.

People always fear change. People feared electricity when it was invented, didn't
they? People feared coal, they feared gas-powered engines... There will
always be ignorance, and ignorance leads to fear. But with time, people
will come to accept their silicon masters.

Success is a lousy teacher. It seduces smart people into thinking they can't lose.

Technology is just a tool. In terms of getting the kids working together
and motivating them, the teacher is the most important.

Television is not real life. In real life people actually have to leave the
coffee shop and go to jobs.

Until we're educating every kid in a fantastic way, until every inner city
is cleaned up, there is no shortage of things to do.

You see, antiquated ideas of kindness and generosity are simply bugs that must
be programmed out of our world. And these cold, unfeeling machines will
show us the way.

Your most unhappy customers are your greatest source of learning.

## RUTH BADER GINSBURG (Supreme Court Justice, 1933 -)

I would not like to be the only woman on the court.

It is not women's liberation, it is women's and men's liberation.

My mother told me to be a lady. And for her, that meant be
your own person, be independent.

So that's the dissenter's hope: that they are writing not
for today but for tomorrow.

The emphasis must be not on the right to abortion but on the
right to privacy and reproductive control.

The state controlling a woman would mean denying
her full autonomy and full equality.

Women will only have true equality when men share with them the
responsibility of bringing up the next generation.

## DIANE GLANCY (Educator, author, Poet, 1941 - )

Words -- as I speak or write them -- make a path on which I walk.

I try. I am trying. I was trying. I will try. I shall in the meantime try. I
sometimes have tried. I shall still by that time be trying.

It is easier th gnaw through bone than the hide of the heart.

Poetry uses the hub of a torque converter for a Jello mold.

## JOHN GLENN (Astronaut, 1921 - )

There is still no cure for the common birthday.

I don't know what you could say about a day in which you have
seen four beautiful sunsets.

The most important thing we can do is inspire young minds and to
advance the kind of science, math and technology education
that will help youngsters take us to the next phase of
space travel.

## ARTHUR GODFREY (Radio Commentator, 1903-1983)

You know, if you don't do nothin,' you don't do nothin.'
You know, it sounds corny, but I believe in myself. And I work hard.

## WHOOPI GOLDBERG (Actor, 1949 - )

An actress can only play a woman. I'm an actor, I can play anything.
And I don't believe that I have to stay on one side of the fence or the other. I
    don't believe that there is any good career move or bad career move. I
    believe there are only the things that make me happy.
Born ham, that's basically me.
For some reason, all artists have self-esteem issues.
I am an artist, art has no color and no sex.
I am the American Dream. I am the epitome of what the American Dream
    basically said. It said, you could come from anywhere and be anything
    you want in this country. That's exactly what I've done.
I am where I am because I believe in all possibilities.
I don't have pet peeves, I have whole kennels of irritation.
I don't look like Halle Berry. But chances are, she's going to end up
    looking like me.
I don't really view communism as a bad thing.
The art of acting is to be other than what you are.
Things happen to you out of luck, and if you get to stick around
    it's because you're talented.
When I listen to these women, it makes what I thought were my hard knocks
    feel like little nudges.
When I started, I knew I didn't fit any visual that anyone was going to lie
    down and take their clothes off about. Work doesn't come to me; I
    go out and look for it.
When you are kind to someone in trouble, you hope they'll remember and be
    kind to someone else. And it'll become like a wildfire.
You know, be an actor because you love to act. Don't be an actor because
    you think you're going to get famous, because that's luck.
You've got to vote for someone. It's a shame, but it's got to be done.

## BARRY GOLDWATER (Senator, 1909-1998)

American business has just forgotten the importance of selling.
If everybody in this town connected with politics had to leave town
    because of chasing women and drinking, you would have no
    government.
The income tax created more criminals than any other single
    act of government
Nixon was the most dishonest individual I have ever met in my life.
    He lied to his wife, his family, his friends, his colleagues in the
    Congress, lifetime members of his own political party, the
    American people and the world.
Equality, rightly understood as our founding fathers understood it,
    leads to liberty and to the emancipation of creative differences;
    wrongly understood, as it has been so tragically in our time, it
    leads first to conformity and then to despotism.
Extremism in the defense of liberty is no vice. And moderation in the
    pursuit of justice is no virtue.

I think every good Christian ought to kick Falwell right in the ass.
I won't say that the papers misquote me, but I sometimes wonder
       where Christianity would be today if some of those reporters
       had been Matthew, Mark, Luke and John.
I wouldn't trust Nixon from here to that phone.
If you don't mind smelling like peanut butter for two or three days,
       peanut butter is darn good shaving cream.
It's a great country, where anybody can grow up to be president... except me.
The only summit meeting that can succeed is the one that does not take place.
When I'm not a politician, I'll be dead.
Where is the politician who has not promised to fight to the death for
       lower taxes- and who has not proceeded to vote for the very
       spending projects that make tax cuts impossible?

## NELSON GOODMAN (Philosopher, 1906-1998)

Coming to understand a painting or a symphony in an unfamiliar style, to
       recognize the work of an artist or school, to see or hear in new ways,
       is as cognitive an achievement as learning to read or write or add.
Truth cannot be defined or tested by agreement with 'the world'; for not
       only do truths differ for different worlds but the nature of agreement
       between a world apart from it is notoriously nebulous.

## BILLY GRAHAM (Evangelist, 1918 -)

A child who is allowed to be disrespectful to his parents will not have
       true respect for anyone.
There is nothing wrong with men possessing riches. The wrong comes when
       riches possess men.
Comfort and prosperity have never enriched the world as much
       as adversity has.
The framers of our Constitution meant we were to have freedom of religion,
       not freedom from religion.
Tears shed for self are tears of weakness, but tears shed for others are a
       sign of strength.
A real Christian is a person who can give his pet parrot to the town gossip.
Nothing can bring a real sense of security into the home except true love.
Only God Himself fully appreciates the influence of a Christian
       mother in the molding of character in her children.
Only those who want everything done for them are bored.
Prayer is simply a two-way conversation between you and God.
Read the Bible. Work hard and honestly. And don't complain.
Suppose you could gain everything in the whole world, and lost
       your soul. Was it worth it?
The Christian life is not a constant high. I have my moments of deep
       discouragement. I have to go to God in prayer with tears in my
       eyes, and say, 'O God, forgive me,' or 'Help me.'
The highest form of worship is the worship of unselfish Christian service.
       The greatest form of praise is the sound of consecrated feet
       seeking out the lost and helpless.
The word 'romance,' according to the dictionary, means excitement,
       adventure, and something extremely real. Romance should
       last a lifetime.

We are not cisterns made for hoarding, we are channels made for sharing.
When wealth is lost, nothing is lost; when health is lost, something is lost;
    when character is lost, all is lost.
The most eloquent prayer is the prayer through hands that heal and bless.
The only time my prayers are never answered is on the golf course.
You're born. You suffer. You die. Fortunately, there's a loophole.
Being a Christian is more than just an instantaneous conversion - it is
    a daily process whereby you grow to be more and more like Christ.
Believers, look up - take courage. The angels are nearer than you think.
Courage is contagious. When a brave man takes a stand, the spines of
    others are often stiffened.
Everybody has a little bit of Watergate in him.
Give me five minutes with a person's checkbook, and I will tell you
    where their heart is.
God has given us two hands, one to receive with and the other to give with.
God is more interested in your future and your relationships than you are.
God proved His love on the Cross. When Christ hung, and bled, and died,
    it was God saying to the world, "I love you."
God will prepare everything for our perfect happiness in heaven, and if it
    takes my dog being there, I believe he'll be there.
God's angels often protect his servants from potential enemies.
I just want to lobby for God.
I've read the last page of the Bible. It's all going to turn out all right.
If a person gets his attitude toward money straight, it will help straighten
    out almost every other area in his life.
If we had more hell in the pulpit, we would have less hell in the pew.
It is not the body's posture, but the heart's attitude that
    counts when we pray.
Man has two great spiritual needs. One is for forgiveness. The
    other is for goodness.
My home is in Heaven. I'm just traveling through this world.

## KELSEY GRAMMAR (Actor, 1955 - )

I think it's your duty to overcome what you inherit in life.
Life is supposed to get tough.
Apologizes are pointless, regrets come too late. What matters is you
    can move, on you can grow.
I'm not sure sophisticated comedy has a place on television any more.
        I'd like to think it still does ... But I'm not sure the networks are
        interested, I'm not sure anybody else is interested in sophisticated
        comedy any more.
Fame obviously has become a premium in everybody's life. Everybody
        thinks they deserve it, everybody thinks they want it and most
        people really don't enjoy it once they get it.
It takes a very strange person to enjoy fame, with all the by-products
        that come with it. It's not necessarily a thrill.

## CARY GRANT (Actor, 1904-1986)

I pretended to be somebody I wanted to be until finally I became that
        person. Or he became me.
Divorce is a game played by lawyers.

When people tell you how young you look, they are telling you how old you are.
Insanity runs in my family. It practically gallops.
I improve on misquotation.
Everyone wants to be.
Do your job and demand your compensation - but in that order.
Everyone wants to be Cary Grant. Even I want to be Cary Grant.
I think that making love is the best form of exercise.
My father used to say, 'Let them see you and not the suit. That
    should be secondary.'
My formula for living is quite simple. I get up in the morning and I
    go to bed at night. In between, I occupy myself as best I can.
To succeed with the opposite sex, tell her you're impotent. She can't
    wait to disprove it.
We have our factory, which is called a stage. We make a product, we
    color it, we title it and we ship it out in cans.

## ULYSSES S. GRANT (President, 1822-1885)
Labor disgraces no man; unfortunately, you occasionally find men
    who disgrace labor.
Leave the matter of religion to the family altar, the church, and the private
    school, supported entirely by private contributions. Keep the church
    and state forever separate.
Let us have peace.
Nations, like individuals, are punished for their transgressions.
The art of war is simple enough. Find out where your enemy is. Get at him as
    soon as you can. Strike him as hard as you can, and keep moving on.

## HORACE GREELY (Journalist, 1811-1872)
Always rise from the table with an appetite, and you will never sit
    down without one.
It is impossible to enslave, mentally or socially, a bible-reading people. The
    principles of the bible are the groundwork of human freedom.
Apathy is a sort of living oblivion.
Common sense is very uncommon.
The way we do things is to begin.
Ease up, the play is over.
Fame is a vapor, popularity an accident, and riches take wings. Only
    one thing endures and that is character.
Go West, young man, and grow up with the country.
I am the inferior of any man whose rights I trample underfoot.
I never said all Democrats were saloonkeepers; what I said was
    all saloonkeepers are Democrats.
While boasting of our noble deeds we're careful to conceal  the ugly fact that by an
    iniquitous money system we have nationalized a system of oppression which,
        though more refined,  is not less cruel than the old system of chattel slavery
Journalism will kill you, but it will keep you alive while you're at it.
The darkest hour in any man's life is when he sits down to plan how
    to get money without earning it.
The illusion that times that were are better than those that are, has
    probably pervaded all ages.
There is no bigotry like that of "free thought" run to seed

## BRIAN GREENE (Physicist, 1963 - )

Sometimes attaining the deepest familiarity with a question is our best
substitute for actually having the answer.

The boldness of asking deep questions may require unforeseen flexibility
if we are to accept the answers.

Physicists are more like avant-garde composers, willing to bend traditional
rules... Mathematicians are more like classical composers.

I have long thought that anyone who does not regularly - or ever - gaze up
and see the wonder and glory of a dark night sky filled with countless
stars loses a sense of their fundamental connectedness to the universe.

## ARLO GUTHRIE (Folk Singer, 1947 - )

Everyone has a responsibility to not only tolerate another person's point of view,
but also to accept it eagerly as a challenge to your own understanding. And
express those challenges in terms of serving other people.

Greed and globalization aren't just America's fault.

I'd rather have friends who care than friends who agree with me.

The death of what's dead is the birth of what's living.

There are people all over the world who are willing to exploit others. You
can't just point the finger at America.

You can't have a light without a dark to stick it in.

## WOODY GUTHRIE (Folk Singer. 1912-1967)

If you play more than two chords, you're showing off.

Left wing, chicken wing, it don't make no difference to me.

Life has got a habit of not standing hitched. You got to ride it like you find it. You
got to change with it. If a day goes by that don't change some of your old
notions for new ones, that is just about like trying to milk a dead cow.

## GENE HACKMAN (Actor, 1930 - )

Dysfunctional families have sired a number of pretty good actors.

I was trained to be an actor, not a star. I was trained to play roles,
not to deal with fame and agents and lawyers and the press.

If I start to become a star, I'll lose contact with the normal
guys I play best.

If you look at yourself as a star, you've already lost something in the
portrayal of any human being.

It really costs me a lot emotionally to watch myself on screen. I think
of myself, and feel like I'm quite young, and then I look at this
old man with the baggy chins and the tired eyes and the
receding hairline and all that.

The difference between a hero and a coward is one step sideways.

## WALTER HAGEN (Athlete, 1892-1969)

They called it golf because all the other four letter words were taken.

It is the addition of strangeness to beauty that constitutes the
romantic character in art.

Make the hard ones look easy and the easy ones look hard.

No one remembers who came in second.

You're only here for a short visit. Don't hurry, don't worry. And be
sure to smell the flowers along the way.

## ALEXANDER HAMILTON (Founding Father, 1755-1804)

A promise must never be broken.

A well adjusted person is one who makes the same mistake
twice without getting nervous.

Constitutions should consist only of general provisions; the reason is that they
must necessarily be permanent, and that they cannot calculate for the
possible change of things.

Even to observe neutrality you must have a strong government.

Here, sir, the people govern; here they act by their immediate representatives.

I never expect to see a perfect work from an imperfect man.

I think the first duty of society is justice.

In framing a government which is to be administered by men over men the great
difficulty lies in this: You must first enable the government to control the
governed, and in the next place, oblige it to control itself.

In politics, as in religion, it is equally absurd to aim at making proselytes by fire
and sword. Heresies in either can rarely be cured by persecution.

In the main it will be found that a power over a man's support (salary) is a
power over his will.

In the usual progress of things, the necessities of a nation in every stage of its
existence will be found at least equal to its resources.

It is the advertiser who provides the paper for the subscriber. It is not to be
disputed, that the publisher of a newspaper in this country, without
a very exhaustive advertising support, would receive less reward for
his labor than the humblest mechanic.

It's not tyranny  we desire;  it's a just, limited, federal government.

Man is a reasoning rather than a reasonable animal.

Men often oppose a thing merely because they have had no agency in planning
it, or because it may have been planned by those whom they dislike.

Nobody expects to trust his body overmuch after the age of fifty.

Power over a man's subsistence is power over his will

Real firmness is good for anything; strut is good for nothing.

The sacred rights of mankind are not to be rummaged for among old parchments
or musty records. They are written, as with a sunbeam, in the whole
volume of human nature, by the hand of the divinity itself; and can
never be erased.

The voice of the people has been said to be the voice of God; and, however
generally this maxim has been quoted and believed, it is not true to fact. The
people are turbulent and changing, they seldom judge or determine right.

There is a certain enthusiasm in liberty, that makes human nature rise above itself,
in acts of bravery and heroism.

Those who stand for nothing fall for anything.

When the sword is once drawn, the passions of men observe no bounds of
moderation.

Why has government been instituted at all? Because the passions of man will not
conform to the dictates of reason and justice without constraint.

## WARREN G. HARDING (President, 1865-1923)

America's present need is not heroics but healing; not nostrums but
normalcy; not revolution but restoration.

I don't know much about Americanism, but it's a damn good word
with which to carry an election.

I have no trouble with my enemies. I can take care of my enemies in
a fight. But my friends, my goddamned friends, they're the ones
who keep me walking the floor at nights!
Only solitary men know the full joys of friendship. Others have their family;
but to a solitary and an exile his friends are everything.

## BENJAMIN HARRISON (President, 1833-1901)
Great lives never go out; they go on.
I pity the man who wants a coat so cheap that the man or woman who
produces the cloth will starve in the process.
No other people have a government more worthy of their respect and
love or a land so magnificent in extent, so pleasant to look upon,
and so full of generous suggestion to enterprise and labor.
The bud of victory is always in the truth.
We Americans have no commission from God to police the world.
When and under what conditions is the black man to have a free ballot?
When is he in fact to have those full civil rights which have so
long been his in law?

## WILLIAM HENRY HARRISON (President, 1773-1841)
All the measures of the Government are directed to the purpose of making
the rich richer and the poor poorer.
There is nothing more corrupting, nothing more destructive of the noblest
and finest feelings of our nature, than the exercise of unlimited power.
I contend that the strongest of all governments is that which is most free.
The chains of military despotism, once fastened upon a nation, ages might
pass away before they could be shaken off.
The only legitimate right to govern is an express grant of power from
the governed.
To Englishmen, life is a topic, not an activity.

## BRET HARTE (Author, 1836-1902)
The creator who could put a cancer in a believer's stomach is above
being interfered with by prayers
We begin to die as soon as we are born, and the end is linked to the beginning
Man has the possibility of existence after death. But possibility is one thing
and the realization of the possibility is quite a different thing.
The only sure thing about luck is that it will change.
One big vice in a man is apt to keep out of a great many smaller ones
A bird in hand is a certainty. But a bird in the bush may sing.
Never a lip is curved with pain that can't be kissed into smiles again.
Never a tear bedims the eye that time and patience will not dry.

## PAUL HARVEY (Radio Commentator, 1918-2009)
Dependency arguments often come from elites - either aid
agencies or governments - and say something about
attitudes to poor people.
Ever occur to you why some of us can be this much concerned with
animals suffering? Because government is not. Why
not? Animals don't vote.
Every pessimist who ever lived has been buried in an unmarked grave.

Tomorrow has always been better than today, and it always will be.
If there is a 50-50 chance that something can go wrong,
    then 9 times out of ten it will
Golf is a game in which you yell "fore," shoot six, and write down five.
I am fiercely loyal to those willing to put their money where my mouth is.
I've never seen a monument erected to a pessimist.
If 'pro' is the opposite of 'con' what is the opposite of 'progress'?
In times like these, it helps to recall that there have always
    been times like these.
When your outgo exceeds your income, the upshot may be your downfall.
Retiring is just practicing up to be dead. That doesn't take any practice.
Like what you do, if you don't like it, do something else.
Now you know the rest of the story.

## STEPHEN HAWKING (Physicist, 1942 - )

I have noticed even people who claim everything is predestined, and
    that we can do nothing to change it, look before they cross the road.
Intelligence is the ability to adapt to change.
It is not clear that intelligence has any long-term survival value.
Even if there is only one possible unified theory, it is just a set of rules
    and equations. What is it that breathes fire into the equations and
    makes a universe for them to describe?
God not only plays dice, He also sometimes throws the dice
    where they cannot be seen.
My goal is simple. It is a complete understanding of the universe, why
    it is as it is and why it exists at all.
To confine our attention to terrestrial matters would be
    to limit the human spirit.
I think computer viruses should count as life. I think it says something
    about human nature that the only form of life we have created so
    far is purely destructive. We've created life in our own image.
If we do discover a complete theory, it should be in time understandable in
    broad principle by everyone. Then we shall all, philosophers,
    scientists, and just ordinary people be able to take part in the
    discussion of why we and the universe exist.
It is no good getting furious if you get stuck. What I do is keep thinking
    about the problem but work on something else. Sometimes it is
    years before I see the way forward. In the case of information loss
    and black holes, it was 29 years.
Most sets of values would give rise to universes that, although they
    might be very beautiful, would contain no one able to wonder
    at that beauty.
Someone told me that each equation I included in the book would
    halve the sales.
The usual approach of science of constructing a mathematical model
    cannot answer the questions of why there should be a universe
    for the model to describe. Why does the universe go to all the
    bother of existing?
The whole history of science has been the gradual realization that events
    do not happen in an arbitrary manner, but that they reflect a certain
    underlying order, which may or may not be divinely inspired.

There are grounds for cautious optimism that we may now be near the
        end of the search for the ultimate laws of nature.
We are just an advanced breed of monkeys on a minor planet of a very
        average star. But we can understand the Universe. That makes us
        something very special.
One cannot really argue with a mathematical theorem.

## GOLDIE HAWN (Actress, 1945 - )

Never apologize for your success because you worked hard for it.
Once you can laugh at your own weaknesses, you can move forward.
        Comedy breaks down walls. It opens up people. If you're good,
        you can fill up those openings with something positive. Maybe
        you can combat some of the ugliness in the world.
I have witnessed the softening of the hardest of hearts by a simple smile.
All I ever wanted to be was happy.
Ditzy dumb blonde? I can be ditzy. I can be.
I'm not afraid of my femininity and I'm not afraid of my sexuality.
It is not the question, what am I going to be when I grow up; you should
        ask the question, who am I going to be when I grow up.
. . . curiosity, I think, is a really important aspect of staying young or youthful.
The biggest lesson we have to give our children is truth.
The only thing that will make you happy is being happy with who you are, and
        not who people think you are.
We have to embrace obstacles to reach the next stage of joy.
Youthfulness is connected to the ability to see things new for the first time. So
        if your eyes still look at life with wonder, then you will seem young,
        even though you may not be chronologically young.

## RUTHERFORD B. HAYES (President, 1822-1893)

As friends go [die] it is less important to live.
Conscience is the authentic voice of God to you.
The unrestricted competition so commonly advocated does not
        leave us the survival of the fittest. The unscrupulous succeed
        best in accumulating wealth.
To vote is like the payment of a debt, a duty never to be neglected, if its
        performance is possible.
Universal suffrage is sound in principle. The radical element is right.
Universal suffrage should rest upon universal education. To this end,
        liberal and permanent provision should be made for the support
        of free schools by the State governments, and, if need be,
        supplemented by legitimate aid from national authority.
Unjust attacks on public men do them more good than unmerited praise.
Virtue is defined to be mediocrity, of which either extreme is vice.
Wars will remain while human nature remains. I believe in my soul in cooperation,
        in arbitration; but the soldier's occupation we cannot
        say is gone until human nature is gone.
Do not let your bachelor ways crystallize so that you can't soften
        them when you come to have a wife and a family of your own.
He serves his party best who serves his country best.
I am a radical in thought (and principle) and a conservative in
        method (and conduct).

I am less disposed to think of a West Point education as requisite
for this business than I was at first. Good sense and energy
are the qualities required.
I am not liked as a President by the politicians in office, in the press,
or in Congress. But I am content to abide the judgment the sober
second thought of the people.
In avoiding the appearance of evil, I am not sure but I have sometimes
unnecessarily deprived myself and others of innocent enjoyments.
It is the desire of the good people of the whole country that sectionalism
as a factor in our politics should disappear...'
Law without education is a dead letter. With education the needed law
follows without effort and, of course, with power to execute itself;
indeed, it seems to execute itself.
Let every man, every corporation, and especially let every village, town,
and city, every county and State, get out of debt and keep out of
debt. It is the debtor that is ruined by hard times.
Must swear off from swearing. Bad habit.
No person connected with me by blood or marriage will be
appointed to office.
One of the tests of the civilization of people is the treatment of its criminals.
The bold enterprises are the successful ones. Take counsel of hopes rather
than of fears to win in this business.
The filth and noise of the crowded streets soon destroy the elasticity
of health which belongs to the country boy.
The independence of all political and other bother is a happiness.
The President of the United States should strive to be always mindful
of the fact that he serves his party best who serves his country best.
The progress of society is mainly the improvement in the condition
of the workingmen of the world.
The truth is, this being errand boy to one hundred and fifty thousand
people tires me so by night I am ready for bed instead of soirees.

## WILLIAM RANDOLPH HEARST (Publisher, 1863-1951)
You must keep your mind on the objective, not on the obstacle.
News is something somebody doesn't want printed; all else is advertising.
Any man who has the brains to think and the nerve to act for the benefit
of the people of the country is considered a radical by those who
are content with stagnation and willing to endure disaster.
Putting out a newspaper without promotion is like winking at a girl in the dark -
well-intentioned, but ineffective.
You can crush a man with journalism.
Don't be afraid to make a mistake, your readers might like it.
You furnish the pictures and I'll furnish the war.
If you make a product good enough . . . the public will make a path to
your door, says the philosopher. But if you want the public in
sufficient numbers, you would better construct a
highway. Advertising is that highway.
Try to be conspicuously accurate in everything, pictures as well as text.
Truth is not only stranger than fiction, it is more interesting.
The coming of the motion picture was as important as that
of the printing press.

A politician will do anything to keep his job, even become a patriot.
In suggesting gifts: Money is appropriate, and one size fits all.

## ROBERT A. HEINLEIN (Author, 1907-1988)
Never insult anyone by accident.
Never underestimate the power of human stupidity.
Theology is never any help; it is searching in a dark cellar at midnight
    for a black cat that isn't there. Theologians can persuade
    themselves of anything.
There is no way that writers can be tamed and rendered civilized or even cured.
    The only solution known to science is to provide the patient with an isolation
    room, where he can endure the acute stages in private and where food can
    be poked in to him with a stick.
The universe never did make sense; I suspect it was built on government contract.
You can have peace. Or you can have freedom. Don't ever
    count on having both at once.
Don't handicap your children by making their lives easy.
I never learned from a man who agreed with me.
It is a truism that almost any sect, cult, or religion will legislate its creed
    into law if it acquires the political power to do so.
No statement should be believed because it is made by an authority.
When any government, or any church for that matter, undertakes to say to
    its subjects, This you may not read, this you must not see, this you are
    forbidden to know, the end result is tyranny and oppression no matter
    how holy the motives.
Women and cats will do as they please, and men and dogs
    should relax and get used to the idea.
Writing is not necessarily something to be ashamed of, but do it in
    private and wash your hands afterwards.
Yield to temptation. It may not pass your way again.
One man's "magic" is another man's engineering. "Supernatural" is
    a null word.
One man's theology is another man's belly laugh.
Political tags - such as royalist, communist, democrat, populist, fascist, liberal,
    conservative, and so forth - are never basic criteria. The human race
    divides politically into those who want people to be controlled and those
    who have no such desire.
A society that gets rid of all its troublemakers goes downhill.
Anyone who considers protocol unimportant has never dealt with a cat.
Everything is theoretically impossible, until it is done.
For me, politeness is a sine qua non of civilization
Don't ever become a pessimist... a pessimist is correct oftener than an optimist,
    but an optimist has more fun, and neither can stop the march of events.
Be wary of strong drink. It can make you shoot at tax collectors... and miss.
Being right too soon is socially unacceptable.
Never worry about theory as long as the machinery does what it's supposed to do.
One could write a history of science in reverse by assembling the solemn
    pronouncements of highest authority about what could not be done
    and could never happen.
One of the sanest, surest, and most generous joys of life comes from
    being happy over the good fortune of others.

Sex without love is merely healthy exercise.

The difference between science and the fuzzy subjects is that science requires reasoning while those other subjects merely require scholarship.

The supreme irony of life is that hardly anyone gets out of it alive.

They didn't want it good, they wanted it Wednesday.

To be matter-of-fact about the world is to blunder into fantasy - and dull fantasy at that, as the real world is strange and wonderful.

When a place gets crowded enough to require ID's, social collapse is not far away. It is time to go elsewhere. The best thing about space travel is that it made it possible to go elsewhere.

A competent and self-confident person is incapable of jealousy in anything. Jealousy is invariably a symptom of neurotic insecurity.

An armed society is a polite society. Manners are good when one may have to back up his acts with his life.

By cultivating the beautiful we scatter the seeds of heavenly flowers, as by doing good we cultivate those that belong to humanity.

I am free because I know that I alone am morally responsible for everything I do. I am free, no matter what rules surround me. If I find them tolerable, I tolerate them; if I find them too obnoxious, I break them. I am free because I know that I alone am morally responsible for everything I do.

I don't see how an article of clothing can be indecent. A person, yes.

It's an indulgence to sit in a room and discuss your beliefs as if they were a juicy piece of gossip.

Love is that condition in which the happiness of another person is essential to your own... Jealousy is a disease, love is a healthy condition. The immature  mind often mistakes one for the other, or assumes that the  greater the love, the greater the jealousy.

May you live as long as you wish and love as long as you live.

## ERNEST HEMINGWAY (Author, 1899-1961)

A man can be destroyed but not defeated.

A man's got to take a lot of punishment to write a really funny book.

A serious writer is not to be confounded with a solemn writer. A serious writer may be a hawk or a buzzard or even a popinjay, but a solemn writer is always a bloody owl.

About  morals, I  know only that what is moral  is what  you feel good after and what is immoral  is what you feel  bad  after.

All  good  books have one thing  in common - they are truer than if they had really happened.

All modern American literature comes from one book by Mark Twain called Huckleberry Finn.

All my life I've looked at words as though I were seeing them for the first time.

All our words from loose using have lost their edge.

All things truly wicked start from innocence.

Always do sober what you said you'd do drunk. That will teach you to keep your  mouth shut.

An intelligent  man is sometimes forced to be drunk to spend time with his fools.

As you get older it is harder to have heroes, but it is sort of necessary.

Bullfighting is the only art in which the artist is in danger of death and in which the degree of brilliance in the performance is left to the fighter's honor.

Courage is grace under pressure.

Cowardice... is almost always simply a lack of ability to suspend
functioning of the imagination.
Decadence is a difficult word to use since it has become little more than a
term of abuse applied by critics to anything they do not yet understand
or which seems to differ from their moral concepts.
Every man's life ends the same  way. It is only the details of how he lived
and how he died that distinguish one man from another.
Fear  of death increases in exact proportion to increase in wealth.
For a long time now I have tried simply to write the best I can. Sometimes I
have good luck and write better than I can.
For a war to be just three conditions are necessary - public authority, just cause,
right motive.
Forget your personal tragedy. We are all bitched from the start and you especially
have to be hurt like hell before you can write seriously. But when
you get the damned hurt, use it-don't cheat with it.
Happiness in intelligent people is the rarest thing I know.
Hesitation increases in relation to risk in equal proportion to age.
His talent was as natural as the pattern that was made by the dust on a
butterfly's wings. At one time he understood it no more than the butterfly
did and he did not know when it was brushed or marred.
I don't like to write like God. It is only because you never do it, though, that
the critics think you can't do it.
I know now that there is no one thing that is true - it is all true.
I know only that what is moral is what you feel good after and what is
immoral is what you feel bad after.
I know war as few other men now living know it, and nothing to me is more
revolting. I have long  advocated its complete abolition, as its very
destructiveness on both friend and foe has rendered it useless as
a method of settling international disputes.
I learned never to empty the well of my writing, but always to stop when there
was still something there in the deep part of the well, and let it refill at
night from the springs that fed it.
I like to listen. I have learned a great deal from listening carefully. Most
people never listen.
I love sleep. My life has the tendency to fall apart when I'm awake, you know?
I never had to choose a subject - my subject rather chose me.
I've tried to reduce profanity but I reduced so much profanity when writing the
book that I'm afraid not much could come out. Perhaps we will have to
consider it simply as a profane book and hope that the next book will be
less profane or perhaps more sacred.
If a writer knows enough about what he is writing about, he may omit things that
he knows. The dignity of movement of an iceberg is due to only one ninth
of it being above water.
If you are lucky enough to have lived in Paris as a young man, then wherever you
go for the rest of your life it stays with you, for Paris is a moveable feast.
If you have a success you have it for the wrong reasons. If you become
popular  it is always because of the worst aspects of your work. .
It's none of their business that you have to learn how to write. Let them
think you were born that way.
Madame, all stories, if continued far enough, end in death, and he is no
true-story teller who would keep that from you.

Man is not made for defeat.

My aim is to put down on paper what I see and what I feel in the
best  and simplest way.

I'm not going to get into the ring with Tolstoy.

Never confuse movement with action.

Never go on trips with anyone you do not love.

Never think that war, no matter how necessary, nor how justified, is not a crime.

No weapon has ever settled a moral problem. It can impose a solution
but it cannot guarantee it to be a just one.

Once we have a war there is only one thing to do. It must be won. For defeat
brings worse things than any that can ever happen in war.

Personal columnists are jackals and no jackal has been known to live on grass
once he had learned about meat - no matter who killed the meat for him.

Pound's crazy. All poets are. They have to be. You don't put a poet
like Pound in the loony bin.

Prose is architecture, not interior decoration, and the Baroque is over.

Somebody just back of you while you are fishing is as bad as someone
looking over your shoulder while you write a letter to your girl.

Switzerland is a small, steep country, much more up and down than
sideways, and is all stuck over with large brown hotels built on
the cuckoo clock style of architecture.

That is what we are supposed to do when we are at our best - make it all up -
but make it up so truly that later it will happen that way.

That terrible mood of depression of whether it's any good or not is what is
known as The Artist's Reward.

The best way to find out if you can trust somebody is to trust them.

The first panacea for a mismanaged nation is inflation of the currency; the second
is war. Both bring a temporary prosperity; both bring a permanent ruin.
But both are the refuge of political and economic opportunists.

The game of golf would lose a great deal if croquet mallets and billiard
cues were allowed on the putting green.

The good parts of a book may be only something a writer is lucky
enough to overhear or it may be the wreck of his whole damn
life and one is as good as the other.

The man who has begun to live more seriously within begins to
live more simply without.

The only thing that could spoil a day was people. People were always the limiters
of happiness except for the very few that were as good as spring itself.

The shortest answer is doing the thing.

The world breaks everyone, and afterward, some are strong
at the broken places.

The world is a fine place and worth the fighting for and I hate
very much to leave it.

There are events which are so great that if a writer has participated in them
his obligation is to write truly rather than assume the presumption
of altering them with invention.

There is no hunting like the hunting of man, and those who have hunted armed
men long enough and liked it, never care for anything else thereafter.

There is no lonelier man in death, except the suicide, than that man who has
lived many years with a good wife and then outlived her. If two people
love each other there can be no happy end to it.

There is no rule on how to write. Sometimes it comes easily and perfectly;
    sometimes it's like drilling rock and then blasting it out with charges.
There is nothing to writing. All you do is sit down at a typewriter and bleed.
There's no one thing that is true. They're all true.
They wrote in the old days that it is sweet and fitting to die for one's country.
    But in modern war, there is nothing sweet nor fitting in your dying. You
    will die like a dog for no good reason.
There is no friend as loyal as a book.
To be a successful father... there's one absolute rule: when you have a kid,
    don't look at it for the first two years.
Wars are caused by undefended wealth.
We are all apprentices in a craft where no one ever becomes a master.
What is moral is what you feel good after, and what is immoral is
    what you feel bad after.
When I have an idea, I turn down the flame, as if it were a little alcohol
    stove, as low as it will go. Then it explodes and that is my idea.
When people talk, listen completely. Most people never listen.
When writing a novel a writer should create living people; people not
    characters. A character is a caricature.
When you have shot one bird flying you have shot all birds flying. They are
    all different and they fly in different ways but the sensation is the
    same and the last one is as good as the first.
Why should anybody be interested in some old man who was a failure?
Writing and travel broaden your ass if not your mind and I like to
    write standing up.
You can wipe out your opponents. But if you do it unjustly you
    become eligible for being wiped out yourself.

## JIMI HENDRIX (Singer, Guitarist, 1942-1970)

Knowledge speaks, but wisdom  listens.
All I'm writing is just what I feel, that's all. I just keep it almost
    naked. And probably the words are so bland.
Blues is easy to play, but hard to feel.
Even Castles made of sand, fall into the sea, eventually.
Every city in the world always has a gang, a street gang, or the so-called outcasts.
You have to give people something to dream on.
You have to go on and be crazy. Craziness is like heaven.
When the power of love overcomes the love of power the world will know peace.

## DON HENLEY (Musician, 1947)

Sometimes you get the best light from a burning bridge.
A man with a briefcase can steal millions more than any man with a gun.
I have a certain pool of subject matter that I like to write about, things that
    interest me: politics, religion, ecology, and relationships between
    men and women. And that's usually what I focus on.
I try to write conversationally; I try to write like people speak and put the
    emphasis on the right syllable.
I'm always jotting things down on pieces of paper. I've got pieces of paper
    all over my house.
Let hope inspire you, but let not idealism blind you. Don't look back, you
    can never look back.

**MARILU HENNER (Actor, 1952 - )**

Babies act out when they're hungry, cold, tired. They do
this for survival.

The more prepared I am, the more I'll be in control, less
nervous, less stressed and more focused.

Being in control of your life and having realistic expectations
about your day-to-day challenges are the keys to stress
management, which is perhaps the most important
ingredient to living a happy, healthy and rewarding life.

Everyone thrives most in his or her own unique environment.

Feeling a little blue in January is normal.

. . .don't let perfectionism become an excuse for
never getting started.

I also think stress is related to control. When you're in charge
of your life, you tend to not care about losing control of
things that don't really matter like traffic jams.

I definitely enjoy being in front of people which gives me
that exciting immediate rush.

I eat all of the time... at least five little meals a day.

I like getting up early. I get up around five.

It is now common knowledge that the average American
gains 7 pounds between Thanksgiving and New
Year's Day.

It's important to determine which surroundings work best
for you, and then build that environment to suit
your needs.

Lack of time is a real health killer.

Like it or not, the world evolves, priorities change and
so do you.

Most of us start out with a positive attitude and a plan to
do our best.

Resolutions are popular because everyone feels they could
use a little improvement.

Silence and solitude are more distracting to me than
chatter and commotion.

Stress is an important dragon to slay - or at least tame -
in your life.

The biggest reason most people fail is that they try to fix
too much at once - join a gym, get out of debt, floss
after meals and have thinner thighs in 30 days.

You know, one of the biggest thrills I have is when famous
people recognize me from Taxi.

**KATHARINE HEPBURN (Actor, 1907-2003)**

Acting is the perfect idiot's profession

I never lose sight of the fact that just being is fun.

Sometimes I wonder if men and women really suit each other. Perhaps they
should live next door and just visit now and then.

Plain women know more about men than beautiful ones do. But beautiful
women don't need to know about men. It's the men who have to
know about beautiful women.

Enemies are so stimulating.

To be loved is very demoralizing

Love has nothing to do with what you are expecting to get - only with
what you are expecting to give - which is everything.

Trying to be fascinating is an asinine position to be in.

It's life, isn't it? You plow ahead and make a hit. And you plow on and
someone passes you. Then someone passes them. Time levels.

Acting is a nice childish profession - pretending you're someone else
and, at the same time, selling yourself

It's a rather rude gesture, but at least it's clear what you mean.

Being a housewife and a mother is the biggest job in the world, but if it doesn't
interest you, don't do it - I would have made a terrible mother.

My greatest strength is... common sense. I'm really a standard brand - like
Campbell's tomato soup or Baker's chocolate.

It would be a terrific innovation if you could get your mind to stretch a
little further than the next wisecrack.

The average Hollywood film star's ambition is to be admired by an American,
courted by an Italian, married to an Englishman and have a
French boyfriend.

As for me, prizes are nothing. My prize is my work.

Acting is the most minor of gifts. After all, Shirley Temple could
do it when she was four.

Death will be a great relief. No more interviews.

To keep your character intact you cannot stoop to filthy acts. It makes it easier
to stoop the next time.I think most of the people involved in any art
always secretly wonder whether they are really there because they're
good or there because they're lucky.

Only the really plain people know about love-the very fascinating ones try so
hard to create an impression that they soon exhaust their talents."

. . . as one goes through life one learns that if you don't paddle your own
canoe, you don't move.

Life is hard. After all, it kills you.

If you always do what interests you, at least one person is pleased.

Never complain. Never explain.

If you obey all the rules, you miss all the fun

Why slap them on the wrist with feather when you can belt them over
the head with a sledgehammer.

If you want to sacrifice the admiration of many men for the criticism
of one, go ahead, get married.

I have many regrets, and I'm sure everyone does. The stupid things you
do, you regret... if you have any sense, and if you don't regret them,
maybe you're stupid.

Without discipline, there's no life at all.

I never realized until lately that women were supposed to be the inferior sex.

Drive on. We'll sweep up the blood later!

I can remember walking as a child. It was not customary to say you
were fatigued. It was customary to complete the goal of the expedition.

Marriage is a series of desperate arguments people feel passionately about.

## HERBERT HOOVER (President, 1874-1964)

A good many things go around in the dark besides Santa Claus.

About the time we can make the ends meet, somebody moves the ends.

All men are equal before fish.

I'm the only person of distinction who has ever had a depression
named for him.

Words without actions are the assassins of idealism.

The thing I enjoyed most were visits from children. They
did not want public office.

America - a great social and economic experiment, noble in motive and
far-reaching in purpose.

Blessed are the young for they shall inherit the national debt.

It is just as important that business keep out of government as that
government keep out of business.

It is a paradox that every dictator has climbed to power on the ladder
of free speech. Immediately on attaining power each dictator has
suppressed all free speech except his own.

Children are our most valuable natural resource.

Competition is not only the basis of protection to the consumer, but is
the incentive to progress.

Economic depression cannot be cured by legislative action or executive
pronouncement. Economic wounds must be healed by the action
of the cells of the economic body - the producers and consumers
themselves.

Fishing is much more than fish. It is the great occasion when we may return
to the fine simplicity of our forefathers.

Freedom is the open window through which pours the sunlight of the human
spirit and human dignity.

Honor is not the exclusive property of any political party.

If the law is upheld only by government officials, then all law is at an end.

In America today, we are nearer a final triumph over poverty
than is any other land.

It is the youth who must inherit the tribulation, the
sorrow... that are the aftermath of war.

Let me remind you that credit is the lifeblood of business, the
lifeblood of prices and jobs.

New discoveries in science will continue to create a thousand
new frontiers for those who still would adventure.

No greater nor more affectionate honor can be conferred on an American
than to have a public school named after him.

No public man can be just a little crooked.

Older men declare war. But it is the youth that must fight and die.

Once upon a time my political opponents honored me as possessing the
fabulous intellectual and economic power by which I created a
worldwide depression all by myself.

Peace is not made at the council table or by treaties, but
in the hearts of men.

Prosperity cannot be restored by raids upon the public Treasury.

The slogan of progress is changing from the full dinner pail to the full
garage. The use of the atomic bomb, with its indiscriminate killing
of women and children, revolts my soul.

We have not yet reached the goal but... we shall soon, with the help
of God, be in sight of the day when poverty shall be
banished from this nation.
When there is a lack of honor in government, the morals
of the whole people are poisoned.
When we are sick, we want an uncommon doctor; when we have a
construction job to do, we want an uncommon engineer, and when
we are at war, we want an uncommon general. It is only when we
get into politics that we are satisfied with the common man.
Wisdom consists not so much in knowing what to do in the ultimate as
knowing what to do next.
With impressive proof on all sides of magnificent progress, no one can
rightly deny the fundamental correctness of our economic system.

## BOB HOPE (Actor, Comedian, 1903-2003)
I do benefits for all religions - I'd hate to blow the hereafter on a technicality.
I don't feel old. I don't feel anything till noon. That's when it's time for my nap.
I've always been in the right place and time. Of course, I steered myself there.
A sense of humor is good for you. Have you ever heard of a laughing
hyena with heart burn?
If you haven't got any charity in your heart, you have the worst
kind of heart trouble.
A bank is a place that will lend you money if you can prove that you don't need it.
I love to go to Washington - if only to be near my money.
I grew up with six brothers. That's how I learned to dance - waiting
for the bathroom.
I have a wonderful make-up crew. They're the same people
restoring the Statue of Liberty.
I have seen what a laugh can do. It can transform almost unbearable
tears into something bearable, even hopeful.
I have too much money invested in sweaters.
I like to play in the low 70's. If it gets any hotter than that I'll stay in the bar!
If you watch a game, it's fun. If you play it, it's recreation. If you work at it, it's golf.
The good news is that Jesus is coming back. The bad news is that he's
really pissed off.
The only thing chicken about Israel is their soup.
There will  always be an England, even if it's in Hollywood.
When they asked Jack Benny to do something for the Actor's
Orphanage - he shot both his parents and moved in.
When we recall the past, we usually find that it is the simplest things - not the
great occasions - that in retrospect give off the greatest glow of happiness.
You know you're getting old when the candles cost more than the cake.
You never get tired unless you stop and take time for it.
Kids are wonderful, but I like mine barbecued.
Middle age is when your age starts to show around your middle.
People who throw kisses are hopelessly lazy.

## HUBERT HUMPHREY (Vice President, Senator,  1911-1978)
To err is human. To blame someone else is politics.
Behind every successful man is a proud wife and a surprised mother-in-law.
Compassion is not weakness, and concern for the unfortunate is not socialism.

It is not what they take away from you that counts. It's what you do
with what you have left.
Freedom is hammered out on the anvil of discussion, dissent, and debate.
Freedom is the most contagious virus known to man.
The impersonal hand of government can never replace the
helping hand of a neighbor.
The President has only 190 million bosses. The Vice President has 190
million and one.
American public opinion is like an ocean, it cannot be stirred by a teaspoon.
The right to be heard does not automatically include the right
to be taken seriously.
It is not enough to merely defend democracy. To defend it may be
to lose it; to extend it is to strengthen it. Democracy is not
property; it is an idea.
Liberalism, above all, means emancipation - emancipation from one's fears,
his inadequacies, from prejudice, from discrimination, from poverty.
To be realistic today is to be visionary. To be realistic is to be starry-eyed.
Today we know that World War II began not in 1939 or 1941 but in the
1920's and 1930's when those who should have known better
persuaded themselves that they were not their brother's keeper.
Unfortunately, our affluent society has also been an effluent society.
We are in danger of making our cities places where business goes on but
where life, in its real sense, is lost.
A politician never forgets the precarious nature of elective life. We
have never established a practice of tenure in public office.
Never give in and never give up.
National isolation breeds national neurosis.
Never answer a question from a farmer.
Propaganda, to be effective, must be believed. To be believed, it must
be credible. To be credible, it must be true.
The difference between hearsay and prophecy is often one of sequence.
Hearsay often turns out to have been prophecy.
The essence of statesmanship is not a rigid adherence to the past, but
a prudent and probing concern for the future.
The greatest gift of life is friendship, and I have received it.
The greatest healing therapy is friendship and love.
The President is the people's lobbyist.
The Senate is a place filled with goodwill and good intentions, and if the
road to hell is paved with them, then it's a pretty good detour.
There are incalculable resources in the human spirit, once
it has been set free.
There are not enough jails, not enough police, not enough courts to
enforce a law not supported by the people.
There is in every American, I think, something of the old Daniel Boone -
who, when he could see the smoke from another chimney, felt
himself too crowded and moved further out into the wilderness.
Anyone who thinks that the vice-president can take a position
independent of the president of his administration simply
has no knowledge of politics or government. You are his
choice in a political marriage, and he expects your
absolute loyalty.

This, then, is the test we must set for ourselves; not to march alone but
       to march in such a way that others will wish to join us

Asia is rich in people, rich in culture and rich in resources. It is
       also rich in trouble.

There are those who say to you - we are rushing this issue of civil
       rights. I say we are 172 years late.

Each child is an adventure into a better life - an opportunity
       to change the old pattern and make it new.

For the first time in the history of mankind, one generation literally
       has the power to destroy the past, the present and the future,
       the power to bring time to an end.

Foreign policy is really domestic policy with its hat on.

I have seen in the Halls of Congress more idealism, more humanness,
       more compassion, more profiles of courage than in any other
       institution that I have ever known.

I learnt more about politics during one South Dakota dust storm than
       in seven years at the university.

If there is dissatisfaction with the status quo, good. If there is ferment,
       so much the better. If there is restlessness, I am pleased. Then l
       et there be ideas, and hard thought, and hard work. If man feels
       small, let man make himself bigger.

In real life, unlike in Shakespeare, the sweetness of the rose depends
       upon the name it bears. Things are not only what they are. They are,
       in very important respects, what they seem to be.

It was once said that the moral test of government is how that government
       treats those who are in the dawn of life, the children; those who are
       in the twilight of life, the elderly; and those who are in the shadows
       of life, the sick, the needy and the handicapped.

Leadership in today's world requires far more than a large stock of gunboats
       and a hard fist at the conference table.

## LEE IACOCCA (Businessman, 1924 - )

We are continually faced by great opportunities brilliantly
       disguised as insoluble problems.

The ability to concentrate and to use time well is everything.

There is no substitute for accurate knowledge. Know yourself, know your
       business, know your men.

The affections are like lightning: you cannot tell where they
       will strike till they have fallen.

The discipline of writing something down is the first
       step toward making it happen.

The thing that lies at the foundation of positive change, the way I
       see it, is service to a fellow human being.

The trick is to make sure you don't die waiting for prosperity to come.

There are times when even the best manager is like the little boy with
       the  big dog, waiting to see where the dog wants to go so
       he can take him there.

Trouble shared is trouble halved.

We've got to pause and ask ourselves: How much clean air do we need?

You can have brilliant ideas, but if you can't get them across, your ideas
       won't get you anywhere.

The greatest discovery of my generation is that human beings can alter their lives by altering their attitudes of mind.

In a completely rational society, the best of us would be teachers and the rest of us would have to settle for something else.

Apply yourself. Get all the education you can, but then, by God, do something. Don't just stand there, make it happen.

I hire people brighter than me and then I get out of their way.

Any supervisor worth his salt would rather deal with people who attempt too much than with those who try too little.

Every business and every product has risks. You can't get around it.

I have always found that if I move with seventy-five percent or more of the facts that I usually never regret it. It's the guys who wait to have everything perfect that drive you crazy.

The most successful businessman is the man who holds onto the old just as long as it is good, and grabs the new just as soon as it is better.

The one word that makes a good manager - decisiveness.

The only rock I know that stays steady, the only institution I know that works, is the family.

I have found that being honest is the best technique I can use. Right up front, tell people what you're trying to accomplish and what you're willing to sacrifice to accomplish it.

I've always found that the speed of the boss is the speed of the team.

If you want to make good use of your time, you've got to know what's most important and then give it all you've got.

In the end, all business operations can be reduced to three words: people, product, and profits.

In times of great stress or adversity, it's always best to keep busy, to plow your anger and your energy into something positive.

Management is nothing more than motivating other people.

Motivation is everything. You can do the work of two people, but you can't be two people. Instead, you have to inspire the next guy down the line and get him to inspire his people.

My father always used to say that when you die, if you've got five real friends, then you've had a great life.

No matter what you've done for yourself or for humanity, if you can't look back on having given love and attention to your own family, what have you really accomplished?

One of the things the government can't do is run anything. The only things our government runs are the post office and the railroads, and both of them are bankrupt.

People want economy and they will pay any price to get it.

So what do we do? Anything. Something. So long as we just don't sit there. If we screw it up, start over. Try something else. If we wait until we've satisfied all the uncertainties, it may be too late.

## WASHINGTON IRVING (Author, 1783-1859)

They who drink beer will think beer.

The tongue is the only tool that gets sharper with use.

Who ever hears of fat men heading a riot, or herding together in turbulent mobs? No - no, your lean, hungry men who are continually worrying society, and setting the whole community by the ears.

Young lawyers attend the courts, not because they have business there, but because they have no business.

Those men are most apt to be obsequious and conciliating abroad, who are under the discipline of shrews at home.

Nothing is enough for the man to whom enough is to little.

One of the greatest and simplest tools for learning more and growing is doing more.

Rising genius always shoots out its rays from among the clouds, but these will gradually roll away and disappear as it ascends to its steady luster.

Some minds seem almost to create themselves, springing up under every disadvantage and working their solitary but irresistible way through a thousand obstacles.

Sweet is the memory of distant friends! Like the mellow rays of the departing sun, it falls tenderly, yet sadly, on the heart.

Temper never mellows with age, and a sharp tongue is the only edged tool that grows keener with constant use.

The easiest thing to do, whenever you fail, is to put yourself down by blaming your lack of ability for your misfortunes.

The idol of today pushes the hero of yesterday out of our recollection; and will, in turn, be supplanted by his successor of tomorrow.

The land of literature is a fairy land to those who view it at a distance, but, like all other landscapes, the charm fades on a nearer approach, and the thorns and briars become visible.

After all, it is the divinity within that makes the divinity without; and I have been more fascinated by a woman of talent and intelligence, though deficient in personal charms, than I have been by the most regular beauty.

Age is a matter of feeling, not of years.

An inexhaustible good nature is one of the most precious gifts of heaven, spreading itself like oil over the troubled sea of thought, and keeping the mind smooth and equable in the roughest weather.

Christmas is a season for kindling the fire for hospitality in the hall, the genial flame of charity in the heart.

Great minds have purposes; others have wishes.

He is the true enchanter, whose spell operates, not upon the senses, but upon the imagination and the heart.

Honest good humor is the oil and wine of a merry meeting, and there is no jovial companionship equal to that where the jokes are rather small and laughter abundant.

I am always at a loss at how much to believe of my own stories.

It is not poverty so much as pretense that harasses a ruined man - the struggle between a proud mind and an empty purse - the keeping up of a hollow show that must soon come to an end.

Kindness in women, not their beauteous looks, shall win my love.

Little minds are tamed and subdued by misfortune; but great minds rise above them.

The natural effect of sorrow over the dead is to refine and elevate the mind.

The natural principle of war is to do the most harm to our enemy with the least harm to ourselves; and this of course is to be effected by stratagem.

The sorrow for the dead is the only sorrow from which we refuse to be divorced. Every other wound we seek to heal - every other affliction to forget: but this wound we consider it a duty to keep open - this affliction we cherish and brood over in solitude.

There is never jealousy where there is not strong regard.

There is in every woman's heart a spark of heavenly fire which lies dormant in the broad daylight of prosperity, but which kindles up and beams and blazes in the dark hour of adversity.

There is a healthful hardiness about real dignity that never dreads contact and communion with others however humble.

There is a sacredness in tears. They are not the mark of weakness, but of power. They speak more eloquently than ten thousand tongues. They are the messengers of overwhelming grief, of deep contrition, and of unspeakable love.

There is a serene and settled majesty to woodland scenery that enters into the soul and delights and elevates it, and fills it with noble inclinations.

There is certain relief in change, even though it be from bad to worse! As I have often found in traveling in a stagecoach, that it is often a comfort to shift one's position, and be bruised in a new place.

Love is never lost. If not reciprocated, it will flow back and soften and purify the heart.

## ANDREW JACKSON (President, 1767-1845)

There is no pleasure in having nothing to do; the fun is having lots to do and not doing it.

One man with courage makes a majority.

Our government is founded upon the intelligence of the people. I for one do not despair of the republic. I have great confidence in the virtue of the great majority of the people, and I cannot fear the result.

Peace, above all things, is to be desired, but blood must sometimes be spilled to obtain it on equable and lasting terms.

Take time to deliberate; but when the time for action arrives, stop thinking and go in.

I weep for the liberty of my country when I see at this early day of its successful experiment that corruption has been imputed to many members of the House of Representatives, and the rights of the people have been bartered for promises of office.

Money is power, and in that government which pays all the public officers of the states will all political power be substantially concentrated.

There are no necessary evils in government. Its evils exist only in its abuses.

It is to be regretted that the rich and powerful too often bend the acts of government to their own selfish purposes.

All the rights secured to the citizens under the Constitution are worth nothing, and a mere bubble, except guaranteed to them by an independent and virtuous Judiciary.

It is a damn poor mind indeed which can't think of at least two ways to spell any word.

The wisdom of man never yet contrived a system of taxation that would operate with perfect equality.

To the victors belong the spoils..

War is a blessing compared with national degradation.

We are beginning a new era in our government. I cannot too strongly urge the necessity of a rigid economy and an inflexible determination not to enlarge the income beyond the real necessities of the government.

You must pay the price if you wish to secure the blessing.

Mischief springs from the power which the moneyed interest derives from a paper
currency which they are able to control, from the multitude of corporations
with exclusive privileges... which are employed altogether for their benefit.

Never take counsel of your fears.

No one need think that the world can be ruled without blood. The civil
sword shall and must be red and bloody.

Americans are not a perfect people, but we are called to a perfect mission.

The brave man inattentive to his duty, is worth little more to his country
than the coward who deserts in the hour of danger.

The great constitutional corrective in the hands of the people against usurpation
of power, or corruption by their agents is the right of suffrage; and this
when used with calmness and deliberation will prove strong enough.

The people are the government, administering it by their agents; they are the
government, the sovereign power.

The planter, the farmer, the mechanic, and the laborer... form the great body of
the people of the United States, they are the bone and sinew of the country
men who love liberty and desire nothing but equal rights and equal laws.

Any man worth his salt will stick up for what he believes right, but it takes a
slightly better man to acknowledge instantly and without reservation
that he is in error.

As long as our government is administered for the good of the people, and is
regulated by their will; as long as it secures to us the rights of persons and
of property, liberty of conscience and of the press, it will be worth defending.

Democracy shows not only its power in reforming governments, but in regenerating
a race of men and this is the greatest blessing of free governments.

Every good citizen makes his country's honor his own, and cherishes it not only as
precious but as sacred. He is willing to risk his life in its defense and its
conscious that he gains protection while he gives it.

Fear not, the people may be deluded for a moment, but cannot be corrupted.

Heaven will be no heaven to me if I do not meet my wife there.

I have always been afraid of banks.

I would sincerely regret, and which never shall happen whilst I am in ]
office, a military guard around the President.

I've got big shoes to fill. This is my chance to do something. I have to seize the
moment.

## JESSE JACKSON (Civil Rights Activist, 1941 - )

Never look down on anybody unless you're helping him up.

In politics, an organized minority is a political majority.

Both tears and sweat are salty, but they render a different result.
Tears will get you sympathy; sweat will get you change.

I hear that melting-pot stuff a lot, and all I can say is that we
haven't melted.

A man must be willing to die for justice. Death is an inescapable reality
and men die daily, but good deeds live forever.

America is not a blanket woven from one thread, one color, one cloth.

At the end of the day, we must go forward with hope and not backward by
fear and division.

It is time for us to turn to each other, not on each other.

When the doors of opportunity swing open, we must make sure that
we are not too drunk or too indifferent to walk through.

Keep hope alive!

Your children need your presence more than your presents.

Leadership cannot just go along to get along. Leadership must meet
the moral challenge of the day.

Leadership has a harder job to do than just choose sides. It must
bring sides together.

No one should negotiate their dreams. Dreams must be free to fly high.
No government, no legislature, has a right to limit your dreams.
You should never agree to surrender your dreams.

Our dreams must be stronger than our memories. We must be pulled
by our dreams, rater than pushed by our memories.

Time is neutral and does not change things. With courage and initiative,
leaders change things.

We must not measure greatness from the mansion down, but from
the manger up.

We've removed the ceiling above our dreams. There are no more
impossible dreams.

When we're [black people] unemployed, we're called lazy; when the
whites are unemployed it's called a depression.

Deliberation and debate is the way you stir the soul of our democracy.

I cast my bread on the waters long ago. Now it's time for you to send
it back to me - toasted and buttered on both sides.

I know they are all environmentalists. I heard a lot of my speeches recycled.

If my mind can conceive it, and my heart can believe it, I know I can
achieve it.

If you run, you might lose. If you don't run, you're guaranteed to lose.

In many ways, history is marked as 'before' and 'after' Rosa Parks. She
sat down in order that we all might stand up, and the walls of
segregation came down.

## THOMAS JEFFERSON (Founding Father, President, 1743-1826)

A Bill of Rights is what the people are entitled to against every government,
and what no just government should refuse, or rest on inference.

A coward is much more exposed to quarrels than a man of spirit.

A strong body makes the mind strong. As to the species of exercises, I advise
the gun. While this gives moderate exercise to the body, it gives boldness,
enterprise and independence to the mind. Games played with the ball,
and others of that nature, are too violent for the body and stamp no
character on the mind. Let your gun therefore be your constant
companion of your walks.

A wise and frugal Government, which shall restrain men from injuring one another,
which shall leave them otherwise free to regulate their own pursuits of
industry and improvement, and shall not take from the mouth of labor the
bread it has earned. This is the sum of good government, and this is
necessary to close the circle of our felicities.

All tyranny needs to gain a foothold is for people of good conscience to
remain silent.

All, too, will bear in mind this sacred principle, that though the will of the
majority is in all cases to prevail, that will to be rightful must be reasonable;
that  the minority possess their equal rights, which equal
law must protect, and to violate would be oppression.

-143-

Always take hold of things by the smooth handle.

Advertisements contain the only truths to be relied on in a newspaper.

An association of men who will not quarrel with one another is a thing  which
    has never yet existed, from the greatest confederacy of nations down
    to a town meeting or a vestry.

An enemy generally says and believes what he wishes.

An injured friend is the bitterest of foes.

As our enemies have found we can reason like men, so now let us show
    them we can fight like men also.

Be polite to all, but intimate with few.

Bodily decay is gloomy in prospect, but of all human contemplations
    the most abhorrent is body without mind.

Books constitute capital. A library book lasts as long as a house, for hundreds of
    years. It is not, then, an article of mere consumption but fairly of capital, and
    often in the case of professional men, setting out in life, it is their
    only capital.

. . . friendship is precious, not only in the shade, but in the sunshine of life, and
    thanks to a benevolent arrangement the greater part of life is sunshine.

Commerce with all nations, alliance with none, should be our motto.

Conquest is not in our principles. It is inconsistent with our government.

Delay is preferable to error.

Dependence begets subservience and venality, suffocates the germ of virtue,
    and prepares fit tools for the designs of ambition.

Determine never to be idle. No person will have occasion to complain of the
    want of time who never loses any. It is wonderful how much may be
    done if we are always doing.

Difference of opinion is advantageous in religion. The several sects perform
    the office of a Censor - over each other.

Do not bite at the bait of pleasure, till you know there is no hook beneath it.

Do you want to know who you are? Don't ask. Act! Action will
    delineate and define you.

Don't talk about what you have done or what you are going to do.

Educate and inform the whole mass of the people... They are the only sure
    reliance for the preservation of our liberty.

Enlighten the people generally, and tyranny and oppressions of body and mind
    will vanish like evil spirits at the dawn of day.

Errors of opinion may be tolerated where reason is left free to combat it.

Every citizen should be a soldier. This was the case with the Greeks and
    Romans, and must be that of every free state.

Every government degenerates when trusted to the rulers of the people alone.
    The people themselves are its only safe depositories.

Experience demands that man is the only animal which devours his own kind, for
    I can apply no milder term to the general prey of the rich on the poor.

Experience hath shewn, that even under the best forms of government those
    entrusted with power have, in time, and by slow operations, perverted
    it into tyranny.

Fix reason firmly in her seat, and call to her tribunal every fact, every opinion.
    Question with boldness even the existence of a God; because, if there
    be one, he must more approve of the homage of reason, than that of
    blindfolded fear.

Force is the vital principle and immediate parent of despotism.

Friendship is but another name for an alliance with the follies and the
        misfortunes of others. Our own share of miseries is sufficient:
        why enter then as volunteers into those of another?
Happiness is not being pained in body or troubled in mind.
For a people who are free, and who mean to remain so, a well-organized and armed
        militia is their best security.
He who knows best knows how little he knows.
He who knows nothing is closer to the truth than he whose mind is filled
        with falsehoods and errors.
History, in general, only informs us of what bad government is.
Honesty is the first chapter in the book of wisdom.
How much pain they have cost us, the evils which have never happened.
I abhor  war and view it as the greatest scourge of mankind.
I am an Epicurean. I consider the genuine (not the imputed) doctrines of
        Epicurus as containing everything rational in moral philosophy which
        Greek and Roman leave to us.
I am mortified to be told that, in the United States of America, the sale of a
        book can become a subject of inquiry, and of criminal inquiry too.
I believe that banking institutions are more dangerous to our
        liberties than standing armies.
I believe that every human mind feels pleasure in doing good to another.
I cannot live without books.
I do not take a single newspaper, nor read one a month, and I feel myself
        infinitely the happier for it.
I find that he is happiest of whom the world says least, good or bad.
I have no ambition to govern men; it is a painful and thankless office.
I have no fear that the result of our experiment will be that men may be
        trusted to govern themselves without a master.
I have seen enough of one war never to wish to see another.
I have sworn upon the altar of God, eternal hostility against every form of
        tyranny over the mind of man.
I hope our wisdom will grow with our power, and teach us, that the less we
        use our power the greater it will be.
I hope we shall crush in its birth the aristocracy of our monied corporations
        which dare already to challenge our government to a trial by strength,
        and bid defiance to the laws of our country.
I know of no safe depository of the ultimate powers of the society but the
        people themselves; and if we think them not enlightened enough to
        exercise their control with a wholesome discretion, the remedy is not
        to take it from them but to inform their discretion.
I like the dreams of the future better than the history of the past.
I never considered a difference of opinion in politics, in religion, in philosophy,
        as cause for withdrawing from a friend.
I never will, by any  word or act, bow to the shrine of intolerance or admit a
        right of inquiry into the religious opinions of others.
I own that I am not a friend to a very energetic government. It is always oppressive.
I predict future happiness for Americans if they can prevent the government from
        wasting the labors of the people under the pretense of taking care of them.
I was bold in the pursuit of knowledge, never fearing to follow truth and reason to
        whatever results they led, and bearding every authority which stood in their
        way.

-145-

I would rather be exposed to the inconveniences attending too much liberty than
those attending too small a degree of it.

I tremble for my country when I reflect that God is just; that his
justice cannot sleep forever.

I think with the Romans, that the general of today should be a soldier
tomorrow if necessary.

If a nation expects to be ignorant and free, in a state of civilization, it
expects what never was and never will be.

If God is just, I tremble for my country.

If there is one principle more deeply rooted in the mind of every
American, it is that we should have nothing to do with conquest.

Ignorance is preferable to error, and he is less remote from the truth
who believes nothing than he who believes what is wrong.

In every country and every age, the priest had been hostile to Liberty.

In matters of style, swim with the current; in matters of principle, stand
like a rock.

In truth, politeness is artificial good humor, it covers the natural want of it, and
ends by rendering habitual a substitute nearly equivalent to the real virtue.

It behooves every man who values liberty of conscience for himself, to resist
invasions of it in the case of others: or their case may, by change of
circumstances, become his own.

It does me no injury for my neighbor to say there are twenty gods or no God.

It is always better to have no ideas than false ones; to believe nothing, than to
believe what is wrong.

It is error alone which needs the support of government. Truth can stand by itself.

It is in our lives and not our words that our religion must be read.

It is incumbent on every generation to pay its own debts as it goes. A principle
which if acted on would save one-half the wars of the world.

It is more dangerous that even a guilty person should be punished
without the forms of law than that he should escape.

It is neither  wealth nor splendor; but tranquility and occupation which
give you happiness.

It is our duty still to endeavor to avoid war; but if it shall actually take place,
no matter by whom brought on, we must defend ourselves. If our house
be on fire, without inquiring whether it was fired from within or without,
we must try to extinguish it.

It takes time to persuade men to do even what is for their own good.

Leave all the afternoon for exercise and recreation, which are as necessary
as reading. I will rather say more necessary because health is worth
more than learning.

Leave no authority existing not responsible to the people.

Mankind are more disposed to suffer, while evils are sufferable, than to right
themselves by abolishing the forms to which they are accustomed.

Merchants have no country. The mere spot they stand on does not constitute
so strong an attachment as that from which they draw their gains.

Money, not morality, is the principle commerce of civilized nations.

My only fear is that I may live too long. This would be a subject of dread to me.

My reading of history convinces me that most bad government results
from too much government.

My theory has always been, that if we are to dream, the flatteries of
hope are as cheap, and pleasanter, than the gloom of despair.

Never put off till tomorrow what you can do today.
No duty the Executive had to perform was so trying as to put the
    right man in the right place.
No freeman shall be debarred the use of arms.
Never spend your money before you have earned it.
No government ought to be without censors; and where the
    press is free no one ever will.
No man will ever carry out of the Presidency the reputation
    which carried him into it.
No occupation is so delightful to me as the culture of the earth, and
    no culture comparable to that of the garden.
Nothing can stop the man with the right mental attitude from achieving his goal;
    nothing on earth can help the man with the wrong mental attitude.
Nothing gives one person so much advantage over another as to remain always cool
    and unruffled under all circumstances.
Nothing is unchangeable but the inherent and unalienable rights of man.
One loves to possess arms, though they hope never to have occasion for them.
One man with courage is a majority.
One travels more usefully when alone, because he reflects more.
Only aim to do your duty, and mankind will give you credit where you fail.
Our country is now taking so steady a course as to show by what road it will pass to
    destruction, to wit: by consolidation of power first, and then corruption, its
    necessary consequence.
Our greatest happiness does not depend on the condition of life in which chance has
    placed us, but is always the result of a good conscience, good health,
    occupation, and freedom in all just pursuits.
Peace and friendship with all mankind is our wisest policy, and I wish
    we may be permitted to pursue it.
Peace, commerce and honest friendship with all nations; entangling
    alliances with none.
Politics is such a torment that I advise everyone I love not to mix with it.
Power is not alluring to pure minds.
Question with boldness even the existence of a God; because, if there be one, he
    must more approve of the homage of reason, than that of blind-folded fear.
Resort is had to ridicule only when reason is against us.
Rightful liberty is unobstructed action according to our will within limits drawn
    around us by the equal rights of others. I do not add 'within the limits
    of the law' because law is often but the tyrant's will, and always so when
    it violates the rights of the individual.
So confident am I in the intentions, as well as wisdom, of the government,
    that I shall always be satisfied that what is not done, either cannot,
    or ought not to be done.
Sometimes it is said that man cannot be trusted with the government of himself.
    Can he, then be trusted with the government of others? Or have we found
    angels in the form of kings to govern him? Let history answer this question
Speeches that are measured by the hour will die with the hour.
Taste cannot be controlled by law.
That government is the strongest of which every man feels himself a part.
The advertisement is the most truthful part of a newspaper.
The care of human life and happiness, and not their destruction, is the first and only
    object of good government.

The constitutions of most of our States assert that all power is inherent in the
     people; that... it is their right and duty to be at all times armed.

The boisterous sea of liberty is never without a wave.

The Creator has not thought proper to mark those in the forehead who are of
     stuff to make good generals. We are first, therefore, to seek them
     blindfold, and then let them learn the trade at the expense of great losses.

The earth belongs to the living, not to the dead.

The  glow of one warm thought is to me worth more than money

The God who gave us life, gave us liberty at the same time.

The good opinion of mankind, like the lever of Archimedes, with the given
     fulcrum, moves the world.

The man who reads nothing at all is better educated than the man
     who reads nothing but newspapers.

The moment a person forms a theory, his imagination sees in
     every object only the traits which favor that theory.

The most successful war seldom pays for its losses.

The natural cause of the human mind is certainly from credulity to skepticism.

The natural progress of things is for liberty to yield and government to
     gain ground.

The republican is the only form of government which is not eternally at
     open or secret war with the rights of mankind.

The second office in the government is honorable and easy; the first is
     but a splendid misery.

The spirit of resistance to government is so valuable on certain occasions
     that I wish it to be always kept alive.

The spirit of this country is totally adverse to a large military force.

The tree of liberty must be refreshed from time to time with the blood
     of patriots and tyrants.

The way to silence religious disputes is to take no notice of them.

The whole commerce between master and slave is a perpetual exercise of the
     most boisterous passions, the most unremitting despotism on the one
     part, and degrading submissions on the other. Our children see this,
     and learn to imitate it.

The world is indebted for all triumphs which have been gained by
     reason and humanity over error and oppression.

There is a natural aristocracy among men. The grounds of this are
     virtue and talents.

There is not a sprig of grass that shoots uninteresting to me.

There is not a truth existing which I fear... or would wish unknown
     to the whole world.

Timid men prefer the calm of despotism to the tempestuous sea of liberty.

To compel a man to furnish funds for the propagation of ideas he
     disbelieves and abhors is sinful and tyrannical.

To penetrate and dissipate these clouds of darkness, the general mind
     must be strengthened by education.

Truth is certainly a branch of morality and a very important one to society.

Walking is the best possible exercise. Habituate yourself to walk very fast.

War is an instrument entirely inefficient toward redressing wrong; and
     multiplies, instead of indemnifying losses.

We are not to expect to be translated from despotism to liberty in a featherbed.

We did not raise armies for glory or for conquest.

We hold these truths to be self-evident: that all men are created equal; that
they are endowed by their Creator with certain unalienable rights; that
among these are life, liberty, and the pursuit of happiness.

We may consider each generation as a distinct nation, with a right, by the
will of its majority, to bind themselves, but none to bind the succeeding
generation, more than the inhabitants of another country.

We never repent of having eaten too little.

Were it left to me to decide whether we should have a government without
newspapers, or newspapers without a government, I should not
hesitate a moment to prefer the latter.

When a man assumes a public trust he should consider himself a public property.

When angry count to ten before you speak. If very angry, count to one hundred.

When the people fear the government, there is tyranny. When the government fears
the people, there is liberty.

When we get piled upon one another in large cities, as in Europe, we shall
become as corrupt as Europe.

When you reach the end of your rope, tie a knot in it and hang on.

Whenever a man has cast a longing eye on offices, a rottenness
begins in his conduct.

Whenever the people are well-informed, they can be trusted with
their own government.

Whenever you do a thing, act as if all the world were watching.

Where the press is free and every man able to read, all is safe.

Wisdom I know is social. She seeks her fellows. But Beauty is jealous,
and illy  bears the presence of a rival.

## STEVE JOBS (Founder of Apple computer, 1955-2011)

Be a yardstick of quality. Some people aren't used to an environment
where excellence is expected

Being the richest man in the cemetery doesn't matter to me. Going to bed at
night saying we've done something wonderful, that's what matters to me.

Creativity is just connecting things. When you ask creative people how they did
something, they feel a little guilty because they didn't really do it, they
just saw something. It seemed obvious to them after a while. That's because
they were able to connect experiences they've had and
synthesize new things.

Design is a funny word. Some people think design means how it looks.
But of course, if you dig deeper, it's really how it  works.

For the past 33 years, I have looked in the mirror every morning and asked myself:
'If today were the last day of my life, would I want to do what
I am about to do today?' And whenever the answer has been 'No' for
too many days in a row, I know I need to change something.

Innovation distinguishes between a leader and a follower.

It's not the tools that you have faith in - tools are just tools. They work, or
they don't work. It's people you have faith in or not. Yeah, sure, I'm
still optimistic I mean, I get pessimistic sometimes  but not for long.

No one wants to die. Even people who want to go to heaven don't want to die to get
there. And yet death is the destination we all share. No one has ever escaped
it. And that is as it should be, because Death is very likely the single best
invention of Life. It is Life's change agent. It clears out
the old to make way for the new.

Remembering that I'll be dead soon is the most important tool I've ever
    encountered to help me make the big choices in life. Because almost
    everything - all external expectations, all pride, all fear of embarrassment or
    failure - these things just fall away in the face of death, leaving only
    what is truly important.
For you to sleep well at night, the aesthetic, the quality, has to be
    carried all the way through.
I want to put a ding in the universe.
Remembering that you are going to die is the best way I know to avoid the trap
    of thinking you have something to lose. You are already naked. There is
    no reason not to follow your heart.
My favorite things in life don't cost any money. It's really clear that the
    most precious resource we all have is time.
Sometimes life hits you in the head with a brick. Don't lose faith.
Sometimes when you innovate, you make mistakes. It is best to admit
    them quickly, and get on with improving your other innovations.
Stay hungry, stay foolish.
Things don't have to change the world to be important.
When you're young, you look at television and think, there's a conspiracy. The
    networks have conspired to dumb us down. But when you get a little
    older, you realize that's not true. The networks are in business to give people
    exactly what they want.
Your time is limited, so don't waste it living someone else's life. Don't be trapped by
    dogma - which is living with the results of other people's thinking.
    Don't let the noise of others' opinions drown out your own inner voice.
    And most important, have the courage to follow your heart and intuition.
Your work is going to fill a large part of your life, and the only way to be truly
    satisfied is to do what you believe is great work. And the only way to do
    great work is to love what you do. If you haven't found it yet, keep looking.
    Don't settle. As with all matters of the heart, you'll know when you find it.

## ANDREW JOHNSON (President, Vice-President, 1808-1875)

The goal to strive for is a poor government but a rich people.
It's a damn poor mind that can only think of one way to spell a word.
If I am shot at, I want no man to be in the way of the bullet.
There are no good laws but such as repeal other laws.
If the rabble were lopped off at one end and the aristocrats at the other,
    all would be well with the country.
Honest conviction is my courage; the Constitution is my guide.
I am sworn to uphold the Constitution as Andy Johnson understands
    it and interprets it.
I feel incompetent to perform duties... which have been so
    unexpectedly thrown upon me.
I hold it the duty of the executive to insist upon frugality in the expenditure,
    and a sparing economy is itself a great national source.
Legislation can neither be wise nor just which seeks the welfare of a single
    interest at the expense and to the injury of many and varied interests.
Outside of the Constitution we have no legal authority more than private
    citizens, and within it we have only so much as that instrument
    gives us. This broad principle limits all our functions and
    applies to all subjects.

Who, then, will govern? The answer must be, Man - for we have no
angels in the shape of men, as yet, who are willing to take
charge of our political affairs.

## LADY BIRD JOHNSON (First Lady, 1912-2007)

Perhaps no place in any community is so totally democratic as the town
library. The only entrance requirement is interest.

The clash of ideas is the sound of freedom.

Any committee is only as good as the most knowledgeable, determined
and vigorous person on it. There must be somebody who
provides the flame.

Become so wrapped up in something that you forget to be afraid.

Children are apt to live up to what you believe of them.

Every politician should have been born an orphan and remain a bachelor.

It's odd that you can get so anesthetized by your own pain or your own
problem that you don't quite fully share the hell of someone
close to you.

No news at 4:30 a.m. is good.

The First Lady is an unpaid public servant elected by one person -
her husband.

## LYNDON B. JOHNSON (President, Vice-President, 1908-1973)

If one morning I walked on top of the water across the Potomac River,
the headline that afternoon would read: "President Can't Swim."

The noblest search is the search for excellence.

If two men agree on everything, you may be sure that one of them
is doing the thinking.

Doing what's right isn't the problem. It is knowing what's right.
Any jackass can kick down a barn but it takes a good carpenter
to build one.

Education is not a problem. Education is an opportunity.

Every man has a right to a Saturday night bath.

Every President wants to do right.
The CIA is made up of boys whose families sent them to Princeton
but wouldn't let them into the family brokerage business.

The fact that a man is a newspaper reporter is evidence of some
flaw of character.

The fifth freedom is freedom from ignorance.

It is important that the United States remain a two-party system.
I'm a fellow who likes small parties and the Republican Party
can't be too small to suit me.

Freedom is not enough.

Yesterday is not ours to recover, but tomorrow is ours to win or lose.

You aren't learning anything when you're talking.

The presidency has made every man who occupied it, no matter
how small, bigger than he was; and no matter how big, not
big enough for its demands.

The Russians feared Ike. They didn't fear me.

The separation of church and state is a source of strength, but the
conscience of our nation does not call for separation between
men of state and faith in the Supreme Being.

The vote is the most powerful instrument ever devised by man for
        breaking down injustice and destroying the terrible walls which
        imprison men because they are different from other men.
There are no favorites in my office. I treat them all with
        the same general inconsideration.
The guns and the bombs, the rockets and the warships, are all
        symbols of human failure.
There are no problems we cannot solve together, and very
        few that we can solve by ourselves.
There are plenty of recommendations on how to get out of trouble
        cheaply and fast. Most of them come down to this: Deny
        your responsibility.
There is but one way for a president to deal with Congress, and that
        is continuously, incessantly, and without interruption. If it is
        really going to work, the relationship has got to be
        almost incestuous.
They call upon us to supply American boys to do the
        job that Asian boys should do.
This administration here and now declares unconditional war on poverty.
This is not Johnson's war. This is America's war. If I drop dead tomorrow,
        this war will still be with you.
To conclude that women are unfitted to the task of our historic society
        seems to me the equivalent of closing male eyes to female facts.
Until justice is blind to color, until education is unaware of race, until
        opportunity is unconcerned with the color of men's skins,
        emancipation will be a proclamation but not a fact.
We are not about to send American boys 9 or 10 thousand miles away from
        home to do what Asian boys ought to be doing for themselves.
We did not choose to be the guardians of the gate, but there is no one else.
We have entered an age in which education is not just a luxury permitting
        some men an advantage over others. It has become a necessity
        without which a person is defenseless in this complex, industrialized
        society. We have truly entered the century of the educated man.
We have talked long enough in this country about equal rights. It is time
        now to write the next chapter - and to write it in the books of law.
We have the opportunity to move not only toward the rich society and the
        powerful society, but upward to the Great Society
A man can take a little bourbon without getting drunk, but if you hold
        his mouth open and pour in a quart, he's going to get sick on it.
A man without a vote is man without protection.
I once told Nixon that the Presidency is like being a jackass caught in a
        hail storm. You've got to just stand there and take it.
I report to you that our country is challenged at home and abroad: that it
        is our will that is being tried and not our strength; our sense of
        purpose and not our ability to achieve a better America.
I seldom think of politics more than eighteen hours a day.
I want to make a policy statement. I am unabashedly in favor of women.
I will do my best. That is all I can do. I ask for your help - and God's.
I'd rather give my life than be afraid to give it.
I'm tired. I'm tired of feeling rejected by the American people. I'm tired
        of waking up in the middle of the night worrying about the war.

If future generations are to remember us more with gratitude than sorrow,
    we must achieve more than just the miracles of technology. We must
    also leave them a glimpse of the world as it was created, not just as
    it looked when we got through with it.
If the American people don't love me, their descendants will.
If you let a bully come in your front yard, he'll be on your
    porch  the next day and the day after that he'll rape
    your wife in your own bed.
I'm the only president you've got.
John F. Kennedy was the victim of the hate that was a part of our
    country. It is a disease that occupies the minds of the few
    but brings danger to the many.
Just like the Alamo, somebody damn well needed to go to their aid. Well,
    by God, I'm going to Viet Nam's aid!
No member of our generation who wasn't a Communist or a dropout
    in the thirties is worth a damn.
One lesson you better learn if you want to be in politics is that you
    never go out on a golf course and beat the President.
Only two things are necessary to keep one's wife happy. One is to
    let her think she is having her own way, and the other is
    to let her have it.
Our most tragic error may have been our inability to establish a
    rapport and a confidence with the press and television
    with the communication media. I don't think the press
    has understood me.
Our numbers have increased in Vietnam because the aggression
    of others has increased in Vietnam. There is not, and there
    will not be, a mindless escalation.
Our purpose in Vietnam is to prevent the success of aggression. It
    is not conquest, it is not empire, it is not foreign bases, it is
    not domination. It is, simply put, just to prevent the forceful
    conquest of South Vietnam by North Vietnam.
Our society is illuminated by the spiritual insights of the Hebrew
    prophets. America and Israel have a common love of human
    freedom, and they have a common faith in a democratic way of life.
Peace is a journey of a thousand miles and it must be
    taken one step at a time.
Poverty must not be a bar to learning and learning must offer
    an escape from poverty.
Presidents quickly realize that while a single act might destroy the
    world they live in, no one single decision can make life
    suddenly better or can turn history around for the good.
The atomic bomb certainly is the most powerful of all weapons, but it
    is conclusively powerful and effective only in the hands of the
    nation which controls the sky.
The moon and other celestial bodies should be free for exploration
    and use by all countries. No country should be permitted to
    advance a claim of sovereignty
It is always a strain when people are being killed. I don't think anybody
    has held this job who hasn't felt personally
    responsible for those being killed.

It is the genius of our Constitution that under its shelter of enduring
  institutions and rooted principles there is ample room for the rich
  fertility of American political invention.
It may be, it just may be, that life as we know it with its humanity is
  more unique than many have thought.
Jack [Kennedy] was out kissing babies while I was out passing bills.
  Someone had to tend the store.
Jerry Ford is so dumb he can't fart and chew gum at the same time.
A President's hardest task is not to do what is right, but
  to know what is right.
I am a freeman, an American, a United States Senator,
  and a Democrat, in that order.
I am concerned about the whole man. I am concerned about what the
  people, using their government as an instrument and a tool, can
do toward building the whole man, which will mean a better society and
  a better world.
I don't believe I'll ever get credit for anything I do in foreign affairs,
  no matter how successful it is, because I didn't go to Harvard.
I feel like I just grabbed a big juicy worm with a right sharp hook
  in the middle of it.
I have learned that only two things are necessary to keep one's wife happy. First, let
  her think she's having her own way. And second, let her have it.
We live in a world that has narrowed into a neighborhood before it has
  broadened into a brotherhood.
We must open the doors of opportunity. But we must also equip our
  people to walk through those doors.
What convinces is conviction. Believe in the argument you're advancing.
  If you don't you're as good as dead. The other person will sense
  that something isn't there, and no chain of reasoning, no matter
  how logical or elegant or brilliant, will win your case for you.
What we won when all of our people united must not be lost in suspicion
  and distrust and selfishness and politics. Accordingly, I shall not
  seek, and I will not accept, the nomination of my party for another
  term as president.
When I was a boy we didn't wake up with Vietnam and
  have Cyprus for lunch and the Congo for dinner.
When I was young, poverty was so common that we
  didn't know it had a name.
When the burdens of the presidency seem unusually heavy, I always
  remind myself it could be worse. I could be a mayor.
When things haven't gone well for you, call in a secretary or a staff
  man and chew him out. You will sleep better and they will
  appreciate the attention.
Whether we are New Dealer, Old Dealer, Liberty Leaguer or Red,
  whether we agree or not, we still have the right to think
  and speak how we feel.
While you're saving your face, you're losing your ass.
You do not examine legislation in the light of the benefits it will
  convey if properly administered, but in the light of the
  wrongs it would do and the harms it would cause
  if improperly administered.

You might say that Lyndon Johnson is a cross between
      a Baptist preacher and a cowboy.
You've got to work things out in the cloakroom, and when you've
      got them worked out, you can debate a little before you vote
In our home there was always prayer - aloud, proud and unapologetic.
Whoever won't fight when the President calls him, deserves
      to be kicked back in his hole and kept there.

## CHIEF JOSEPH (Nez Pierce Chief, 1840-1904)
I hope that no more groans of wounded men and women will ever go to the ear
      of the Great Spirit Chief above, and that all people may be one people.
I only ask of the government to be treated as all other men are treated.
I pressed my father's hand and told him I would protect his grave with my
      life. My father smiled and passed away to the spirit land.
I said in my heart that, rather than have war, I would give up my country.
I want the white people to understand my people.
I will obey every law, or submit to the penalty.
I will speak with a straight tongue.
I would have given my own life if I could have undone
      the killing of white men by my people.
If the white man wants to live in peace with the Indian he can live in peace.
It does not require many words to speak the truth.
It makes my heart sick when I remember all the good words
      and the broken promises.
Let me be a free man - free to travel, free to stop, free to work.
Some of you think an Indian is like a wild animal. This is a great mistake.
The earth is the mother of all people, and all people should have
      equal rights upon it.
The Indian race are waiting and praying.
Treat  all men alike. Give them the same law. Give them
      an even chance to live and grow.
War can be avoided, and it ought to be avoided. I want no war.
We ask to be recognized as men.
We gave up some of our country to the white men, thinking that then we could
      have peace. We were mistaken. The white man would not let us alone.
We soon found that the white men were growing rich very fast, and were greedy.
When an Indian fights, he only shoots to kill.
When my young men began the killing, my heart was hurt.
Words do not pay for my dead people.
A man who would not love his father's grave is worse than a wild animal.
All men were made by the Great Spirit Chief. They are all brothers.
An Indian respects a brave man, but he despises a coward.
Good words will not give me back my children.
Hear me, my chiefs! I am tired. My heart is sick and sad. From where
      the sun now stands, I will fight no more forever.
I  am tired of talk that comes to nothing.
I believe much trouble would be saved if we opened our hearts more.
I have heard talk and talk, but nothing is done.
I hope that no more groans of wounded men and women will ever go to the ear
      of the Great Spirit Chief above, and that all people may be one people.
I only ask of the government to be treated as all other men are treated.

If the white man wants to live in peace with the Indian he can live in peace.
Let me be a free man - free to travel, free to stop, free to work.

### DARYN KAGAN (Entertainment Reporter, 1963 -)

Times might be tough, your head and thoughts might be spinning, but
  I find it's physically impossible to do that spiral thing when your
  mind is focused on giving and creating opportunity.
Your mind simply can't focus forward and downward all at the same time.
Bad things do happen in the world, like war, natural disasters, disease.
  But out of those situations always arise stories of ordinary people
  doing extraordinary things.
Everyday I meet folks who show me how to look at challenges differently.
I think most people live in a space where they are looking for meaning in
  life and good in the world and that is not necessarily reflected in
  straight news coverage right now.
If you don't take your clothes seriously, why should your
  viewers take you seriously?
If you're really invested in feeling bad about the world, there are
  a lot of media outlets out there that you can turn to.
It's important to be informed but I also think it's important to be inspired.
  I'm creating a space where people can be inspired.

### HENRY J. KAISER (Businessman, 1882-1967)

Having an aim is the key to achieving your best.
Problems are only opportunities in work clothes.
When your work speaks for itself, don't interrupt.
I always have to dream up there against the stars. If I don't dream I
  will make it, I won't even get close.
I make progress by having people around me who are smarter than I am
  and listening to them. And I assume that everyone is smarter about
  something than I am.
Live daringly, boldly, fearlessly. Taste the relish to be found in
  competition - in having put forth the best within you.
You can't sit on the lid of progress. If you do, you will be blown to pieces.

### CASEY KASUM (Radio Announcer, DJ, 1932 - )

Always be consistent.
I like the storytelling and reading the letters, the long-distance dedications. Anytime
  in radio that you can reach somebody on an emotional level,
  you're really connecting. The stories are success stories. The letters
  from listeners often touch the heart and can be inspiring.
Anytime in radio that you can reach somebody on an emotional level,
  you're really connecting.
If the beat gets to the audience, and the message touches them, you've got a hit.

### DANNY KAYE (Actor, 1913-1987)

Life is a great big canvas; throw all the paint you can at it.
To travel is to take a journey into yourself.
You bet I arrived overnight. Over a few hundred nights in the
  Catskills, in vaudeville, in clubs and on Broadway.

**BARNABY C. KEENEY (Educator, 20th century)**

At college age, you can tell who is best at taking tests and going to school, but you can't tell who the best people are. That worries the hell out of me.

The scramble to get into college is going to be so terrible in the next few years that students are going to put up with almost anything, even an education.

**HELEN KELLER (Author, 1880-1968)**

It is a terrible thing to see and have no vision.

It is hard to interest those who have everything in those who have nothing.

Walking with a friend in the dark is better than walking alone in the light.

People do not like to think. If one thinks, one must reach conclusions. Conclusions are not always pleasant.

The highest result of education is tolerance.

Life is either a great adventure or nothing.

Science may have found a cure for most evils; but it has found no remedy for the worst of them all - the apathy of human beings.

Optimism is the faith that leads to achievement. Nothing can be done without hope and confidence.

Avoiding danger is no safer in the long run than outright exposure. The fearful are caught as often as the bold.

Literature is my Utopia. Here I am not disenfranchised. No barrier of the senses shuts me out from the sweet, gracious discourses of my book friends. They talk to me without embarrassment or awkwardness.

So long as the memory of certain beloved friends lives in my heart, I shall say that life is good.

I am only one, but still I am one. I cannot do everything, but still I can do something; and because I cannot do everything, I will not refuse to do something that I can do.

Death is no more than passing from one room into another. But there's a difference for me, you know. Because in that other room I shall be able to see.

Instead of comparing our lot with that of those who are more fortunate than we are, we should compare it with the lot of the great majority of our fellow men. It then appears that we are among the privileged.

It is for us to pray not for tasks equal to our powers, but for powers equal to our tasks, to go forward with a great desire forever beating at the door of our hearts as we travel toward our distant goal.

Unless we form the habit of going to the Bible in bright moments as well as in trouble, we cannot fully respond to its consolations because we lack equilibrium between light and darkness.

I do not want the peace which passeth understanding, I want the understanding which bringeth peace.

Until the great mass of the people shall be filled with the sense of responsibility for each other's welfare, social justice can never be attained.

Security is mostly a superstition. It does not exist in nature, nor do the children of men as a whole experience it. Avoiding danger is no safer in the long run than outright exposure. Life is either a daring adventure, or nothing.

Self-pity is our worst enemy and if we yield to it, we can never do anything wise in this world.

Smell is a potent wizard that transports you across thousands of miles and all the years you have lived.

Strike against war, for without you no battles can be fought!

All the world is full of suffering. It is also full of overcoming.

The best and most beautiful things in the world cannot be seen or even
touched - they must be felt with the heart.

The heresy of one age becomes the orthodoxy of the next.

The marvelous richness of human experience would lose something of rewarding
joy if there were no limitations to overcome. The hilltop hour would
not be half so wonderful if there were no dark valleys to traverse.

The most beautiful things in the world cannot be seen or even touched,
they must be felt with the heart.

The world is moved along, not only by the mighty shoves of its heroes, but
also by the aggregate of tiny pushes of each honest worker.

There is no king who has not had a slave among his ancestors, and no
slave who has not had a king among his.

To me a lush carpet of pine needles or spongy grass is more
welcome than the most luxurious Persian rug.

Toleration is the greatest gift of the mind; it requires the same effort
of the brain that it takes to balance oneself on a bicycle.

True happiness... is not attained through self-gratification, but through
fidelity to a worthy purpose.

We can do anything we want to if we stick to it long enough.

We could never learn to be brave and patient, if there were only joy in the world.

We may have found a cure for most evils; but we have found no remedy
for the worst of them all, the apathy of human beings.

What a blind person needs is not a teacher but another self.

What I am looking for is not out there, it is in me.

What we have once enjoyed we can never lose. All that we love
deeply becomes a part of us.

When we do the best that we can, we never know what miracle is
wrought in our life, or in the life of another

Alone we can do so little; together we can do so much.

Although the world is full of suffering, it is also full of the overcoming of it.

As selfishness and complaint pervert the mind, so love with its joy
clears and sharpens the vision.

As the eagle was killed by the arrow winged with his own feather, so
the hand of the world is wounded by its own skill.

Character cannot be developed in ease and quiet. Only through experience
of trial and suffering can the soul be strengthened, ambition
inspired, and success achieved.

College isn't the place to go for ideas.

It is not possible for civilization to flow backwards while there is youth in the
world. Youth may be headstrong, but it will advance it allotted length.

It is wonderful how much time good people spend fighting the devil. If they
would only expend the same amount of energy loving their fellow
men, the devil would die in his own tracks of ennui.

It's wonderful to climb the liquid mountains of the sky. Behind me and
before me is God and I have no fears.

Keep your face to the sunshine and you cannot see a shadow.

Knowledge is love and light and vision.

Life is a succession of lessons which must be lived to be understood.

Life is an exciting business, and most exciting when it is lived for others.

Love is like a beautiful flower which I may not touch, but whose
fragrance makes the garden a place of delight just the same.
Many people know so little about what is beyond their short range of experience.
They look within themselves - and find nothing! Therefore they conclude that
there is nothing outside themselves either.
Many persons have a wrong idea of what constitutes true happiness. It is not
attained through self-gratification but through fidelity to a worthy purpose.
My share of the work may be limited, but the fact that it is work makes it precious.
Never bend your head. Always hold it high. Look the world straight in the eye
No matter how dull, or how mean, or how wise a man is, he feels that
happiness is his indisputable right.
No one has a right to consume happiness without producing it.
No pessimist ever discovered the secret of the stars, or sailed to an
uncharted land, or opened a new doorway for the human spirit.
Of all the senses, sight must be the most delightful.
Once I knew only darkness and stillness... my life was without past or
future... but a little word from the fingers of another fell into my hand
that clutched at emptiness, and my heart leaped to the rapture of living.
One can never consent to creep when one feels an impulse to soar.
Everything has its wonders, even darkness and silence, and I learn,
whatever state I may be in, therein to be content.
Faith is the strength by which a shattered world shall emerge into the light.
I can see, and that is why I can be happy, in what you call the dark, but which
to me is golden. I can see a God-made world, not a manmade world.
I long to accomplish a great and noble task, but it is my chief duty to
accomplish small tasks as if they were great and noble.
I seldom think about my limitations, and they never make me sad. Perhaps
there is just a touch of yearning at times; but it is vague, like a breeze
among flowers.

## EDWARD KENNEDY (Senator, 1932-2009)

For all my years in public life, I have believed that America must sail toward the
shores of liberty and justice for all. There is no end to that journey, only
the next great voyage. We know the future will outlast all of us, but I believe
that all of us will live on in the future we make.
Frankly, I don't mind not being President. I just mind that someone else is.
Integrity is the lifeblood of democracy. Deceit is a poison in its veins.
The Constitution does not just protect those whose views we share; it
also protects those with whose views we disagree.
The Republicans are looking after the financial interests of the wealthiest individuals
in this country.
The work goes on, the cause endures, the hope still lives and the
dreams shall never die.
Thus, the controversy about the Moral Majority arises not only from its views, but
from its name - which, in the minds of many, seems to imply that only one
set of public policies is moral and only one majority can possibly be right.

## ETHEL KENNEDY (Wife of Robert Kennedy, 1928 - )

For anyone to achieve something, he will have to show a little courage. You're
only on this earth once. You must give it all you've got.

## JACKIE KENNEDY (First Lady, Reporter, 1929-1994)

A camel makes an elephant feel like a jet plane.

I want to live my life, not record it.

You have to have been a Republican to know how good it is to be a Democrat.

There are many little ways to enlarge your child's world. Love
of books is the best of all.

An Editor becomes kind of your mother. You expect love and
encouragement from an Editor.

Now, I think that I should have known that he [Jack Kennedy] was magic all
along. I did know it - but I should have guessed that it would be too
much to ask to grow old with and see our children grow up together.
So now, he is a legend when he would have preferred to be a man.

Being a reporter seems a ticket out to the world.

Can anyone understand how it is to have lived in the White House
and then, suddenly, to be living alone as the President's widow?

Dear God, please take care of your servant John Fitzgerald Kennedy.

Even though people may be well known, they hold in their hearts the
emotions of a simple person for the moments that are the most
important of those we know on earth: birth, marriage and death.

He didn't even have the satisfaction of being killed for civil rights. it
had to be some silly little Communist.

I always wanted to be some kind of writer or newspaper reporter. But
after college... I did other things.

I am a woman above everything else.

I don't think there are any men who are faithful to their wives.

I don't understand it. Jack will spend any amount of money to buy votes
but he balks at investing a thousand dollars in a beautiful painting.

I think the best thing I can do is to be a distraction. A husband lives and
breathes his work all day long. If he comes home to more table
thumping, how can the poor man ever relax?

I want minimum information given with maximum politeness.

I'll be a wife and mother first, then First Lady.

If you bungle raising your children, I don't think whatever
else you do matters very much.

If you mess up your children, nothing else you do really matters.

It looks like it's been furnished by discount stores.

One must not let oneself be overwhelmed by sadness.

Sex is a bad thing because it rumples the clothes.

The children have been a wonderful gift to me, and I'm thankful to have
once again seen our world through their eyes. They restore
my faith in the family's future.

The first time you marry for love, the second for money, and
the third for companionship.

The one thing I do not want to be called is First Lady. It sounds
like a saddle horse.

There are two kinds of women, those who want power in
the world and those who want power in bed.

What is sad for women of my generation is that they weren't supposed
to work if they had families. What were they going to do when
the  children are grown - watch the raindrops coming down the
window pane?

Whenever I was upset by something in the papers, Jack always told me to be
more tolerant, like a horse flicking away flies in the summer.
The only routine with me is no routine at all.

## JOHN F. KENNEDY (President, 1917-1963)

A child miseducated is a child lost.

A man may die, nations may rise and fall, but an idea lives on.

I just received the following wire from my generous Daddy: "Dear Jack, Don't
buy a single vote more than is necessary. I'll be damned if I'm going to
pay for a landslide.

A nation that is afraid to let its people judge the truth and falsehood in
an open market is a nation that is afraid of its people.

A nation which has forgotten the quality of courage which in the past has been
brought to public life is not as likely to insist upon or regard that quality
in its chosen leaders today - and in fact we have forgotten.

A young man who does not have what it takes to perform military service is not
likely to have what it takes to make a living. Today's military rejects
include tomorrow's hard-core unemployed.

All free men, wherever they may live, are citizens of Berlin. And therefore,
as a free man, I take pride in the words "Ich bin ein Berliner!"

America has tossed its cap over the wall of space.

And so, my fellow Americans, ask not what your country can do for you;
ask what you can do for your country.

As we express our gratitude, we must never forget that the highest
appreciation is not to utter words, but to live by them.

Change is the law of life. And those who look only to the past or
present are certain to miss the future.

Communism has never come to power in a country that was not
disrupted by war or corruption, or both.

Conformity is the jailer of freedom and the enemy of growth.

Do not pray for easy lives. Pray to be stronger men.

Do you realize the responsibility I carry? I'm the only person standing
between Richard Nixon and the White House.

Domestic policy can only defeat us; foreign policy can kill us.

Efforts and courage are not enough without purpose and direction.

For time and the world do not stand still. Change is the law of life. And those
who look only to the past or the present are certain to miss the future.

Forgive your enemies, but never forget their names.

Geography has made us neighbors. History has made us friends. Economics has
made us partners, and necessity has made us allies. Those whom God
has so joined together, let no man put asunder.

History is a relentless master. It has no present, only the past rushing into the
future. To try to hold fast is to be swept aside.
I am not the Catholic candidate for President. I am the Democratic
Party's candidate for President, who happens also to be a Catholic.

I am sorry to say that there is too much point to the wisecrack that life is extinct
on other planets because their scientists were more advanced than ours.

I am the man who accompanied Jacqueline Kennedy to
Paris, and I have enjoyed it.

I don't think the intelligence reports are all that hot. Some days I get
more out of the New York Times.

I hope that no American will waste his franchise and throw away his vote by
    voting either for me or against me solely on account of my religious
    affiliation. It is not relevant.
I just received the following wire from my generous Daddy; Dear Jack, Don't
    buy a single vote more than is necessary. I'll be damned if I'm going
    to pay for a landslide.
I look forward to a great future for America - a future in which our country will
    match its military strength with our moral restraint, its wealth with our
    wisdom, its power with our purpose.
I think 'Hail to the Chief' has a nice ring to it.
I think this is the most extraordinary collection of talent, of human knowledge,
    that has ever been gathered at the White House - with the possible
    exception of when Thomas Jefferson dined alone.
I'm always rather nervous about how you talk about women who are active in
    politics, whether they want to be talked about as women or as politicians.
I'm an idealist without  illusions.
If a free society cannot help the many who are poor, it cannot save
    the few who are rich.
If anyone is crazy enough to want to kill a president of the United States, he
    can do it. All he must be prepared to do is give his life for the president's.
If art is to nourish the roots of our culture, society must set the artist free
    to follow his vision wherever it takes him.
If we cannot now end our differences, at least we can help make the
    world safe for diversity.
In a very real sense, it will not be one man going to the moon it will
    be an entire nation. For all of us must work to put him there.
In the long history of the world, only a few generations have been granted the
    role of defending freedom in its hour of maximum danger. I do not
    shrink from this responsibility - I welcome it.
Israel was not created in order to disappear - Israel will endure and flourish. It
    is the child of hope and the home of the brave. It can neither be broken
    by adversity nor demoralized by success. It carries the shield of
    democracy and it honors the sword of freedom.
It is an unfortunate fact that we can secure peace only by preparing for war.
It might be said now that I have the best of both worlds. A Harvard
    education and a Yale degree.
Our progress as a nation can be no swifter than our progress in
    education. The human mind is our fundamental resource.
Peace is a daily, a weekly, a monthly process, gradually changing
    opinions, slowly eroding old barriers, quietly building new structures.
Physical fitness is not only one of the most important keys to a healthy
    body, it is the basis of dynamic and creative intellectual activity.
Politics is like football; if you see daylight, go through the hole.
Sure it's a big job; but I don't know anyone who can do it better than I can.
The basic problems facing the world today are not susceptible to a
    military solution.
The cost of freedom is always high, but Americans have always paid it. And
    one path we shall never choose, and that is the path of surrender,
    or submission.
The courage of life is often a less dramatic spectacle than the courage of a final
    moment; but it is no less a magnificent mixture of triumph and tragedy.

The goal of education is the advancement of knowledge and the
dissemination of truth.

The best road to progress is freedom's road.

The great enemy of the truth is very often not the lie, deliberate, contrived
and dishonest, but the myth, persistent, persuasive and unrealistic.

The greater our knowledge increases the more our ignorance unfolds.

The human mind is our fundamental resource.

The ignorance of one voter in a democracy impairs the security of all.

The path we have chosen for the present is full of hazards, as all paths
are. The cost of freedom is always high, but Americans have always
paid it. And one path we shall never choose, and that is the path of
surrender, or submission.

The pay is good and I can walk to work.

The problems of the world cannot possibly be solved by skeptics or cynics
whose horizons are limited by the obvious realities. We need men
who can dream of things that never were.

The time to repair the roof is when the sun is shining.

The United States has to move very fast to even stand still.

The very word 'secrecy' is repugnant in a free and open society; and we are
as a people inherently and historically opposed to secret societies, to
secret oaths, and to secret proceedings.

The world is very different now. For  man holds in his mortal hands the power
to abolish all forms of human poverty, and all forms of human life.

There are many people in the world who really don't understand-or say they
don't-what is the great issue between the free world and the
Communist world. Let them come to Berlin!

There are risks and costs to action. But they are far less than the long
range risks of comfortable inaction.

There is always inequality in life. Some men are killed in a war and some
men are wounded and some men never leave the country. Life is unfair.

Things do not happen. Things are made to happen.

Those who dare to fail miserably can achieve greatly.

Those who make peaceful revolution impossible will make
violent revolution inevitable.

To state the facts frankly is not to despair the future nor indict the past.
The prudent heir takes careful inventory of his legacies and gives a
faithful accounting to those whom he owes an obligation of trust.

Tolerance implies no lack of commitment to one's own beliefs. Rather it
condemns the oppression or persecution of others.

Too often we... enjoy the comfort of opinion without the discomfort of thought.

Unconditional war can no longer lead to unconditional victory. It can no
longer serve to settle disputes... can no longer be of concern to
great powers alone.

Victory has a thousand fathers, but defeat is an orphan.

War will exist until that distant day when the conscientious objector enjoys
the same reputation and prestige that the warrior does today.

Washington is a city of Southern efficiency and Northern charm.

We are not afraid to entrust the American people with unpleasant facts, foreign
ideas, alien philosophies, and competitive values. For a nation that is
afraid to let its people judge the truth and falsehood in an open market
is a nation that is afraid of its people.

We are tied to the ocean. And when we go back to the sea, whether it is to
sail or to watch - we are going back from whence we came.
We believe that if men have the talent to invent new machines that put men
out of work, they have the talent to put those men back to work.
We cannot expect that all nations will adopt like systems, for conformity
is the jailer of freedom and the enemy of growth.
We have the power to make this the best generation of mankind in the
history of the world or to make it the last.
We must use time as a tool, not as a couch.
We prefer world law in the age of self-determination to world war in
the age of mass extermination.
We stand today on the edge of a new frontier - the frontier of the 1960's - a frontier
of unknown opportunities and perils - a frontier of unfulfilled
hopes and threats.
We would like to live as we once lived, but history will not permit it.
When power leads man toward arrogance, poetry reminds him of his limitations.
When power narrows the area of man's concern, poetry reminds him of the
richness and diversity of existence. When power corrupts, poetry cleanses.
When we got into office, the thing that surprised me most was to find that
things were just as bad as we'd been saying they were.
When written in Chinese, the word "crisis" is composed of two characters. One
represents danger and the other represents opportunity.

## ROBERT KENNEDY (Attorney General, Senator, 1925-1968)

All of us , from the wealthiest and most powerful of men, to the weakest and
hungriest of children, share one precious possession: the name American.
As long as men are not free--in their lives and their opinions, their speech and
knowledge-- that long will the American Revolution not be finished.
Our gross national product does not allow for the health of our children, the quality
of their education, or the joy of their play. It does not include the beauty of
our poetry or the strength of our marriages, the intelligence of our public
debate or the integrity of our public officials. It measures neither our wit nor
our courage, neither our wisdom nor our learning, neither our compassion
nor our devotion to our country; it measures everything, in short, except that
which makes life worth while. And it can tell us everything about America
except why we are proud that we are Americans.
On this generation of Americans falls the burden of proving to the world that we
really mean it when we say all men are created free and are equal before the
law. All of us might wish at times that we lived in a more tranquil world, but
we don't. And if our times are difficult and perplexing, so are they
challenging and filled with opportunity.
Since the days of Greece and Rome when the word 'citizen' was a title of honor, we
have often seen more emphasis put on the rights of citizenship than on its
responsibilities. And today, as never before in the free world, responsibility is
the greatest right of citizenship and service is the greatest of freedom's
privileges.
What we need in the United States is not division; what we need in the United
States is not hatred; what we need in the United States is not violence or
lawlessness; but love and wisdom, and compassion toward one another, and
a feeling of justice toward those who still suffer within our country, whether
they be white or they be black.

Democracy is no easy form of government. Few nations have been able to sustain it.
        For it requires that we take the chances of freedom; that the liberating play
        of reason be brought to bear on events filled with passion; that dissent be
        allowed to make its appeal for acceptance; that men chance error in their
        search for the truth.
Justice delayed is democracy denied.
The sharpest criticism often goes hand in hand with the deepest idealism
        and love of country.
We must recognize the full human equality of all our people - before God, before the
        law, and in the councils of government. We must do this not because it is
        economically advantageous - although it is; not because the laws of God and
        man command it - although they do command it; not because people in
        other lands wish it so. We must do it for the single and fundamental reason
        that it is the right thing to do.
 What is objectionable, what is dangerous about extremists is not that they are
        extreme, but that they are intolerant. The evil is not what they say about
        their causes, but what they say about their opponents.
 The future is not a gift: it is an achievement. Every generation helps make      its
        own future. This is the essential challenge of the present.
The future does not belong to those who are content with today, apathetic toward
        common problems and their fellow man alike, timid and fearful in the face of
        bold projects and new ideas. Rather, it will belong to those who can
        blend passion, reason and courage in a personal commitment to the
        great enterprises and ideals of American society.
Only those who dare to fail greatly, can ever achieve greatly.
At the heart of that Western freedom and democracy is the belief that the
        individual man, the child of God, is the touchstone of value, and all
        society, groups, the state, exist for his benefit. Therefore the enlargement
        of liberty for individual human beings must be the supreme goal and the
        abiding practice of any Western society.
 First, is the danger of futility; the belief there is nothing one man or woman can do
        against the enormous array of the worlds ills--against misery and ignorance,
        injustice and violence. Yet many of the world's great movements, of thought
        and action, have flowed from the work of a single man. A young monk began
        the Protestant Reformation, a young general extended an empire from
        Macedonia to the borders of the earth, and a young woman reclaimed the
        territory of France. It was a young Italian explorer who discovered the New
        World, and the thirty-two year old
        Thomas Jefferson who proclaimed that all men are created equal.
How do you tell if Lyndon is lying? If he wiggles his ears, that doesn't mean
        he's lying. If he raises his eyebrows, that doesn't mean he's lying. But
        when he moves his lips, he's lying.'
You knew that what is given or granted can be taken away, that what is
        begged can be refused; but that what is earned is kept.
We know that if one man's rights are denied, the rights of all are endangered.
One-fifth of the people are against everything all the time.
There are people in every time and every land who want to stop history in its
        tracts. They fear the future, mistrust the present, and invoke the security
        of the comfortable past which , in fact, never existed
 He knows all the facts, and he's against all the solutions.
I believe that, as long as there is plenty, poverty is evil.

The problem of power is how to achieve its responsible use rather than its
      irresponsible and indulgent use -- of how to get men of power to live
      for the public rather than off the public.
Men without hope, resigned to despair and oppression, do not make revolutions.
      It is when expectation replaces submission, when despair is touched with the
      awareness of possibility, that the forces of human desire and the passion for
      justice are unloosed.
A revolution is coming--a revolution which will be peaceful if we are wise enough;
      compassionate if we care enough; successful if we are fortunate enough--
      But a revolution which is coming whether we will it or not. We can affect
      its character; we cannot alter its inevitability.
We can master change not though force or fear, but only though the free work
      of an understanding mind, though an openness to new knowledge and
      fresh outlooks, which can only strengthen the most fragile and most
      powerful of human gifts: the gift of reason.
Too much and too long, we seem to have surrendered community excellence
      and community values in the mere accumulation of material things.
 Few will have the greatness to bend history; but each of us can work to change a
      small portion of events, and in the total of all those acts will be written the
      history of this generation ... It is from numberless diverse acts of courage
      and belief that human history is thus shaped. Each time a man stands up for
      an ideal, or acts to improve the lot of others, or strikes out against injustice,
      he sends forth a tiny ripple of hope, and crossing each other from a million
      different centers of energy and daring, those ripples build a current which
      can sweep down the mightiest walls of oppression and resistance.
That which unites us is, must be, stronger than that which divides us. We can
      concentrate on what unites us, and secure the future for all our children;
      or we can concentrate on what divides us, and fail our duty through
      argument and resentment and waste.
What has violence ever accomplished? What has it ever created? No martyr's cause
      has ever been stilled by an assassin's bullet. No wrongs have ever been
      righted by riots and civil disorders. A sniper is only a coward, not a hero; and
      an uncontrolled, uncontrollable mob is only the voice of madness, not the
      voice of reason. Whenever any American's life is taken by another American
      unnecessarily - whether it is done in the name of the law or in the defiance
      of the law, by one man or a gang, in cold blood or in passion, in an attack of
      violence or in response to violence - whenever we tear at the fabric of the life
      which another man has painfully and clumsily woven for himself and his
      children, the whole nation is degraded.
My views on birth control are somewhat distorted by the fact that I
      was seventh of nine children.
Our answer is the world's hope; it is to rely on youth. The cruelties and obstacles of
      this swiftly changing planet will not yield to obsolete dogmas and outworn
      slogans. It cannot be moved by those who cling to a present which is already
      dying, who prefer the illusion of security to the excitement of danger. It
      demands the qualities of youth: not a time of life but a state of mind, a
      temper of the will, a quality of the imagination, a predominance of courage
      over timidity, of the appetite for adventure over the love of ease.
All of us might wish at times that we lived in a more tranquil world, but we don't.
      And if our times are difficult and perplexing, so are they challenging and
      filled with opportunity.

But suppose God is black? What if we go to Heaven and we, all our lives, have
  treated the Negro as an inferior, and God is there, and we look up and
  He is not white? What then is our response?
Every society gets the kind of criminal it deserves. What is equally true is that
  every community gets the kind of law enforcement it insists on.
Few will have the greatness to bend history itself; but each of us can work to
  change a small portion of events, and in the total; of all those
  acts will be written the history of this generation.
I believe that, as long as there is plenty, poverty is evil.
I was the seventh of nine children. When you come from that far down
  you have to struggle to survive.
It is not enough to understand, or to see clearly. The future will be shaped
  in the arena of human activity, by those willing to commit their
  minds and their bodies to the task.
Let us dedicate ourselves to what the Greeks wrote so many years ago: to
  tame the savageness of man and make gentle the life of this world
People say I am ruthless. I am not ruthless. And if I find the man who
  is calling me ruthless, I shall destroy him.
Progress is a nice word. But change is its motivator. And change has its enemies.
The free way of life proposes ends, but it does not prescribe means.
There are those who look at things the way they are, and ask why... I
  dream of things that never were, and ask why not?
Tragedy is a tool for the living to gain wisdom, not a guide by which to live.
Ultimately, America's answer to the intolerant man is diversity, the very
  diversity which our heritage of religious freedom has inspired.
Whenever men take the law into their own hands, the loser is the
  law. And when the law loses, freedom languishes.

## ROSE KENNEDY (Kennedy Family Matron, 1890-1995)
I'm like old wine. They don't bring me out very often, but I'm well preserved.
Life isn't a matter of milestones, but of moments.
Birds sing after a storm;  why shouldn't people feel as free to
  delight in whatever remains to them?
I tell myself that God gave my children many gifts - spirit, beauty,
  intelligence, the capacity to make friends and to inspire respect.
  There was only one gift he held back - length of life.
I've had an exciting time; I married for love and got a little money along with it.
If you can keep your head about you when all about you are losing theirs,
  its just possible you haven't grasped the situation.
It's our money, and we're free to spend it any way we please.
Make sure you never, never argue at night. You just lose a good
  night's sleep, and you can't settle anything until morning anyway.
More business is lost every year through neglect than through any other cause.
Neither comprehension nor learning can take place in an atmosphere of anxiety.
Prosperity tries the fortunate, adversity the great.
The time will come when it will disgust you to look in the mirror.
There's nothing I like less than bad arguments for a view that I hold dear.

## JACK KEROUAC (Author, 1922-1969)
Accept loss forever.
All human beings are also dream beings. Dreaming ties all mankind together.

All of life is a foreign country.
Avoid the world, it's just a lot of dust and drag and means nothing in the end.
Great things are not accomplished by those who yield to trends
        and fads and popular opinion.
I had nothing to offer anybody except my own confusion.
I hope it is true that a man can die and yet not only live in others but
        give them life, and not only life, but that great consciousness of life.
If moderation is a fault, then indifference is a crime.
It is not my fault that certain so-called bohemian elements have found in my
        writings something to hang their peculiar beatnik theories on.
Mankind is like dogs, not gods - as long as you don't get mad they'll bite
        you - but stay mad and you'll never be bitten. Dogs don't respect
        humility and sorrow.
Maybe that's what life is... a wink of the eye and winking stars.
My fault, my failure, is not in the passions I have, but in my lack of
        control of them.
My witness is the empty sky.
Offer them what they secretly want and they of course
        immediately become panic-stricken.
Whither goest thou, America, in thy shiny car in the night?
Write in recollection and amazement for yourself.
You can't teach the old maestro a new tune.

## JOHN KERRY (Politician, 1943 - )

Real Democrats don't abandon the middle class.
I saw courage both in the Vietnam War and in the struggle to stop it.
        I learned that patriotism includes protest, not just military service.
Being lectured by the president [G.W. Bush] on fiscal responsibility
        is a little bit like Tony Soprano talking to me about law and
        order in this country.
I want to start by saying something nice about President Bush. Of all the presidents
        we've had with the last name of Bush, his economic
        plan ranks in the top two.
I would rather be the candidate of the NAACP than the NRA.
I'm fascinated by rap and by hip-hop. I think there's a lot of poetry in it.
        There's a lot of anger, a lot of social energy in it. And I think you'd
        better listen to it pretty carefully, 'cause it's important.
The best way to begin genuine bipartisanship to make America stronger is to
        work together on the real crises facing our country, not to manufacture
        an artificial crisis to serve a special interest agenda out of touch with
        the needs of Americans.
You get the feeling that if George Bush had been President during other
        periods in American history, he would have sided with the candle
        lobby against electricity, the buggy-makers against cars, and
        typewriter companies against computers.
Did the training wheels fall off?" [after being told by reporters that
        President G.W. Bush took a tumble during a bike ride].
Invading Iraq in response to 9/11 would be like Franklin Roosevelt invading Mexico
        in response to Pearl Harbor.[In regards to G.W. Bush's plan to invade Iraq].
I'm glad the President finally found an economic development program. I'm just sad
        that it's only in Baghdad."

My friends, that's trickle-down economics, and I believe every worker
in America is tired of being trickled on by George W. Bush.
George Bush thought he could play dress-up on an aircraft carrier
and you wouldn't notice. Ask yourself, whose mission is accomplished?
In the event of emergency, my hair can be used as a flotation device
The consequences of a crime should not be out of proportion to the crime itself.
We [in Iraq] have traded a dictator for a chaos that has left America less secure.
When we walk away from global warming, Kyoto, when we are irresponsibly
slow in moving toward AIDS in Africa, when we don't advance and live
up to our own rhetoric and standards, we set a terrible message
of duplicity and hypocrisy.
I figured out Karl Rove's political strategy -- make gas so expensive, no
Democrats can afford to go to the polls.

## CORETTA SCOTT KING (Civil Rights Activist, 1927-2006)

Freedom and justice cannot be parceled out in pieces to suit political
convenience. I don't believe you can stand for freedom for one
group of people and deny it to others.
Hate is too great a burden to bear. It injures the hater more
than it injures the hated.
Homophobia is like racism and anti-Semitism and other forms of bigotry
in that it seeks to dehumanize a large group of people, to deny their
humanity, their dignity and personhood.
I believe all Americans who believe in freedom, tolerance and human
rights have a responsibility to oppose bigotry and prejudice
based on sexual orientation.
I'm fulfilled in what I do. I never thought that a lot of money or fine clothes -
the finer things of life - would make you happy. My concept of
happiness is to be filled in a spiritual sense.
If American women would increase their voting turnout by ten percent,
I think we would see an end to all of the budget cuts in programs
benefitting women and children.
Mama and Daddy King represent the best in manhood and womanhood,
the best in a marriage, the kind of people we are trying to become.
Segregation was wrong when it was forced by white people, and I believe
it is still wrong when it is requested by black people.
Struggle is a never ending process. Freedom is never really won, you earn
it and win it in every generation.
There is a spirit and a need and a man at the beginning of every great
human advance. Every one of these must be right for that
particular moment of history, or nothing happens.
Women, if the soul of the nation is to be saved, I believe that you
must become its soul.

## MARTIN LUTHER KING, JR. (Minister, Civil Rights Activist, 1929-1968)

A genuine leader is not a searcher for consensus but a molder of consensus.
A lie cannot live.
A man who won't die for something is not fit to live.
A nation or civilization that continues to produce soft-minded men
purchases its own spiritual death on the installment plan.

A nation that continues year after year to spend more money on military
        defense than on programs of social uplift is approaching spiritual doom.
A right delayed is a right denied.
A riot is the language of the unheard.
A man can't ride your back unless it's bent.
All labor that uplifts humanity has dignity and importance and should be
        undertaken with painstaking excellence.
Almost always, the creative dedicated minority has made the world better.
An individual has not started living until he can rise above the narrow confines
        of his individualistic concerns to the broader concerns of all humanity.
An individual who breaks a law that conscience tells him is unjust, and who
        willingly accepts the penalty of imprisonment in order to arouse the
        conscience of the community over its injustice, is in reality expressing
        the highest respect for the law.
At the center of non-violence stands the principle of love.
All progress is precarious, and the solution of one problem brings us
        face to face with another problem.
Change does not roll in on the wheels of inevitability, but comes through
        continuous struggle. And so we must straighten our backs and work
        for our freedom. A man can't ride you unless your back is bent.
Darkness cannot drive out darkness; only light can do that. Hate cannot
        drive out hate; only love can do that.
Discrimination is a hellhound that gnaws at Negroes in every waking moment
        of their lives to remind them that the lie of their inferiority is accepted
        as truth in the society dominating them.
Every man must decide whether he will walk in the light of creative
        altruism or in the darkness of destructive selfishness.
Everything that we see is a shadow cast by that which we do not see.
Faith is taking the first step even when you don't see the whole staircase.
Freedom is never voluntarily given by the oppressor; it must be
        demanded by the oppressed.
Have we not come to such an impasse in the modern world that we must love
        our enemies - or else? The chain reaction of evil - hate begetting hate,
        wars producing more wars - must be broken, or else we shall be
        plunged into the dark abyss of annihilation.
He who passively accepts evil is as much involved in it as he who helps to
        perpetrate it. He who accepts evil without protesting against it is
        really cooperating with it.
History will have to record that the greatest tragedy of this period of social
        transition was not the strident clamor of the bad people, but the
        appalling silence of the good people.
Human progress is neither automatic nor inevitable... Every step toward the
        goal of justice requires sacrifice, suffering, and struggle; the tireless
        exertions and passionate concern of dedicated individuals.
Human salvation lies in the hands of the creatively maladjusted.
I believe that unarmed truth and unconditional love will have the final
        word in reality. This is why right, temporarily defeated, is stronger
        than evil triumphant.
I have a dream that my four little children will one day live in a nation
        where they will not be judged by the color of their skin, but by
        the content of their character.

I have a dream that one day every valley shall be exalted, every hill and mountain
        shall be made low, the rough places will be made straight and the glory of
        the Lord shall be revealed and all flesh shall see it together.
I have a dream that one day on the red hills of Georgia, the sons of former
        slaves and the sons of former slave owners will be able to sit together
        at the table of brotherhood.
        I am not interested in power for power's sake, but I'm interested
        in power that is moral, that is right and that is good.
I have decided to stick with love. Hate is too great a burden to bear.
I just want to do God's will. And he's allowed me to go to the mountain. And
        I've looked over, and I've seen the promised land! I may not get there
        with you, but I want you to know tonight that we as a people will get
        to the promised land.
I look to a day when people will not be judged by the color of their skin,
        but by the content of their character.
I refuse to accept the view that mankind is so tragically bound to the starless
        midnight of racism and war that the bright daybreak of peace and
        brotherhood can never become a reality... I believe that unarmed
        truth and unconditional love will have the final word.
I submit that an individual who breaks the law that conscience tells him is
        unjust and willingly accepts the penalty by staying in jail to arouse the
        conscience of the community over its injustice, is in reality expressing
        the very highest respect for law.
I submit to you that if a man hasn't discovered something
        that he will die for, he isn't fit to live.
I want to be the white man's brother, not his brother-in-law.
If physical death is the price that I must pay to free my white brothers and sisters
        from a permanent death of the spirit, then nothing can be more redemptive.
If we are to go forward, we must go back and rediscover those precious values -
        that all reality hinges on moral foundations and that all
        reality has spiritual control.
In the End, we will remember not the words of our enemies,
        but the silence of our friends.
Injustice anywhere is a threat to justice everywhere.
It is not enough to say we must not wage war. It is necessary
        to love peace and sacrifice for it.
It may be true that the law cannot make a man love me, but it can keep
        him from lynching me, and I think that's pretty important.
Law and order exist for the purpose of establishing justice and when they
        fail in this purpose they become the dangerously structured dams
        that block the flow of social progress.
Life's most persistent and urgent question is, 'What are you doing for others?'
Love is the only force capable of transforming an enemy into friend.
Means we use must be as pure as the ends we seek.
Never forget that everything Hitler did in Germany was legal.
Never succumb to the temptation of bitterness.
Nonviolence is a powerful and just weapon. which cuts without wounding
        and ennobles the man who wields it. It is a sword that heals.
Nonviolence means avoiding not only external physical violence but also
        internal violence of spirit. You not only refuse to shoot a man, but
        you refuse to hate him.

Nothing in all the world is more dangerous than sincere
        ignorance and conscientious stupidity.
Man must evolve for all human conflict a method which rejects revenge,
        aggression and retaliation. The foundation of such a method is love.
One who breaks an unjust law that conscience tells him is unjust,
        and who willingly accepts the penalty of imprisonment in order
        to arouse the conscience of the community over its injustice,
        is in reality expressing the highest respect for law.
Our lives begin to end the day we become silent about things that matter
Our scientific power has outrun our spiritual power. We have guided
        missiles and misguided men.
Peace is not merely a distant goal that we seek, but a means by
        which we arrive at that goal.
Philanthropy is commendable, but it must not cause the philanthropist
        to overlook the circumstances of economic injustice which
        make philanthropy necessary.
Pity may represent little more than the impersonal concern which prompts
        the mailing of a check, but true sympathy is the personal concern
        which demands the giving of one's soul.
Property is intended to serve life, and no matter how much we surround it
        with rights and respect, it has no personal being. It is part of the
        earth man walks on. It is not man.
Rarely do we find men who willingly engage in hard, solid thinking. There is
        an almost universal quest for easy answers and half-baked solutions.
        Nothing pains some people more than having to think.
Science investigates religion interprets. Science gives man knowledge
        which is power  religion gives man wisdom which is control.
Seeing is not  always believing.
Shallow understanding from people of good will is more frustrating than
        absolute misunderstanding from people of ill will.
Take the first step in faith. You don't have to see the whole staircase, just
        take the first step.
That old law about 'an eye for an eye' leaves everybody blind. The time
        is always right to do the right thing.
The art of acceptance is the art of making someone who has just done you a
        small favor wish that he might have done you a greater one.
The first question which the priest and the Levite asked was: "If I stop to help
        this man, what will happen to me?" But... the good Samaritan reversed
        the question: "If I do not stop to help this man, what will happen to him?"
The function of education is to teach one to think intensively and to think critically.
        Intelligence plus character - that is the goal of true education.
The hope of a secure and livable world lies with disciplined nonconformists
        who are dedicated to justice, peace and brotherhood.
The hottest place in Hell is reserved for those who remain neutral in times
        of great moral conflict.
The limitation of riots, moral questions aside, is that they cannot win and their
        participants know it. Hence, rioting is not revolutionary but reactionary
        because it invites defeat. It involves an emotional catharsis, but it must
        be followed by a sense of futility.
The Negro needs the white man to free him from his fears. The white man
        needs the Negro to free him from his guilt.

The past is prophetic in that it asserts loudly that wars are poor chisels for
    carving out peaceful tomorrows.

The moral arc of the universe bends at the elbow of justice.

The quality, not the longevity, of one's life is what is important.

The question is not whether we will be extremists, but what kind of extremists we
    will be... The nation and the world are in dire need of creative extremists.

The sweltering summer of the Negro's legitimate discontent will not pass
    until there is an invigorating autumn of freedom and equality.

The time is always right to do what is right.

The ultimate measure of a man is not where he stands in moments of comfort and
    convenience, but where he stands at times of challenge and controversy.

The ultimate tragedy is not the oppression and cruelty by the bad people but the
    silence over that by the good people.

There can be no deep disappointment where there is not deep love.

There is nothing more tragic than to find an individual bogged down in the
    length of life, devoid of breadth.

To be a Christian without prayer is no more possible than
    to be alive without breathing.

War is a poor chisel to carve out tomorrow.

Wars are poor  chisels for carving out peaceful tomorrows.

We are not makers of history. We are made by history.

We have guided missiles and misguided men.

We may have all come on different ships, but we're in the same boat now.

We must accept finite disappointment, but never lose infinite hope.

We must build dikes of courage to hold back the flood of fear.

We must concentrate not merely on the negative expulsion of war but the
    positive affirmation of peace.

We must develop and maintain the capacity to forgive. He who is devoid of
    the power to forgive is devoid of the power to love. There is some good
    in the worst of us and some evil in the best of us. When we discover this, we
    are less prone to hate our enemies.

We must learn to live together as brothers or perish together as fools.

*We must use* time creatively.

We who in engage in nonviolent direct action are not the creators of tension.
    We merely bring to the surface the hidden tension that is already alive.

We will have to repent in this generation not merely for the vitriolic words and
    actions of the bad people, but for the appalling silence of the good people.

Whatever affects one directly, affects all indirectly. I can never be what I ought
    to be until you are what you ought to be. This is the interrelated structure
    of reality.

Whatever your life's work is, do it well. A man should do his job so well
    that the living, the dead, and the unborn could do it no better.

When you are right you cannot be too radical; when you are wrong, you
    cannot be too conservative.

## EARTHA KITT (Actress, 1927 -)

Just because you are different does not mean that you have to be rejected.

I was given away. If your mother gives you away, you think everybody
    who comes into your life is going to give you away.

Don't depend on other people to be responsible for you. Don't make yourself
    stressed out over nonsensical things like material things.

Dr. Einstein was not successful in school, but he found something in the air
from his own imagination and his own brain power, and look what he did.
Having my animals or my children with me exorcizes that feeling of
not being wanted.
I am learning all the time. The tombstone will be my diploma.
I never take anything for granted. I may slip any minute.
I punish myself more than anybody else does if I am stupid about my
actions, and I suffer, really suffer.
Jewelry, to me, is a pain in the derriere, because you have to be watching
it all the time.
Let's take care of the necessities first: give people jobs, and find a way
to get us out of poverty.
Live theater to me is much more free than the movies or television.
My house was bugged. They couldn't find any information on me being a
subversive because I happen to love America; I just don't like some
of the things the government is doing.
My recipe for life is not being afraid of myself, afraid of
what I think or of my opinions.
Orson Welles was one of these people who was defying everything the doctors
told him he wasn't supposed to be doing. He was really enjoying himself
when he was eating what he wanted to eat.
The public has become my fairy godmother.
The river is constantly turning and bending and you never know where it's going
to go and where you'll wind up. Following the bend in the river and
staying on your own path means that you are on the right track. Don't
let anyone deter you from that.
We're not thought of in terms of color because we are entertainers. We are
there to entertain you not because we are black, white, pink, or green
or gay or straight or because we are Catholic or Protestant.
When the people who are responsible for our country ask you a direct question,
I expect them to accept a direct answer, not to be blackballed because
you are telling the truth.
When we want to have our own style of living, it is nobody's business but
ours. What we do in private is our private business.
You don't move just because you want to go from this point to that point - the
body has to be using the words as well as you vocally use the words.

## WALTER KOENIG (Actor, 1036 - )

Religious tolerance is something we should all practice; however, there have
been more persecution and atrocities committed in the name of religion
and religious freedom than anything else.
Movies can be effective in influencing people to think in ways they might not
otherwise be exposed to. Social commentary in films is most effective
when you're not aware of a soapbox. Making the point without
force-feeding the audience is the most desirable approach.

## CHARLES KURALT (Journalist, Commentator, 1934-1997)

A country so rich that it can send people to the moon still has hundreds of
thousands of its citizens who can't read. That's terribly troubling to me.

It does no harm just once in a while to acknowledge that the whole country
    isn't in flames, that there are people in the country besides politicians,
    entertainers, and criminals.
Thanks to the Interstate Highway System, it is now possible to travel
    across the country from coast to coast without seeing anything.
The everyday kindness of the back roads more than makes up for the
    acts of greed in the headlines.
For a while there, I was a stringer. The expression comes from the old habit
    of stringing together the column inches that you had written. They'd
    measure it and pay you 10 cents an inch for your printed copy.
Good teachers know how to bring out the best in students.
I believe that writing is derivative. I think good writing comes
    from good reading.
I can't say that I've changed anybody's life, ever, and that's the
    real work of the world, if you want a better society.
I could tell you which writer's rhythms I am imitating. It's not
    exactly plagiarism, it's falling in love with good language
    and trying to imitate it.
I didn't like the competitiveness of big-time journalism.
I don't have any well-developed philosophy about journalism.
    Ultimately it is important in a society like this, so people
    can know about everything that goes wrong.
I don't think one should ever come to my stage of life and have to
    look back and say, Gosh. I wish I hadn't spent all those years
    doing that job I was never really interested in.
I had a little insight into life that most kids probably didn't
    have. My mother was a schoolteacher, and my father was a
    social worker. Through his eyes I saw the underside of society.
I remember being in the public library and my jaw just aching as I looked
    around at all those books I wanted to read. There just wasn't time
    enough to read everything I wanted to read.
I saw how many people were poor and how many kids my age went to
    school hungry in the morning, which I don't think most of my
    contemporaries in racially segregated schools in the South
    thought very much about at the time.
I would love to write something that people would still read 50
    or 100 years from now. That comes with growing older, I think.
I'm not any kind of social reformer.
In television, everything is gone with the speed of light, literally.
    It is no field for anybody with intimations of immortality.
It was so much fun to have the freedom to wander America, with no
    assignments. For 25 or 30 years I never had an assignment. These
    were all stories I wanted to do myself.
It's best to leap into something you know you love. You might
    change your mind later, but that is the privilege of youth.
Just by luck, I picked good heroes to worship.
When we become a really mature, grown-up, wise society, we will put
    teachers at the center of the community, where they belong. We
    don't honor them enough, we don't pay them enough.
You can find your way across this country using burger joints the
    way a navigator uses stars.

The first books I was interested in were all about baseball. But I
    can't think of one single book that changed my life in any way.
The love of family and the admiration of friends is much more important
    than wealth and privilege.
Look for joy in your life; it's not always easy to find.
There are a lot of people who are doing wonderful things, quietly,
    with no motive of greed, or hostility toward other people, or
    delusions of superiority.
There is such a thing as a national conscience, and it can be touched.
I suppose I was a little bit of what would be called today a nerd. I didn't
    have girlfriends, and really I wasn't a very social boy.
I think all those people I did stories about measured their own
    success by the joy their work was giving them.
I used to think that driving, sleepless, ambitious labor was what you
    needed to succeed.
I wasn't a very discriminating reader. I read just about
    everything that came along.

## MERCEDES LACKEY (Author, 1950 - )

I always work from an outline, so I know all the of the broad events and
    some of the finer details before I begin writing the book.
It makes sense for people who are good at fighting to go out and do it-because
    if they're good at it, that means the fewest number of other people die.
Magic, like technology, is a tool

## NORMAN LAMM (Educator, 1927 -)

No religious position is loyally served by refusing to consider
    annoying theories which may well turn out to be facts.
Judaism is an intellectually based religion, and the single most
    important theme is that of study.
Conventional dogmas, even if endowed with the authority of an Aristotle -
    ancient or modern - must be tested vigorously. If they are found
    wanting, we need not bother with them. But if they are found to be
    substantially correct, we may not overlook them.
. . . the word madda in modern Hebrew specifically means science.
I showed that privacy was an implicit right in Jewish law, probably going back
    to the second or third century, when it was elaborated on in a legal way.
In Judaism, there are 613 biblical commandments, and the Talmud says that
    the chief commandment of all is study.
Maimonides taught that it is better that 10 criminals go free than let one
    innocent man be executed. The Innocence Project represents that
    point of view.

## LOUIS L'AMOUR (Author, 1908-1988)

For one who reads, there is no limit to the number of lives that may be lived,
    for fiction, biography, and history offer an inexhaustible number of lives
    in many parts of the world, in all periods of time.
To make democracy work, we must be a notion of participants, not simply
    observers. One who does not vote has no right to complain.
Anger is a killing thing: it kills the man who angers, for each rage leaves
    him less than he had been before - it takes something from him.

No memory is ever alone; it's at the end of a trail of memories, a dozen
     trails that each have their own associations.
No one can get an education, for of necessity education is a continuing process.
A good beginning makes a good end.
A wise man fights to win, but he is twice a fool who has no plan for possible defeat.
Knowledge is like money: to be of value it must circulate, and in circulating
     it can increase in quantity and, hopefully, in value.
Nobody got anywhere in the world by simply being content.
To disbelieve is easy; to scoff is simple; to have faith is harder.
Too often I would hear men boast of the miles covered that day,
     rarely of what they had seen.

### BURT LANCASTER (Actor, 1913-1994)

Sell yourself first, if you want to sell anything.
Can anything be more Un-American than the Un-American committee?
Sometimes I only succeed in beating myself to death.
Take the feeling of hunger out of your gut, and you're no longer a champion.
A circus is like a mother in whom one can confide and who rewards
     and punishes.
I always try to improve, to find new ways of expressing myself, to
     keep looking for truth and originality.
I am interested in being in pictures that I would like to see.
I am reasonably happy, providing I keep busy.
I hate looking backward, but every once in a while it sneaks up on you.
I judge a restaurant by the bread and by the coffee.
I've always wanted to get an education, and tonight's as good a time as any.

### DOROTHEA LANGE (Photographer, 1895-1965)

One should really use the camera as though tomorrow you'd be stricken blind.
Photography takes an instant out of time, altering life by holding it still.
Pick a theme and work it to exhaustion... the subject must be something
     you truly love or truly hate.
While there is perhaps a province in which the photograph can tell us nothing
     more than what we see with our own eyes, there is another in
     which it proves to us how little our eyes permit us to see.
The camera is an instrument that teaches people how to see without a camera.
The best way to go into an unknown territory is to go in ignorant, ignorant as
     possible, with your mind wide open, as wide open as possible and not having
     to meet anyone else's requirement but my own.
Photographers stop photographing a subject too soon before they have
     exhausted the possibilities.

### ROBERT E. LEE (Soldier, 1807-1870)

I cannot trust a man to control others who cannot control himself.
It is good that war is so horrible, or we might grow to like it.
The devil's name is dullness.
The education of a man is never completed until he dies.
A true man of honor feels humbled himself when he
     cannot help humbling others.
Do your duty in all things. You cannot do more, you
     should never wish to do less.

Get correct views of life, and learn to see the world in its true
	light. It will enable you to live pleasantly, to do good,
		and, when summoned away, to leave without regret.
I like whiskey. I always did, and that is why I never drink it.
I think it better to do right, even if we suffer in so doing,
		than to incur the reproach of our consciences and posterity.
In all my perplexities and distresses, the Bible has never failed
		to give me light and strength.
My chief concern is to try to be an humble, earnest Christian.
Never do a wrong thing to make a friend or to keep one.
Obedience to lawful authority is the foundation of manly character

## ANNIE LEIBOVITZ (Photographer, 1949 - )
When I say I want to photograph someone, what it really means is
		that I'd like to know them. Anyone I know I photograph.
Sometimes I enjoy just photographing the surface because I think it
		can be as revealing as going to the heart of the matter.
A thing that you see in my pictures is that I was not afraid to fall in
		love with these people.
If it makes you cry, it goes in the show.
A very subtle difference can make the picture or not.
Computer photography won't be photography as we know it. I think
		photography will always be chemical.
I am impressed with what happens when someone stays in the same place
		and you took the same picture over and over and it would be
		different, every single frame.
I didn't want to let women down. One of the stereotypes I see breaking is
		the idea of aging and older women not being beautiful.
I still need the camera because it is the only reason anyone is talking to me.
My hope is that we continue to nurture the places that we love, but that
		we also look outside our immediate worlds.
Nature is so powerful, so strong. Capturing its essence is not easy -
		your work becomes a dance with light and the weather. It
		takes you to a place within yourself.
When you are younger, the camera is like a friend and you can go places
		and feel like you're with someone, like you have a companion.
When you go to take someone's picture, the first thing they say is, what
		you want me to do? Everyone is very awkward.
You don't have to sort of enhance reality. There is nothing stranger than truth.

## JAY LENO (Talk show Host, Comedian, 1950 - )
Here's something to think about: How come you never see a
		headline like 'Psychic Wins Lottery'?
I think high self-esteem is overrated. A little low self-esteem is actually quite
		good. Maybe you're not the best, so you should work a little harder.
According to the Mayans, the world is supposed to end in the
		year 2012. Are you buying that? When's the last time you
		even ran into a Mayan?
According to the latest poll, a record 73 percent of Americans think the country
		is headed in the wrong direction. But the good news: Gas is so
		expensive that we'll never get there.

According to New York publishers, Bill Clinton will get more money for his
    book than Hillary Clinton got for hers. Well, duh. At least
    his book has some sex in it.
Do you know what White House correspondents call actors who
    pose as reporters? Anchors.
Politics is just show business for ugly people.
For the first time ever, overweight people outnumber average people in
    America. Doesn't that make overweight the average then? Last month
    you were fat, now you're average - hey, let's get a pizza!
I went into a McDonald's yesterday and said, "I'd like some fries." The girl
    at the counter said, "Would you like some fries with that?"
If God doesn't destroy Hollywood Boulevard, he owes Sodom and
    Gomorrah an apology.
If God had wanted us to vote, he would have given us candidates.
If you don't want your dog to have bad breath, do what I do: Pour a
    little Lavoris in the toilet.
Nineteen percent of doctors say that they'd be able to give their patients a
    lethal injection. But they also went on to say that the patient would
The New England Journal of Medicine reports that 9 out of 10 doctors
    agree that 1 out of 10 doctors is an idiot.
The Supreme Court has ruled that they cannot have a nativity scene in
    Washington, D.C. This wasn't for any religious reasons. They
    couldn't find three wise men and a virgin.
The reason there are two senators for each state is so that one
    can be the designated driver.
You can't stay mad at somebody who makes you laugh.
You're not famous until my mother has heard of you
The University of Nebraska says that elderly people that drink beer or wine
    at least four times a week have the highest bone density. They
    need it - they're the ones falling down the most.
The Washington Bullets are changing their name. They don't want their team to be
    associated with crime. From now on, they'll just be known as the Bullets.
Give a man a fish and he will eat for a day. Teach a man to fish and he will eat
    for a lifetime. Teach a man to create an artificial shortage of fish and
    he will eat steak.
A new poll shows only 3 percent strongly approve of the job Congress is doing,
    with a margin of error of 4 percent, so it's possible that "less than
    no one thinks they're doing a good job.
Researchers found a frog in new guinea that is so tiny, they believe it's
    the smallest vertebrate on the planet. It has the tiniest backbone
    of any living creature, except members of Congress.
Scientists are complaining that the new Dinosaur movie shows dinosaurs with
    lemurs, who didn't evolve for another million years. They're afraid the
    movie will give kids a mistaken impression. What about the fact that the
    dinosaurs are singing and dancing?
Here's an uplifting story. Congratulations to the Little League team from Huntington
    Beach, California. Yeah, they beat Japan to win the Little
    League World Series. That's pretty good. See, that proves that when
    math and science aren't involved, our kids can beat anybody.
Britney Spears told an interviewer if she weren't famous, she would be a
    teacher. So thank God she's famous.

The good news is, the stock market is closed and it can't hurt
     us again until tomorrow.
Today is Valentine's Day - or, as men like to call it, Extortion Day!
A new study found that people who are depressed have a greater risk
     of stroke. Well that should cheer them up.
The new specialty at the Iowa fair this year is fried butter on a stick. Of
     course, if you're like me and you want like to eat healthy,
     get your stick of butter baked.
The Republican debate got pretty heated. They spent most of their
     time arguing over who God called first.
Scientists say that Texas and Antarctica were connected at one time. In fact,
     early Mexicans used to go through Texas to try to sneak into Antarctica.
Michele Bachmann said that if she is elected president, she would
     consider eliminating the Department of Education because "the states
     could do a gooder job."
China is now expected to surpass Japan as the 2nd richest country in the
     world. They could become the richest, but that's only if we pay
     them the money we owe them, and that's not going to happen.
There are 249 millionaires in Congress. Remember a couple of years ago
     when this new Congress told us they had the solution to the
     recession? Apparently, they didn't share it with the rest of us.
Denmark is charging a fat food tax on cheese, meat, and oil. Here, we
     call that the Denny's Grand Slam breakfast

## DAVID LETTERMAN (Talk Show Host, 1947 - )

Somebody threw a book at President Obama. If you're trying to scare a
     president by throwing a book at him, you're one president too late.
People say New Yorkers can't get along. Not true. I saw two New Yorkers,
     complete strangers, sharing a cab. One guy took the tires and the
     radio; the other guy took the engine.
President Bush has been silent on Schwarzenegger. Of course, he can't
     pronounce Schwarzenegger.
President Bush has said that he does not need approval from the UN to wage
     war, and I'm thinking, well, hell, he didn't need the approval of
     the American voters to become president, either.
President Bush says he needs a month off to unwind. Unwind? When
     the hell does this guy wind?
I'm just trying to make a smudge on the collective unconscious.
The White House is giving George W. Bush intelligence briefings. You
     know, some of these jokes just write themselves.
The worst tempered people I have ever met were those who
     knew that they were wrong.
Sarah Palin, part-time Governor of Alaska, is angry because Michele Obama
     is encouraging kids to eat healthy. Sarah Palin believes the
     government shouldn't tell us what to do. Sarah Palin
     believes she should tell us what to do.
They say there are about 12 million illegal immigrants in this country. But
     if you ask a Native American, that number is more like 300 million.
There is no off position on the genius switch.
There's no business like show business, but there are several
     businesses like accounting.

Traffic signals in New York are just rough guidelines.
USA Today has come out with a new survey - apparently, three out of
every four people make up 75% of the population.
I cannot sing, dance or act; what else would I be but a talk show host?
New York now leads the world's great cities in the number of people
around whom you shouldn't make a sudden move.
New York... when civilization falls apart, remember, we
were way ahead of you.
Next in importance to having a good aim is to recognize
when to pull the trigger.

## SINCLAIR LEWIS (Author, 1885-1951)

When fascism comes to America it will be wrapped in the flag and carrying a cross.
Intellectually I know that America is no better than any other country;
emotionally I know she is better than every other country.
What is love? It is the morning and the evening star.
Advertising is a valuable economic factor because it is the cheapest
way of selling goods, particularly if the goods are worthless.
People will buy anything that is 'one to a customer.'
The trouble with this country is that there are too many people going
about saying, "The trouble with this country is..."
When audiences come to see us authors lecture, it is largely in the
hope that we'll be funnier to look at than to read.
Damn the great executives, the men of measured merriment, damn the
men with careful smiles oh, damn their measured merriment.
Winter is not a season, it's an occupation.
Don't be a writer. Writing is an escape from something. You be a scientist.
Every compulsion is put upon writers to become safe, polite, obedient, and sterile.
He who has seen one cathedral ten times has seen something; he who has
seen ten cathedrals once has seen but little; and he who has spent
half an hour in each of a hundred cathedrals has seen nothing at all.
Our American professors like their literature clear and cold and
pure and very dead.
Pugnacity is a form of courage, but a very bad form.
The middle class, that prisoner of the barbarian 20th century.
There are two insults no human being will endure: that he has no
sense of humor, and that he has never known trouble.
Whatever poet, orator or sage may say of it, old age is still old age.

## CHARLES LINDBERGH (Pilot, Adventurer, 1902-1974)

Decades spent in contact with science and its vehicles have directed my mind and
senses to areas beyond their reach. I now see scientific accomplishments as
a path, not an end; a path leading to and disappearing in mystery. Science,
in fact, forms many paths branching from the trunk of human progress; and
on every periphery they end in the miraculous. Following these paths far
enough, one must eventually conclude that science itself is a miracle—like
the awareness of man arising from and then disappearing in the apparent
nothingness of space. Rather than nullifying religion and proving that 'God is
dead,' science enhances spiritual values by revealing the magnitudes and
minitudes—from cosmos to atom—through which man extends and
of which he is composed.

I owned the world that hour as I rode over it. free of the earth, free of the
        mountains, free of the clouds, but how inseparably I was bound to them.
Real freedom lies in wildness, not in civilization.
I have seen the science I worshiped, and the aircraft I loved,
        destroying the civilization I expected them to serve.
If I had to choose, I would rather have birds than airplanes.
In wilderness I sense the miracle of life, and behind it our
        scientific accomplishments fade to trivia.
Is he alone who has courage on his right hand and faith on his left hand?
Isn't it strange that we talk least about the things we think about most?
It is the greatest shot of adrenaline to be doing what you have wanted to do so
        badly. You almost feel like you could fly without the plane.
Life is a culmination of the past, an awareness of the present, an
        indication of a future beyond knowledge, the quality that gives
        a touch of divinity to matter.
Life is like a landscape. You live in the midst of it but can describe it
        only from the vantage point of distance.
Living in dreams of yesterday, we find ourselves still dreaming of
        impossible future conquests.
Man must feel the earth to know himself and recognize his values... God
        made life simple. It is man who complicates it.
To a person in love, the value of the individual is intuitively known. Love
        needs no logic for its mission.
If I were entering adulthood now instead of in the environment of fifty years ago, I
        would choose a career that kept me in touch with nature more than science.
        ... Too few natural areas remain; both by intent and by indifference we have
        insulated ourselves from the wilderness that produced us.
If we can combine our knowledge of science with the wisdom of wildness, if we
        can nurture civilization through roots in the primitive, man's potentialities
        appear to be unbounded, Through this evolving awareness, and his
        awareness of that awareness, he can emerge with the miraculous—to which
        we can attach what better name than 'God'? And in this merging, as long
        sensed by intuition but still only vaguely perceived by rationality, experience
        may travel without
Our emphasis on science has resulted in an alarming rise in world populations,
        the demand and ever-increasing emphasis of science to improve their
        standards and maintain their vigor. I have been forced to the conclusion
        that an over-emphasis of science weakens character and upsets life's
        essential balance.
Our survival, the future of our civilization, possibly the existence of
        mankind, depends on American leadership
Unless science is controlled by a greater moral force, it will become the
        Antichrist prophesied by the early Christians.
We are in the grip of a scientific materialism, caught in a vicious cycle where
        our security today seems to depend on regimentation and weapons
        which will ruin us tomorrow.
I grew up as a disciple of science. I know its fascination. I have felt the
        godlike power man derives from his machines.
Science intensifies religious truth by cleansing it of ignorance and superstition

## RUSH LIMBAUGH (Conservative Radio Commentator, 1951 - )

Being stuck is a position few of us like. We want something new but cannot let
go of the old - old ideas, beliefs, habits, even thoughts. We are out of
contact with our own genius. Sometimes we know we are stuck;
sometimes we don't. In both cases we have to DO something.

Character matters; leadership descends from character.

Compassion is no substitute for justice.

Feminism was established to allow unattractive women easier
access to the mainstream.

Football is like life and I know life.

I don't need equal time, I am equal time!

I must be honest. I can only read so many paragraphs of a
New York Times story before I puke.

I want anyone who believes in life, liberty, pursuit of happiness to succeed.
And I want any force, any person, any element of an overarching Big
Government that would stop your success, I want that organization,
that element or that person to fail. I want you to succeed.

If Thomas Jefferson thought taxation without representation was bad,
he should see how it is with representation.

If you commit a crime, you're guilty.
Let me tell you who we conservatives are: we love people. When we look out
over the United States of America, when we are anywhere, when we see
a group of people, such as this or anywhere, we see Americans. We see
human beings. We don't see groups. We don't see victims.

Liberal Democrats are inexorably opposed to tax cuts, because tax cuts give
people more power, and take away from the role of government.

Most people's historical perspective begins with the day of their birth.

No nation ever taxed itself into prosperity.

Poverty is not the root cause of crime.

Ronald Reagan was the greatest president of the twentieth century.

The Los Angeles riots were not caused by the Rodney King verdict. The
Los Angeles riots were caused by rioters.

The truth does not require a majority to prevail, ladies and gentlemen. The
truth is its own power. The truth will out. Never forget that.

There is one other business where the customer is always wrong and
that's the media.

There's a simple way to solve the crime problem: obey the
law; punish those who do not.

We are born to action; and whatever is capable of suggesting and
guiding action has power over us from the first.

We can take this country back. All we need is to nominate the right
candidate. It's no more complicated than that.

You could afford your house without the government if it
weren't for the government.

You know why there's a Second Amendment? In case the
government fails to follow the first one.

We want everybody to succeed. You know why? We want the country to succeed,
and for the country to succeed, its people - its individuals - must succeed.

## MAYA LIN (Architect, 1959 - )

It's funny, as you live through something you're not aware of it.

To me, the American Dream is being able to follow your own personal calling. To be able to do what you want to do is incredible freedom.

It's only in hindsight that you realize what indeed your childhood was really like.

A lot of my works deal with a passage, which is about time. I don't see anything that I do as a static object in space. It has to exist as a journey in time.

Growing up, I thought I was white. It didn't occur to me I was Asian-American until I was studying abroad in Denmark and there was a little bit of prejudice.

Nothing is ever guaranteed, and all that came before doesn't predicate what you might do next.

It's funny, as you live through something you're not aware of it.

It's only in hindsight that you realize what indeed your childhood was really like.

I went through withdrawal when I got out of graduate school. It's what you learn, what you think. That's all that counts.

I deliberately did not read anything about the Vietnam War because I felt the politics of the war eclipsed what happened to the veterans. The politics were irrelevant to what this memorial was.

OK, it was black, it was below grade, I was female, Asian American, young, too young to have served. Yet I think none of the opposition in that sense hurt me.

When I was building the Vietnam Memorial, I never once asked the veterans what it was like in the war, because from my point of view, you don't pry into other people's business.

I probably have fundamentally antisocial tendencies. I never took one extracurricular activity. I just failed utterly at that level. Part of me still rebels against that.

How we are using up our home, how we are living and polluting the planet is frightening. It was evident when I was a child. It's more evident now.

You have to let the viewers come away with their own conclusions. If you dictate what they should think, you've lost it.

All my work is much more peaceful than I am.

Art is very tricky because it's what you do for yourself. It's much harder for me to make those works than the monuments or the architecture.

Even though I build buildings and I pursue my architecture, I pursue it as an artist. I deliberately keep a tiny studio. I don't want to be an architectural firm. I want to remain an artist.

Every memorial in its time has a different goal.

For the most part things never get built the way they were drawn.

I didn't have anyone to play with so I made up my own world.

I had very few friends. We always ate dinner with our parents. We didn't want to go out. American adolescence was a lot wilder than I would have felt comfortable with.

I left science, then I went into art, but I approach things very analytically. I choose to pursue both art and architecture as completely separate fields rather than merging them.

I loved logic, math, computer programming. I loved systems and logic approaches. And so I just figured architecture is this perfect combination.

I probably spent the first 20 years of my life wanting to be as American as possible. Through my 20s, and into my 30s, I began to become aware of how so much of my art and architecture has a decidedly Eastern character.

I really enjoyed hanging out with some of the teachers. This one chemistry teacher,
        she liked hanging out. I liked making explosives. We would
        stay after school and blow things up.
I loved school. I studied like crazy. I was a Class A nerd.
I started studying what the nature of a monument is and what a monument
        should be. And for the World War III memorial I designed a futile,
        almost terrifying passage that ends nowhere.
It was a requirement by the veterans to list the 57,000 names. We're reaching
        a time that we'll acknowledge the individual in a war on a national level.
I try to give people a different way of looking at their
        surroundings. That's art to me.
I was always making things. Even though art was what I did every day, it
        didn't even occur to me that I would be an artist.
I was probably the first kid in my high school to go to Yale. I applied almost as
        a lark. Then, when I got there, I was the dumbest person in your class.
If we can't face death, we'll never overcome it. You have to look it straight in
        the eye. Then you can turn around and walk back out into the light.
It terrified me to have an idea that was solely mine to be no longer a part
        of my mind, but totally public.
Math, it's a puzzle to me. I love figuring out puzzles.
My dad was dean of fine arts at the university. I was casting bronzes in
        the school foundry. I was using the university as a playground.
My goal is to strip things down so that you need just the right amount of words or
        shape to convey what you need to convey. I like editing. I like it very tight.
My grandfather, on my father's side, helped to draft one of the first
        constitutions of China. He was a fairly well-known scholar.
My parents are both college professors, and it made me want to question
        authority, standards and traditions.
Our parents decided not to teach us Chinese. It was an era when they
        felt we would be better off if we didn't have that complication.
Some artists want to confront. Some want to invoke thought. They're all
        necessary and they're all valid.
Sometimes you have to stop thinking. Sometimes you shut down
        completely. I think that's true in any creative field.
The definition of a modern approach to war is the acknowledgment of
        individual lives lost.
The only thing that mattered was what you were to do in life, and it
        wasn't about money. It was about teaching, or learning.
The process I go through in the art and the architecture, I actually
        want it to be almost childlike. Sometimes I think it's magical.
The role of art in society differs for every artist.
We were unusually brought up; there was no gender differentiation. I
        was never thought of as any less than my brother.
When I was very little, we would get letters from China, in Chinese,
        and they' be censored. We were a very insular little family.
You couldn't put me in a social group setting. I'm probably a terrible
        anarchist deep down.
You have to have conviction and completely question everything and anything
        you do. No matter how much you study, no matter how much you know, the
        side of your brain that has the smarts won't necessarily help you
        in making art.

You should be having more fun in high school, exploring things because you
  want to explore them and learning because you love learning-not
  worrying about competition.
To fly we have to have resistance.


## ABRAHAM LINCOLN (President, 1809-1865)

A friend is one who has the same enemies as you have.
A house divided against itself cannot stand.
All my life I have tried to pluck a thistle and plant a flower wherever
  the flower would grow in thought and mind.
Allow the president to invade a neighboring nation, whenever he shall deem
  it necessary to repel an invasion, and you allow him to do so whenever
  he may choose to say he deems it necessary for such a purpose - and
  you allow him to make war at pleasure.
Always bear in mind that your own resolution to succeed is more
  important than any other.
Am I not destroying my enemies when I make friends of them?
America will never be destroyed from the outside. If we falter and lose
  our freedoms, it will be because we destroyed ourselves.
Any people anywhere, being inclined and having the power, have the right to
  rise up, and shake off the existing government, and form a new one
  that suits them better. This is a most valuable - a most sacred right -
  a right, which we hope and believe, is to liberate the world.
As I  would not be a slave, so I would not be a master. This expresses
  my idea of democracy.
As our case is new, we must think and act anew.
Avoid popularity if you would have peace.
Ballots are the rightful and peaceful successors to bullets.
Be sure you put your feet in the right place, then stand firm.
Better to remain silent and be thought a fool than to
  speak out and remove all doubt.
Books serve to show a man that those original thoughts of
  his aren't very new at all.
Character is like a tree and reputation like a shadow. The shadow
  is what we think of it; the tree is the real thing.
Common looking people are the best in the world: that  is the
  reason the Lord makes so many of them.
Discourage litigation. Persuade your neighbors to compromise whenever you
  can. As a peacemaker the lawyer has superior opportunity of being a
  good man. There will still be business enough.
Don't interfere with anything in the Constitution. That must be
  maintained, for  it is the only safeguard of our liberties.
Don't worry when you are not recognized, but strive to be worthy of recognition.
Every man is said to have his peculiar ambition. Whether it be true or not, I can
  say for one that I have no other so great as that of being truly esteemed
  of my fellow men, by rendering myself worthy of their esteem.
Every one desires to live long, but no one would be old.
Everybody likes a compliment.
Give me six hours to chop down a tree and I will
  spend the first four sharpening the axe.
God must love the common man, he made so many of them.

Government of the people, by the people, for the people, shall
    not perish from the Earth.
He has a right to criticize, who has a heart to help.
Hold on with a bulldog grip, and chew and choke as much as possible.
I am a firm believer in the people. If given the truth, they can be depended upon
    to meet any national crisis. The great point is to bring them the real facts.
I am not bound to win, but I am bound to be true. I am not bound to succeed,
    but I am bound to live by the light that I have. I must stand with
    anybody that stands right, and stand with him while he is right, and
    part with him when he goes wrong.
I can make more generals, but horses cost money.
I care not much for a man's religion whose dog and cat are not the better for it.
I do not think much of a man who is not wiser today than he was yesterday.
I do the very best I know how - the very best I can; and I mean to keep
    on doing so until the end.
I don't know who my grandfather was; I am much more concerned to
    know what his grandson will be.
I don't like that man. I must get to know him better.
I have always found that mercy bears richer fruits than strict justice.
I like to see a man proud of the place in which he lives. I like to see a
    man live so that his place will be proud of him.
I never had a policy; I have just tried to do my very best each and every day.
I will prepare and some day my chance will come.
I'm a slow walker, but I never walk back.
If I were to try to read, much less answer, all the attacks made on
    me, this shop might as well be closed for any other business.
If I were two-faced, would I be wearing this one?
If once you forfeit the confidence of your fellow-citizens, you can never
    regain their respect and esteem.
If there is anything that a man can do well, I say let him do it. Give him a chance.
If you look for the bad in people expecting to find it, you surely will.
In great contests each party claims to act in accordance with the will
    of God. Both may be, and one must be wrong.
In the end, it's not the years in your life that count. It's the life in your years.
It has been my experience that folks who have no vices have very few virtues.
It is better to remain silent and be thought a fool than to open one's
    mouth and remove all doubt.
Knavery and flattery are blood relations.
Labor is prior to, and independent of, capital. Capital is only the fruit of labor,
    and could never have existed if labor had not first existed. Labor is the
    superior of capital, and deserves much the higher consideration.
Let not him who is houseless pull down the house of another, but let him work
    diligently and build one for himself, thus by example assuring
    that his own shall be safe from violence when built.
Lets have faith that right makes might; and in that faith let us, to the
    end, dare to do our duty as we understand it.
Marriage is neither heaven nor hell, it is simply purgatory.
My dream is of a place and a time where America will once again be
    seen as the last best hope of earth.
My great concern is not whether you have failed, but whether you are
    content with your failure.

Nearly all men can stand adversity, but if you want to test a man's
    character, give him power.
Important principles may, and must, be inflexible.
Never stir up litigation. A worse man can scarcely be found than one who does this.
No man has a good enough memory to be a successful liar.
No man is good enough to govern another man without that other's consent.
No matter how much cats fight, there always seem to be plenty of kittens.
People are just as happy as they make up their minds to be.
Some single mind must be master, else there will be no agreement in anything.
Stand with anybody that stands right, stand with him while he is right
    and part with him when he goes wrong.
Surely God would not have created such a being as man, with an ability to grasp the
    infinite, to exist only for a day! No, no, man was made for immortality.
Tact is the ability to describe others as they see themselves.
That some achieve great success, is proof to all that others can achieve it as well.
The assertion that "all men are created equal" was of no practical use in
    effecting our separation from Great Britain and it was placed in the
    Declaration not for that, but for future use.
The ballot is stronger than the bullet.
The best thing about the future is that it comes one day at a time.
The best way to get a bad law repealed is to enforce it strictly.
The people themselves, and not their servants, can safely
    reverse their own deliberate decisions.
The people will save their government, if the government itself will allow them.
The philosophy of the school room in one generation will be the
    philosophy of government in the next.
The probability that we may fail in the struggle ought not to deter us
    from the support of a cause we believe to be just.
The shepherd drives the wolf from the sheep's for which the sheep thanks the
    shepherd as his liberator, while the wolf denounces him for the same
    act as the destroyer of liberty. Plainly, the sheep and the wolf
    are not agreed upon a definition of liberty.
The things I want to know are in books; my best friend is the
    man who'll get me a book I ain't read.
The way for a young man to rise is to improve himself in every way
    he can, never suspecting that anybody wishes to hinder him.
There is another old poet whose name I do not now remember who
    said, "Truth is the daughter of Time."
There is nothing true anywhere, The true is nowhere to be seen; If you
    say you see the true, This seeing is not the true one.
These capitalists generally act harmoniously and in concert, to fleece the people.
Things may come to those who wait, but only the things left by those who hustle.
Those who deny freedom to others deserve it not for themselves.
To give victory to the right, not bloody bullets, but peaceful
    ballots only, are necessary.
To stand in silence when they should be protesting makes cowards out of men.
Towering genius disdains a beaten path. It seeks regions hitherto unexplored.
We should be too big to take offense and too noble to give it.
We the people are the rightful masters of both Congress and the
    courts, not to overthrow the Constitution but to overthrow
    the men who pervert the Constitution.

What kills a skunk is the publicity it gives itself.
Whatever you are, be a good one.
The time comes upon every public man when it is best for his lips closed.
When I am getting ready to reason with a man, I spend one-third of my time
thinking about myself and what I am going to say and two-thirds
about him and what he is going to say.
When I do good, I feel good. When I do bad, I feel bad. That's my religion.
When I hear a man preach, I like to see him act as if he were fighting bees.
When you have got an elephant by the hind legs and he is trying to run
away, it's best to let him run.
Whenever I hear anyone arguing for slavery, I feel a strong impulse
to see it tried on him personally.
You can fool all the people some of the time, and some of the people
all the time, but you cannot fool all the people all the time.
You cannot build character and courage by taking away a man's
initiative and independence.
You cannot escape the responsibility of tomorrow by evading it today.
You cannot help men permanently by doing for them what they
could and should do for themselves.
You have to do your own growing no matter how tall your grandfather was.

## HAROLD LLOYD (Actor [silent film era], 1893-1971)
Comedy comes from inside. It comes from your face. It
comes from your body.
I do not believe the public will want spoken comedy. Motion pictures
and the spoken arts are two distinct arts.
My humor was never cruel or cynical. I just took life and poked fun at it.
We made it so it could be understood the world over, without
language barriers. We seem to have conquered the time
barrier, too. [comments in 1970]
At a cost of 75 cents they provide a trademark recognized instantly
wherever pictures are shown. [discussing his horn-rimmed glasses].

## JAMES RUSSELL LOWELL (Poet, 1819-1891)
One thorn of experience is worth a whole wilderness of warning.
True scholarship consists in knowing not what things exist, but what
they mean; it is not memory but judgment.
Toward no crimes have men shown themselves so cold- bloodedly
cruel as in punishing differences of belief.
Usually when people are sad, they don't do anything.
They just cry over their condition. But when they get angry,
they bring about a change.
What a sense of security in an old book which time has criticized for us.
As life runs on, the road grows strange with faces new - and near the end.
The milestones into headstones change, Neath every one a friend.
Blessed are they who have nothing to say and who cannot be persuaded to say it.
Books are the bees which carry the quickening pollen from one to another mind.
Poetry is something to make us wiser and better, by continually revealing
those types of beauty and truth, which God has set in all men's souls.
Good luck is the willing handmaid of a upright and
energetic character, and conscientious observance of duty.

The foolish and the dead alone never change their opinions.
The greatest homage we can pay to truth, is to use it.
The eye is the notebook of the poet.
Where one person shapes their life by precept and example,
    there are a thousand who have shaped it by
    impulse and circumstances.
Mishaps are like knives, that either serve us or cut us,
    as we grasp them by the blade or the handle.
No man can produce great things who is not thoroughly
    sincere in dealing with himself.
Truth, after all, wears a different face to everybody, and it
    would be too tedious to wait till all were agreed.
What men prize most is a privilege, even if it
    be that of chief mourner at a funeral.
Reputation is only a candle, of wavering and uncertain
    flame, and easily blown out, but it is the light by
    which the world looks for and finds merit.
Sincerity is impossible, unless it pervade the whole being,
    and the pretense of it saps the very foundation of character.
Solitude is as needful to the imagination as society
    is wholesome for the character.
Thank God every morning when you get up that
    you have something to do that day, which must
    be done, whether you like it or not.
The heart forgets its sorrow and ache.
The mind can weave itself warmly in the cocoon of its own
    thoughts, and dwell a hermit anywhere.
The only faith that wears well and holds its color in
    all weathers is that which is woven of conviction and set
    with the sharp mordant of experience.
There are two kinds of weakness, that which breaks and that which bends.
There is no good in arguing with the inevitable. The only
    argument available with an east wind is to put on your overcoat.
There is nothing so desperately monotonous as the sea,
    and I no longer wonder at the cruelty of pirates.
To educate the intelligence is to expand the
    horizon of its wants and desires.
A weed is no more than a flower in disguise, Which is
    seen through at once, if love give a man eyes.
All the beautiful sentiments in the world weigh less than a single lovely action.
Fortune is the rod of the weak, and the staff of the brave.
Freedom is the only law which genius knows.
Greatly begin. Though thou have time,
    but for a line, be that sublime. Not failure, but low aim is crime.
He who is firmly seated in authority soon learns to think security,
    and not progress, the highest lesson in statecraft.
I have always been of the mind that in a democracy
    manners are the only effective weapons against the bowie-knife.
If youth be a defect, it is one that we outgrow only too soon.
In creating, the only hard thing is to begin: a grass blade's
    no easier to make than an oak.

In the ocean of baseness, the deeper we get, the easier the sinking.
Incredulity robs us of many pleasures, and gives us nothing in return.
It is by presence of mind in untried emergencies that the
      native metal of man is tested.
It is the privilege of genius that life never grows
      common place, as it does for the rest of us.
Joy comes, grief goes, we know not how.
Let us be of good cheer, however, remembering that the
      misfortunes hardest to bear are those which never come.
Light is the symbol of truth.
Not failure, but low aim, is crime.
On one issue at least, men and women agree; they both distrust women.
Once to every person and nation come the moment to decide.
      In the conflict of truth with falsehood, for the good or evil side.
An appeal to the reason of the people has never been
      known to fail in the long run.
And what is so rare as a day in June? Then, if ever, come perfect days.
Children are God's Apostles, sent forth, day by day, to preach
      of love, and hope, and peace.
Compromise makes a good umbrella, but a poor roof;
      it is temporary expedient, often wise in party politics,
      almost sure to be unwise in statesmanship.
Creativity is not the finding of a thing, but the making something
      out of it after it is found.
Death is delightful. Death is dawn, The waking from a weary night Of
      fevers unto truth and light.
Democracy gives every man the right to be his own oppressor.
Each day the world is born anew for him who takes it rightly.
Endurance is the crowning quality, And patience all the
      passion of great hearts.
Every man feels instinctively that all the beautiful sentiments in the
      world weigh less than a single lovely action.
Fate loves the fearless.
Folks never understand the folks they hate.

## DOUGLAS MACARTHUR (Soldier, 1880-1964)

A better world shall emerge based on faith and understanding.
A general is just as good or just as bad as the troops under his
      command make him.
Age wrinkles the body. Quitting wrinkles the soul.
Always there has been some terrible evil at home or some monstrous
      foreign power that was going to gobble us up if we did not
      blindly rally behind it.
Could I have but a line a century hence crediting a contribution to
      the advance of peace, I would yield every honor which has
      been accorded by war.
Duty, Honor, Country. Those three hallowed words reverently dictate
      what you ought to be, what you can be, what you will be.
I am concerned for the security of our great Nation; not so much because
      of any threat from without, but because of the insidious forces
      working from within.

I have just returned from visiting the Marines at the front, and there is
      not a finer fighting organization in the world!

I have known war as few men now living know it. It's very destructiveness
      on both friend and foe has rendered it useless as a means of settling
      international disputes.

I've looked that old scoundrel death in the eye many times but this time
      I think he has me on the ropes.

In my dreams I hear again the crash of guns, the rattle of musketry,
      the strange, mournful mutter of the battlefield.
      Americans never quit.

In war there is no substitute for victory.

In war, you win or lose, live or die - and the difference is just an eyelash.

It is fatal to enter any war without the will to win it.

It is part of the general pattern of misguided policy that our country is
      now geared to an arms economy which was bred in an artificially
      induced psychosis of war hysteria and nurtured upon an
      incessant propaganda of fear.

Life is a lively process of becoming.

My first recollection is that of a bugle call.

Never give an order that can't be obeyed.

Old soldiers never die; they just fade away.

One cannot wage war under present conditions without the support
      of public opinion, which is tremendously molded by the press
      and other forms of propaganda.

Only those are fit to live who are not afraid to die.

Our government has kept us in a perpetual state of fear - kept us in
      a continuous stampede of patriotic fervor - with the cry of
      grave national emergency.

Part of the American dream is to live long and die young. Only those
      Americans who are willing to die for their country are fit to live.

The best luck of all is the luck you make for yourself.

The soldier above all others prays for peace, for it is the soldier who
      must suffer and bear the deepest wounds and scars of war.

The world is in a constant conspiracy against the brave. It's the age-old
      struggle: the roar of the crowd on the one side, and the voice of
      your conscience on the other.

There is no security on this earth; there is only opportunity.

They died hard, those savage men - like wounded wolves at bay.
      They were filthy, and they were lousy, and they stunk.
      And I loved them.

We are not retreating - we are advancing in another direction.

You are remembered for the rules you break.

## JAMES MADISON (President, 1751-1836)

In no instance have... the churches been guardians of the
      liberties of the people.

Religious bondage shackles and debilitates the mind and
      unfits it for every noble enterprise, every
      expanded prospect.

The advancement and diffusion of knowledge is the only
      guardian of true liberty.

The purpose of separation of church and state is to keep
     forever from these shores the ceaseless strife that
     has soaked the soil of Europe with blood for centuries.
The truth is that all men having power ought to be mistrusted.
The means of defense against foreign danger historically
     have become the instruments of tyranny at home.
And I have no doubt that every new example will succeed,
     as every past one has done, in showing that religion
     and Government will both exist in greater purity, the
     less they are mixed together.
Philosophy is common sense with big words.
The capacity of the female mind for studies of the highest
     order cannot be doubted, having been
     sufficiently  illustrated by its works of genius, of
     erudition, and of science.
The circulation of confidence is better than the
     circulation of money.
Religion flourishes in greater purity, without than with
     the aid of Government.
The number, the industry, and the morality of the priesthood,
     and the devotion of the people have been manifestly
     increased by the total separation of the church
     from the state.
The people are the only legitimate fountain of power, and
     it is from them that the constitutional charter, under
     which the several branches of government hold their
     power, is derived.
The happy Union of these States is a wonder; their Constitution
     a miracle; their example the hope of Liberty throughout
     the world.
A well-instructed people alone can be permanently a free people.
All men having power ought to be distrusted to a certain degree.
It is a universal truth that the loss of liberty at home is to be charged to
     the provisions against danger, real or pretended, from abroad.
It will be of little avail to the people that the laws are made by men of
     their own choice if the laws be so voluminous that they cannot be
     read, or so incoherent that they cannot be understood.
Knowledge will forever govern ignorance; and a people who mean to be
     their own governors must arm themselves with the power which
     knowledge gives.
I believe there are more instances of the abridgement of freedom of the
     people by gradual and silent encroachments by those in power
     than by violent and sudden usurpations.
I have no doubt but that the misery of the lower classes will be found to
     abate whenever the Government assumes a freer aspect and the
     laws favor a subdivision of Property.
If Tyranny and Oppression come to this land, it will be in
     the guise of fighting a foreign enemy.
If we are to take for the criterion of truth the majority of suffrages,
     they ought to be gotten from those philosophic and patriotic
     citizens who cultivate their reason.

In framing a government which is to be administered by men over men you
must first enable the government to control the governed; and in the
next place oblige it to control itself.
I should not regret a fair and full trial of the entire abolition of capital punishment.
In Republics, the great danger is, that the majority may not sufficiently
respect the rights of the minority.
Learned Institutions ought to be favorite objects with every free people.
They throw that light over the public mind which is the best security
against crafty and dangerous encroachments on the public liberty.
If men were angels, no government would be necessary.
Let me recommend the best medicine in the world: a long journey, at a
mild season, through a pleasant country, in easy stages.
Liberty may be endangered by the abuse of liberty, but also by the
abuse of power.
No nation could preserve its freedom in the midst of continual warfare.
Of all the enemies of public liberty, war is perhaps the most to be
dreaded, because it comprises and develops the germ of every other.
I must not write a word to you about politics, because you are a woman.
I must study politics and war that my sons may have liberty to study
mathematics and philosophy.
If we do not lay out ourselves in the service of
mankind whom should we serve?
Let us tenderly and kindly cherish, therefore, the means of knowledge.
Let us dare to read, think, speak, and write.
Liberty cannot be preserved without general knowledge among the people
To suppose that any form of government will secure
liberty or happiness without any virtue in the
people, is a chimerical idea.
To the press alone, chequered as it is with abuses, the world is
indebted  for all the triumphs which have been gained
by reason and humanity over error and oppression.
Union of religious sentiments begets a surprising confidence.
War contains so much folly, as well as wickedness, that much
is to be hoped from the progress of reason.
War should only be declared by the authority of the people,
whose toils and treasures are to support its burdens,
instead of the government which is to reap its fruits.
We are right to take alarm at the first experiment upon our liberties.
What prudent merchant will hazard his fortunes in any new
branch of commerce when he knows not that his plans
may be rendered unlawful before they can be executed?
What spectacle can be more edifying or more seasonable, than
that of Liberty and Learning, each leaning on the other
for their mutual and surest support?
Whenever a youth is ascertained to possess talents meriting
an education which his parents cannot afford, he should
be carried forward at the public expense.
Where an excess of power prevails, property of no sort is duly
respected. No man is safe in his opinions, his person,
his faculties, or his possessions.
Wherever there is interest and power to do wrong, wrong will generally be done.

A man has a property in his opinions and the free communication of them.
A popular government without popular information or the means
of acquiring it, is but a prologue to a farce, or a tragedy, or perhaps both.
A pure democracy is a society consisting of a small number of citizens, who
assemble and administer the government in person.
A well regulated militia, composed of the body of the  people, trained in arms,
is the best most natural defense of a free country.
Ambition must be made to counteract ambition.
In politics the middle way is none at all.
America was indebted to immigration for her settlement and prosperity. That
part of America which had encouraged  them most had advanced most
rapidly in population, agriculture and the arts.
As a man is said to have a right to his property, he may be
equally said to have a property in his rights.
As long as the reason of man continues fallible, and he is at
liberty to exercise it, different opinions will be formed.
By rendering the labor of one, the property of the other, they cherish pride, luxury,
and vanity on one side; on the other, vice and servility, or hatred and revolt.
Commercial shackles are generally unjust, oppressive, and impolitic.
Despotism can only exist in darkness, and there are too many lights now in the
political firmament to permit it to remain anywhere, as it has heretofore
done, almost everywhere.
Do not separate text from historical background. If you do, you will have
perverted and subverted the Constitution, which can only end in a
distorted, bastardized form of illegitimate government.
Each generation should be made to bear the burden of its own wars, instead of
carrying them on, at the expense of other generations.
The class of citizens who provide at once their own food and their own raiment,
may be viewed as the most truly independent and happy.
The Constitution preserves the advantage of being armed which Americans
possess over the people of almost every other nation where the
governments are afraid to trust the people with arms.
The essence of Government is power; and power, lodged as it
must be in human hands, will ever be liable to abuse.
The executive has no right, in any case, to decide the question,
whether there is or is not cause for declaring war.
The internal effects of a mutable policy poisons the blessings of liberty itself.
The personal right to acquire property, which is a natural  right, gives to
property, when acquired, a right to protection, as a social right.

## BILL MAHER (Talk Show Host, Comedian, 1956 - )
If you think you have it tough, read history books.
We have the Bill of Rights. What we need is a Bill of Responsibilities.
Things aren't right. If a burglar breaks into your home and you shoot
him, he can sue you. For what, restraint of trade?
I think flying planes into a building was a faith-based initiative. I think
religion is a neurological disorder.
We are a nation that is unenlightened because of religion. I do believe that. I
think religion stops people from thinking. I think it justified crazies.
We need more people speaking out. This country is not overrun with
rebels and free thinkers. It's overrun with sheep and conformists.

Women cannot complain about men anymore until they start
getting better taste in them.
Clinton left the White House with all the class of an XFL halftime show.
Curious people are interesting people, I wonder why that is.
To me a real patriot is like a real friend. Who's your real friend? It's the person
who tells you the truth. That's who my real friends are. So, you know, I
think as far as our country goes, we need more people who will do that.
What Democratic congressmen do to their women staffers, Republican
congressmen do to the country.
Everything that used to be a sin is now a disease.
Religion, to me, is a bureaucracy between man and God that I don't need.
Suicide is man's way of telling God, "You can't fire me - I quit."
The Bible looks like it started out as a game of Mad Libs.
The Clinton White House today said they would start to give national security
and intelligence briefings to George Bush. I don't know how well this is
working out. Today after the first one Bush said, 'I've got one question:
What color isthe red phone?'
The country has become much more conservative, partly because it's
been taken over by the religious right.
The tea baggers. The one thing they hate is when you call them racist. The
other thing they hate is black people. But they won't say it.
They're talking about banning cigarette smoking now in any place that's used
by ten or more people in a week, which, I guess, means that Madonna
can't even smoke in bed.
This has been a learning experience for me. I also thought that privacy was
something we were granted in the Constitution. I have learned from this
when in fact the word privacy does not appear in the Constitution.
This is a ridiculous heat wave we're in right now, and to contribute, Newt Gingrich
said that for the entire month of June, he will stop blowing hot air.
We have been the cowards lobbing cruise missiles from 2,000 miles away. That's
cowardly. Staying in the airplane when it hits the building, say what you
want about it, it's not cowardly.
When you want to make it clear to the rest of the world that you are not an
imperialist, the best countries to have with you are Britain and Spain.
Whenever the people are for gay marriage or medical marijuana or assisted
suicide, suddenly the "will of the people" goes out the window.
Fame has sent a number of celebrities off the deep end, and in the case
of Michael Jackson, to the kiddy pool.
Hi, I'm Bill. I'm a birth survivor.
I do think the patriotic thing to do is to critique my country. How else do you
make a country better but by pointing out its flaws?
I don't want my president to be a TV star. You don't have to be on television
every minute of every day - you're the president, not a rerun of
'Law & Order'. TV stars are too worried bout being popular and too
concerned about being renewed.
I never thought I'd say this, what Obama needs in his personality
is a little George Bush.
I think capital punishment works great. Every killer you kill never kills again.
It's all been satirized for your protection.
Jim Bakker spells his name with two k's because three would be too obvious.
Kids. They're not easy. But there has to be some penalty for sex.

Let's face it; God has a big ego problem. Why do we always have to worship him?

Maybe every other American movie shouldn't be based on a comic book. Other
countries will think Americans live in an infantile fantasy land where reality is
whatever we say it is and every problem can be solved with violence.

Men are only as loyal as their options.

## BERNARD MALAMUD (Author, 1914-1986)

A writer is a spectator, looking at everything with a highly critical eye.

I work with language. I love the flowers of afterthought.

If you ever forget you're a Jew, a Gentile will remind you.

Life is a tragedy full of joy.

Revision is one of the exquisite pleasures of writing.

The idea is to get the pencil moving quickly.

There comes a time in a man's life when to get where he has to go -
if there are no doors or windows he walks through a wall.

Those who write about life, reflect about life. you see in others who you are.

We have two lives the one we learn with and the life we live after that.

Without heroes, we are all plain people and don't know how far we can go.

## PEYTON MANNING (Athlete, 1976 - )

Pressure is something you feel when you don't know what the hell you're doing.

You hear about how many fourth quarter comebacks that a guy has and I
think it means a guy screwed up in the first three quarters.

## GEORGE C. MARSHALL (Soldier, 1880-1959)

Don't fight the problem, decide it.

If man does find the solution for world peace it will be the most
revolutionary reversal of his record we have ever known.

When a thing is done, it's done. Don't look back. Look forward to
your next objective.

## THURGOOD MARSHALL (Supreme Court Justice, 1908-1993)

Sometimes history takes things into its own hands.

None of us got where we are solely by pulling ourselves up by our bootstraps.
We got here because somebody - a parent, a teacher, an Ivy League crony
or a few nuns - bent down and helped us pick up our boots.

What is the quality of your intent?  Certain people have a way of saying things that
shake us at the core. Even when the words do not seem harsh or offensive,
the impact is shattering. What we could be experiencing is the intent behind
the words. When we intend to do good, we do. When we intend to do harm,
it happens. What each of us must come to realize is that our intent always
comes through. We cannot sugarcoat the feelings in our heart of hearts. The
emotion is the energy that motivates. We cannot ignore what we really want
to create. We should be honest and do it the way we feel it. What we owe to
ourselves and everyone around is to examine the reasons of our true intent.
My intent will be evident in the results.

In recognizing the humanity of our fellow beings, we pay ourselves
the highest tribute.

If the 1st Amendment means anything, it means that a state has no business telling
a man, sitting alone in his own house, what books he may read or what films
he may watch.

Mere access to the courthouse doors does not by itself assure a proper functioning
	of the adversary process.
Our whole constitutional heritage rebels at the thought of giving government the
	power to control men's minds.
Surely the fact that a uniformed police officer is wearing his hair below his collar will
	make him no less identifiable as a policeman.
Today's Constitution is a realistic document of freedom only because of several
	corrective amendments. Those amendments speak to a sense of decency and
	fairness that I and other Blacks cherish.
A child born to a Black mother in a state like Mississippi... has exactly the same
	rights as a white baby born to the wealthiest person in the United States.
	It's not true, but I challenge anyone to say it is not a goal worth working for.
If the First Amendment means anything, it means that a state has no business
	telling a man, sitting alone in his house, what books he may read
	or what films he may watch.
Ending racial discrimination in jury selection can be accomplished only by
	eliminating peremptory challenges entirely.

## STEVE MARTIN (Actor, Comedian, 1945 - )

A day without sunshine is like, you know, night.
Boy, those French: they have a different word for everything!
Chaos in the midst of chaos isn't funny, but chaos in the midst of order is.
Comedy may be big business but it isn't pretty.
Don't have sex man. It leads to kissing and pretty soon
	you have to start talking to them.
Hosting the Oscars is much like making love to a woman. It's something I
	only get to do when Billy Crystal is out of town.
I believe entertainment can aspire to be art, and can become art, but
	if you set out to make art you're an idiot.
I believe Ronald Reagan can make this country what it once was... a
	large Arctic region covered with ice.
I believe that sex is one of the most beautiful, natural, wholesome
	things that money can buy.
I like a woman with a head on her shoulders. I hate necks.
I think I did pretty well, considering I started out with nothing but
	a bunch of blank paper.
I've got to keep breathing. It'll be my worst business mistake if I don't.
Love is a promise delivered already broken.
Talking about music is like dancing about architecture.
The real joy is in constructing a sentence. But I see myself as an actor first
	because writing is what you do when you are ready and acting is what
	you do when someone else is ready.
There is one thing I would break up over, and that is if she caught me with
	another woman. I won't stand for that.
Well, excuuuuuse me!
What is comedy? Comedy is the art of making people laugh
	without making them puke.
When your hobbies get in the way of your work - that's OK; but when
	your hobbies get in the way of themselves... well.
You know what your problem is, it's that you haven't seen enough
	movies - all of life's riddles are answered in the movies.

## LEE MARVIN (Actor, 1924-1987)

I only make movies to finance my fishing.

Ah, stardom! They put your name on a star in the sidewalk on Hollywood Boulevard and you walk down and find a pile of dog manure on it. That tells the whole story, baby.

I love Marlon Brando. Never seem him bad, just less good.

Tequila. Straight. There's a real polite drink. You keep drinking until you finally take one more and it just won't go down. Then you know you've reached your limit.

Stimulation? Thursdays. Motivation? Thursdays. Paydays. That`s it. It`s important not to think too much about what you do. You see, with my way of thinking there are always Thursdays -- no matter how the picture works out.

There was that very credible virility of guys like Spencer Tracy or Humphrey Bogart. I don`t think that I could one day resemble them, but in life and in movies I profoundly admired Bogart, both personally and professionally.

If I have any appeal at all, it`s to the fellow who takes out the garbage.

The beauty of that man. He`s so still. He`s moving and yet he`s not moving. [about Robert Mitchum]

## GROUCHO MARX (Actor, Comedian, 1890-1977 )

I intend to live forever, or die trying.

The secret of life is honesty and fair dealing. If you can fake that, you've got it made.

I must confess, I was born at a very early age.

There's one way to find out if a man is honest - ask him. If he says, "Yes," you know he is a crook.

Quote me as saying I was mis-quoted.

I, not events, have the power to make me happy or unhappy today. I can choose which it shall be. Yesterday is dead, tomorrow hasn't arrived yet. I have just one day, today, and I'm going to be happy in it.

I find television very educating. Every time somebody turns on the set, I go into the other room and read a book.

I never forget a face, but in your case I'll be glad to make an exception.

I worked my way up from nothing to a state of extreme poverty.

Those are my principles, and if you don't like them... well, I have others.

Outside of a dog, a book is man's best friend. Inside of a dog it's too dark to read.

Money frees you from doing things you dislike. Since I dislike doing nearly everything, money is handy.

From the moment I picked up your book until I laid it down, I was convulsed with laughter. Some day I intend reading it.

My favorite poem is the one that starts 'Thirty days hath September' because it actually tells you something.

Age is not a particularly interesting subject. Anyone can get old. All you have to do is live long enough.

Either this man is dead or my watch has stopped.

Why should I care about posterity? What's posterity ever done for me?

Why, I'd horse-whip you if I had a horse.

Wives are people who feel they don't dance enough.

I never forget a face, but in your case I'll be glad to make an exception.

I've had a perfectly wonderful evening. But this wasn't it.
Who are you going to believe, me or your own eyes?
Whoever  named it necking was a poor judge of anatomy
It isn't necessary to have relatives in Kansas City in order to be unhappy.
Military intelligence is a contradiction in terms.
Military justice is to justice what military music is to music.
My mother loved children -- she would have given anything if I had been one.
The first thing which I can record concerning myself is, that I was born. These
	are wonderful words. This life, to which neither time nor eternity can
	bring diminution - this everlasting living soul, began. My mind loses
	itself in these depths.
Politics is the art of looking for trouble, finding it everywhere,
	diagnosing it incorrectly and applying the wrong remedies.
Practically everybody in New York has half a mind to write a book, and does.
She got her looks from her father. He's a plastic surgeon.
Next time I see you, remind me not to talk to you.
No man goes before his time - unless the boss leaves early.
One morning I shot an elephant in my pajamas. How he got into my
	pajamas I'll never know.
Time flies like an arrow. Fruit  flies like a banana.
A child of five would understand this. Send someone to fetch a child of five.
Women should be obscene and not heard.
A black cat crossing your path signifies that the animal is going somewhere.
A man's only as old as the woman he feels.
A woman is an occasional pleasure but a cigar is always a smoke.
Alimony  is like buying hay for a dead horse.
All people are born alike - except Republicans and Democrats.
Anyone who says he can see through women is missing a lot.
Before I speak, I have something important to say.
Behind every successful man is a woman, behind her is his wife.
Humor is reason gone mad.
I didn't like the play, but then I saw it under adverse
	conditions - the curtain was up.
I read in the newspapers they are going to have 30 minutes of intellectual
	stuff on television every Monday from 7:30 to 8. to educate America.
	They couldn't educate America if they started at 6:30.
I remember the first time I had sex - I kept the receipt.
I was married by a judge. I should have asked for a jury.
I wish to be cremated. One tenth of my ashes shall be given to my
	agent, as written in our contract.
I'm not feeling very well - I need a doctor immediately. Ring the
	nearest golf course.
I've got the brain of a four year old. I'll bet he was glad to be rid of it.
If you've heard this story before, don't stop me, because I'd like to hear it again.
In Hollywood, brides keep the bouquets and throw away the groom.

## ANTHONY CLEMENT MCAULIFFE (Soldier, 1898-1979)
"NUTS! [when surrounded by Germans who demanded the surrender of his 101st
	airborne troops in Bastogne, Belgium during the battle of the bulge].

## CHRISTA MCAULIFFE (Teacher, Astronaut, 1948-1986)

I touch the future. I teach.

Space is going to be commonplace.

The president felt that it was important to send an ordinary citizen to experience
the excitement of space travel as a representative for all Americans.

The Twilight Zone' wasn't around with the kids. They think going up in space is
neat. Within their lifetime, there will be paying passengers on the shuttle.

My sympathies have always been for working-class people.

NASA was going to pick a public school teacher to go into space, observe
and make a journal about the space flight, and I am a teacher who
always dreamed of going up into space.

Reach for it. Push yourself as far as you can.

Reach for the stars.

## GEORGE MCGOVERN (Politician, 1922 - )

You know, sometimes, when they say you're ahead of your time, it's
just a polite way of saying you have a real bad sense of timing.

The highest patriotism is not a blind acceptance of official policy, but a love
of one's country deep enough to call her to a higher plain.

I am fed up with a system which busts the pot smoker and lets the
big dope racketeer go free.

I'm fed up to the ears with old men dreaming up wars for young men to die in.

No man should advocate a course in private that he's ashamed to admit in public.

Politics is an act of faith; you have to show some kind of confidence
in the intellectual and moral capacity of the public.

The Establishment center... has led us into the stupidest and cruelest war in all
history. That war is a moral and political disaster - a terrible cancer eating
away at the soul of our nation.

The longer the title, the less important the job.

## WILLIAM MCKINLEY (President, 1843-1901)

Expositions are the timekeepers of progress.

I have never been in doubt since I was old enough to think intelligently
that I would someday be made president.

In the time of darkest defeat, victory may be nearest.

Let us ever remember that our interest is in concord, not in conflict; and that
our real eminence rests in the victories of peace, not those of war.

Our differences are policies; our agreements, principles.

That's all a man can hope for during his lifetime - to set an example -
and when he is dead, to be an inspiration for history.

The free man cannot be long an ignorant man.

The mission of the United States is one of benevolent assimilation.

War should never be entered upon until every agency of peace has failed.

We need Hawaii just as much and a good deal more than we did California.
It is Manifest Destiny.

## DENNIS MILLER (Comedian, commentator, 1953 - )

There's nothing wrong with being shallow as long as you're insightful about it.

You've got bad eating habits if you use a grocery cart in 7-Eleven.

A recent police study found that you're much more likely to get shot by
a fat cop if you run.

Born again?! No, I'm not. Excuse me for getting it right the first time.
Elected office holds more perks than Elvis' nightstand.
Here in Hollywood you can actually get a marriage license
        printed on an Etch-A-Sketch.
Human beings are human beings. They say what they want, don't they?
        They used to say it across the fence while they were hanging wash.
        Now they just say it on the Internet.
Washington, DC is to lying what Wisconsin is to cheese.
I lapsed into rude.
I rant, therefore I am.
I'm a comedian, for God's sake. Viewers shouldn't trust me. And you
        know what? They're hip enough to know they shouldn't trust me.
        I'm just doing stand-up comedy.
I'm like Bush, I see the world more like checkers than chess.
It's ironic that in our culture everyone's biggest complaint is about not having
        enough time; yet nothing terrifies us more than the  thought of eternity.
The radical right is so homophobic that they're blaming
        global warming on the AIDS quilt.
What is guilt? Guilt is the pledge drive constantly hammering in our heads
        that keeps us from fully enjoying the show. Guilt is the reason they
        put the articles in Playboy.
You know there is a problem with the education system when you realize that
        out of the 3 R's only one begins with an R.
Just put down 9/11... I think, on most things I'm liberal, except on defending
        ourselves and keeping half the money. Those things I'm kind of
        conservative on.
Liberals should not overplay this weapons of mass destruction card, because
        you want me to tell you the truth? Most of us are not going to care if
        they don't find these weapons of mass destruction. It's enough for a
        lot of us to see those kids smiling on that street again.
Never ever discount the idea of marriage. Sure, someone might tell you that
        marriage is just a piece of paper. Well, so is money, and what's more
        life-affirming than cold, hard cash?
Now, I don't want to get off on a rant here, but guilt is simply God's way of
        letting you know that you're having too good a time.
One man's Voltaire is another man's Screech.
Police in Washington D.C. are now using cameras to catch drivers who go
        through red lights. Many congressmen this week opposed the use of
        the red light cameras incorrectly assuming they were being used for
        surveillance at local brothels.
President Bush gave his first-ever presidential radio address in both English
        and Spanish. Reaction was mixed, however, as people were trying to
        figure out which one was which.

### ROBERT MITCHUM (Actor, 1917-1997)
I started out to be a sex fiend, but I couldn't pass the physical
There just isn't any pleasing some people. The trick is to stop trying.
People think I have an interesting walk. Hell, I'm just trying to hold my gut in.
John Wayne had four inch lifts in his shoes. He had the overheads on his boat
        accommodated to fit him. He had a special roof put in his station wagon.
        The son of a bitch, they probably buried him in his goddamn lifts.

Sure I was glad to see John Wayne win the Oscar ... I`m always glad to
          see the fat lady win the Cadillac on TV, too.
I came back from the war and ugly heroes were in.
This is not a tough job. You read a script. If you like the part and the money
          is O.K., you do it. Then you remember your lines. You show up on time.
Every two or three years I knock off for a while. That way I'm constantly the
          new girl in the whorehouse.
Maybe love is like luck. You have to go all the way to find it
I kept the same suit for six years and the same dialogue. They just
          changed the title of the picture and the leading lady.
I`ve survived because I work cheap and don`t take up too much time.
Movies bore me, especially my own.
The only difference between me and my fellow actors is that I`ve
          spent more time in jail.
I gave up being serious about making pictures around the time I made a film with
          Greer Garson and she took a hundred and twenty-five takes to say no.
I`ve still got the same attitude I had when I started. I haven`t changed
          anything but my underwear.
Listen. I got three expressions: looking left, looking right and
          looking straight ahead.
They`re all true - booze, brawls, broads, all true. Make up
          some more if you want to.
When I drop dead and they rush to the drawer, there`s going to
          be nothing in it but a note saying `later`.
Years ago, I saved up a million dollars from acting, a lot of money in those
          days, and I spent it all on a horse farm in Tucson. Now when I go down
          there, I look at that place and I realize my whole acting career adds
          up to a million dollars worth of horse shit.
I have two acting styles: with and without a horse.
I never changed anything, except my socks and my underwear. And I never
          did anything to glorify myself or improve my lot. I took what came
          and did the best I could with it.
You`ve got to realize that a Steve McQueen performance lends itself to monotony.
Not that I`m a complete whore, understand. There are movies I won`t do for any
          amount. I turned down Patton (1970) and I turned down Dirty Harry (1971).
          Movies that piss on the world. If I`ve got five bucks in my pocket, I don`t
          need to make money that f***ing way, daddy.
You know what the average Robert Mitchum fan is? He`s full of warts and dandruff
          and he`s probably got a hernia too, but he sees me up there on the screen
          and he thinks if that bum can make it, I can be president.
Young actors love me. They think if that big slob can make
          it, there`s a chance for us.
How do I keep fit? I lay down a lot.
I got a great life out of the movies. I`ve been all over the world and met the
          most fantastic people. I don`t really deserve all I`ve gotten. It`s a
          privileged life, and I know it.
Sometimes, I think I ought to go back and do at least one thing really well. But
          again, indolence will probably cause me to hesitate about finding a place
          to start. Part of that indolence perhaps is due to shyness because I`m a
          natural hermit. I`ve been in constant motion of escape all my life. I never
          really found the right corner to hide in.

Up there on the screen you`re thirty feet wide, your eyeball is six feet high, but
    it doesn`t mean that you really amount to anything or have anything
    important to say.
I often regret my good reviews, because there is no point in doing something I
    know to be inferior and then I find I have come off the best in the film.
    Wouldn`t you find that worrying?
The Rin Tin Tin method is good enough for me. That dog never worried about
    motivation or concepts and all that junk.
I only read the reviews of my films if they`re amusing. Six books have been written
    about me but I`ve only met two of the authors. They get my name and
    birthplace wrong in the first paragraph. From there it`s all downhill.
Where are the real artists? Today it`s four-barreled carburetors and that`s it.
I never will believe there is such a thing as a great actor.
When asked what he looked for in a script before accepting a job,
    Mitchum said, "*Days off.*"
When Mitchum, who served time for marijuana possession, was asked what it was
    like in jail, he replied, "It`s like Palm Springs without the riff-raff.
When asked why in his mid-sixties he took on the arduous task of starring in an
    18-hour mini-series "The Winds of War" (1983) (mini): "It promised
    a year of free lunches."
Asked his opinion of the Vietnam War in 1968: "If they won`t listen to
    reason over there, just kill `em. Nuke `em all."

## JAMES MONROE (President, 1758-1851)

A little flattery will support a man through great fatigue.
It is only when the people become ignorant and corrupt, when they
    degenerate into a populace, that they are incapable of
    exercising their sovereignty.
National honor is the national property of the highest value.
Our country may be likened to a new house. We lack many things,
    but we possess the most precious of all - liberty!
Preparation for war is a constant stimulus to suspicion and ill will.
The best form of government is that which is most likely to prevent
    the greatest sum of evil.
The public lands are a public stock, which ought to be disposed of to
    the best advantage for the nation.

## MARILYN MONROE (Actor, 1926-1962)

Dogs never bite me. Just humans.
Hollywood is a place where they'll pay you a thousand
    dollars for a kiss and fifty cents for your soul.
What do I wear in bed? Why, Chanel No. 5, of course.
I restore myself when I'm alone.
I'm very definitely a woman and I enjoy it.
I've been on a calendar, but I've never been on time.
I've never dropped anyone I believed in.
If I'd observed all the rules, I'd never have got anywhere.
If I'm a star, then the people made me a star.
It's all make believe, isn't it?
It's better to be unhappy alone than unhappy with someone - so far.
A career is wonderful, but you can't curl up with it on a cold night.

A sex symbol becomes a thing. I just hate to be a thing.
An actress is not a machine, but they treat you like a
        machine. A money machine.
I don't mind living in a man's world as long as I can be a woman in it.
I don't mind making jokes, but I don't want to look like one.
I don't want to make money, I just want to be wonderful.
Before marriage, a girl has to make love to a man to hold him. After
        marriage, she has to hold him to make love to him.
Dreaming about being an actress, is more exciting then being one.
Fame will go by and, so long, I've had you, fame. If it goes by, I've
        always known it was fickle. So at least it's something I experience,
        but that's not where I live.
First, I'm trying to prove to myself that I'm a person. Then
        maybe I'll convince myself that I'm an actress.
Husbands are chiefly good as lovers when they are betraying their wives.
I am invariably late for appointments - sometimes as much as two hours.
        I've tried to change my ways but the things that make me late
        are too strong, and too pleasing.
I am involved in a freedom ride protesting the loss of the minority rights
        belonging to the few remaining earthbound stars. All we
        demanded was our right to twinkle.
I guess I have always been deeply terrified to really be someone's
        wife since I know from life one cannot love another, ever, really.
I have feelings too. I am still human. All I want is to be
        loved, for myself and for my talent.
I have too many fantasies to be a housewife. I guess I am a fantasy.
I knew I belonged to the public and to the world, not because I was
        talented or even beautiful, but because I had never
        belonged to anything or anyone else.
It's not true I had nothing on, I had the radio on.
Men are so willing to respect anything that bores them.
No one ever told me I was pretty when I was a little girl. All little
        girls should be told they're pretty, even if they aren't.
Sex is a part of nature. I go along with nature.
The body is meant to be seen, not all covered up.
The trouble with censors is that they worry if a girl has cleavage. They
        ought to worry if she hasn't any.
To put it bluntly, I seem to have a whole superstructure with no
        foundation. But I'm working on the foundation.

## AUDIE MURPHY (Soldier, Actor, 1924-1971)
. . .freedom is what America means to the world.
Lead from the front.
They were singing in French, but the melody was freedom
        and any American could understand that.
The true meaning of America, you ask? It's in a Texas rodeo, in a policeman's
        badge, in the sound of laughing children, in a political rally, in a newspaper...
        In all these things, and many more, you'll find America. In all these things,
        you'll find freedom. And freedom is what America means to the world.
America will never be destroyed from the outside. If we falter
        and lose our freedoms, it will be because we destroyed ourselves.

## RALPH NADER (Consumer Advocate, Presidential Candidate, 1934 - )

Once you don't vote your ideals... that has serious undermining affects. It
erodes the moral basis of our democracy.

I start with the premise that the function of leadership is to produce
more leaders, not more followers.

A leader has the vision and conviction that a dream can be achieved. He
inspires the power and energy to get it done.

Addiction should never be treated as a crime. It has to be treated as a health
problem. We do not send alcoholics to jail in this country. Over 500,000
people are in our jails who are nonviolent drug users.

For almost seventy years the life insurance industry has been a smug sacred cow
feeding the public a steady line of sacred bull.

I don't think meals have any business being deductible. I'm for
separation of calories and corporations.

John D. Rockefeller wanted to dominate oil, but Microsoft wants it all,
you name it: cable, media, banking, car dealerships.

Power has to be insecure to be responsive.

A society that has more justice is a society that needs less charity.

Like sex in Victorian England, the reality of Big Business today is
our big dirty secret.

No presidential candidate should visit Las Vegas without
condemning organized gambling.

[about Nixon] Our founders did not oust George III in order for
us to crown Richard I.

People are stunned to hear that one company has data files
on 185 million Americans.

President Reagan was elected on the promise of getting government off the
backs of the people and now he demands that government wrap itself
around the waists of the people.

Sanctions against polluters are feeble and out of date, and are rarely invoked.

The corporate lobby in Washington is basically designed to stifle all legislative
activity on behalf of consumers.

## JOHN NAISBITT (Businessman, 1929 -)

Value is what people are willing to pay for it.

We are drowning in information but starved for knowledge.

Lawyers are like beavers: They get in the mainstream and dam it up.

Leadership involves finding a parade and getting in front of it.

In a world that is constantly changing, there is no one subject or set of subjects
that will serve you for the foreseeable future, let alone for the rest of your
life. The most important skill to acquire now is learning how to learn.

In an information society, education is no mere amenity; it is the prime
tool for growing people and profits.

In their search for quality, people seem to be looking for permanency in
a time of change.

Intuition becomes increasingly valuable in the new information society
precisely because there is so much data.

One of the best kept secrets in America is that people are aching to
make a commitment, if they only had the freedom and environment
in which to do so.

Strategic planning is worthless - unless there is first a strategic vision.

The most reliable way to forecast the future is to try to understand the present.
The new leader is a facilitator, not an order giver.
Trends, like horses, are easier to ride in the direction they are going.
We are shifting from a managerial society to an entrepreneurial society.
We must learn to balance the material wonders of technology with the
      spiritual demands of our human race.

## JOE NAMATH (Athlete, 1943 - )

First, I prepare. Then I have faith.
If you aren't going all the way, why go at all?
Till I was 13, I thought my name was "Shut Up."
I think that at some point in your life you realize you don't have to worry if
      you do everything you're supposed to do right. Or if not right, if you
      do it the best you can... what can worry do for you? You are already
      doing the best you can.
To be a leader, you have to make people want to follow you, and nobody
      wants to follow someone who doesn't know where he is going.
What I do is prepare myself until I know I can do what I have to do.
When we won the league championship, all the married guys on the club had to
      thank their wives for putting up with all the stress and strain all season. I
      had to thank all the single broads in New York.
When you have confidence, you can have a lot of fun. And when you
      have fun, you can do amazing things.
When you win, nothing hurts

## RICKY NELSON (Musician, 1940-1985)

You can't please everyone so you have to please yourself.
Just believe in what you're doing, and keep doing it.
 A career is a series of comebacks.

## MICHAEL NESMITH (Musician, Author, Originator of MTV, 1942 - )

As an artist, you don't think about the parabola or the arc you're describing or
      where you're going to ultimately end up, you're just kind of crawling
      around, seeing what's out there.
You can't tru and walk down two different roads, and look to both of them
      to bring you home.  You must take your own way, though it is the
      long way, and sometimes you find yourself alone.  I know, for this
      all happened once before.
Buzzwords and cliches - those are stock in trade. There's nothing
      wrong with them.
I never feel like I have to hang on to the music. I don't expect that the music will go
      away. Ideas are the only thing I can point to that are permanent and fixed.
It's important to be precise about words, because of the thought value of
      them-they frame and shape so much of the way we understand things.
Linear thinking typifies a highly developed industry. It starts to get these
      patterns built into it somehow. I'm not sure how that happens, but
      certainly you take a look at dinosaurs.
People recognize intellectual property the same way they recognize real estate.
      People understand what property is. But it's a new kind of property, and
      so the understanding uses new control surfaces. It uses a new way of
      defining the property.

Some ways of using our thinking are really inspiring. There are people who use
their thinking to race cars. People use their thinking to build rockets to
the moon. It's all just a use of your thinking.
I coined a word the other day, but I forgot what it was. It was a
good one, it came to me in a dream.
The Internet provides the access to resources, so it's incumbent upon the
people who control those resources to make sure that the economic
engine stays intact.
The only people who steal are thieves, and that's a very small percentage of
civilization. Most people want to have some way to make the economic
transaction valid. They want to return the favor, if you will... return the
benefit and reciprocate.
The rock sitting on the shelf has potential because it can fall-it's the
same way with the Internet. It has this potential. It's not really
doing it yet, but it's about to.
There are more honest people and more good people than there are thieves
and bad people. It's just always been that way.
There is a certain logic to events that pushes you along a certain path. You
go along the path that feels the most true, and most according to the
principles that are guiding you, and that's the way the decisions are made.
There's a certain logic to systems, and that logic is fairly self-evident. It's very
straightforward, usually. It might take a little research, it might take a
little bit of industry to prize it out, but it's there to be seen.
There's this notion that allows people to create their own collection of songs, so it
rewrites what a song is. They may only want 10 seconds of something, or
they may only want this particular song, or they want this group of songs.
It becomes much more user-controlled.
Typically what happens is, somebody drags an idea from the past that worked in an
old set of logics that they try to apply to the new one. And it doesn't work.

## LOUISE BERLIAWSKY NEVELSON ( Sculptor, 1899-1988)

The freer that women become, the freer men will be. Because when you
enslave someone, you are enslaved.
A woman may not hit a ball stronger than a man, but it is
different. I prize that difference.
I think all great innovations are built on rejections.
I think most artists create out of despair. The very nature of creation  is not
a performing glory on the outside, it's a painful, difficult search within.
True strength is delicate.
What we call reality is an agreement that people have arrived at
to make life more livable.

## PAUL NEWMAN (ACTOR, 1925-2008)

Acting isn't really a creative profession. It's an interpretative one.
You only grow when you are alone.
I picture my epitaph: "Here lies Paul Newman, who died a failure
because his eyes turned brown
The embarrassing thing is that the salad dressing is outgrossing my films.
If you don't have enemies, you don't have character.
If you're playing a poker game and you look around the table and
can't tell who the sucker is, it's you.

Money won is twice as sweet as money earned.
Newman's first law: It is useless to put on your brakes when you're upside down.
Newman's second law: Just when things look darkest, they go black.
People stay married because they want to, not because the doors are locked.
Show me a good loser and I will show you a loser.
The star of oil and vinegar and the oil and vinegar of the stars.
To be an actor you have to be a child.
You can't be as old as I am without waking up with a surprised look on your
    face every morning: 'Holy Christ, whaddya know - I'm still around!' It's
    absolutely amazing that I survived all the booze and smoking and the
    cars and the career.
The ozone hole is actually bigger than the entire continent of North America this
    year, and that's a record.
I just try to get through the day.
Who's to say who's an expert?

## BOB NEWHART (Comedian, Actor, 1929 - )

All I can say about life is, 'Oh God, enjoy it!'
Comedians are never really on vacation because you're always at
    attention... that antenna is always out there.
Funny is funny is funny.
I don't know how many sacred cows there are today. I think there's a little confusion
    between humor and gross passing for humor. That's kind of regrettable.
I don't like country music, but I don't mean to denigrate those who do. And for the
    people who like country music, denigrate means 'put down'.
I think you should be a child for as long as you can. I have been successful
    for 74 years being able to do that. Don't rush into adulthood, it isn't
    all that much fun.
I was influenced by every comedian I ever saw work. That's the only way
    you learn how to do it.
I'm most proud of the longevity of my marriage, my kids, and my
    grandchildren. If you don't have that, you really don't have very much.

## NICHELLE NICHOLS (Actress, 1932 - )

All the people in Star Trek will always be known as those characters. And what
    characters to have attached to your name in life! The show is such a
    phenomenon all over the world.
I think anybody with any intelligence sits down and sees Star Trek is not a kids'
    show.

## JACK NICHOLSON (Actor, 1937 - )

I used to think that one of the great signs of security was the
    ability to just walk away.
I'll tell you one thing: Don't ever give anybody your best advice, because
    they're not going to follow it
I'm Irish. I think about death all the time.
I only take Viagra when I'm with more than one woman.
I've been too many places. I'm like the bad penny.
I've never been able to say I've been influenced by a list of artists I like
    because I like thousands and thousands and I've been influenced
    in some way by all of them.

In my last year of school, I was voted Class Optimist and Class
        Pessimist. Looking back, I realize I was only half right.
In other words, I wouldn't like to be an actor if I could only be real. I like
        to get wild, behaviorally wild, and it's crazy to think of any form
        where it's just one way.
I'm not hard to get along with.
In this industry, there are only two ways up the ladder. Rung by rung or
        claw your way to the top. It's sure been tough on my nails.
It's a slight stretch of the imagination but most people are alike in most ways so
        I've never had any trouble identifying with the character that I'm playing.
Most of the early part of an actor's career, you do the jobs you get.
My mother never saw the irony in calling me a son-of-a-bitch.
My whole career strategy has been to build a base so that I could take the
        roles I want to play. I'd hate to think that a shorter part might not be
        available because I was worried about my billing.
Once you've been really bad in a movie, there's a certain
        kind of fearlessness you develop.
Just let the wardrobe do the acting.
The minute that you're not learning I believe you're dead.
There is no way you can get people to believe you on screen if they
        know who you really are through television.
There's only two people in your life you should lie to... the police
        and your girlfriend.
We are going as fast as we can as soon as we can. We're in a
        race against time, until we run out of money.
Well, a girlfriend once told me never to fight with anybody you don't love.
Well, a younger woman is a type, but not necessarily a type for me. And what
        is a younger woman? I mean, I'm pretty old. Almost everyone is younger.
Well, I'm not going to sit here and pretend that I haven't been a
        rogue most of my life.
What's beautiful is all that counts, pal. That's ALL that counts.
When I was in high school, I earned the pimple award and every
        other gross-out award.
With my sunglasses on, I'm Jack Nicholson. Without them, I'm fat and 60.

## LEONARD NIMOY (Actor, Photographer, Poet, 1931 - )

I think it's my adventure, my trip, my journey, and I guess my attitude
        is, let the chips fall where they may.
I'm touched by the idea that when we do things that are useful and helpful -
        collecting these shards of spirituality - that we may be helping to
        bring about a healing.
Logic is the beginning of wisdom, not the end.
My dream concept is that I have a camera and I am trying to photograph
        what is essentially invisible. And every once in a while I get a glimpse
        of her and I grab that picture.
That is the exploration that awaits you! Not mapping stars and studying
        nebula, but charting the unknown possibilities of existence.
The miracle is this: the more we share the more we have.
You know, for a long time I have been of the opinion that artists don't
        necessarily know what they're doing. You don't necessarily know
        what kind of universal concept you're tapping into

# RICHARD NIXON (President, 1913-1994)

A public man must never forget that he loses his usefulness when he as an
individual, rather than his policy, becomes the issue.

Always remember that others may hate you but those who hate you don't win
unless you hate them. And then you destroy yourself.

Americans admire a people who can scratch a desert and produce a garden. The
Israelis have shown qualities that Americans identify with: guts, patriotism,
idealism, a passion for freedom. I have seen it. I know. I believe that.

Any change is resisted because bureaucrats have a vested interest in
the chaos in which they exist.

Any lady who is first lady likes being first lady. I don't care what
they say, they like it.

As this long and difficult war ends, I would like to address a few special words to the
American people: Your steadfastness in supporting our insistence on peace
with honor has made peace with honor possible.

By the time you get dressed, drive out there, play 18 holes and come
home, you've blown seven hours. There are better things
you can do with your time.

A man is not finished when he is defeated. He is finished when he quits.

Castro couldn't even go to the bathroom unless the Soviet Union put
the nickel in the toilet.

Certainly in the next 50 years we shall see a woman president, perhaps
sooner than you think. A woman can and should be able to do any
political job that a man can do.

Defeat doesn't finish a man, quit does. A man is not finished when he's
defeated. He's finished when he quits.

Don't get the impression that you arouse my anger. You see, one can
only be angry with those he respects.

Finishing second in the Olympics gets you silver. Finishing second
in politics gets you oblivion.

I am not a crook.

I believe in the battle-whether it's the battle of a campaign or the
battle of this office, which is a continuing battle.

I brought myself down. I impeached myself by resigning.

I can see clearly now... that I was wrong in not acting more decisively
and more forthrightly in dealing with Watergate.

I can take it. The tougher it gets, the cooler I get.

I don't know anything that builds the will to win better than competitive sports.

I don't think that a leader can control, to any great extent, his destiny. Very
seldom can he step in and change the situation if the forces of history
are running in another direction

I gave 'em a sword. And they stuck it in, and they twisted it with relish. And I
guess if I had been in their position, I'd have done the same thing.

I have never been a quitter. To leave office before my term is completed is
opposed to every instinct in my body. But as president I must put
the interests of America first Therefore, I shall resign the presidency
effective at noon tomorrow.

I let the American people down.

I wish I could give you a lot of advice, based on my experience of winning
political debates. But I don't have that experience. My only experience
is at losing them.

I'm glad I'm not Brezhnev. Being the Russian leader in the Kremlin. You
never know if someone's tape recording what you say.

I've never canceled a subscription to a newspaper because of bad cartoons
or editorials. If that were the case, I wouldn't have any newspapers
or magazines to read.

I played by the rules of politics as I found them.

I reject the cynical view that politics is a dirty business.

If an individual wants to be a leader and isn't controversial, that means
he never stood for anything.

If we take the route of the permanent handout, the American character
will itself be impoverished.

If you take no risks, you will suffer no defeats. But if you take no risks, you win

If you think the United States has stood still, who built the
largest shopping center in the world?

If you want to make beautiful music, you must play the black
and the white notes together.

In the long term we can hope that religion will change the nature of man and
reduce conflict. But history is not encouraging in this respect. The
bloodiest wars in history have been religious wars.

In the television age, the key distinction is between the candidate who
can speak poetry and the one who can only speak prose.

It is necessary for me to establish a winner image. Therefore,
I have to beat somebody.

It's a piece of cake until you get to the top. You find you can't stop playing
the game the way you've always played it.

Let us begin by committing ourselves to the truth to see it like it is, and tell it
like it is, to find the truth, to speak the truth, and to live the truth.

Let us move from the era of confrontation to the era of negotiation.

Life isn't meant to be easy. It's hard to take being on the top - or on the bottom.
I guess I'm something of a fatalist. You have to have a sense of history, I
think, to survive some of these things... Life is one crisis after another.

My concern today is not with the length of a person's hair but with his conduct.

My own view is that taping of conversations for historical purposes was a bad
decision on the part of all the presidents. I don't think Kennedy should
have done it. I don't think Johnson should have done it, and I don't think
we should have done it.

My strong point, if I have a strong point, is performance. I always do
more than I say. I always produce more than I promise.

Never let your head hang down. Never give up and sit down and grieve. Find
another way. And don't pray when it rains if you don't
pray when the sun shines.

Never say no when a client asks for something, even if it is the moon. You can
always try, and anyhow there is plenty of time afterwards to explain
that it was not possible.

Once you get into this great stream of history, you can't get out.

Only if you have been in the deepest valley, can you ever know how
magnificent it is to be on the highest mountain.

Our chief justices have probably had more profound and lasting influence
on their times and on the direction of the nation than most presidents.

People have got to know whether or not their president is a crook. Well, I'm
not a crook. I earned everything I've got.

People react to fear, not love; they don't teach that in Sunday School, but it's true.
Politics would be a helluva good business if it weren't for the goddamned people.
President Johnson and I have a lot in common. We were both born in small
    towns and we're both fortunate in the fact that we think we married
    above ourselves.
Remember, always give your best. Never get discouraged. Never be petty.
    Always remember, others may hate you. But those who hate you don't
    win unless you hate them. And then you destroy yourself.
Scrubbing  floors and emptying bedpans has as much dignity as the Presidency.
Solutions are not the answer.
Sure there are dishonest men in local government. But there are dishonest
    men in national government too.
Tell them to send everything that can fly.
The American people are entitled to see the president and to hear his
    views directly, and not to see him only through the press.
The Cold War isn't thawing; it is burning with a deadly heat. Communism
    isn't sleeping; it is, as always, plotting, scheming, working, fighting.
The finest steel has to go through the hottest fire.
The greatest honor history can bestow is that of peacemaker.
The mark of a true politician is that he is never at a loss for words because
    he is always half-expecting to be asked to make a speech.
The more you stay in this kind of job, the more you realize that a public
    figure, a major public figure, is a lonely man.
The presidency has many problems, but boredom is the least of them.
The press is the enemy.
There are some people, you know, they think the way to be a big man is to
    shout  and stomp and raise hell-and then nothing ever really happens.
    I'm not like that I never shoot blanks.
There will be no whitewash in the White House.
Those who hate you don't win unless you hate them, and then
    you destroy yourself.
Tonight - to you, the great silent majority of my fellow Americans - I ask
    for your support.
Under the doctrine of separation of powers, the manner in which the president
    personally exercises his assigned executive powers is not subject to
    questioning by another branch of government.
Unless a president can protect the privacy of the advice he gets, he
    cannot get the advice he needs.
Voters quickly forget  what a man says.
We cannot learn from one another until we stop shouting at one another - until we
    speak quietly enough so that our words can be heard as well as our voices.
We do not learn by inference and deduction and the application of mathematics to
    philosophy, but by direct intercourse and sympathy.
We must always remember that America is a great nation today not because of
    what government did for people but because of what people did for
    themselves and for one another.
Well, I screwed it up real good, didn't I?
What starts the process, really, are laughs and slights and snubs when you are a
    kid. If your anger is deep enough and strong enough, you learn that you
    can change those attitudes by excellence, personal gut performance.
When the President does  it, that means that it's not illegal.

You must never be satisfied with losing. You must get angry, terribly angry, about
      losing. But the mark of the good loser is that he takes his anger out on
      himself and not his victorious opponents or on his teammates.
You won't have Nixon to kick around anymore, because, gentlemen, this
      is my last press conference.
You've got to learn to survive a defeat. That's when you develop character

## ANDRE NORTON (Author, 1912-2005)
Always the cat remains a little beyond the limits we
      try to set for him in our blind folly.
As for courage and will - we cannot measure how much of each lies
      within us, we can only trust there will be sufficient to carry
      through trials which may lie ahead.
I think the human race made a big mistake at the beginning of the industrial
      revolution, we leaped for the mechanical things, people need the use
      of their hands to feel creative.
Perhaps it is because cats do not live by human patterns, do not fit themselves into
      prescribed behavior, that they are so united to creative people.
There's no night without stars.
Either the law exists, or it does not.
Victory belongs to the most persevering.

## BARACK OBAMA (President, 1961 - )
A good compromise, a good piece of legislation, is like a good sentence;
      or a good piece of music. Everybody can recognize it. They
      say, 'Huh. It works. It makes sense.'
Americans... still believe in an America where anything's
      possible - they just don't think their leaders do.
As a nuclear power - as the only nuclear power to have used a nuclear
      weapon - the United States has a moral responsibility to act.
Change will not come if we wait for some other person or some other time. We
      are the ones we've been waiting for. We are the change that we seek.
Community colleges play an important role in helping people transition between
      careers by providing the retooling they need to take on a new career.
Focusing your life solely on making a buck shows a certain poverty of ambition. It
      asks too little of yourself. Because it's only when you hitch your wagon to
      something larger than yourself that you realize your true potential.
I cannot swallow whole the view of Lincoln as the Great Emancipator.
I consider it part of my responsibility as President of the United States to fight
      against negative stereotypes of Islam wherever they appear.
I don't care whether you're driving a hybrid or an SUV. If you're headed for a
      cliff, you have to change direction. That's what the American people
      called for in November, and that's what we intend to deliver.
I don't oppose all wars. What I am opposed to is a dumb
      war. What I am opposed to is a rash war.
I found this national debt, doubled, wrapped in a big bow waiting for
      me as I stepped into the presidency.
I know my country has not perfected itself. At times, we've struggled to keep the
      promise of liberty and equality for all of our people. We've made our share
      of mistakes, and there are times when our actions around the world have
      not lived up to our best intentions.

I think when you spread the wealth around it's good for everybody.

I've got two daughters. 9 years old and 6 years old. I am going to teach them first of all about values and morals. But if they make a mistake, I don't want them punished with a baby.

If the people cannot trust their government to do the job for which it exists - to protect them and to promote their common welfare - all else is lost.

If you're walking down the right path and you're willing to keep walking, eventually you'll make progress.

In America, there's a failure to appreciate Europe's leading role in the world.

It took a lot of blood, sweat and tears to get to where we are today, but we have just begun. Today we begin in earnest the work of making sure that the world we leave our children is just a little bit better than the one we inhabit today.

My administration is the only thing between you [CEO's] and the pitchforks.

My job is not to represent Washington to you, but to represent you to Washington.

My parents shared not only an improbable love, they shared an abiding faith in the possibilities of this nation. They would give me an African name, Barack, or blessed, believing that in a tolerant America your name is no barrier to success.

Money is not the only answer, but it makes a difference.

No one is pro-abortion.

Issues are never simple. One thing I'm proud of is that very rarely will you hear me simplify the issues.

One of the great strengths of the United States is... we have a very large Christian population - we do not consider ourselves a Christian nation or a Jewish nation or a Muslim nation. We consider ourselves a nation of citizens who are bound by ideals and a set of values.

Over the last 15 months, we've traveled to every corner of the United States. I've now been in 57 states? I think one left to go.

People of Berlin - people of the world - this is our moment. This is our time.

The fact that my 15 minutes of fame has extended a little longer than 15 minutes is somewhat surprising to me and completely baffling to my wife.

The thing about hip-hop today is it's smart, it's insightful. The way they can communicate a complex message in a very short space is remarkable.

The United States has been enriched by Muslim Americans. Many other Americans have Muslims in their families or have lived in a Muslim-majority country - I know, because I am one of them.

There are patriots who opposed the war in Iraq and there are patriots who supported the war in Iraq. We are one people, all of us pledging allegiance to the stars and stripes, all of us defending the United States of America.

There is not a liberal America and a conservative America - there is the United States of America. There is not a black America and a white America and latino America and asian America - there's the United States of America.

This is the moment when we must build on the wealth that open markets have created, and share its benefits more equitably. Trade has been a cornerstone of our growth and global development. But we will not be able to sustain this growth if it favors the few, and not the many.

Today we are engaged in a deadly global struggle for those who would intimidate, torture, and murder people for exercising the most basic freedoms. If we are to win this struggle and spread those freedoms, we must keep our own moral compass pointed in a true direction.

Tonight, we gather to affirm the greatness of our nation - not because of the height of our skyscrapers, or the power of our military, or the size of our economy. Our pride is based on a very simple premise, summed up in a declaration made over two hundred years ago.

This is the moment when we must come together to save this planet. Let us resolve that we will not leave our children a world where the oceans rise and famine spreads and terrible storms devastate our lands.

We can't drive our SUVs and eat as much as we want  and keep our homes on 72 degrees at all times... and then just expect that other countries are going to say OK. That's not leadership. That's not going to happen.

We cannot continue to rely only on our military in order to achieve the national security objectives that we've set. We've got to have a civilian national security force that's just as powerful, just as strong, just as well-funded.

We have an obligation and a responsibility to be investing in our students and our schools. We must make sure that people who have the grades, the desire and the will, but not the money, can still get the best education possible.

We need somebody who's got the heart, the empathy, to recognize what it's like to be a young teenage mom, the empathy to understand what it's like to be poor or African-American or gay or disabled or old - and that's the criterion by which I'll be selecting my judges.

We need to internalize this idea of excellence. Not many folks s
pend a lot of time trying to be excellent.

We have real enemies in the world. These enemies must be found. They
must be pursued and they must be defeated.

We need to steer clear of this poverty of ambition, where people want to drive fancy cars and wear nice clothes and live in nice apartments but don't want to work hard to accomplish these things. Everyone should try to realize their full potential.

What Washington needs is adult supervision.

With the changing economy, no one has lifetime employment. But
community colleges provide lifetime employability.

You know, my faith is one that admits some doubt.

## MICHELLE OBAMA (First Lady, 1964 -)

Although the circumstances of our lives may seem very disengaged, with me standing here as the First Lady of the United States of America and you just getting through school, I want you to know  we have very much in common. For nothing in my life ever would  have predicted that I would standing here as the first African-American First Lady.

. . . Barack and I were raised with so many of the same values, like you work hard for what you want in life. That your word is your bond; that  you do what you say you're going to do. That you treat people with  dignity and respect, even if you don't know them and even if you don't  agree with them.

And in my own life, in my own small way, I've tried to give back to this country that has given me so much. That's why I left a job at a law firm for a career in public service, working to empower young people to volunteer in their communities. Because I believe that each of us - no matter what our age or background or walk of life - each of us has something to contribute to the life of this nation.

And let's be clear: It's not enough just to limit ads for foods that aren't healthy. It's also going to be critical to increase marketing for foods that are healthy.

America is just downright mean.

As a mom, I know it is my responsibility, and no one else's, to raise my kids. But we have to ask ourselves, what does it mean when so many parents are finding their best efforts undermined by an avalanche of advertisements aimed at our kids.

Even if we give parents all the information they need and we improve school meals and build brand new supermarkets on every corner, none of that matters if when families step into a restaurant, they can't make a healthy choice.

Exercise is really important to me - it's therapeutic. So if I'm ever feeling tense or stressed or like I'm about to have a meltdown, I'll put on my iPod and head to the gym or out on a bike ride along Lake Michigan with the girls.

I am an example of what is possible when girls from the very beginning of their lives are loved and nurtured by people around them. I was surrounded by extraordinary women in my life who taught me about quiet strength and dignity.

I like to talk about my obsession with french fries because I don't want people to think that 'Let's Move' is about complete, utter deprivation. It's about moderation and real-life changes and ideas that really work for families.

I never cut class. I loved getting As, I liked being smart. I liked being on time. I thought being smart is cooler than anything in the world.

I was not raised with wealth or resources or any social standing to speak of.

I'm a fry lover.

I'm not asking any of you to make drastic changes to every single one of your recipes or to totally change the way you do business. But what I am asking is that you consider reformulating your menu in pragmatic and incremental ways to create healthier versions of the foods that we all love.

## CONAN O'BRIEN (Talk Show Host, 1963 - )

President Clinton signed a $10 million deal to write a book by 2003. Isn't that amazing? Yes, and get this, not only that, President Bush signed a $10 million deal to read a book by 2003.

Apparently Arnold [Schwarzenegger] was inspired by President Bush, who proved you can be a successful politician in this country even if English is your second language.

Starbucks says they are going to start putting religious quotes on cups. The very first one will say, 'Jesus! This cup is expensive!'

Republicans have called for a National African-American Museum. The plan is being held up by finding a location that isn't in their neighborhood.

Scientists announced that they have located the gene for alcoholism. Scientists say they found it at a party, talking way too loudly.

Several hard-core Star Wars fans who had tickets for the first showing actually said that when the movie finally began, they started crying. Mainly because they realized that it's 22 years later, and they still haven't lost their virginity.

The U.S. army confirmed that it gave a lucrative fire fighting contract in Iraq to the firm once run by the Vice President Dick Cheney without any competitive bidding. When asked if this could be conceived as Cheney's friends profiting from the war, the spokesman said 'Yes.'

CBS news anchor Dan Rather has interviewed Iraqi dictator Saddam Hussein. When asked what it was like to talk to a crazy man, Saddam said, 'It's not so bad.'

Earlier today, Arnold Schwarzenegger criticized the California school system, calling it disastrous. Arnold says California's schools are so bad that its graduates are willing to vote for me.

. . . the new high-tech Star Wars toys will be in stores any day now. The toys can talk and are interactive, so they can be easily distinguished from Star Wars fans.

Early on, they were timing my contract with an egg timer.

Fish recognize a bad leader.

If life gives you lemons, make some kind of fruity juice.

In Cleveland there is legislation moving forward to ban people from wearing  pants that fit too low. However, there is lots of opposition from the plumber' union.

Nobody in life gets exactly what they thought they were going to get, but if you work really hard and you're kind, amazing things will happen.

Officials at the White House are saying that President Bush hasn't changed his schedule much since the war started. The main difference, they say, is that he's started watching the news and taping Sponge Bob.

President Bush left for Canada today to attend a trade summit. Reportedly, the trade summit got off to an awkward start when the president pulled out his baseball cards.

## MADALYN MURRAY O'HAIR (Author, Atheist, 1919-1995)

Religion has caused more misery to all of mankind in every stage of human history than any other single idea.

In an unconstitutional partnership with the state, the church can impose the most irresistible, if covert, controls conceivable.

An Atheist believes that a hospital should be built instead of a church. An atheist believes that deed must be done instead of prayer said. An atheist strives for involvement in life and not escape into death. He wants disease conquered, poverty vanished, war eliminated.

I feel that everyone has a right to be insane.

I feel that everyone who wants to say anything, do anything, should be able to say anything or do anything, within the limits of not hurting another person.

I want three words: Woman, Atheist, Anarchist. That's me.

No god ever gave any man anything, nor ever answered any prayer at any time - nor ever will.

## GEORGIA O'KEEFFE (Artist, 1887-1986)

I found I could say things with color and shapes that I couldn't say any other way - things I had no words for.

One can not be an American by going about saying that one is an American. It is necessary to feel America, like America, love America and then work.

I hate flowers - I paint them because they're cheaper than models and they don't move.

I have things in my head that are not like what anyone has taught me - shapes
and ideas so near to me - so natural to my way of being and thinking that
it hasn't occurred to me to put them down.
I know now that most people are so closely concerned with themselves that they
are not aware of their own individuality, I can see myself, and it has helped
me to say what I want to say in paint.
I often painted fragments of things because it seemed to make my statement
as well as or better than the whole could.
I've been absolutely terrified every moment of my life - and I've never let
it keep me from doing a single thing I wanted to do.
Marks on paper are free - free speech - press - pictures all go together I suppose.
Nobody sees a flower really; it is so small. We haven't time, and to see takes
time - like to have a friend takes time.
The days you work are the best days.
To create one's world in any of the arts takes courage.
When you take a flower in your hand and really look at it, it's your world for the
moment. I want to give that world to someone else. Most people in the
city rush around so, they have no time to look at a flower. I want them
to see it whether they want to or not.
You get whatever accomplishment you are willing to declare
One can't paint New York as it is, but rather as it is felt.

## JACK PAAR (Talk Show Host, 1916-2004)

Immigration is the sincerest form of flattery.
Poor people have more fun than rich people, they say; and I notice
it's the rich people who keep saying it.
Looking back, my life seems like one long obstacle race, with me as
the chief obstacle.
To restore a sense of reality, I think Walt Disney should have a Hardluckland.
I have never seen a bad television program, because I refuse to. God gave
me a mind, and a wrist
Last week, I decided to go to the movies, so I got a GI loan and a ticket.
Forest Lawn is like a Disneyland for shut-ins.
I came from a poor family. We never had meat at our house. And
whenever I would go by a butcher's window I thought there had
been a terrible accident.
Doing the show was like painting the George Washington Bridge. As soon
as you finished one end, you started right in on the other.

## THOMAS PAINE (Founding Father, Statesman, 1737-1809)

A long habit of not thinking a thing wrong gives it a superficial
appearance of being right.
A thing moderately good is not so good as it ought to be. Moderation in
temper is always a virtue; but moderation in principle is always a vice.
All national institutions of churches, whether Jewish, Christian or Turkish, appear
to me no other than human inventions, set up to terrify and enslave
mankind, and monopolize power and profit.
An army of principles can penetrate where an army of soldiers cannot.
Arms discourage and keep the invader and plunderer in awe, and preserve
order in the world as well as property... Horrid mischief would ensue
were the law-abiding deprived of the use of them.

Belief in a cruel God makes a cruel man.

But such is the irresistible nature of truth, that all it asks, and all it
wants is the liberty of appearing.

Any system of religion that has anything in it that shocks the mind of a
child, cannot be true.

Character is much easier kept than recovered.

Every religion is good that teaches man to be good; and I know of none
that instructs him to be bad.

Every science has for its basis a system of principles as fixed and unalterable
as those by which the universe is regulated and governed. Man cannot
make principles; he can only discover them.

Government, even in its best state, is but a necessary evil; in its worst
state, an intolerable one.

He that rebels against reason is a real rebel, but he that in defense of reason
rebels against tyranny has a better title to Defender of the Faith, than
George the Third.

He that would make his own liberty secure, must guard even his enemy from
oppression; for if he violates this duty, he establishes a precedent that
will reach to himself.

He who is the author of a war lets loose the whole contagion of hell and
opens a vein that bleeds a nation to death.

I believe in the equality of man; and I believe that religious duties consist in doing
justice, loving mercy, and endeavoring to make our fellow-creatures happy.

I love the man that can smile in trouble, that can gather  strength from distress,
and grow brave by reflection. 'Tis the business of little minds to shrink,
but he whose heart is firm, and whose conscience approves his conduct,
will pursue his principles unto death.
Human nature is not of itself vicious.

I prefer peace. But if trouble must come, let it come in my time, so that
my children can live in peace

Is it not a species of blasphemy to call the New Testament revealed religion,
when we see in it such contradictions and absurdities.

It is an affront to treat falsehood with complaisance.

It is error only, and not truth, that shrinks from inquiry.

It is necessary to the happiness of man that he be mentally faithful to himself.
Infidelity does not consist in believing, or in disbelieving, it consists in
professing to believe what he does not believe.

It is not a God, just and good, but a devil, under the name of God,
that the Bible describes.

It is the direction and not the magnitude which is to be taken into consideration.

Lead, follow, or get out of the way.

Moderation in temper is always a virtue; but moderation in principle
is always a vice.

My country is the world, and my religion is to do good.

Of all the tyrannies that affect mankind, tyranny in religion is the worst.

One good schoolmaster is of more use than a hundred priests.

Persecution is not an original feature in any religion; but it is always the
strongly marked feature of all religions established by law.

Reason obeys itself; and ignorance submits to whatever is dictated to it.

Reputation is what men and women think of us; character is what God and
angels know of us.

Society in every state is a blessing, but government, even in its best stage, is
　　　　but a necessary evil; in its worst state an intolerable one.

Suspicion is the companion of mean souls, and the bane of all good society.

That God cannot lie, is no advantage to your argument, because it is no proof
　　　　that priests can not, or that the Bible does not.

That which we obtain too easily, we esteem too lightly.

The abilities of man must fall short on one side or the other, like too scanty a
　　　　blanket when you are abed. If you pull it upon your shoulders, your feet are
　　　　left bare; if you thrust it down to your feet, your shoulders are uncovered.

The greatest remedy for anger is delay.

The harder the conflict, the more glorious the triumph.

The instant formal government is abolished, society begins to act. A general
　　　　association takes place, and common interest produces common security.

The real man smiles in trouble, gathers strength from distress, and
　　　　grows brave by reflection.

The strength and power of despotism consists wholly in the fear of resistance.

The Vatican is a dagger in the heart of Italy.

The whole religious complexion of the modern world is due to the absence from
　　　　Jerusalem of a lunatic asylum.

The World is my country, all mankind are my brethren, and to do
　　　　good is my religion.

There are matters in the Bible, said to be done by the express
　　　　commandment of God, that are shocking to humanity and
　　　　to every idea  we have of moral justice.

There are two distinct classes of what are called thoughts: those that we
　　　　produce in ourselves by reflection and the act of thinking and those
　　　　that bolt into the mind of their own accord.

These are the times that try men's souls.

My mind is my own church.

Those who expect to reap the blessings of freedom must, like men,
　　　　undergo the fatigue of supporting it.

Time makes more converts than reason.

'Tis the business of little minds to shrink; but he whose heart is firm, and whose
　　　　conscience approves his conduct, will pursue his principles unto death.

Titles are but nicknames, and every nickname is a title.

To say that any people are not fit for freedom, is to make poverty their
　　　　choice, and to say they had rather be loaded with taxes than not.

Virtues are acquired through endeavor, Which rests wholly upon yourself. So, to
　　　　praise others for their virtues Can but encourage one's own efforts.

War involves in its progress such a train of unforeseen circumstances that no
　　　　human wisdom can calculate the end; it has but one thing certain,
　　　　and that is to increase taxes.

We can only reason from what is; we can reason on actualities, but
　　　　not on possibilities.

We have it in our power to begin the world over again.

What we obtain too cheap, we esteem too lightly; it is dearness only
　　　　that gives everything its value.

When men yield up the privilege of thinking, the last
　　　　shadow of liberty quits the horizon.

When we are planning for posterity, we ought to remember
　　　　that virtue is not hereditary.

## SARAH PALIN (Politician, governor of Alaska, 1964 - )

But obviously, we've got to stand with our North Korean allies

I want to help clean up the state that is so sorry today of journalism.
And I have a communications degree.

Go back to what our founders and our founding documents meant -- they're
quite clear -- that we would create law based on the God of the Bible
and the Ten Commandments.[This comment is in total disagreement
with almost every comment about government and religion by our
founding fathers].

As for that VP talk all the time, I'll tell you, I still can't answer that
question until somebody answers for me what is it exactly
that the VP does every day?

I'm the mayor, I can do whatever I want until the courts tell me I can't.

They are also building schools for the Afghan children so that there is hope
and opportunity in our neighboring country of Afghanistan.

I have not, and I think if you go back in history and if you ask that question
of many vice presidents, they may have the same answer that I just
gave you. [Asked if she had never met a foreign head of state - every
US vice-president in the last 32 years had met a foreign head of state
Before taking office]

I may not answer the questions that either the moderator or you want to hear,
but I'm going to talk straight to the American people and let them know
my track record also. [On not answering questions in the vice presidential
debate, St. Louis, Missouri, October 2, 2008]

When we talk about fighting for our country, we're talking
about our vote, our vote is our arms.

We need leaders who will stand up for the little guy and listen once again.

People have a constitutional right to burn a Koran if they want to, but doing
so is insensitive and an unnecessary provocation - much like building
a mosque at Ground Zero.

People know something has gone terribly wrong with our government and it
has gotten so far off track. But people also know that there is nothing
wrong in America that a good old-fashioned election can't fix.

Politics isn't just a game of clashing parties and competing interests. The right
reason is to challenge the status quo, to serve the common good, and
to leave this nation better than we found it.

Well, let's see. There's -- of course -- in the great history of America rulings
there have been rulings. [Unable to name a Supreme Court decision
she disagreed with other than Roe vs. Wade, interview with Katie Couric]

All of 'em, any of 'em that have been in front of me over all these years. [Unable
to name a single newspaper or magazine she reads, interview with Katie
Couric].

## BRUCE PALTROW (Producer, 1943-2002)

It's a prizefight. Get off the stool, take your beating, go back to your corner,
rest, and take a beating again. Believe in your own talent. Marry well.

Everything has been homogenized. Over time, with television and jet travel,
everybody has blended together. Some of our wonderful charm
has been lost.

Don't dumb it down. The audience is smart and gets what you are doing.

## DOLLY PARTON (Musician, 1946 - )

You'll never do a whole lot unless you're brave enough to try.
I look just like the girls next door... if you happen to live
    next door to an amusement park.
I modeled my looks on the town tramp.
I still close my eyes and go home - I can always draw from that.
I was the first woman to burn my bra - it took the fire
    department four days to put it out.
I'm not going to limit myself just because people won't accept
    the fact that I can do something else.
I'm not offended by all the dumb blonde jokes because I know
    I'm not dumb... and I also know that I'm not blonde.
I'm old enough and cranky enough now that if someone tried to
    tell me what to do, I'd tell them where to put it.
If you don't like the road you're walking, start paving another one.
If you talk bad about country music, it's like saying bad things about
    my momma. Them's fightin' words.
It's a good thing I was born a girl, otherwise I'd be a drag queen.
My weaknesses have always been food and men - in that order.
Storms make trees take deeper roots.
The way I see it, if you want the rainbow, you gotta put up with the rain.
We cannot direct the wind, but we can adjust the sails.
When I'm inspired, I get excited because I can't wait to see
    what I'll come up with next.
You'd be surprised how much it costs to look this cheap!

## JOHN PATRICK (Playwright, 1905-1995)

Pain makes man think. Thought makes man
    wise. Wisdom makes life endurable.
I don't feel any older now than when I was 70.

## GEORGE PATTON (Soldier, 1885-1945)

A good plan, violently executed now, is better than a perfect plan next week.
Battle is an orgy of disorder.
Better to fight for something than live for nothing.
Do your damnedest in an ostentatious manner all the time.
If everyone is thinking alike, then somebody isn't thinking.
Courage is fear holding on a minute longer.
A piece of spaghetti or a military unit can only be led from the front end.
A pint of sweat, saves a gallon of blood.
If we take the generally accepted definition of bravery as a quality which
    knows no fear, I have never seen a brave man. All men are frightened.
    The more intelligent they are, the more they are frightened.
It is foolish and wrong to mourn the men who died. Rather we should
    thank God that such men lived.
No bastard ever won a war by dying for his country. He won it by
    making the other poor dumb bastard die for his country.
Accept the challenges so that you can feel the exhilaration of victory.
All very successful commanders are prima donnas and must be so treated.
Don't tell people how to do things, tell them what to do and let them
    surprise you with their results.

If you tell people where to go, but not how to get
        there, you'll be amazed at the results.
If a man does his best, what else is there?
I don't measure a man's success by how high he climbs but how
        high he bounces when he hits bottom.
Nobody ever defended anything successfully, there is only attack
        and attack and attack some more.
Prepare for the unknown by studying how others in the past have
        coped with the unforeseeable and the unpredictable.
Take calculated risks. That is quite different from being rash.
The time to take counsel of your fears is before you make an important battle
        decision. That's the time to listen to every fear you can imagine! When
        you have collected all the facts and fears and made your decision, turn
        off all your fears and go ahead!
Watch what people are cynical about, and one can often discover what they lack.
Always do everything you ask of those you command.
Americans love to fight. All real Americans love the sting of battle
Americans play to win at all times. I wouldn't give a hoot and hell for a man who
        lost and laughed. That's why Americans have never lost nor ever lose a war.
Battle is the most magnificent competition in which a human being can indulge. It
        brings out all that is best; it removes all that is base. All men are afraid in
        battle. The coward is the one who lets his fear overcome his sense of duty.
        Duty is the essence of manhood.

### PAT PAULSEN (Comedian, 1927-1997)

I must choose my words carefully in order to avoid any
        negative interpretation. Among politicians, this is
        a tactic known as lying.
All the problems we face in the United States today can be
        traced to an unenlightened immigration policy
        on the part of the American Indian.
I feel proud to be living in a country where people are not afraid to
        laugh at themselves and where political satire is tolerated by the
        government, if not the television network.
Without guns, how are we gonna shoot anybody? We need guns.
        You never can tell when you're walking down the street
        you'll spot a moose. Suppose a man comes home early and
        finds another man with his wife? What's he supposed to do?
        Poison him? How about suicide? Can you imagine trying to
        beat yourself to death with a stick?  But let's be objective about
        this. Guns are not the real problem. The real problem is bullets.
A good many people feel that our present draft laws are unjust.
        These people are called soldiers. [This quote was made in the
        late 1960s, when the draft was still in force]
Censorship does not interfere with the constitutional rights of every American to
        sit alone in a dark room in the nude and cuss. There are realistic taboos,
        especially regarding political comments. Our leaders were not elected to
        be tittered at. For example, we're allowed to say Ronald Reagan is a lousy
        actor, but we're not allowed to say he's a lousy governor—which is ridiculous.
        We know he's a good actor. And we're not allowed to make fun of President
        'Johnson'. But if we praise him, who would believe it?

I am neither left wing nor right wing. I am middle-of-the-bird.
I belong to the Straight Talking American Government Party,
        or STAG Party for short.
Every child has a right to go to high school and end up
        with a third grade education.
I don't want to say too much about illegal immigration. I'm afraid
        my views will be reported on the Cinco O'Clock News.
I'm often asked why I travel around the country talking politics. Is it for
        humanitarian reasons, community spirit, or is it for the money, the
        limousines or the girls? The answers are: no, no, yes yes yes!
If Iowa is the 'heart' land, what part of the human body is Los Angeles?
Many of you have asked why it's taken me so long to select a running mate. I have
        no intention of reaching into the political grab bag and grabbing any man to
        be my running mate. I'm going to reach in and grab a woman!
Marijuana should be licensed and kept out of the hands of
        teenagers. It's too good for them.
Assuming that either the left wing or the right wing gained
        control of the country, it would probably fly around in circles
Divorce is painful. There's an easy way to save yourself
        a lot of trouble. Just find a woman you hate and
        buy her a house.
I took biology two years in a row just to eat the specimens.
We are upping our standards ---- up yours too!.

## SAUL PERLMUTTER (Astronomer, Nobel Price Winner, 1959 - )

You want your mind to be boggled. That is a pleasure in and of itself. And
        it's more a pleasure if it's boggled by something that you can then
        demonstrate is really, really true.
What we were seeing was a little bit like throwing the apple up in the air
        and seeing it blast off into space.
As a scientist, you feel a sense of team spirit for your country but you also
        have a sense of team spirit for the international community.
I tend not to dwell too much on ultimates.
I was one of those kids who always thought that we should know how the
        world works around us.
I will say that growing up as a kid in an urban environment and having lived
        in cities all my life, the one achievement that everyone can look forward
        to is getting the perfect parking spot.
There are still so many questions to answer. When you look at any part of the
        universe, you have to feel humbled.

## ROSS PEROT (Businessman, Presidential Candidate, 1930 - )

Written reports stifle creativity.
Eagles don't flock, you have to find them one at a time.
If we did not have such a thing as an airplane today, we would probably create
        something the size of N.A.S.A. to make one.
If you can't stand a little sacrifice and you can't stand a trip across the desert
        with limited water, we're never going to straighten this country out.
If you see a snake, just kill it - don't appoint a committee on snakes.
Failures are like skinned knees, painful but superficial.
If someone is blessed as I am is not willing to clean out the barn, who will?

In plain Texas talk, it's 'do the right thing'

Which one of the three candidates would you want your daughter to marry?
(Referring to himself, George H. Bush, and Bill Clinton)

A weak currency is the sign of a weak economy, and a weak economy
leads to a weak nation.

Anybody can cut prices, but it takes brains to produce a better article.

Action is greater than writing. A good man is a nobler object of contemplation
than a great author. There are but two things worth living for: to do what
is worthy of being written; and to write what is worthy of being read.

Business is not just doing deals; business is having great products, doing great
engineering, and providing tremendous service to customers. Finally,
business is a cobweb of human relationships.

You don't have to be the biggest to beat the biggest.

## ROGER TORY PETERSON (Environmentalist, 1908-1996)

Birds have wings; they're free; they can fly where they want when they
want. They have the kind of mobility many people envy.

I consider myself to have been the bridge between the shotgun and the
binoculars in bird watching. Before I came along, the primary way
to observe birds was to shoot them and stuff them.

Birds are indicators of the environment. If they are in trouble, we know
we'll soon be in trouble.

Not all is doom and gloom. We are beginning to understand the natural
world and are gaining a reverence for life - all life.

## FRANKLIN PIERCE (President, 1804-1869)

A Republic without parties is a complete anomaly. The histories of
all popular governments show absurd is the idea of their
attempting to exist without parties.

Frequently the more trifling the subject, the more
animated and protracted the discussion.

The dangers of a concentration of all power in the general government
of a confederacy so vast as ours are too obvious to be disregarded.

## EDGAR ALLAN POE (Author, 1809-1849)

To vilify a great man is the readiest way in which a little
man can himself attain greatness.

Of puns it has been said that those who most dislike them
are those who are least able to utter them.

Poetry is the rhythmical creation of beauty in words.

Science has not yet taught us if madness is or is not the
sublimity of the intelligence.

Stupidity is a talent for misconception.

That man is not truly brave who is afraid either to seem
or to be, when it suits him, a coward.

That pleasure which is at once the most pure, the most elevating
and the most intense, is derived, I maintain, from the
contemplation of the beautiful.

The boundaries which divide Life from Death are at best
shadowy and vague. Who shall say where the one ends,
and where the other begins?

The death of a beautiful woman, is unquestionably the
most poetical topic in the world.
All religion, my friend, is simply evolved out of fraud, fear, greed,
imagination, and poetry.
All that we see or seem is but a dream within a dream.
Beauty of whatever kind, in its supreme development, invariably
excites the sensitive soul to tears.
Experience has shown, and a true philosophy will always show, that a vast,
perhaps the larger portion of the truth arises from the seemingly irrelevant.
I have great faith in fools; self-confidence my friends call it.
I have no faith in human perfectability. I think that human exertion will have
no appreciable effect upon humanity. Man is now only more active - not
more happy - nor more wise, than he was 6000 years ago.
I wish I could write as mysterious as a cat.
If you wish to forget anything on the spot, make a note that
this thing is to be remembered.
In one case out of a hundred a point is excessively discussed
because it is obscure; in the ninety-nine remaining it is obscure
because it is excessively discussed.
It is the nature of truth in general, as of some ores in particular,
to be richest when most superficial.
With me poetry has not been a purpose, but a passion.
Words have no power to impress the mind without the
exquisite horror of their reality.
Man's real life is happy, chiefly because he is ever
expecting that it soon will be so.
The ninety and nine are with dreams, content but the hope of the
world made new, is the hundredth man who is grimly bent
on making those dreams come true.
The nose of a mob is its imagination. By this, at any time, it
can be quietly led.
The rudiment of verse may, possibly, be found in the spondee.
The true genius shudders at incompleteness - and usually prefers
silence to saying something which is not everything it should be.
There are few cases in which mere popularity should be considered a
proper test of merit; but the case of song-writing is, I think, one
of the few.
There is an eloquence in true enthusiasm.
There is something in the unselfish and self-sacrificing love of a brute,
which goes directly to the heart of him who has had frequent
occasion to test the paltry friendship and gossamer fidelity of
mere Man.
They who dream by day are cognizant of many things which escape
those who dream only by night.

## SIDNEY POITIER (Actor, 1924 - )
As a man, I've been representative of the values I hold dear. And
the values I hold dear are carryovers from the lives of
my parents.
. . .I always had the ability to say no. That's how
I called my own shots.

History passes the final judgment.

So much of life, it seems to me, is determined by pure randomness.

So I'm OK with myself, with history, my work, who I am and who I was.

So it's been kind of a long road, but it was a good journey altogether.

The journey has been incredible from its beginning.

There is not racial or ethnic domination of
hopelessness. It's everywhere.

To simply wake up every morning a better person
than when I went to bed.

We all suffer from the preoccupation that there
exists... in the loved one, perfection.

I decided in my life that I would do nothing that did not
reflect positively on my father's life.

I had chosen to use my work as a reflection of my values.

I never had an occasion to question color, therefore, I only saw
myself as what I was... a human being.

I wanted to explore the values that are at work, underpinning my life.

I wanted to look at them because I feel, internally, that I am an
ordinary person who has had an extraordinary life.

If you apply reason and logic to this career of mine, you're not going to
get very far. You simply won't.

Mine was an easy ride compared to Jackie Robinson's.

My autobiography was simply the story of my life.

## JAMES K. POLK (President, 1795-1849)

I am heartily rejoiced that my term is so near its close. I will soon
cease to be a servant and will become a sovereign.

There is more selfishness and less principle among members of Congress
than I had any conception of, before I became President of the U.S.

It becomes us in humility to make our devout acknowledgments to the
Supreme Ruler of the Universe for the inestimable civil and religious
blessings with which we are favored.

Minorities have a right to appeal to the Constitution as a
shield against such oppression.

No president who performs his duties faithfully and
conscientiously can have any leisure.

One great object of the Constitution was to restrain majorities from
oppressing minorities or encroaching upon their just rights.

The passion for office among members of Congress is very great, if not
absolutely disreputable, and greatly embarrasses the operations
of the Government. They create offices by their own
votes and then seek to fill them themselves.

The world has nothing to fear from military ambition in our Government.

With me it is exceptionally true that the Presidency is no bed of roses.

## COLIN POWELL (Soldier, 1937 - )

Excellence is not an exception, it is a prevailing attitude.

Bad news isn't wine. It doesn't improve with age.

If you are going to achieve excellence in big things, you
develop the habit in little matters.

You don't know what you can get away with until you try.

Don't be afraid to challenge the pros, even in their own backyard.
Don't bother people for help without first trying to solve the
    problem yourself.
It ain't as bad as you think. It will look better in the morning.
A dream doesn't become reality through magic; it takes sweat,
    determination and hard work.
Leadership is solving problems. The day soldiers stop bringing you
    their problems is the day you have stopped leading them. They
    have either lost confidence that you can help or concluded you
    do not care. Either case is a failure of leadership.
Never let your ego get so close to your position that when your
    position goes, your ego goes with it.
Experts often possess more data than judgment.
Fit no stereotypes. Don't chase the latest management fads. The situation
    dictates which approach best accomplishes the team's mission.
Get mad, then get over it.
Giving back involves a certain amount of giving up.
Great leaders are almost always great simplifiers, who can cut
    through argument, debate and doubt, to offer a solution
    everybody can understand.
Never neglect details. When everyone's mind is dulled or distracted
    the leader must be doubly vigilant.
No battle plan survives contact with the enemy.
Organization charts and fancy titles count for next to nothing.
Perpetual optimism is a force multiplier.
Politics is not bean bags. It's serious, tough stuff.
The United States is not stingy. We are the greatest contributor
    to international relief efforts in the world.
There are no secrets to success. It is the result of preparation,
    hard work, and learning from failure.
Success is the result of perfection, hard work, learning from
    failure, loyalty, and persistence.
Surround yourself with people who take their work seriously, but
    not themselves, those who work hard and play hard.
The chief condition on which, life, health and vigor depend on,
    is action. It is by action that an organism develops its faculties,
    increases its energy, and attains the fulfillment of its destiny.
The commander in the field is always right and the rear echelon is
    wrong, unless proved otherwise.
The healthiest competition occurs when average people
    win by putting above average effort.

## ELVIS PRESLEY (Singer, Actor, 1935-1977)
Ambition is a dream with a V8 engine.
Truth is like the sun. You can shut it out for a time, but it ain't goin' away.
The image is one thing and the human being is another.
    It's very hard to live up to an image, put it that way.
More than anything else, I want the folks back at home to think right of me.
People ask me where I got my singing style. I didn't copy my style from anybody.
Rhythm is something you either have or don't have,
    but when you have it, you have it all over.

Rock and roll music, if you like it, if you feel it,  you can't help but move
      to it. That's what happens to me. I can't help it.'
The army teaches boys to think like men.
The colored folks been singing it and playing it just like I'm doin'
      now, man, for more years than I know. I got it from them.
The Lord can give, and the Lord can take away.
      I might be herding sheep next year.
There are too many people that depend on me. I'm too obligated.
      I'm in too far to get out.
Until we meet again, may God bless you as he has blessed me.
Whatever I will become will be what God has chosen for me.
When I get married, it'll be no secret.
When I was a boy, I always saw myself as a hero in comic books and
      in movies. I grew up believing this dream.
Too much TV hurts movies.
Adversity is sometimes hard upon a man; but for one man who can
      stand prosperity, there are a hundred that will stand adversity.
I was training to be an electrician. I suppose I got wired the wrong way
      round somewhere along the line.
I'll never feel comfortable taking a strong drink, and I'll never feel easy
      smoking a cigarette. I just don't think those  things are right for me.
I'm not trying to be sexy. It's just my way of expressing
      myself when I move around.
I'm strictly for Stevenson [for president]. I don't dig the intellectual bit,
      but I'm telling you, man, he knows the most.
I'm trying to keep a level head. You have to be careful out in the world.
      It's so easy to get turned.
I've been getting some bad publicity - but you got to expect that.
I'm so nervous. I've always been nervous, ever since I was a kid.
I've never written a song in my life. It's all a big hoax.
I've tried to lead a straight, clean life, not set any kind of a bad example.
Just because I managed to do a little something, I don't want anyone back
      home to think I got the big head.
After a hard day of basic training, you could eat a rattlesnake.
Every time I think that I'm getting old, and gradually going to
      the grave, something else happens.
From the time I was a kid, I always knew something was going to
      happen to me. Didn't know exactly what.
I don't do any vulgar movements.
I don't know anything about music. In my line you don't have to.
I don't think I'm bad for people. If I did think I was bad for people,
      I would go back to driving a truck, and I really mean this.
I happened to come along in the music business when there was no trend.
      I knew by heart all the dialogue of James Dean's films; I could
      watch Rebel Without a Cause a hundred times over.
I never expected to be anybody important.

## JOSEPH PULITZER (Publisher, 1847-1911)
Newspapers should have no friends.
Objectivity is to a newspaper what virtue is to a woman
Our Republic and its press will rise or fall together.

Publicity, publicity, publicity is the greatest moral
    factor and force in our public life.
A cynical, mercenary, demagogic press will in time
    produce a people as base as itself.
An able, disinterested, public-spirited press, with trained intelligence to
    know the right and courage to do it, can preserve that public virtue
    without which popular government is a sham and a mockery.
I am deeply interested in the progress and elevation of journalism, having
    spent my life in that profession, regarding it as a noble profession
    and one of unequaled importance for its influence upon the minds
    and morals of the people.
I desire to assist in attracting to this profession young men of character
    and ability, also to help those already engaged in the profession
    to acquire the highest moral and intellectual training.
Put it before them briefly so they will read it, clearly so they will
    appreciate it, picturesquely so they will remember it and,
    above all, accurately so they will be guided by its light.
The power to mold the future of the Republic will be in the hands of
    the journalists of future generations.

## ERNIE PYLE (War Correspondent, WW2, 1900-1945)

War makes strange giant creatures out of us little routine
    men who inhabit the earth.
All the rest of us - you and me and even the thousands of soldiers behind the lines
    in Africa - we want terribly yet only academically for the war to get over.
At last we are in it up to our necks, and everything is
    changed, even your outlook on life.
. . . to the fighting soldier that phase of the war is behind. It was left behind
    after his first battle. His blood is up. He is fighting for his life, and
    killing now for him is as much a profession as writing is for me.
I've been immersed in it too long. My spirit is wobbly and my mind is
    confused. The hurt has become too great.
If I can just see the European war out I think I might feel justified in
    quitting the war. [Erine did not quit; he died in the Pacific
    theatre of WW2]
In their eyes as they pass is not hatred, not excitement, not despair, not
    the tonic of their victory - there is just the simple expression of
    being here as though they had been here doing this forever,
    and nothing else.
Someday when peace has returned to this odd world I want to come to
    London again and stand on a certain balcony on a moonlit night
    and look down upon the peaceful silver curve of the Thames with
    its dark bridges.
Swinging first and swinging to kill is all that matters now.
The American soldier is quick in adapting himself to a new mode of living.
    Outfits which have been here only three days have dug vast networks
    of ditches three feet deep in the bare brown earth. They have rigged
    up a light here and there with a storage battery.
The front-line soldier wants it to be got over by the physical process of his
    destroying enough Germans to end it. He is truly at war. The rest of
    us, no matter how hard we work, are not.

If you go long enough without a bath, even the fleas will leave you alone.
The men are walking. They are fifty feet apart, for dispersal. Their walk is
        slow, for they are dead weary, as you can tell even when looking at
        them from behind. Every line and sag of their bodies speaks their
        inhuman exhaustion.

## DAN QUAYLE (Vice President, 1947 - )

A low voter turnout is an indication of fewer people going to the polls.
Bank failures are caused by depositors who don't deposit enough
        money to cover losses due to mismanagement.
Bobby Knight told me this: 'There is nothing that a good defense cannot
        beat a better offense.' In other words a good offense wins.
El Salvador is a democracy so it's not surprising that there are many voices
        to be heard here. Yet in my conversations with Salvadorans... I have
        heard a single voice.
Every once in a while, you let a word or phrase out and you want to catch
        it and bring it back. You can't do that. It's gone, gone forever.
For NASA, space is still a high priority.
Great American sport. Horseshoes is a very great game. I love it.
Hawaii has always been a very pivotal role in the Pacific. It is in the
        Pacific. It is a part of the United States that is an island that is right here.
I am not part of the problem. I am a Republican.
I believe we are on an irreversible trend toward more freedom and
        democracy - but that could change.
I couldn't help but be impressed by the magnitude of the earthquake.
I deserve respect for the things I did not do.
I do have a political agenda. It's to have as few regulations as possible.
I don't watch it, but I know enough to comment on it.
I have a very good family. I'm very fortunate to have a very good family.
        I believe very strongly in the family. It's one of the things we have
        in our platform, is to talk about it.
I have made good judgments in the past. I have made good
        judgments in the future.
I just don't believe in the basic concept that someone should make
        their whole career in public service.
I love California, I practically grew up in Phoenix.
I pledge allegiance to the Christian flag, and to the Savior, for whose
        Kingdom it stands, one Savior, crucified, risen, and coming again,
        with life and liberty for all who believe.
I spend a great deal of time with the President. We have a very close, personal,
        loyal relationship. I'm not, as they say, a potted plant in these meetings
I stand by all the misstatements that I've made.
I want to be Robin to Bush's Batman.
I was known as the chief grave robber of my state.
I was recently on a tour of Latin America, and the only regret I have was that I
        didn't study Latin harder in school so I could converse with those people.
I've never professed to be anything but an average student.
If Al Gore invented the Internet, I invented spell check.
If we don't succeed we run the risk of failure.
If you give a person a fish, they'll fish for a day. But if you train a person
        to fish, they'll fish for a lifetime.

Illegitimacy is something we should talk about in terms of not having it.

It isn't pollution that's harming the environment. It's the impurities in
our air and water that are doing it.

It shows 'us vs. them,' and I'm on the 'us' side.

It's a question of whether we're going to go forward into the
future, or past to the back.

It's a very good historical book about history.

It's rural America. It's where I came from. We always refer to ourselves
as real America. Rural America, real America, real, real, America.

It's time for the human race to enter the solar system.

It's wonderful to be here in the great state of Chicago.

Japan is an important ally of ours. Japan and the United States of the
Western industrialized capacity, 60 percent of the GNP, two
countries. That's a statement in and of itself.

Let me just be very clear that the Republican Party will select a nominee
that will beat Bill Clinton.

My friends, no matter how rough the road may be, we can and we will,
never never surrender to what is right.

People that are really very weird can get into sensitive positions
and have a tremendous impact on history.

People who bowl vote. Bowlers are not the cultural elite.

Quite frankly, teachers are the only profession that teach our children.

Republicans have been accused of abandoning the poor. It's the other
way around. They never vote for us.

Republicans understand the importance of bondage between a mother and child.

Space is almost infinite. As a matter of fact, we think it is infinite.

The American people would not want to know of any misquotes
that Dan Quayle may or may not make.

The future will be better tomorrow.

The global importance of the Middle East is that it keeps the Far East
and the Near East from encroaching on each other.

The Holocaust was an obscene period in our nation's history. I mean in this
century's history. But we all lived in this century. I didn't
live in this century.

The loss of life will be irreplaceable.

The other day the President said, I know you've had some rough times, and
I want to do something that will show the nation what faith that I have
in you, in your maturity and sense of responsibility. He paused, then
said, would you like a puppy?

The President is going to benefit from me reporting directly to him when I arrive.

This President is going to lead us out of this recovery.

Tobacco exports should be expanded aggressively because
Americans are smoking less.

Unfortunately, the people of Louisiana are not racists.

Votes are like trees, if you are trying to build a forest. If you have more
trees than you have forests, then at that point the pollsters
will probably say you will win.

We have a firm commitment to NATO, we are a part of NATO. We have a firm
commitment to Europe. We are a part of Europe.

We have to do more than just elect a new President if we
truly want to change this country.

We should develop anti-satellite weapons because we could not
have prevailed without them in 'Red Storm Rising'.
We are ready for any unforeseen event that may or may not occur.
We shouldn't have to be burdened with all the technicalities that come up
from time to time with shrewd, smart lawyers interpreting what the
laws or what the Constitution may or may not say.
We will invest in our people, quality education, job opportunity, family,
neighborhood, and yes, a thing we call America.
We will move forward, we will move upward, and yes, we will move onward.
We're all capable of mistakes, but I do not care to enlighten you on the
mistakes we may or may not have made.
We're going to have the best-educated American people in the world.
Welcome to President Bush, Mrs. Bush, and my fellow astronauts.
What a terrible thing to have lost one's mind. Or not to have a mind at
all. How true that is.
What a waste it is to lose one's mind. Or not to have a mind is being
very wasteful. How true that is.
What you guys want, I'm for.
When I have been asked during these last weeks who caused the riots and
the killing in L.A., my answer has been direct and simple: Who is to
blame for the riots? The rioters are to blame. Who is to blame for the
killings? The killers are to blame.
When you make as many speeches and you talk as much as I do and
you get away from the text, it's always a possibility to get a few
words tangled here and there.
You all look like happy campers to me. Happy campers you are, happy
campers you have been, and, as far as I am concerned, happy
campers you will always be.
You do the policy, I'll do the politics

## QWATSINAS [Nuxalk Indian Nation, died 2010]
We must protect the forests for our children, grandchildren and children yet
to be born. We must protect the forests for those who can't speak for
themselves such as the birds, animals, fish and trees.

## GILDA RADNER (Actor, 1946-1989)
Adopted kids are such a pain - you have to teach them how to look like you.
I'd much rather be a woman than a man. Women can cry, they can wear cute
clothes, and they're the first to be rescued off sinking ships.
Comedy is very controlling - you are making people laugh.
I can always be distracted by love, but eventually I get horny for my creativity.
I wanted a perfect ending. Now I've learned, the hard way, that some poems don't
rhyme, and some stories don't have a clear beginning, middle and end.
Life is about not knowing, having to change, taking the moment and making the
best of it, without knowing what's going to happen next.
The goal is to live a full, productive life even with all that ambiguity. No matter what
happens, whether the cancer never flares up again or whether you die, the
important thing is that the days that you have had you will have lived.
While we have the gift of life, it seems to me the only tragedy is to allow part of us
to die - whether it is our spirit, our creativity or our glorious uniqueness.

You feel completely in control when you hear a wave of laughter coming back at you that you have caused.

Dreams are like paper, they tear so easily.

I base my fashion taste on what doesn't itch.

## DAN RATHER (Journalist, News Commentator, 1931 - )

Courage is being afraid but going on anyhow.

If all difficulties were known at the outset of a long journey, most of us would never start out at all.

Don't taunt the alligator until after you've crossed the creek.

Americans will put up with anything provided it doesn't block traffic.

An intellectual snob is someone who can listen to the William Tell Overture and not think of The Lone Ranger.

A tough lesson in life that one has to learn is that not everybody wishes you well.

The dream begins with a teacher who believes in you, who tugs and pushes and leads you to the next plateau, sometimes poking you with a sharp stick called "truth".

I'm proud to say I've never been anybody's lapdog.

Those market researchers... are playing games with you and me and with this entire country. Their so-called samples of opinion are no more accurate or reliable than my grandmother's big toe was when it came to predicting the weather.

To err is human but to really foul up requires a computer.

What I say or do here won't matter much, nor should it.

## ROBERT RAUSCHENBERG (Artist, 1925-2008)

An empty canvas is full.

. . . I think a painting has such a limited life anyway.

I always have a good reason for taking something out but I never have one for putting something in. And I don't want to, because that means that the picture is being painted predigested.

I don't mess around with my subconscious.

Every time I've moved, my work has changed radically.

I don't think any one person, whether artist or not, has been given permission by anyone to put the responsibility of the way things are on anyone else.

I think a painting is more like the real world if it's made out the real world.

I'm sure we don't read old paintings the way they were intended.

If you don't have trouble paying the rent, you have trouble doing something else; one needs just a certain amount of trouble.

The artist's job is to be a witness to his time in history.

There was a whole language that I could never make function for myself in relationship to painting and that was attitudes like tortured, struggle, pain.

Very quickly a painting is turned into a facsimile of itself when one becomes so familiar with with it that one recognizes it without looking at it.

## NANCY REAGAN (First Lady, 1921 - )

A lot of what acting is paying attention.

I am a big believer that eventually everything comes back to
you. You get back what you give out.

I believe that people would be alive today if there were a death penalty.

I do not believe in abortion at will. I do not believe that if a woman just
wants to have an abortion she should... I do believe if you have
an abortion you are committing murder.

I don't talk about political matters. That's not my department.

I don't think most people associate me with leeches or how to get them
off. But I know how to get them off. I'm an expert at it.

I must say acting was good training for the political life
which lay ahead for us.

I see the first lady as another means to keep a
president from becoming isolated.

I think a woman gets more if she acts feminine.

I think people would be alive today if there were a death penalty.

Just say no to drugs!

My life really began when I married my husband.

Pornography is pornography, what is there to see? Movies are attempting
to destroy something that's supposed to be the most beautiful thing
a man and a woman can have by making it cheap and common. It's
what you don't see that's attractive.

The movies were custard compared to politics.

## RONALD REAGAN (President, 1911-2004)

A people free to choose will always choose peace.

I've noticed that everyone who is for abortion has already been born.

A tree's a tree. How many more do you need to look at?

Above all, we must realize that no arsenal, or no weapon in the arsenals of the
world, is so formidable as the will and moral courage of free men and
women. It is a weapon our adversaries in today's world do not have.

All great change in America begins at the dinner table.

All the waste in a year from a nuclear power plant can be stored under a desk.

Approximately 80% of our air pollution stems from hydrocarbons released by
vegetation, so let's not go overboard in setting and enforcing tough
emission standards from man-made sources.

Before I refuse to take your questions, I have an opening statement.

But there are advantages to being elected President. The day after I was
elected, I had my high school grades classified Top Secret.

Concentrated power has always been the enemy of liberty.

Democracy is worth dying for, because it's the most deeply honorable
form of government ever devised by man.

Don't be afraid to see what you see.

Each generation goes further than the generation preceding it because it
stands on the shoulders of that generation. You will have opportunities
beyond anything we've ever known.

Facts are stubborn things.

Freedom is never more than one generation away from extinction. We didn't
pass it to our children in the bloodstream. It must be fought for,
protected, and handed on for them to do the same.

Freedom prospers when religion is vibrant and the rule of law
under God is acknowledged.

Entrepreneurs and their small enterprises are responsible for almost all the
economic growth in the United States.

Going to college offered me the chance to play football for four more years.

Government always finds a need for whatever money it gets.

Government does not solve problems; it subsidizes them.

Government exists to protect us from each other. Where government has
gone beyond its limits is in deciding to protect us from ourselves.

Government is like a baby. An alimentary canal with a loud voice at
one end and no responsibility at the other.

Government's first duty is to protect the people, not run their lives.

Governments tend not to solve problems, only to rearrange them.

Heroes may not be braver than anyone else. They're
just braver five minutes longer.

History teaches that war begins when governments believe
the price of aggression is cheap.

How can a president not be an actor?

How do you tell a communist? Well, it's someone who reads Marx
and Lenin. And how do you tell an anti-Communist?
It's someone who understands Marx and Lenin.

I call upon the scientific community in our country, those who gave us
nuclear weapons, to turn their great talents now to the cause of
mankind and world peace: to give us the means of rendering
these nuclear weapons impotent and obsolete.

I favor the Civil Rights Act of 1964 and it must be
enforced at gunpoint if necessary.

I have left orders to be awakened at any time in case of
national emergency, even if I'm in a cabinet meeting.

I have wondered at times what the Ten Commandments would have
looked like if Moses had run them through the US Congress.

I know in my heart that man is good. That what is right will always eventually
triumph. And there's purpose and worth to each and every life.

I never drink coffee at lunch. I find it keeps me awake for the afternoon.

I'm not worried about the deficit. It is big enough to take care of itself.

I've never been able to understand why a Republican contributor is a
'fat cat' and a Democratic contributor of the same amount of
money is a 'public-spirited philanthropist'.

I've often said there's nothing better for the inside of a man
than the outside of a horse.

If the federal government had been around when the Creator was
putting  His hand to this state, Indiana wouldn't be here. It'd still
be waiting for an environmental impact statement.

If the Soviet Union let another political party come into existence, they would
still be a one-party state, because everybody would join the other party.

If we love our country, we should also love our countrymen.

Information is the oxygen of the modern age. It seeps through the walls
topped by barbed wire, it wafts across the electrified borders.

It doesn't do good to open doors for someone who doesn't have the price to
get in. If he has the price, he may not need the laws. There is no law
saying the Negro has to live in Harlem or Watts.

It's difficult to believe that people are still starving in this country
        because food isn't available.
Inflation is as violent as a mugger, as frightening as
        an armed robber and as deadly as a hit man.
It's silly talking about how many years we will have to spend in the jungles of
        Vietnam when we could pave the whole country and put parking stripes
        on it and still be home by Christmas.
Let us be sure that those who come after will say of us in our time, that in
        our time we did everything that could be done. We finished the race;
        we kept them free; we kept the faith.
Let us not forget who we are. Drug abuse is a repudiation of everything America is.
Life is one grand, sweet song, so start the music.
Man is not free unless government is limited.
My fellow Americans, I am pleased to tell you I just signed legislation
        which outlaws Russia forever. The bombing begins in five minutes.
My philosophy of life is that if we make up our mind what we are going to
        make of our lives, then work hard toward that goal, we never lose -
        somehow we win out.
No government ever voluntarily reduces itself in size. Government programs,
        once launched, never disappear. Actually, a government bureau is the
        nearest thing to eternal life we'll ever see on this earth!
No matter what time it is, wake me, even if it's in the middle of a Cabinet meeting.
No mother would ever willingly sacrifice her sons for territorial gain, for
        economic advantage, for ideology.
Of the four wars in my lifetime, none came about because the U.S. was too strong.
One picture is worth 1,000 denials.
One way to make sure crime doesn't pay would be to let the government run it.
Peace is not the absence of conflict, it is the ability to handle conflict
        by peaceful means.
People do not make wars; governments do.
Politics I supposed to be the second-oldest profession. I have come to
        realize that it bears a very close resemblance to the first.
Politics is just like show business. You have a hell of an opening, coast
        for a while, and then have a hell of a close.
Politics is not a bad profession. If you succeed there are many rewards, if you
        disgrace yourself you can always write a book.
Protecting the rights of even the least individual among us is basically
        the only excuse the government has for even existing.
Recession is when a neighbor loses his job. Depression is when you lose yours.
Republicans believe every day is the Fourth of July, but the democrats
        believe every day is April 15.
Some people wonder all their lives if they've made a difference. The
        Marines don't have that problem.
Status quo, you know, is Latin for 'the mess we're in'.
Surround yourself with the best people you can find, delegate authority, and don't
        interfere as long as the policy you've decided upon is being carried out.
The best minds are not in government. If any were, business
        would steal them  away.
The government's view of the economy could be summed up in a few short
        phrases: If it moves, tax it. If it keeps moving, regulate it. And if it
        stops moving, subsidize it.

The greatest security for Israel is to create new Egypts.

The most terrifying words in the English language are: I'm from the
government and I'm here to help.

The problem is not that people are taxed too little, the problem is that
government spends too much.

The taxpayer - that's someone who works for the federal government
but doesn't have to take the civil service examination.

The thought of being President frightens me and I do not think I want the job.

There are no constraints on the human mind, no walls around the human
spirit, no barriers to our progress except those we ourselves erect.

There are no easy answers' but there are simple answers. We must have the
courage to do what we know is morally right.

There are no great limits to growth because there are no limits of human
intelligence, imagination, and wonder.

They say hard work never hurt anybody, but I figure why take the chance.

They say the world has become too complex for simple answers. They are wrong.

Thomas Jefferson once said, 'We should never judge a president by his age,
only by his works.' And ever since he told me that, I stopped worrying.

To paraphrase Winston Churchill, I did not take the oath I have just taken with the
intention of presiding over the dissolution of the world's strongest economy.

To sit back hoping that someday, some way, someone will make things right is to
go on feeding the crocodile, hoping he will eat you last - but eat you he will.

Today we did what we had to do. They counted on America to be
passive. They counted wrong.

Today, if you invent a better mousetrap, the government
comes along with a better mouse.

Trust, but verify.

Unemployment insurance is a pre-paid vacation for freeloaders.

We are never defeated unless we give up on God.

We can not play innocents abroad in a world that is not innocent.

We can't help everyone, but everyone can help someone.

We have the duty to protect the life of an unborn child.

We might come closer to balancing the Budget  if  all of us lived closer
to the Commandments and the Golden Rule.

We must reject the idea that every time a law's broken, society is guilty rather
than the lawbreaker. It is time to restore the American precept that each
individual is accountable for his actions.

We should measure welfare's success by how many people leave
welfare, not by how many are added.

We will always remember. We will always be proud. We will always be
prepared, so we will always be free.

We're in greater danger today than we were the day after Pearl Harbor. Our
military is absolutely incapable of defending this country.

Welfare's purpose should be to eliminate, as far as possible, the need
for its own existence.

When you can't make them see the light, make them feel the heat.

While I take inspiration from the past, like most Americans, I live for the future.

You can tell a lot about a fellow's character by his way of eating jellybeans.

## HARRY REASONER (News Commentator, 1923-1991)

The thing is helicopters are different from airplanes An airplane by it's nature wants to fly, and if not interfered with too strongly by unusual events or incompetent piloting, it will fly.

We're all controlled neurotics.

When 25 percent of the population believe the President should be impeached and 51 percent of the population believe in UFOs, you may or may not need a new President, but you definitely need a new population.

## ROBERT REDFORD (Actor, 1936 - )

Sport is a wonderful metaphor for life. Of all the sports that I played - skiing, baseball, fishing - there is no greater example than golf, because you're playing against yourself and nature.

Generally speaking, I went through that. I came to a place where I realized what true value was. It wasn't money. Money is a means to achieving an end, but it's not the end.

Health food may be good for the conscience but Oreos taste a hell of a lot better.

I believe in mythology. I guess I share Joseph Campbell's notion that a culture or society without mythology would die, and we're close to that.

I don't know what your childhood was like, but we didn't have much money. We'd go to a movie on a Saturday night, then on Wednesday night my parents would walk us over to the library. It was such a big deal, to go in and get my own book.

I think the environment should be put in the category of our national security. Defense of our resources is just as important as defense abroad. Otherwise what is there to defend?

I'm not a facelift person. I am what I am.

I'm not interested in a film about golf but I am interested in golf as a metaphor.

In fact you've got your hands tied behind your back when somebody chooses to take a low road in to you, there is nothing you can do about it, and so you just live with it and move on.

It's an honor putting art above politics. Politics can be seductive in terms of things reductive to the soul.

## BURT REYNOLDS (Actor, 1936 - )

I can sing as well as Fred Astaire can act.

Marriage is about the most expensive way for the average man to get laundry done.

My movies were the kind they show in prisons and airplanes, because nobody can leave.

I've always gotten along well with Texans. You've got to.

The moment you grab someone by the lapels, you're lost.

You can only hold your stomach in for so many years.

## SALLY RIDE (Astronaut, 1951 - )

All adventures, especially into new territory, are scary.

Because I was a tennis player, Billie Jean King was a hero of mine.

But when I wasn't working, I was usually at a window looking down at Earth.

For quite some time, women at NASA only had scientific backgrounds.

I didn't really decide that I wanted to be an astronaut for sure until the end of college.

I had both male and female heroes.
When you're getting ready to launch into space, you're
         sitting on a big explosion waiting to happen.
Yes, I did feel a special responsibility to be the first
         American woman in space.

## JAMES WHITCOMB RILEY (Poet, 1849-1916)
The ripest peach is highest on the tree.
It is no use to grumble and complain; It's just as cheap and easy to rejoice;
When God sorts out the weather and sends rain - Why, rain's my choice.
The anger of a person who is strong, can always bide its time.
The most essential factor is persistence - the determination never to allow
         your energy or enthusiasm to be dampened by the discouragement
         that must inevitably come.
When I see a bird that walks like a duck and swims like a duck and
         quacks like a duck, I call that bird a duck.
When you awaken some morning and hear that somebody or other has
         been discovered, you can put it down as a fact that he
         discovered himself years ago - since that time he has
         been toiling, working, and striving  to make himself worthy
         of general discovery.

## PAT RILEY (Basketball Coach, 1945 -)
If you have a positive attitude and constantly strive to give your
         best effort, eventually you will overcome your immediate
         problems and find you are ready for greater challenges.
Look for your choices, pick the best one, then go with it.
People who create 20% of the results will begin believing they
         deserve 80% of the rewards.
The Ten Commandments were not a suggestion.
There can only be one state of mind as you approach any profound test;
         total concentration, a spirit of togetherness, and strength.
There's always the motivation of wanting to win. Everybody has that.
         But a champion needs, in his attitude, a motivation
         above and beyond winning.
There's no such thing as coulda, shoulda, or woulda. If you
         shoulda and coulda, you woulda done it.
You can never have enough talent.
You have no choices about how you lose, but you do have a choice
         about how you come back and prepare to win again.
Discipline is not a nasty word.
Don't let other people tell you what you want.
Excellence is the gradual result of always striving to do better.
Giving yourself permission to lose guarantees a loss.
Great effort springs naturally from great attitude.
A champion needs a motivation above and beyond winning.
Being a part of success is more important than being
         personally indispensable.
Being ready isn't enough; you have to be prepared for a promotion
         or any other significant change.
Don't let other people tell you what you want.

Each Warrior wants to leave the mark of his will, his signature, on
        important acts he touches. This is not the voice of ego but
        of the human spirit, rising up and declaring that it has
        something to contribute to the solution of the hardest
        problems, no matter how vexing!
Excellence is the gradual result of always striving to do better.
Giving yourself permission to lose guarantees a loss.
Great effort springs naturally from great attitude.

## ORAL ROBERTS (Evangelist. 1918-2009)

God wants you well. God wants you prosperous. God wants you a whole person.
I am charismatic with roots of the Pentecostal
Well, I can't figure out God.

## JOHN D. ROCKEFELLER (Businessman, 1839-1937)

A friendship founded on business is better than a
        business founded on friendship.
 Competition is a sin.
Do you know the only thing that gives me pleasure? It's
        to see my dividends coming in.
Charity is injurious unless it helps the recipient to become independent of it.
If you want to succeed you should strike out on new paths, rather
        than travel the worn paths of accepted success.
If your only goal is to become rich, you will never achieve it.
It is wrong to assume that men of immense wealth are always happy.
Next to doing the right thing, the most important thing is to let people
        know you are doing the right thing.
Singleness of purpose is one of the chief essentials for success in life,
        no matter what may be one's aim.
The ability to deal with people is as purchasable a commodity
        as sugar or coffee and I will pay more for that ability than for
        any other under the sun.
The most important thing for a young man is to establish
        a credit... a reputation, character.
The only question with wealth is, what do you do with it?
The way to make money is to buy when blood is running in the streets.
There is nothing in this world that can compare with the Christian
        fellowship; nothing that can satisfy but Christ.
After it is all over, the religion of man is his most important possession.
And we are never too old to study the Bible. Each time the lessons
        are studied comes some new meaning, some new thought
        which will make us better.
Don't be afraid to give up the good to go for the great.
Don't blame the marketing department. The buck stops with
        the chief executive.
Every right implies a responsibility; Every opportunity, an
        obligation, Every possession, a duty.
I always tried to turn every disaster into an opportunity.
I believe in the dignity of labor, whether with head or hand; that the
        world owes no man a living but that it owes every man an
        opportunity to make a living.

I believe that thrift is essential to well-ordered living.
Good leadership consists of showing average people how
to do the work of superior people.
I can think of nothing less pleasurable than a life devoted to pleasure.
I do not think that there is any other quality so essential to success of
any kind as the quality of perseverance. It overcomes almost
everything, even nature.
I have ways of making money that you know nothing of.
I know of nothing more despicable and pathetic than a man who devotes
all the hours of the waking day to the making of money for
money's sake.
I would rather earn 1% off a 100 people's efforts than 100% of
my own efforts.

## NELSON ROCKEFELLER (Politician, 1908-1979)

There are three periods in life: youth, middle age and "how well you look.
The chief problem of low-income farmers is poverty.
America is not just a power, it is a promise. It is not enough for our country
to be extraordinary in might; it must be exemplary in meaning.
It is essential that we enable young people to see themselves as participants
in one of the most exciting eras in history, and to have a sense of
purpose in relation to it.
Never forget that the most powerful force on earth is love.
The secret to success is to own nothing, but control everything.

## NORMAN ROCKWELL (Painter, 1894-1978)

I'm the oldest antique in town.  I'm tired, but proud.
Without thinking too much about it in specific terms, I was showing the America
I knew and observed to others who might not have noticed. My
fundamental purpose is to interpret the typical American. I am a story teller.
If a picture wasn't going very well, I'd put a puppy in it.
Commonplaces never become tiresome. It is we who become tired when
we cease to be curious and appreciative.
I unconsciously decided that, even if it wasn't an ideal world, it should be and
so painted only the ideal aspects of it—pictures in which there are no
drunken slatterns or self-centered mothers ... only foxy grandpas who
played baseball with the kids and boys who fished from logs and got up
circuses in the backyard.
The view of life I communicate in my pictures excludes the sordid and
ugly. I paint life as I would like it to be.
I learned to draw everything except glamorous women. No matter how
much I tried to make them look sexy, they always ended up l
ooking silly ... or like somebody's mother.
If there was sadness in this creative world of mine, it was a pleasant
sadness. If there were problems, they were humorous problems.
Some folks think I painted Lincoln from life, but I haven't been around
that long. Not quite.
I cannot convince myself that a painting is good unless it is popular. If the
public dislikes one of my Post covers, I can't help disliking it myself.

## GENE RODDENBERRY (Creator of Star Trek, 1921-1991)

A man either lives life as it happens to him, meets it head-on and
  licks it, or he turns his back on it and starts to wither away.

Time is the fire in which we burn.

We must question the story logic of having an all-knowing all-powerful God,
  who creates faulty Humans, and then blames them for his own mistakes.

If man is to survive, he will have learned to take a delight in the essential
  differences between men and between cultures. He will learn that
  differences in ideas and attitudes are a delight, part of life's exciting
  variety, not something to fear.

It is the struggle itself that is most important. We must strive to be more
  than we are. It does not matter that we will not reach our ultimate
  goal. The effort itself yields its own reward.

The network told me to get rid of Number One, the woman first lieutenant, and
  also get rid of 'that Martian fellow'... meaning, of course, Spock. I knew I
  couldn't keep both, so I gave the stoicism of the female officer to Spock,
  and married the actress who played Number One. Thank God it wasn't
  the other way around. I mean Leonard's cute, but...

Ancient astronauts didn't build the pyramids. Human beings built
  the pyramids, because they're clever and they work hard.

## WILL ROGERS (Humorist, 1879-1935)

A difference of opinion is what makes horse racing and missionaries.

A fool and his money are soon elected.

A holding company is a thing where you hand an accomplice the
  goods while the policeman searches you.

A man only learns in two ways, one by reading, and the other by
  association with smarter people.

A remark generally hurts in proportion to its truth.

About all I can say for the United States Senate is that it opens with a
  prayer and closes with an investigation.

Advertising is the art of convincing people to spend money they
  don't have for something they don't need.

Alexander Hamilton started the U.S. Treasury with nothing, and that
  was the closest our country has ever been to being even.

All I know is just what I read in the papers, and that's an alibi for my ignorance

America is a nation that conceives many odd inventions for getting
  somewhere but it can think of nothing to do once it gets there.

America is becoming so educated that ignorance will be a novelty. I
  will belong to the select few.

An economist's guess is liable to be as good as anybody else's.

An ignorant person is one who doesn't know what you have just found out.

An onion can make people cry but there's never been a vegetable that
  can make people laugh.

Ancient Rome declined because it had a Senate, now what's going to
  happen to us with both a House and a Senate?

Anything important is never left to the vote of the people. We only get
to vote on some man; we never get to vote on what he is to do.

Be thankful we're not getting all the government we're paying for.

Being a hero is about the shortest-lived profession on earth.

Buy land. They ain't making any more of the stuff.

Chaotic action is preferable to orderly inaction.
Communism to me is one-third practice and two-thirds explanation.
Democrats never agree on anything, that's why they're Democrats. If
      they agreed with each other, they would be Republicans.
Diplomacy is the art of saying "Nice doggie" until you can find a rock.
Diplomats are just as essential to starting a war as soldiers are for finishing  it...
      You take diplomacy out of war, and the thing would fall flat in a week.
Do the best you can, and don't take life too serious.
Don't gamble; take all your savings and buy some good stock and hold
      it till it goes up, then sell it. If it don't go up, don't buy it.
Even if you're on the right track, you'll get run over if you just sit there.
Even though you are on the right track - you will get run over if you just sit there.
Everybody is ignorant, only on different subjects.
Everything is changing. People are taking their comedians
      seriously and the politicians as a joke.
Everything is funny, as long as it's happening to somebody else.
Get someone else to blow your horn and the sound will carry twice as far.
Good judgment comes from experience, and a lot of that comes
      from bad judgment.
Half our life is spent trying to find something to do with the time
      we have rushed through life trying to save.
I am not a member of any organized political party. I am a Democrat.
I bet after seeing us, George Washington would sue us for calling him "father."
I don't make jokes. I just watch the government and report the facts.
I guess there is nothing that will get your mind off everything like golf. I have
      never been depressed enough to take up the game, but they say you
      get so sore at yourself you forget to hate your enemies.
I have a scheme for stopping war. It's this - no nation is allowed to enter
      a war till they have paid for the last one.
I never expected to see the day when girls would get
      sunburned in the places they now do.
I read about eight newspapers in a day. When I'm in a town with
      only one newspaper, I read it eight times.
I'm not a real movie star. I've still got the same wife I started out
      with twenty-eight years ago.
If advertisers spent the same amount of money on improving their products
      as they do on advertising then they wouldn't have to advertise them.
If I studied all my life, I couldn't think up half the number of funny
      things passed in one session of congress.
If Stupidity got us into this mess, then why can't it get us out?
If the other fellow sells cheaper than you, it is called dumping. 'Course, if
      you sell cheaper than him, that's mass production.
If you ever injected truth into politics you have no politics.
If you make any money, the government shoves you in the creek once a
      year with it in your pockets, and all that don't get wet you can keep.
If you want to be successful, it's just this simple. Know what you are
      doing. Love what you are doing. And believe in what you are doing.
In Hollywood the woods are full of people that learned to write but
      evidently can't read. If they could read their stuff, they'd stop writing.
In Hollywood you can see things at night that are fast enough to be
      in the Olympics in the day time.

Instead of giving money to found colleges to promote learning, why don't they
        pass a constitutional amendment prohibiting anybody from learning
        anything? If it works as good as the Prohibition one did, why, in five
        years we would have the smartest race of people on earth.
If you can build a business up big enough, it's respectable.
It isn't what we don't know that gives us trouble, it's what we know that ain't  so.
It's a good thing we don't get all the government we pay for.
It's easy being a humorist when you've got the whole government working for you.
It's not what you pay a man, but what he costs you that counts.
Last year we said, 'Things can't go on like this', and they didn't, they got worse.
Let advertisers spend the same amount of money improving their product
        that they do on advertising and they wouldn't have to advertise it.
Lettin' the cat outta the bag is a whole lot easier 'n puttin' it back in.
Liberty doesn't work as well in practice as it does in speeches.
Make crime pay. Become a lawyer.
Money and women are the most sought after and the
        least known about of any two things we have.
Never let yesterday use up too much of today.
Now if there is one thing that we do worse than any other nation, it
        is try and manage somebody else's affairs.
Ohio claims they are due a president as they haven't had one since Taft.
        Look at the United States, they have not had one since Lincoln.
On account of being a democracy and run by the people, we are the only nation in
        the world that has to keep a government four years, no matter what it does.
One Ad is worth more to a paper than forty Editorials.
One-third of the people in the United States promote, while the
        other two-thirds provide.
Our constitution protects aliens, drunks and U.S. Senators.
People are getting smarter nowadays; they are letting lawyers, instead of
        their conscience, be their guide.
People who fly into a rage always make a bad landing.
People's minds are changed through observation and not through argument.
Politics has become so expensive that it takes a lot of money even to be defeated.
Politics is applesauce.
Prohibition is better than no liquor at all.
So let's be honest with ourselves and not take ourselves too serious,
        and never condemn the other fellow for doing what we are doing
        every day, only in a different way.
So live that you wouldn't be ashamed to sell the family parrot to the town gossip.
Take the diplomacy out of war and the thing would fall flat in a week.
The 1928 Republican Convention opened with a prayer. If the Lord can see His
        way clear to bless the Republican Party the way it's been carrying on,
        then the rest of us ought to get it without even asking.
The best way out of a difficulty is through it.
The difference between a Republican and a Democrat is the Democrat is a
        cannibal they have to live off each other, while the Republicans, why,
        they live off the Democrats.
The farmer has to be an optimist or he wouldn't still be a farmer.
The fellow that can only see a week ahead is always the popular fellow, for he
        is looking with the crowd. But the one that can see years ahead, he
        has a telescope but he can't make anybody believe that he has it.

The income tax has made liars out of more Americans than golf.

The man with the best job in the country is the vice-president. All he has t
o do is get up every morning and say, "How is the president?"

The more that learn to read the less learn how to make a living. That's one
thing about a little education. It spoils you for actual work. The more
you know the more you think somebody owes you a living.

The more you observe politics, the more you've got to admit that each
party is worse than the other.

The movies are the only business where you can go out front and applaud yourself.

The only difference between death and taxes is that death doesn't get
worse every time Congress meets.

The only time people dislike gossip is when you gossip about them.

The only way you can beat the lawyers is to die with nothing.

The schools ain't what they used to be and never was.

The time to save is now. When a dog gets a bone, he doesn't go out and make a
down payment on a bigger bone. He buries the one he's got.

The United States never lost a war or won a conference.

The worst thing that happens to you may be the best thing for you if you
don't let it get the best of you.

There are three kinds of men. The one that learns by reading. The few
who learn by observation. The rest of them have to pee on the
electric fence for themselves.

There is no more independence in politics than there is in jail.

There is nothing so stupid as the educated man if you get him
off the thing he was educated in.

There ought to be one day - just one - when there is open season on senators.

There's no trick to being a humorist when you have the whole
government working for you.

There's only one thing that can kill the movies, and that's education.

Things ain't what they used to be and never were.

Things in our country run in spite of government, not by aid of it.

This country has come to feel the same when Congress is in session as
when the baby gets hold of a hammer.

This thing of being a hero, about the main thing to it is to know when to die.

We are all here for a spell, get all the good laughs you can.

We can't all be heroes, because somebody has to sit on the
curb and applaud when they go by.

We don't seem to be able to check crime, so why not legalize
it and then tax it out of business?

We will never have true civilization until we have learned to
recognize the rights of others.

What the country needs is dirtier fingernails and cleaner minds.

When should a college athlete turn pro? Not until he has earned all
he can in college as an amateur.

When the Oakies left Oklahoma and moved to California, it
raised the I.Q. of both states.

When you put down the good things you ought to have done, and leave
out the bad ones you did do well, that's Memoirs.

Why don't they pass a constitutional amendment prohibiting anybody from
learning anything? If it works as well as prohibition did, in five years
Americans would be the smartest race of people on Earth.

Worrying is like paying on a debt that may never come due.
You can't say civilization don't advance... in every war they kill you in a new way.
You've got to go out on a limb sometimes because that's where the fruit is.
When ignorance gets started it knows no bounds.

## ELEANOR ROOSEVELT (First Lady, 1884-1962)

A woman is like a tea bag - you can't tell how strong she is until you
     put her in hot water.
Perhaps nature is our best assurance of immortality.
No one can make you feel inferior without your consent.
It takes as much energy to wish as it does to plan.
Justice cannot be for one side alone, but must be for both.
If life were predictable it would cease to be life, and be without flavor.
Remember always that you not only have the right to be an individual,
     you have an obligation to be one.
The battle for the individual rights of women is one of long standing
     and none of us should countenance anything which undermines it.
The Bible illustrated by Dore occupied many of my hours - and I think
     probably gave me many nightmares.
The future belongs to those who believe in the beauty of their dreams.
The giving of love is an education in itself.
When you cease to make a contribution, you begin to die.
Ambition is pitiless. Any merit that it cannot use it finds despicable.
A little simplification would be the first step toward rational living, I think.
Anyone who knows history, particularly the history of Europe, will,
     I think, recognize that the domination of education or of
     government by any one particular religious faith is never a
     happy arrangement for the people.
When will our consciences grow so tender that we will act to
     prevent human misery rather than avenge it?
With the new day comes new strength and new thoughts.!
You can never really live anyone else's life, not even your child's. The
     influence you exert is through your own life, and what
     you've become yourself.
You can't move so fast that you try to change the mores faster than people
     can accept it. That doesn't mean you do nothing, but it means that
     you do the things that need to be done according to priority.
You gain strength, courage, and confidence by every experience in which
     you really stop to look fear in the face. You are able to say to
     yourself, 'I lived through this horror. I can take the next
     thing that comes along.'
You have to accept whatever comes and the only important thing is that
     you meet it with courage and with the best that you have to give.
People grow through experience if they meet life honestly and
     courageously. This is how character is built.
Probably the happiest period in life most frequently is in middle age,
     when the eager passions of youth are cooled, and the infirmities of
     age not yet begun; as we see that the shadows, which are at morning
     and evening so large, almost entirely disappear at midday.
Since you get more joy out of giving joy to others, you should put a good
     deal of thought into the happiness that you are able to give.

I think that somehow, we learn who we really are and then live with that decision.

Actors are one family over the entire world.

I think, at a child's birth, if a mother could ask a fairy godmother to
endow it with the most useful gift, that gift should be curiosity.

I used to tell my husband that, if he could make me 'understand' something,
it would be clear to all the other people in the country.

I'm so glad I never feel important, it does complicate life!

In all our contacts it is probably the sense of being really needed and
wanted which gives us the greatest satisfaction and
creates the most lasting bond.

In the long run, we shape our lives, and we shape ourselves. The process
never ends until we die. And the choices we make are ultimately
our own responsibility.

It is better to light a candle than curse the darkness.

It is not fair to ask of others what you are not willing to do yourself.

It is not more vacation we need - it is more vocation.

It isn't enough to talk about peace. One must believe in it. And
it isn't enough to believe in it. One must work at it.

Life must be lived and curiosity kept alive. One must never,
for whatever reason, turn his back on life.

My experience has been that work is almost the best way to
pull oneself out of the depths.

Never allow a person to tell you no who doesn't have the power to say yes.

Old age has deformities enough of its own. It should never add
to them the deformity of vice.

One's philosophy is not best expressed in words; it is expressed in the choices one
makes... and the choices we make are ultimately our responsibility.

Only a man's character is the real criterion of worth.

Sometimes I wonder if we shall ever grow up in our politics and say definite
things which mean something, or whether we shall always go on using
generalities to which everyone can subscribe, and which mean very little.

The only advantage of not being too good a housekeeper is that your guests
are so pleased to feel how very much better they are.

The only things one can admire at length are those one
admires without knowing why.

Too often the great decisions are originated and given form in bodies made up
wholly of men, or so completely dominated by them that whatever of special
value women have to offer is shunted aside without expression.

Understanding is a two-way street.

There are practical little things in housekeeping which no man really understands.

We are afraid to care too much, for fear that the other person does not care at all.

We gain strength, and courage, and confidence by each experience in
which we really stop to look fear in the face... we must do that
which we think we cannot.

What one has to do usually can be done.

What you don't do can be a destructive force.

Anyone who thinks must think of the next war as they would of suicide.

As for accomplishments, I just did what I had to do as things came along.

Autobiographies are only useful as the lives you read about and
analyze may suggest to you something that you may find useful
in your own journey through life.

Campaign behavior for wives: Always be on time. Do as little talking as
humanly possible. Lean back in the parade car so everybody can
see the president.
When life is too easy for us, we must beware or we may not be ready to
meet the blows which sooner or later come to everyone, rich or poor.
Do what you feel in your heart to be right - for you'll be criticized anyway.
You'll be damned if you do, and damned if you don't.
Freedom makes a huge requirement of every human being. With freedom comes
responsibility. For the person who is unwilling to grow up, the person who
does not want to carry is own weight, this is a frightening prospect.
Friendship with ones self is all important, because without it one
cannot be friends with anyone else in the world.
Great minds discuss ideas; average minds discuss events;
small minds discuss people.
Happiness is not a goal; it is a by-product.
Hate and force cannot be in just a part of the world
without having an effect on the rest of it.
Have convictions. Be friendly. Stick to your beliefs as they
stick to theirs. Work as hard as they do.
I believe that anyone can conquer fear by doing the things he fears to do,
provided he keeps doing them until he gets a record of successful
experience behind him.
I can not believe that war is the best solution. No one
won the last war, and no one will win the next war.
I have spent many years of my life in opposition, and I rather like the role.
I once had a rose named after me and I was very flattered. But I was not
pleased to read the description in the catalogue: no good in a bed,
but fine up against a wall.

## FRANKLIN D. ROOSEVELT (President, 1882-1945)
A conservative is a man with two perfectly good legs who, however,
has never learned how to walk forward.
A reactionary is a somnambulist walking backwards.
Art is not a treasure in the past or an importation from another land, but
part of the present life of all living and creating peoples.
Be sincere; be brief; be seated.
But  while they prate of economic laws, men and women are starving. We
must lay hold of the fact that economic laws are not made by nature.
They are made by human beings.
Competition has been shown to be useful up to a certain point and no further,
but cooperation, which is the thing we must strive for today, begins
where competition leaves off.
Confidence... thrives on honesty, on honor, on the sacredness of obligations, on
faithful protection and on unselfish performance. Without them it cannot live.
Democracy cannot succeed unless those who express their choice are prepared to
choose wisely. The real safeguard of democracy, therefore, is education.
Don't forget what I discovered that over ninety percent of all national deficits from
1921 to 1939 were caused by payments for past, present, and future wars.
Favor comes because for a brief moment in the great space of human
change and progress some general human purpose finds in him a
satisfactory embodiment.

Happiness lies in the joy of achievement and the thrill of creative effort.

Here is my principle: Taxes shall be levied according to ability to pay. That
is the only American principle.

A nation that destroys its soils destroys itself. Forests are the lungs of
our land, purifying the air and giving fresh strength to our people.

Human kindness has never weakened the stamina or softened the
fiber of a free  people. A nation does not have to be cruel to be tough.

I am a Christian and a Democrat, that's all.

I am neither bitter nor cynical but I do wish there was less
immaturity in political thinking.

I ask you to judge me by the enemies I have made.

I believe that in every country the people themselves are more
peaceably and liberally inclined than their governments.

I do not look upon these United States as a finished product. We
are still in the making.

I think we consider too much the good luck of the early bird and not
enough the bad luck of the early worm.

I'm not the smartest fellow in the world, but I can sure pick smart colleagues.

If civilization is to survive, we must cultivate the science of human relationships -
the ability of all peoples, of all kinds, to live together, in the same
world at peace.

If I went to work in a factory the first thing I'd do is join a union.

If we can boondoggle ourselves out of this depression, that word is going to
be enshrined in the hearts of the American people for years to come.

If you treat people right they will treat you right... ninety percent of the time.

In our personal ambitions we are individualists. But in our seeking for
economic and political progress as a nation, we all go up
or else all go down as one people.

In our seeking for economic and political progress, we all
go up - or else we all go down.

In politics, nothing happens by accident. If it happens, you can
bet it was planned that way.

It is an unfortunate human failing that a full pocketbook
often groans more loudly than an empty stomach.

It is fun to be in the same decade with you.

It is the duty of the President to propose and it is the
privilege of the Congress to dispose.

It isn't sufficient just to want - you've got to ask yourself what you are
going to do to get the things you want.

It takes a long time to bring the past up to the present.

Let us never forget that government is ourselves and not an alien power over us.
The ultimate rulers of our democracy are not a President and senators
and congressmen and government officials, but the voters of this country.

Men are not prisoners of fate, but only prisoners of their own minds.

More than an end to war, we want an end to the beginning of all wars - yes, an
end to this brutal, inhuman and thoroughly impractical method of settling
the differences between governments.

No government can help the destinies of people who insist in putting sectional
and class consciousness ahead of general good.

No group and no government can properly prescribe precisely what should
constitute the body of knowledge with which true education is concerned.

Nobody will ever deprive the American people of the right to vote except the
American people themselves and the only way they could
do this is by not voting.
Not only our future economic soundness but the very soundness of our
democratic institutions depends on the determination of our government
to give employment to idle men.
One thing is sure. We have to do something. We have to do the best we know
how at the moment... If it doesn't turn out right, we can modify
it as we go along.
Our national determination to keep free of foreign wars and foreign
entanglements cannot prevent us from feeling deep concern when
ideals and principles that we have cherished are challenged.
Physical strength can never permanently withstand the impact of spiritual force.
Prosperous farmers mean more employment, more prosperity for the workers
and the business men of every industrial area in the whole country.
Put two or three men in positions of conflicting authority. This will force them
to work at loggerheads, allowing you to be the ultimate arbiter.
Remember you are just an extra in everyone else's play.
Rules  are not necessarily sacred, principles are.
Self-interest is the enemy of all true affection.
Selfishness is the only real atheism; aspiration, unselfishness,
the only real religion.
Somoza may be a son of a bitch, but he's our son of a bitch.
Take  a method and try it. If it fails, admit it frankly, and try
another. But by all means, try something.
The nation that destroys its soil destroys itself.
The only limit to our realization of tomorrow will be our doubts of today.
The only sure bulwark of continuing liberty is a government strong enough to
protect the interests of the people, and a people strong enough and well
enough informed to maintain its sovereign control over the government.
The only thing we have to fear is fear itself.
The overwhelming majority of Americans are possessed of two great
qualities a sense of humor and a sense of proportion.
The point in history at which we stand is full of promise and danger. The
world will either move forward toward unity and widely shared
prosperity - or it will move apart.
The school is the last expenditure upon which America should
be willing to economize.
The test of our progress is not whether we add more to the abundance of those
who have much it is whether we provide enough for those who have little.
The truth is found when men are free to pursue it.
The United States Constitution has proved itself the most marvelously elastic
compilation of rules of government ever written.
The virtues are lost in self-interest as rivers are lost in the sea.
There are as many opinions as there are experts.
There are many ways of going forward, but only one way of standing still.
There is a mysterious cycle in human events. To some generations much is
given. Of other generations much is expected. This generation of ]
Americans has a rendezvous with destiny.
There is nothing I love as much as a good fight.
This generation of Americans has a rendezvous with destiny.

To reach a port, we must sail - sail, not tie at anchor - sail, not drift.
True individual freedom cannot exist without economic security and
      independence. People who are hungry and out of a job are
      the stuff of which dictatorships are made.
War is a contagion.
We are trying to construct a more inclusive society. We are going to
      make a country in which no one is left out.
We continue to recognize the greater ability of some to earn more than others.
      But we do assert that the ambition of the individual to obtain for him a
      proper security is an ambition to be preferred to the appetite for
      great wealth and great power.
We have always held to the hope, the belief, the conviction that there is
      a better life, a better world, beyond the horizon.
We must lay hold of the fact that economic laws are not made by
      nature. They are made by human beings.
When you get to the end of your rope, tie a knot and hang on.
When you see a rattlesnake  poised to strike, you do not wait until
      he has struck to crush him.
Whoever seeks to set one religion against another seeks to destroy all religion.
Yesterday, December seventh, 1941, a date which will live in infamy, the
      United States of America was suddenly and deliberately attacked by
      naval and air forces of the Empire of Japan.

## THEODORE (TEDDY) ROOSEVELT (President, 1858-1919)

A man who has never gone to school may steal from a freight car; but if
      he has a university education, he may steal the whole railroad.
A man who is good enough to shed his blood for the country is good
      enough to be given a square deal afterwards.
A typical vice of American politics is the avoidance of
      saying anything real on real issues.
A vote is like a rifle; its usefulness depends upon the character of the user.
Absence and death are the same - only that in death there is no suffering.
Appraisals are where you get together with your team leader and agree what an
      outstanding member of the team you are, how much your contribution
      has been valued, what massive potential you have and, in recognition
      of all this, would you mind having your salary halved.
Behind the ostensible government sits enthroned an invisible government
      owing no allegiance and acknowledging no responsibility to the people.
Believe you can and you're halfway there.
Big jobs usually go to the men who prove their ability to outgrow small ones.
Do what you can, with what you have, where you are.
Don't hit at all if it is honorably possible to avoid hitting; but never hit soft.
Every immigrant who comes here should be required within five
      years to learn English or leave the country.
Every reform movement has a lunatic fringe.
Far and away the best prize that life has to offer is the
      chance to work hard at work worth doing.
Far better is it to dare mighty things, to win glorious triumphs, even though
      checkered by failure... than to rank with those poor spirits who
      neither enjoy nor suffer much, because they live in a gray twilight
      that knows not victory nor defeat.

For unflagging interest and enjoyment, a household of children, if
      things go reasonably well, certainly all other forms of success and
      achievement lose their importance by comparison.
Character, in the long run, is the decisive factor in the
      life of an individual and of nations alike.
Courtesy is as much a mark of a gentleman as courage.
Freedom from effort in the present merely means that there has
      been effort stored up in the past.
Get action. Seize the moment. Man was never intended to become an oyster.
Great thoughts speak only to the thoughtful mind, but great
      actions speak to all mankind.
I am a part of everything that I have read.
I am only an average man but, by George, I work harder at it
      than the average man.
I care not what others think of what I do, but I care very much
      about what I think of what I do! That is character!
I don't pity any man who does hard work worth doing. I admire
      him. I pity the creature who does not work, at whichever
      end of the social scale he may regard himself as being.
I think there is only one quality worse than hardness of heart
      and that is softness of head.
I took the Canal Zone and let Congress debate; and while the
      debate goes on, the canal does also.
I wish to preach, not the doctrine of ignoble ease, but the
      doctrine of the strenuous life.
If there is not the war, you don't get the great general; if there is not a
      great occasion, you don't get a great statesman; if Lincoln had lived
      in a time of peace, no one would have known his name.
If you could kick the person in the pants responsible for most of
      your trouble, you wouldn't sit for a month.
In a moment of decision the best thing you can do is the right
      thing. The worst thing you can do is nothing.
It behooves every man to remember that the work of the critic is of
      altogether secondary importance, and that, in the end, progress
      is accomplished by the man who does things.
It is difficult to make our material condition better by the best law,
      but it is easy enough to ruin it by bad laws.
It is essential that there should be organization of labor. This is an era of
      organization. Capital organizes and therefore labor must organize.
It is hard to fail, but it is worse never to have tried to succeed.
It is only through labor and painful effort, by grim energy and
      resolute courage, that we move on to better things.
Keep your eyes on the stars, and your feet on the ground.
Leave it as it is. The ages have been at work on it and man can only mar it.
Never throughout history has a man who lived a life of ease
      left a name worth remembering.
No man is above the law and no man is below it: nor do we ask
      any man's permission when we ask him to obey it.
No man is justified in doing evil on the ground of expedience.
No man is worth his salt who is not ready at all times to risk his
      well-being, to risk his body, to risk his life, in a great cause.

No people is wholly civilized where a distinction is drawn between
      stealing an office and stealing a purse.
Nine-tenths of wisdom is being wise in time.
Nobody cares how much you know, until they know how much you care.
Obedience of the law is demanded; not asked as a favor.
Old age is like everything else. To make a success of it, you've got to start young.
Order without liberty and liberty without order are equally destructive.
People ask the difference between a leader and a boss. The leader
      leads, and the boss drives.
Probably the greatest harm done by vast wealth is the harm that we
      of moderate means do ourselves when we let the vices of envy
      and hatred enter deep into our own natures.
Rhetoric is a poor substitute for action, and we have trusted only to rhetoric. If we
      are really to be a great nation, we must not merely talk; we must act big.
Some men can live up to their loftiest ideals without ever
      going higher than a basement.
Speak softly and carry a big stick; you will go far.
The American people abhor a vacuum.
The best executive is one who has sense enough to pick good people to do
      what he wants done, and self-restraint enough to keep from
      meddling with them while they do it.
The boy who is going to make a great man must not make up his
      mind merely to overcome a thousand obstacles, but to win
      in spite of a thousand repulses and defeats.
The first requisite of a good citizen in this republic of ours is that he
      shall be able and willing to pull his own weight.
The government is us; we are the government, you and I.
The human body has two ends on it: one to create with and one to sit on.
Sometimes people get their ends reversed. When this happens
      they need a kick in the seat of the pants.
The man who loves other countries as much as his own stands on a level
      with the man who loves other women as much as he loves his own wife.
The most important single ingredient in the formula of success
      is knowing how to get along with people.
The most practical kind of politics is the politics of decency.
The most successful politician is he who says what the people
      are thinking most often in the loudest voice.
The only man who never makes a mistake is the man who never does anything.
The only time you really live fully is from thirty to sixty. The young are slaves
      to dreams; the old servants of regrets. Only the middle-aged have all
      their five senses in the keeping of their wits.
The reactionary is always willing to take a progressive
      attitude on any issue that is dead.
The one thing I want to leave my children is an honorable name.
The things that will destroy America are prosperity-at-any-price,
      peace-at-any-price, safety-first instead of duty-first, the
      love of soft living, and the get-rich-quick theory of life.
The unforgivable crime is soft hitting. Do not hit at all if it can be
      avoided; but never hit softly.
There has never yet been a man in our history who led a life of
      ease whose name is worth remembering.

To announce that there must be no criticism of the president... is
      morally treasonable to the American public.
To educate a man in mind and not in morals is to educate a menace to society.
Wars are, of course, as a rule to be avoided; but they are far
      better than certain kinds of peace.
We can have no "50-50" allegiance in this country. Either a man is
      an American and nothing else, or he is not an American at all.
When they call the roll in the Senate, the Senators do not know
      whether to answer "Present" or "Not guilty."
When you are asked if you can do a job, tell 'em, 'Certainly I can!' Then
      get busy and find out how to do it.
When you play, play hard; when you work, don't play at all.
With self-discipline most anything is possible.

## ELIHU ROOT (Lawyer, 1845 -1937)

Honest people, mistakenly believing in the justice of their
      cause, are led to support injustice.
Cruelty to men and to the lower animals as well, which would have
      passed unnoticed a century ago, now shocks the sensibilities
      and is regarded as wicked and degrading.
The popular tendency is to listen approvingly to the most extreme
      statements and claims of politicians and orators who seek
      popularity by declaring their own country right in
      everything and other countries wrong in everything.
The theoretical postulate of all diplomatic discussion between nations
      is the assumed willingness of every nation to do justice.
There is so much of good in human nature that men grow to like each
      other upon better acquaintance, and this points to another way
      in which we may strive to promote the peace of the world.
To deal with the true causes of war one must begin by recognizing as
      of prime relevancy to the solution of the problem the familiar
      fact that civilization is a partial, incomplete, and, to a great
      extent, superficial modification of barbarism.
Gradually, everything that happens in the world is coming to be of
      interest everywhere in the world, and, gradually, thoughtful
      men and women everywhere are sitting in judgment
      upon the conduct of all nations.
It is not uncommon in modern times to see governments straining
      every nerve to keep the peace, and the people whom they
      represent, with patriotic enthusiasm and resentment over
      real or fancied wrongs, urging them forward to war.
Men do not fail; they give up trying.
Nobody knows through how many thousands of years fighting men
      have made a place for themselves while the weak and
      peaceable have gone to the wall.
Prejudice and passion and suspicion are more dangerous than the
      incitement of self-interest or the most stubborn adherence to
      real differences of opinion regarding rights.
The growth of modern constitutional government compels for its successful
      practice the exercise of reason and considerate judgment by the
      individual citizens who constitute the electorate.

The law of the survival of the fittest led inevitably to the survival and
       predominance of the men who were effective in war and who
       loved it because they were effective.
The wolf always charges the lamb with muddying the stream.

## DIANA ROSS (Singer, Actor, 1944 -)

Criticism, even when you try to ignore it, can hurt. I have cried
       over  many articles written about me, but I move on and
       I don't hold on to that .
Instead of looking at the past, I put myself ahead twenty years and try
       to look at what I need to do now in order to get there then.
I don't judge people by their sexual orientation or the color of their skin,
       so I find it really hard to identify someone by saying that they're
       a gay person or a black person or a Jewish person.
With the Supremes I made so much money so fast all I wanted to
       do was buy clothes and pretty things. Now I'm comfortable
       with money and it's comfortable with me.
You can't just sit there and wait for people to give you that golden dream.
       You've got to get out there and make it happen for yourself.
You know, you do need mentors, but in the end, you really just
       need to believe in yourself.
I learned something from that. If someone asks me something that
       I really don't want to do, I say no. I have to trust that. And
       I'm not afraid to talk money.
I think a responsibility comes with notoriety, but I never think of it
       as power. It's more like something you hold, like grains of sand.
       If you keep your hand closed, you can have it and possess it, but
       if you open your fingers in any way, you can lose it just as quickly.
If I have someone who believes in me, I can move mountains.
Just because I have my standards they think I'm a bitch.
My travels led me to where I am today. Sometimes these steps
       have felt painful, difficult, but led me to greater happiness
       and opportunities.

## DEAN RUSK (Diplomat, 1909-1994)

Continuity does not rule out fresh approaches to fresh situations.
The best way to persuade people is with your ears - by listening to them.
We have tried to make it clear that the United States is not just an old
       cow that gives more milk the more it is kicked in the flanks.
We were eyeball-to-eyeball and the other fellow just blinked.
       [regarding the Cuban missile crisis]
When you solve a problem, you ought to thank God and go on to the next one.
While we are sleeping, two-thirds of the world is plotting to do us in.

## CARL SAGAN (Astronomer, 1934-1996)

All of the books in the world contain no more information than is broadcast as video
       in a single large American city in a single year. Not all bits have equal value.
. . . the fact that some geniuses were laughed at does not imply that all
       who are laughed at are geniuses. They laughed at Columbus, they
       laughed at Fulton, they laughed at the Wright Brothers. But they also
       laughed at Bozo the Clown.

For me, it is far better to grasp the Universe as it really is than to
       persist in delusion, however satisfying and reassuring.
For small creatures such as we the vastness is bearable only through love.
I am often amazed at how much more capability and enthusiasm for science
       there is among elementary school youngsters than among college students.
I can find in my undergraduate classes, bright students who do not know that the
       stars rise and set at night, or even that the Sun is a star
A celibate clergy is an especially good idea, because it tends
       to suppress any hereditary propensity toward fanaticism.
If we long to believe that the stars rise and set for us, that we are the reason there
       is a Universe, does science do us a disservice in deflating our conceits?
If you wish to make an apple pie from scratch, you must first invent the universe.
Imagination will often carry us to worlds that never were. But
       without it we go nowhere.
Our species needs, and deserves, a citizenry with minds wide
       awake and a basic understanding of how the world works.
Personally, I would be delighted if there were a life after death, especially if it
       permitted me to continue to learn about this world and others, if it
       gave me a chance to discover how history turns out.
Science is a way of thinking much more than it is a body of knowledge.
Skeptical scrutiny is the means, in both science and religion, by which deep
       thoughts can be winnowed from deep nonsense.
Somewhere, something incredible is waiting to be known.
The brain is like a muscle. When it is in use we feel very good.
Understanding is joyous.
The universe is not required to be in perfect harmony with human ambition.
The universe seems neither benign nor hostile, merely indifferent.
We have also arranged things so that almost no one understands science and
       technology. This is a prescription for disaster. We might get away with
       it for a while, but sooner or later this combustible mixture of
       ignorance and power is going to blow up in our faces.
We live in a society exquisitely dependent on science and technology, in
       which hardly anyone knows anything about science and technology
We've arranged a civilization in which most crucial elements
       profoundly depend on science and technology.
When you make the finding yourself - even if you're the last
       person on Earth to see the light - you'll never forget it.
Who are we? We find that we live on an insignificant planet of a humdrum star
       lost in a galaxy tucked away in some forgotten corner of a universe in
       which there are far more galaxies than people.

## J. D. SALINGER (Author, 1919-2010)

An artist's only concern is to shoot for some kind of perfection,
       and on his own terms, not anyone else's.
I am a kind of paranoid in reverse. I suspect people of plotting to make me happy.
How do you know you're going to do something, until you do it?
People never notice anything.
The worst thing that being an artist could do to you would be
       that it would make you slightly unhappy constantly.
You take somebody that cries their goddam eyes out over phoney stuff in the
       movies, and nine times out of ten they're mean bastards at heart.

All morons hate it when you call them a moron.
Goddam money. It always ends up making you blue as hell.
He had a theory, Walt did, that the religious life, and all the agony that goes with it,
      is just something God sics on people who have the gall
      to accuse Him of having created an ugly world.
How long should a man's legs be? Long enough to touch the ground.
I don't even like old cars. I'd rather have a goddam horse. A horse
      is at least human, for God's sake.
I don't exactly know what I mean by that, but I mean it
I'm quite illiterate, but I read a lot.
I'm sick of just liking people. I wish to God I could meet somebody I could respect.
I'm sick of not having the courage to be an absolute nobody.
I'm the most terrific liar you ever saw in your life.
If a girl looks swell when she meets you, who gives a damn if she's late? Nobody.
It's funny. All you have to do is say something nobody understands
      and they'll do practically anything you want them to
Its really hard to be roommates with people if your suitcases are
      much better than theirs.
Mothers are all slightly insane.
People never believe you.

## CARL SANDBURG (Poet, 1878-1967)

I won't take my religion from any man who never works except with his mouth.
After the sunset on the prairie, there are only the stars
Love your neighbor as yourself; but don't take down the fence.
A baby is God's opinion that life should go on.
Slang is a language that rolls up its sleeves, spits on its hands and goes to work.
We can never possibly know what is about to happen: it is
      happening, each time, for the first time, for the only time
I never made a mistake in grammar but one in my life and as
      soon as I done it I seen it.
There are 10 men in me and I do not know or understand one of them.
A book is never a masterpiece: it becomes one. Genius is the talent of a dead man.
A man may be born, but in order to be born he must first die, and
      in order to die he must first awake.
I'm either going to be a writer or a bum.
I've written some poetry I don't understand myself.
In these times you have to be an optimist to open your eyes
      when you awake in the morning.
Let a joy keep you. Reach out your hands and take it when it runs by.
Let the gentle bush dig its root deep and spread upward to split the boulder.
Life is like an onion. You peel it off one layer at a time, and sometimes you weep.
Poetry is a phantom script telling how rainbows are made and why they go away.
Poetry is an echo, asking a shadow to dance.
Poetry is the opening and closing of a door, leaving those who look
      through to guess about what is seen during the moment.
A politician should have three hats. One for throwing into the ring, one
      for talking through, and one for pulling rabbits out of if elected.
All human actions are equivalent... and all are on principle doomed to failure.
There have been as many varieties of socialists as there are wild birds that
      fly in the woods and sometimes go up and on through the clouds.

Anger is the most impotent of passions. It effects nothing it goes about,
      and hurts the one who is possessed by it more than the one against
      whom it is directed.

Poetry is the synthesis of hyacinths and biscuits.

Arithmetic is where the answer is right and everything is nice and you can look
      out of the window and see the blue sky - or the answer is wrong and you
      have to start over and try again and see how it comes out this time.

Back of every mistaken venture and defeat is the laughter of wisdom, if you listen.

Calling it off comes easy enough if you haven't told the girl you
      are smitten with her.

Every blunder behind us is giving a cheer for us, and only for those who
      were willing to fail are the dangers and splendors of life.

Here is the difference between Dante, Milton, and me. They wrote about
      hell and never saw the place. I wrote about Chicago after looking
      the town over for years and years.

I a m an idealist. I don't know where I'm going but I'm on my way.

I can remember only a few of the strange and curious words now dead
      but living and spoken by the English people a thousand years ago.

I couldn't see myself filling some definite niche in what is called
      a career. This was all misty.

I doubt if you can have a truly wild party without liquor.

I have always felt that a woman has the right to treat the subject of her age
      with ambiguity until, perhaps, she passes into the realm of over ninety.
      Then it is better she be candid with herself and with the world.

I have become infected, now that I see how beautifully a book
      is coming out of all this.

I have in later years taken to Euclid, Whitehead, Bertrand
      Russell, in an elemental way.

I have often wondered what it is an old building can do to you when you happen
      to know a little about things that went on long ago in that building.

I knew I would read all kinds of books and try to get at what it is that makes
      good writers good. But I made no promises that I would write
      books a lot of people would like to read.

I learned you can't trust the judgment of good friends.

I make it clear why I write as I do and why other poets write as they do. After
      hundreds of experiments I decided to go my own way in
      style and see what would happen.

I stayed away from mathematics not so much because I knew it would be
      hard work as because of the amount of time I knew it would
      take, hours spent in a field where I was not a natural.

I tell you the past is a bucket of ashes, so live not in your yesterdays, no just
      for tomorrow, but in the here and now. Keep moving and forget the
      post mortems; and remember, no one can get the jump on the future.

I took to wearing a black tie known as the Ascot, with long drooping ends. I
      had seen pictures of painters, sculptors, poets, wearing this style of tie.

I wrote poems in my corner of the Brooks Street station. I sent them to two
      editors who rejected them right off. I read those letters of
      rejection years later and I agreed with those editors.

I had taken a course in Ethics. I read a thick textbook, heard the class
      discussions and came out of it saying I hadn't learned a thing I didn't
      know before about morals and what is right or wrong in human conduct.

There is an eagle in me that wants to soar, and there is a
        hippopotamus in me that wants to wallow in the mud.
I fell in love, not deep, but I fell several times and then fell out.
There was always the consolation that if I didn't like what I wrote I
        could throw it away or burn it
Time is the coin of your life. It is the only coin you have, and only
        you can determine how it will be spent. Be careful lest you
        let other people spend it for you.
To be a good loser is to learn how to win.
To work hard, to live hard, to die hard, and then go to hell after
        all would be too damn hard.
Valor is a gift. Those having it never know for sure whether they
        have it till the test comes. And those having it in one test
        never know for sure if they will have it when the next test comes.
We don't have to think up a title  till we get the doggone book written.
We had two grand antique professors who had been teaching at Lombard since
        before I was born. We read Robert Browning's poetry. Here we needed no
        guidance from the professor: the poems themselves were enough.
When a nation goes down, or a society perishes, one condition may
        always be found; they forgot where they came from. They lost
        sight of what had brought them along.
When I was writing pretty poor poetry, this girl with midnight
        black hair told me to go on.
Where was I going? I puzzled and wondered about it til I actually
        enjoyed the puzzlement and wondering.
You remember some bedrooms you have slept in. There are
        bedrooms you like to remember and others you would like to forget
My room for books and study or for sitting and thinking about nothing in
        particular to see what would happen was at the end of a hall.
Nearly all the best things that came to me in life have been
        unexpected, unplanned by me.
Nothing happens unless first we dream.
Often I look back and see that I had been many kinds of a fool -
        and that I had been happy in being this or that kind of fool.
One of the greatest necessities in America is to discover creative solitude.
Ordering a man to write a poem is like commanding a pregnant
        woman to give birth to a red-headed child.
Shame is the feeling you have when you agree with the woman
        who loves you that you are the man she thinks you are.
Sometime they'll give a war and nobody will come.
Strange things blow in through my window on the wings of the
        night wind and I don't worry about my destiny.
The greatest cunning is to have none at all.
The moon is a friend for the lonesome to talk to.
The scholars and poets of an earlier time can be read only
        with a dictionary to help.
I am an idealist. I believe in everything — I am only looking for proofs.
I am the people — the mob — the crowd — the mass.
Do you know that all the great work of the world is done through me?
The sea speaks a language polite people never repeat. It is a
        colossal scavenger slang and has no respect.

The secret of happiness is to admire without desiring
I take you and pile high the memories. Death will break her claws on some I keep.
God, let me remember all good losers.
I see America, not in the setting sun of a black night of despair ahead of
  us, I see America in the crimson light of a rising sun fresh from the
  burning, creative hand of God. I see great days ahead, great days
  possible to men and women of will and vision

## CHARLES SCHULTZ (Cartoonist, 1922-2000)

A whole stack of memories never equal one little hope.
All you need is love. But a little chocolate now and then doesn't hurt.
Aunt Marion was right... Never marry a musician, and never answer the door.
Decorate your home. It gives the illusion that your life
  is more interesting than it really is.
Don't worry about the world coming to an end today. It
  is already tomorrow in Australia.
That's the secret to life... replace one worry with another.
There's a difference between a philosophy and a bumper sticker.
Try not to have a good time... this is supposed to be educational
I think I've discovered the secret of life - you just hang
  around until you get used to it.
If I were given the opportunity to present a gift to the next generation, it
  would be the ability for each individual to learn to laugh at himself.
It doesn't matter what you believe just so long as you're sincere.
Jogging is very beneficial. It's good for your legs and your feet. It's also
  very good for the ground. It makes it feel needed.
Life is like a ten speed bicycle. Most of us have gears we never use.
Life is like an ice-cream cone, you have to lick it one day at a time.
My life has no purpose, no direction, no aim, no meaning, and yet I'm
  happy. I can't figure it out. What am I doing right?
No problem is too big to run away from.
Sometimes I lie awake at night, and ask, 'Where have I gone wrong?' Then
  a voice says to me, 'This is going to take more than one night.'

## ARNOLD SCHWARZENEGGER (Governor of California, Actor, 1947 - )

My relationship to power and authority is that I'm all for it. People need
  somebody to watch over them. Ninety-five percent of the people
I think that gay marriage should be between a man and a woman.
  in the world need to be told what to do and how to behave.
Milk is for babies. When you grow up you have to drink beer.
And now, of course this is another thing I didn't count on, that now as the
  governor of the state of California, I am selling California worldwide.
  You see that? Selling.
As long as I live, I will never forget that day 21 years ago when I raised
  my hand and took the oath of citizenship. Do you know how proud
  I was? I was so proud that I walked around with an American flag
  around my shoulders all day long.
As you know, I'm an immigrant. I came over here as an immigrant,
  and what gave me the opportunities, what made me to be here
  today, is the open arms of Americans. I have been received. I
  have been adopted by America.

Bodybuilding is much like any other sport. To be successful, you must
     Dedicate yourself 100% to your training, diet and mental approach.
Everything I have, my career, my success, my family, I owe to America.
My own dreams fortunately came true in this great state. I became Mr.
     Universe; I became a successful businessman. And even though
     some people say I still speak with a slight accent, I have reached
     the top of the acting profession.
I have inhaled, exhaled everything.
No matter the nationality, no matter the religion, no matter the
     ethnic background, America brings out the best in people.
Political courage is not political suicide.
Start wide, expand further, and never look back.
Strength does not come from winning. Your struggles develop your
     strengths. When you go through hardships and decide not to
     surrender, that is strength.
The best activities for your health are pumping and humping.
The biggest problem that we have is that California is being run now by special
     interests. All of the politicians are not anymore making the moves for
     the people, but for special interests and we have to stop that.
The mind is the limit. As long as the mind can envision the fact that you can do
     something, you can do it, as long as you really believe 100 percent.
The resistance that you fight physically in the gym and the resistance
     that you fight in life can only build a strong character.
The worst thing I can be is the same as everybody else. I hate that.
There is no place, no country, more compassionate more generous more
     accepting and more welcoming than the United States of America.
To restore the trust of the people, we must reform the way
     the government operates.
Training gives us an outlet for suppressed energies created by stress
     and thus tones the spirit just as exercise conditions the body.
We are a forward-looking people, and we must have
     a forward-looking government.
What we face may look insurmountable. But I learned something from all those
     years of training and competing. I learned something from all those sets
     and reps when I didn't think I could lift another ounce of weight. What I
     learned is that we are always stronger than we know.
When the people become involved in their government, government
     becomes more accountable, and our society is stronger, more
     compassionate, and better prepared for the challenges of the future.
Failure is not an option. Everyone has to succeed.
For me life is continuously being hungry. The meaning of life is not simply
     to exist, to survive, but to move ahead, to go up, to achieve, to conquer.
Freedom is a right ultimately defended by the sacrifice of
     America's servicemen and women.
Government's first duty and highest obligation is public safety.
Help others and give something back. I guarantee you will discover that while
     public service improves the lives and the world around you, its greatest
     reward is the enrichment and new meaning it will bring your own life.
I am a big believer in education, because when I grew up in Austria - when I
     grew up in Austria I had a great education. I had great teachers.
I have a love interest in every one of my films: a gun.

I believe with all my heart that America remains 'the great idea' that
      inspires the world. It is a privilege to be born here. It is an honor
      to become a citizen here. It is a gift to raise your family here,
      to vote here, and to live here.
I speak directly to the people, and I know that the people of California
      want to have better leadership. They want to have great leadership.
      They want to have somebody that will represent them. And it
      doesn't matter if you're a Democrat or a Republican, young or old.
I was born in Europe... and I've traveled all over the world. I can tell
      you that there is no place, no country, that is more compassionate,
      more generous, more accepting, and more welcoming than
      the United States of America.
I welcome and seek your ideas, but do not bring me
      small ideas; bring me big ideas to match our future.
If you work hard and play by the rules, this country is
      truly open to you. You can achieve anything.
In our society, the women who break down barriers are those who ignore limits.
In this country, it doesn't make any difference where you were born.
      It doesn't make any difference who your parents were. It doesn't
      make any difference if, like me, you couldn't even speak English
      until you were in your twenties.
Learned helplessness is the giving-up reaction, the quitting response
      that follows from the belief that whatever you do doesn't matter.
Money doesn't make you happy. I now have $50 million but I was just
      as happy when I had $48 million.
Women are the engine driving the growth in California's economy.
      Women make California's economy unique.
I just use my muscles as a conversation piece, like someone
      walking a cheetah down 42nd Street.
I knew I was a winner back in the late sixties. I knew I was destined for great
      things. People will say that kind of thinking is totally immodest.
      I agree. Modesty is not a word that applies to me in any way - I
      hope it never will.

**PETE SEEGER (Folk Singer, 1919 - )**
Down through the centuries, this trick has been tried by various establishments
      throughout the world. They force people to get involved in the kind of
      examination that has only one aim and that is to stamp out dissent.
I am not going to answer any questions as to my association, my philosophical
      or religious beliefs or my political beliefs, or how I voted in any election,
      or any of these private affairs.
I am saying voluntarily that I have sung for almost every religious
      group in the country, from Jewish and Catholic, and
      Presbyterian and Holy Rollers and Revival Churches.
I feel that my whole life is a contribution.
I fought for peace in the fifties.
I have sung for Americans of every political persuasion, and I am proud that
      I never refuse to sing to an audience, no matter what religion or color
      of their skin, or situation in life. I have sung in hobo jungles, and I
      have sung for the Rockefellers, and I am proud that I have never
      refused to sing for anybody.

I like to say I'm more conservative than Goldwater. He just
     wanted to turn the clock back to when there was no income tax.
     Do you know the difference between education and experience? Education is
     when you read the fine print; experience is what you get when you don't.
I love my country very dearly, and I greatly resent the implication that some of
     the places that I have sung and some of the people that I have known,
     and some of my opinions, whether they are religious or philosophical,
     make me less of an American.
I still call myself a communist, because communism is no more what Russia
     made of it than Christianity is what the churches make of it.
I want to turn the clock back to when people lived in small villages
     and took care of each other.
One of the things I'm most proud of about my country is the fact that we
     did lick  McCarthyism back in the fifties.

## AL SHARPTON (Politican, Minister, Promoter, 1954 - )

Dr. King used Gandhi's commitment to non-violence and to passive resistance.
Dr. King's general principles are universal. But the things he
     confronted took place in another era.
During my 2004 presidential campaign, I was fond of saying that it was
     high time for the Christian right to meet the right Christians.
Evangelicals catapulted George W. Bush back to the White House.
How do you make things fair?
I do believe the Democratic party has moved far to the right. I do believe
     that the party has a bunch of elephants running around in donkey clothes.
I grew up in the 1950s and '60s, when it was almost a holiday
     when a black act would go on Ed Sullivan.
I very rarely read any fiction. I love biographies; I read about all
     kinds of people. I love theology and some philosophy.
I was raised by a single mother who made a way for me. She used to scrub floors
     as a domestic worker, put a cleaning rag in her pocketbook and ride the
     subways in Brooklyn so I would have food on the table. But she taught me
     as I walked her to the subway that life is about not where you start, but
     where you're going. That's family values.
I was the first candidate to come out against this war, spoke at
     every anti-war march.
I won vice president of my student body in high school. That
     doesn't mean anything.
I'm a patriot in the truest sense of the word.
I've never done anything else in my life other than preach
     and be an activist. Way before I was known.
I've seen enough things to know that if you just keep on going,
     if you turn the corner, the sun will be shining.
I've seen too much in life to give up.
If Charlton Heston can have a constitutional right carry a rifle,
     why can't grandma have a constitutional right to health care?
If O.J. had been accused of killing his black wife, you would
     not have seen the same passion stirred up.
If you can get the proper definition of trouble, then we can
     find out who the real troublemakers are
If you play the theatrics too much, you get in the way of your own cause.

It is true that Mr. Lincoln signed the Emancipation Proclamation, after which
there was a commitment to give 40 acres and a mule. That's where the
argument, to this day, of reparations starts. We never got the 40 acres.
We went all the way to Herbert Hoover, and we never got the 40 acres.
We didn't get the mule. So we decided we'd ride this
donkey as far as it would take us.
It seems some have chosen to ignore or have simply forgotten the big-picture
vision promoted by Dr. King and his kin.
My ministry's always been one of social activism. I think a responsible
minister must be at some levels involved in the social order.
My ordination in the Church of God in Christ was at age 9, and I
later became a Baptist minister, which I am today.
One of the reasons I get so much joy out of my own children's
childhoods is that I'm having my first childhood myself.
The boxing world is full of all kinds of corruption.
The dream was not to put one black family in the White House,
the dream was to make everything equal in everybody's house.
The promise of America is one immigration policy for all who seek to enter our
shores, whether they come from Mexico, Haiti or Canada, there must be
one set of rules for everybody. We cannot welcome those to come and
then try and act as though any culture will not be respected or treated
inferior. We cannot look at the Latino community and preach "one
language." No one gave them an English test before they sent them
to Iraq to fight for America.
The right wing always mobilizes around constitutional
amendments: the right to bear arms, school prayer.
The United States government has the obligation to educate
all young people in this country.
The United States has got to adopt a policy of befriending and
creating allies around the world.
We have defeated Jim Crow, but now we have to deal with his
son, James Crow Jr., esquire.
We need an amendment that gives us the right to vote protected
by the federal government and the Constitution.
We're not anti-police... we're anti-police brutality.
We're not willing to give black leaders second chances because, in
most cases, we're not willing to give them first chances.
Who defines terrorists? Today's terrorist is tomorrow's friend

## PAUL SIMON (Musician, 1941 - )
A man sees what he wants to see, And disregards the rest.
Anybody can do bad work, but not everybody does good work.
As long as you have capital punishment there is no guarantee
that innocent people won't be put to death.
Being an artist doesn't mean that you're a good artist. That was the bargain I
first made with myself: I'd say, I'm an artist, but I'm not really very good.
Facts can be turned into art if one is artful enough.
Faith is an island in the setting sun, But proof is the bottom line for everyone.
I don't very often think I've done a good job. I don't like the majority of
what I do. I shouldn't say I don't like it, but I'm not satisfied with
almost everything that I do.

I lived in an attached house. My father used to drive into the wrong driveway all the
      time. He'd say, Damn it, how do you tell one of these houses from another?
I question what emotion Manilow touches. People are entertained by him. But are
      they emotionally moved? I don't believe anything that Barry Manilow sings
I suppose an artist takes the elements of his life and rearranges them and then has
      them perceived by others as though they were the elements of their lives.
I always get very calm with baseball.
I don't like fashion. It's very heartless.
I think I have a superior brain and an inferior stature, if you
      really want to get brutal about it.
I try to open up my heart as much as I can and keep a real keen
      eye out that I don't get sentimental. I think we're all afraid
      to reveal our hearts. It's not at all in fashion.
I was eating in a Chinese restaurant downtown. There was a dish called Mother
      and Child Reunion. It's chicken and eggs. And I said, I gotta use that one.
I'm more interested in what I discover than what I invent.
I'm not in it for the money. I like music. I love to write music. I
      can't imagine myself not playing or singing or writing. It
      would just drive me crazy if I didn't.
If you can get humor and seriousness at the same time, you've
      created a special little thing, and that's what I'm looking
      for, because if you get pompous, you lose everything.
Improvisation is too good to leave to chance.
It's a big error to think that because you like somebody's
      work, you're going to like him.
It's pointless to be critical of your stuff once it's done. I don't spend a lot
      of time agonizing over it. It's of no importance once it's finished.
Music is forever; music should grow and mature with you, following
      you right on up until you die.
My life so common it disappears and sometimes even music
      cannot substitute for tears.
My whole artistic life has always been about change, change,
      change, move on, move on. It's the only thing I find interesting.
Not every song I write is ecstasy. And it can happen only one time. After
      that, when you sing the same melody and words, it's pleasure,
      but you don't get wiped out.
People often called us perfectionists, but we were not looking for
      perfection. We were looking for some kind of magic in the music.
The thought that life could be better is woven indelibly into
      our hearts and our brains.
The words of the prophets are written on the subway walls and
      tenements halls and whispered in the sounds of silence.
There's something about the sound of a train that's very romantic
      and nostalgic and hopeful.
We've survived by believing our life is going to get better.
Who am I to blow against the wind?
You want to be a writer, don't know how or when? Find a
      quiet place, use a humble  pen.

## ALFRED E. SMITH (Politician, 1873-1944)

All the ills of democracy can be cured by more democracy.

It is the right of our people to organize to oppose any law and any
part of the Constitution with which they are not in sympathy.

The American people never carry an umbrella. They prepare
to walk in eternal sunshine.

Be simple in words, manners, and gestures. Amuse as well as
instruct. If you can make a man laugh, you can make
him think and make him like and believe you.

Nobody shoots at Santa Claus.

## TOMMY SMOTHERS (Comedian, Folk Singer, 1937 - )

Red meat is not bad for you. Now blue-green meat, that's bad for you!

The only valid censorship of ideas is the right of people not to listen.

The ultimate censorship is the flick of the dial.

When you don't know what you're talking about, it's hard to
know when you're finished.

## THEODORE C. SORENSEN (Lawyer, Political aide to RFK, 1928 - )

I think Democrats made a mistake running away from liberalism. Liberalism, uh,
Franklin Roosevelt, Harry Truman, John and Robert Kennedy - that's what
the Democratic party ought to reach for.

The damage done to this country by its own misconduct in the last
few months and years, to its very heart and soul, is far
greater and longer lasting than any damage that any
terrorist could possibly inflict upon us.

We will be safer from terrorist attack only when we have earned the
respect of all other nations instead of their fear, respect for our
values and not merely our weapons.

I believe in an America in which the fruits of productivity and
prosperity are shared by all, by workers as well as owners,
by those at the bottom as well as those at the top; an
America in which the sacrifices required by national
security are shared by all, by profiteers in the back offices
as well as volunteers on the front lines.

Al Gore is not just whistling in the wind. Global warming is for real.
Every scientist knows that now, and we are on our way to
the destruction of every species on earth, if we don't pay
attention and reverse our course.

Presidential candidates don't chew gum.

If we can but tear the blindfold of self-deception from our eyes and
loosen the gag of self-denial from our voices, we can restore
our country to greatness.

Military strength in reserve is better than military strength being
reigned upon the other side including all of its innocent civilians.

Now people all across America are starting to believe in America
again. We are coming back, back to the heights of
greatness, back to America's proud role as a temple of
justice and a champion of peace.

Our surest protection against assault from abroad has been not all
  our guards, gates and guns, or even our two oceans, but
  our essential goodness as a people. Our richest asset has
  been not our material wealth but our values.

The good news, to relieve all this gloom, is that a democracy is
  inherently self-correcting. Here, the people are sovereign.
  Inept political leaders can be replaced. Foolish policies can
  be changed. Disastrous mistakes can be reversed.

We have convinced over one billion members of the Islamic faith that we
  are prejudiced against their religion, that we would deny
  them freedom of religion, that we want suppress their
  culture and invade their governments.

We have treated our most serious adversaries, such as Iran and North Korea,
  in the most juvenile manner - by giving them the silent treatment. In
  so doing, we have weakened, not strengthened, our bargaining
  position and our leadership.

## SONIA SOTOMAYOR (Supreme Court Justice, 1954 - )

It's not the heart that compels conclusions in cases, it's the law.

I strive never to forget the real-world consequences of my
  decisions on individuals, businesses, and government

I firmly believe in the rule of law as the foundation for all of our basic rights.

I would hope that a wise Latina woman with the richness of her experiences
  would more often than not reach a better conclusion than a
  white male who hasn't lived that life.

Personal experiences affect the facts that judges choose to see.

Although I grew up in very modest and challenging circumstances,
  I consider my life to be immeasurably rich.

We apply law to facts. We don't apply feelings to facts.

Whether born from experience or inherent physiological or cultural
  differences our gender and national origins may and will
  make a difference in our judging.

## JOHN STEINBECK (Author, 1902-1968)

Journey is a person in itself; no two are alike. And all plans, safeguards,
  policing, and coercion are fruitless. We find that after years
  of struggle that we do not take a trip; a trip takes us.

A journey is like marriage. The certain way to be wrong is to
  think you control it.

A sad soul can kill quicker than a germ.

Four hoarse blasts of a ship's whistle still raise the hair on my
  neck and set my feet to tapping.

Give a critic  an inch, he'll write a play.

I am impelled, not to squeak like a grateful and apologetic mouse,
  but to roar like a lion out of pride in my profession.

I hate cameras. They are so much more sure than I am about everything.

I have come to believe that a great teacher is a great artist and that there are as
  few as there are any other great artists. Teaching might even be the greatest
  of the arts since the medium is the human mind and spirit.

I have never smuggled anything in my life. Why, then, do I feel an
  uneasy sense of guilt on approaching a customs barrier?

I have owed you this letter for a very long time-but my fingers
        have avoided the pencil as though it were an old and poisoned tool.
I hold that a writer who does not passionately believe in the perfectibility of man
        has no dedication nor any membership in literature.
I've lived in good climate, and it bores the hell out of me. I like
        weather rather than climate.
I've seen a look in dogs' eyes, a quickly vanishing look of amazed contempt, and I
        am convinced that basically dogs think humans are nuts.
Ideas are like rabbits. You get a couple and learn how to handle
        them, and pretty soon you have a dozen.
If you're in trouble, or hurt or need - go to the poor people.
        They're the only ones that'll help - the only ones.
In the souls of the people the grapes of wrath are filling and growing
        heavy, growing heavy for the vintage.
In utter loneliness a writer tries to explain the inexplicable.
It has always been my private conviction that any man who
        puts his intelligence up against a fish and loses had it coming.
It is a common experience that a problem difficult at night is resolved in the
        morning after the committee of sleep has worked on it.
It is true that we are weak and sick and ugly and quarrelsome but if that is all we
        ever were, we would millenniums ago have disappeared
        from the face of the earth.
It seems to me that if you or I must choose between two courses of thought or
        action, we should remember our dying and try so to live
        that our death brings no pleasure on the world.
Man is the only kind of varmint sets his own trap, baits it, then steps in it.
Man, unlike anything organic or inorganic in the universe, grows beyond his work,
        walks up the stairs of his concepts, emerges ahead of his accomplishments.
Many a trip continues long after movement in time and space have ceased.
Men do change, and change comes like a little wind that ruffles the curtains atdawn,
        and it comes like the stealthy perfume of wildflowers hidden in the grass.
No man really knows about other human beings. The best he
        can do is to suppose that they are like himself.
No one wants advice - only corroboration.
One can find so many pains when the rain is falling.
Power does not  corrupt. Fear corrupts... perhaps the fear of a loss of power.
Syntax, my lad. It has been restored to the highest place in the republic.
The discipline of the written word punishes both stupidity and dishonesty.
The impulse of the American woman to geld her husband and
        castrate her sons is very strong.
The profession of book writing makes horse racing seem like a
        solid, stable business.
The writer  must believe that what he is doing is the most important thing in the
        world. And he must hold to this illusion even when he knows it is not true.
These words dropped into my childish mind as if you should accidentally drop a ring
        into a deep well. I did not think of them much at the time, but there came a
        day in my life when the ring was fished up out of the well, good as new.
Time is the only critic  without  ambition.
Unless a reviewer  has the courage to give you unqualified praise,
        I say ignore the bastard.

We spend our time searching for security and hate it when we get it.

Where does discontent start? You are warm enough, but you shiver. You are fed,
yet hunger gnaws you. You have been loved, but your yearning wanders in
new fields. And to prod all these there's time, the Bastard Time.

Writers are a little below clowns and a little above trained seals.

## ADLAI E. STEVENSON (Politician, Ambassador, 1900-1965)

A free society is one where it is safe to be unpopular.

Freedom rings where opinions clash.

Man is a strange animal. He generally cannot read the handwriting
on the wall until his back is up against it.

A hungry man is not a free man.

Laws are never as effective as habits

I believe that if we really want human brotherhood to spread and
increase until it makes life safe and sane, we must also be
certain that there is no one true faith or path by which it may spread.

I have been thinking that I would make a proposition to my Republican friends...
that if they will stop telling lies about the Democrats, we will stop
telling the truth about them.

It's hard to lead a cavalry charge if you think you look funny on a horse.

The first principle of a free society is an untrammeled flow of
words in an open forum.

Public confidence in the integrity of the Government is indispensable to
faith in democracy; and when we lose faith in the system, we have
lost faith in everything we fight and spend for.

All progress has resulted from people who took unpopular positions.

Change is inevitable. Change for the better is a full-time job.

There is a spiritual hunger in the world today - and it cannot be
satisfied by better cars on longer credit terms.

There was a time when a fool and his money were soon parted, but
now it happens to everybody.

Nature is indifferent to the survival of the human species, including Americans.

On the plains of hesitation lie the blackened bones of countless
millions who at the dawn of victory lay down to rest, and in resting died.

On this shrunken globe, men can no longer live as strangers.

Patriotism is not short, frenzied outbursts of emotion, but the tranquil
and steady dedication of a lifetime.

Peace is the one condition of survival in this nuclear age.

Saskatchewan is much like Texas- except it's more friendly
to the United States.

Some people approach every problem with an open mouth.

That which seems the height of absurdity in one generation often
becomes the height of wisdom in another.

The best reason I can think of for not running for President of the
United States is that you have to shave twice a day.

The hardest thing about any political campaign is how to win
without proving that you are unworthy of winning.

I believe in the forgiveness of sin and the redemption of ignorance.

I think that one of the most fundamental responsibilities is to give
testimony in a court of law, to give it honestly and willingly.

Ignorance is stubborn and prejudice is hard.

In America any boy may become President and I suppose it's just
        one of the risks he takes.
In quiet places, reason abounds.
It is not the years in your life but the life in your years that counts.
It will be helpful in our mutual objective to allow every man in America
        to look his neighbor in the face and see a man-not a color.
Law is not a profession at all, but rather a
        business service station and repair shop.
Making peace is harder than making war.
Man does not live by words alone, despite the fact that
        sometimes he has to eat them.
The idea that you can merchandise candidates for high office like breakfast
        cereal - that you can gather votes like box tops - is, I think,
        the ultimate indignity to the democratic process.
The journey of a thousand leagues begins with a single step. So we must never
        neglect any work of peace within our reach, however small.
The New Dealers have all left Washington to make way for the car dealers.
Those who corrupt the public mind are just as evil as those who
        steal from the public purse.
Communism is the corruption of a dream of justice.
A hypocrite is the kind of politician who would cut down a redwood
        tree, then mount the stump and make a speech for conservation.
A beauty is a woman you notice; a charmer is one who notices you.
A politician is a statesman who approaches every question with an open mouth.
Accuracy to a newspaper is what virtue is to a lady; but a
        newspaper can always print a retraction.
The time to stop a revolution is at the beginning, not the end.
To act coolly, intelligently and prudently in perilous circumstances
        is the test of a man - and also a nation.
We can chart our future clearly and wisely only when we know the path
        which has led to the present.
We have confused the free with the free and easy.
We mean by "politics" the people's business - the most important
        business there is.
After four years at the United Nations I sometimes yearn for the
        peace and tranquility of a political convention.
An editor is someone who separates the wheat from the chaff
        and then prints the chaff.
An Independent is someone who wants to take the politics out of politics.
As citizens of this democracy, you are the rulers and the ruled, the law-givers
        and the law-abiding, the beginning and the end.
Communism is the death of the soul. It is the organization of total conformity -
        in short, of tyranny - and it is committed to making tyranny universal.
Every age needs men who will redeem the time by living with a
        vision of the things that are to be.
Flattery is all right so long as you don't inhale.
Freedom is not an ideal, it is not even a protection, if it means
        nothing more than the freedom to stagnate.
Freedom rings where opinions clash.
He who slings mud generally loses ground.
You can tell the size of a man by the size of the thing that makes him mad.

We must recover the element of quality in our traditional pursuit of equality.
We must not, in opening our schools to everyone, confuse
the idea that all should have equal chance with the notion
that all have equal endowments.

We travel together, passengers on a little spaceship, dependent on its
vulnerable reserves of air and soil, all committed, for our safety, to
its security and peace. Preserved from annihilation only by
the care, the work and the love we give our fragile craft.

What a man knows at fifty that he did not know at twenty is for
the most part incommunicable.

Your days are short here; this is the last of your springs. And now in the
serenity and quiet of this lovely place, touch the depths of
truth, feel the hem of Heaven. You will go away with old,
good friends. And don't forget when you leave why you came.

## JIMMY SWAGGART (Evangelist, 1935 -)

Evolution is a bankrupt speculative philosophy, not a scientific fact.
Only a spiritually bankrupt society could ever believe it. Only
atheists could accept this Satanic theory.

The Media is ruled by Satan. But yet I wonder if many Christians fully
understand that.

If I do not return to the pulpit this weekend, millions of
people will go to hell.

I have sinned against you, my Lord.

I'm gonna be blunt and plain, if one ever looks at me like that
I'm gonna kill him and tell God he died.

I've never seen a man in my life I wanted to marry.

It's a humorous statement that doesn't mean anything. You can't
lie to God - it's ridiculous.

Philosophies change by the day while God never changes, simply
because, being perfect, He does not have to change!

## CHUCK SWINDOLL (Christian Pastor, Motivational Speaker, 1934 - )

Alleged "impossibilities" are opportunities for our capacities to be stretched.

A family is a place where principles are hammered and honed on the
anvil of everyday living.

I cannot even imagine where I would be today were it not for that
handful of friends who have given me a heart full of joy.
Let's face it, friends make life a lot more fun.

When intimidated by who's sitting in the audience, we should
remember the King of Kings is also here, and it's his message.

The world's smallest package is a man wrapped up in himself

When God is involved, anything can happen. Be open. Stay that way. God has a
beautiful way of bringing good vibrations out of broken chords.

The habit of always putting off an experience until you can afford it, or until the
time is right, or until you know how to do it is one of the greatest
burglars of joy. Be deliberate, but once you've made up your mind-jump in.

Few things are more infectious than a godly lifestyle. The people you rub
shoulders with everyday need that kind of challenge. Not prudish. Not
preachy. Just cracker jack clean living. Just honest to goodness,
bone - deep, non-hypocritical integrity.

Laughter is the most beautiful and beneficial therapy God ever granted humanity

If you're running a 26-mile marathon, remember that every mile is run one step at a time. If you are writing a book, do it one page at a time. If you're trying to master a new language, try it one word at a time. There are 365 days in the average year. Divide any project by 365 and you'll find that no job is all that intimidating

The difference between something good and something great is attention to detail.

We are all faced with a series of great opportunities brilliantly disguised as impossible situations.

When I think of vision, I have in mind the ability to see above and beyond the majority.

When you have vision it affects your attitude. Your attitude is optimistic rather than pessimistic.

The remarkable thing is, we have a choice everyday regarding the attitude we will embrace for that day.

The secret of living a life of excellence is merely a matter of thinking thoughts of excellence. Really, it's a matter of programming our minds with the kind of information that will set us free.

Words can never adequately convey the incredible impact of our attitudes toward life. The longer I live the more convinced I become that life is 10 percent what happens to us and 90 percent how we respond to it.

If we want the advantages of love, then we must be willing to take the risks of love. And that requires vulnerability. Of course, we can refuse this path and trod another one devoid of openness. But the toll on such a road is extremely high.

When you suffer and lose, that does not mean you are being disobedient to God. In fact, it might mean you're right in the centre of His will. The path of obedience is often marked by times of suffering and loss.

We cannot change our past. We can not change the fact that people act in a certain way. We can not change the inevitable. The only thing we can do is play on the one string we have, and that is our attitude.

In vain I have searched the Bible, looking for examples of early believers whose lives were marked by rigidity, predictability, inhibition, dullness, and caution. Fortunately, grim, frowning, joyless saints in Scriptures are conspicuous by their absence. Instead, the examples I find are of adventurous, risk-taking, enthusiastic, and authentic believers whose joy was contagious even in times of full trial. Their vision was broad even when death drew near. Rules were few and changes were welcome. The contrast between then and now is staggering.

A saying I heard years ago: 'It doesn't matter what you do. Just do something, even if it's wrong!' That's the most stupid counsel I've ever heard. Never do what's wrong! Do nothing until it's right. Then do it with all your might. That's wise counsel.

The swift wind of compromise is a lot more devastating than the sudden jolt of misfortune.

Each day of our lives we make deposits in the memory banks of our children.

Encouragement is awesome. It (can) actually change the course of another person's day, week, or life.

## WILLIAM HOWARD TAFT (President, 1857-1930)

A government is for the benefit of all the people.

I do not believe in the divinity of Christ, and there are many other
of the postulates of the orthodox creed to which I cannot subscribe.

No tendency is quite so strong in human nature as the desire to
lay down rules of conduct for other people.

A system in which we may have an enforced rest from
legislation for two years is not bad.

Anti-Semitism is a noxious weed that should be cut
out. It has no place in America.

Don't write so that you can be understood, write so
that you can't be misunderstood.

Enthusiasm for a cause sometimes warps judgment.

Failure to accord credit to anyone for what he may
have done is a great weakness in any man.

I am afraid I am a constant disappointment to my party. The fact of the matter
is, the longer I am president the less of a party man I seem to become.

I am in favor of helping the prosperity of all countries
because, when we are all prosperous, the trade with
each becomes more valuable to the other.

I am president now, and tired of being kicked around.

I have come to the conclusion that the major part of the work of
a President is to increase the gate receipts of expositions
and fairs and bring tourists to town.

I love judges, and I love courts. They are my ideals, that typify on earth
what we shall meet hereafter in heaven under a just God.

I think I might as well give up being a candidate. There are so many
people in the country who don't like me.

I'll be damned if I am not getting tired of this. It seems to be
the profession of a President simply to hear other people talk.

If this humor be the safety of our race, then it is due largely to the
infusion into the American people of the Irish brain.

Politics makes me sick.

Presidents come and go, but the Supreme Court goes on forever.

Socialism proposes no adequate substitute for the motive of
enlightened selfishness that today is at the basis of all
human labor and effort, enterprise and new activity.

Substantial progress toward better things can rarely be taken
without developing new evils requiring new remedies.

The trouble with me is that I like to talk too much.

The world is not going to be saved by legislation.

We are all imperfect. We can not expect perfect government.

We live in a stage of politics, where legislators seem to regard the passage
of laws as much more important than the results of their enforcement.

## GEORGE TAKEI (ACTOR, 1937 - )

. . . it seems to me important for a country, for a nation to certainly know
about its glorious achievements but also to know where its ideals
failed, in order to keep that from happening again.

. . . the ideals of a country are only as good as the people who
give it flesh and blood.

This is supposed to be a participatory democracy and if we're not in there
    participating then the people that will manipulate and exploit the
    system will step in there.
. . . when we came out of camp, that's when I first realized that being in
    camp, that being Japanese-American, was something shameful.
Every time we had a hot war going on in Asia, it was
    difficult for Asian Americans here.
I spent my boyhood behind the barbed wire fences of American
    internment camps and that part of my life is something that
    I wanted to share with more people.
I'm an anglophile. I visit England regularly,
    sometimes three or four times a year, at least once a year.
STAR TREK is a show that had a vision about a future that was positive.
. . . the whole history of Star Trek is the market demand.
Yes, I remember the barbed wire and the guard towers and the machine
    guns, but they became part of my normal landscape. What would
    be abnormal in normal times became my normality in camp.
I grew up in two American internment camps, and at that time I was
    very young.

## ZACHARY TAYLOR (President, 1784-1850)

It would be judicious to act with magnanimity towards a prostrate foe.
The power given by the Constitution to the Executive to interpose his
    veto is a high conservative power; but in my opinion it should
    never be exercised except in cases of clear violation of the
    Constitution, or manifest haste and want of due
    consideration by Congress.
As American freemen we can not but sympathize in all efforts to extend
    the blessings of civil and political liberty, but at the same time
    we are warned by the admonitions of history and the voice of our
    own beloved Washington to abstain from entangling alliances with
    foreign nations. In all disputes between conflicting governments it
    is our interest not less than our duty to remain strictly neutral,
    while our geographical position, the genius of our institutions and
    our people, the advancing spirit of civilization, and, above all, the
    dictates of religion direct us to the cultivation of peaceful and friendly
    relations with all other power
I have always done my duty. I am ready to die. My only regret
    is for the friends I leave behind me.
It eminently becomes a government like our own, founded on the
    morality and intelligence of its citizens and upheld by their
    affections, to exhaust every resort of honorable diplomacy before
    appealing to arms.

## NIKOLA TESLA (Inventor, 1856-1943)

We build but to tear down. Most of our work and resource
    is squandered. Our onward march is marked by
    devastation. Everywhere there is an appalling loss of
    time, effort and life. A cheerless view, but true.
Our virtues and our failings are inseparable, like force and matter.
    When they separate, man is no more.

Most certainly, some planets are not inhabited, but others
are, and among these there must exist life under all
conditions and phases of development.

There is no conflict between the ideal of religion and the ideal
of science, but science is opposed to theological dogmas
because science is founded on fact. To me, the universe is
simply a great machine which never came into being and
never will end. The human being is no exception to the
natural order. Man, like the universe, is a machine.
Nothing enters our minds or determines our actions which
is not directly or indirectly a response to stimuli beating
upon our sense organs from without.

From childhood I was compelled to concentrate attention upon
myself. This caused me much suffering, but to my present
view, it was a blessing in disguise for it has taught me to appreciate
the inestimable value of introspection in the preservation of life, as
well as a means of achievement.

If Edison had a needle to find in a haystack, he would proceed
at once with the diligence of the bee to examine straw after
straw until he found the object of his search. ... I was a sorry witness
of such doings, knowing that a little theory and
calculation would have saved him ninety per cent of his labor.

Let the future tell the truth, and evaluate each one according to
his work and accomplishments. The present is theirs; the
future, for which I have really worked, is mine.

The scientific man does not aim at an immediate result. He does
not expect that his advanced ideas will be readily taken up.
His work is like that of the planter — for the future. His duty
is to lay the foundation for those who are to come, and point
the way. He lives and labors and hopes.

I do not think there is any thrill that can go through the
human heart like that felt by the inventor as he sees some
creation of the brain unfolding to success... such emotions
make a man forget food, sleep, friends, love, everything.

The scientists of today think deeply instead of clearly. One must
be sane to think clearly, but one can think deeply and be
quite insane.

The spread of civilization may be likened to a fire;
first, a feeble spark, next a flickering flame, then
a mighty blaze, ever increasing in speed and power.

Today's scientists have substituted mathematics for
experiments, and they wander off through equation
after equation, and eventually build a structure which
has no relation to reality.

**TWYLA THARP (Dancer, 1941 - )**

The only thing I fear more than change is no change. The
business of being static makes me nuts.

It is extremely arrogant and very foolish to think that you
can ever outwit your audience.

The formal education that I received made little sense to me.

My mother was a dominant force in my life. She had a very specific
idea about education, which was: you should know everything
about everything. It was quite simple. There was no
exclusivity, and there really was no judgment.
Optimism with some experience behind it is much more energizing
than  plain old experience with a certain degree of cynicism.
There's this expression called postmodernism, which is kind of
silly, and destroys a perfectly good word called modern,
which now no longer means anything.

## LEWIS THOMAS (Physician, Educator 1913-1993)
The great thing about human language is that it prevents us from
tackling the matter at hand
I have always had a bad memory, as far back as I can remember.
Statistically the probability of any one of us being here is so small that you
would think the mere fact of existence would keep us all in a contented
dazzlement of surprise. We are alive against the stupendous odds of
genetics, infinitely outnumbered by all the alternates who might, except
for luck, be in our places.
The need to make music, and to listen to it, is universally expressed
by human beings. I cannot imagine, even in our most primitive times,
the emergence of talented painters to make cave paintings without
there having been, near at hand, equally creative people making song.
It is, like speech, a dominant aspect of human biology.
It is my belief, based partly on personal experience but partly also arrived at
by looking around at others, that childhood lasts considerably longer in
the males of our species than in the females.
Everything here is alive thanks to the living of everything else.
Left to ourselves, mechanistic and autonomic, we hanker for friends.
We hanker to go on, even in the face of plain evidence that long, long lives are not
necessarily pleasurable in the kind of society we have arranged thus far. We
will be lucky if we can postpone the search for new technologies for a while,
until we have discovered some satisfactory things to do with the extra time.
Ants are more like the parts of an animal than entities on their own. They are
mobile cells, circulating through a dense connective tissue of other ants in a
matrix of twigs. The circuits are so intimately interwoven that the anthill
meets all the essential criteria of an organism.
If we have learned anything at all in this century, it is that all new technologies
will be put to use, sooner or later, for better or worse, as it is in our
nature to do.
If you want to use a cliche you must take full responsibility for it
yourself and not try to fob it off on anon., or on society.
The great secret of doctors, known only to their wives, but still hidden from the
public, is that most things get better by themselves; most things, in fact,
are better in the morning.
We are built to make mistakes, coded for error.
We are, perhaps, uniquely among the earth's creatures, the worrying animal.
We worry away our lives, fearing the future, discontent with the present,
unable to take in the idea of dying, unable to sit still.
Music is the effort we make to explain to ourselves how our brains work. We
listen to Bach transfixed because this is listening to a human mind.

Sometimes you get a glimpse of a semicolon coming, a few lines farther on, and
     it is like climbing a steep path through woods and seeing a wooden bench
     just at a bend in the road ahead, a place where you can expect to sit for a
     moment, catching your breath.
Human language... prevents us from sticking to the matter at hand.
The cloning of humans is on most of the lists of things to worry about from
     Science, along with behavior control, genetic engineering, transplanted
     heads, computer poetry and the unrestrained growth of plastic flowers.

## HUNTER S. THOMPSON (Journalist, 1937-2005)

America... just a nation of two hundred million used car salesmen with all the
     money we need to buy guns and no qualms about killing anybody else
     in the world who tries to make us uncomfortable.
A word to the wise is infuriating.
Call on God, but row away from the rocks.
Politics is the art of controlling your environment.
In a closed society where everybody's guilty, the only crime is getting
     caught. In a world of thieves, the only final sin is stupidity.
It was the Law of the Sea, they said. Civilization ends at the waterline. Beyond
     that, we all enter the food chain, and not always right at the top.
No man is so foolish but he may sometimes give another good counsel, and no
     man so wise that he may not easily err if he takes no other counsel than
     his own. He that is taught only by himself has a fool for a master.
Of all the men that have run for president in the twentieth century, only
     George McGovern truly understood what a monument America
     could be to the human race.
That was always the difference between Muhammad Ali and the rest of us. He
     came, he saw, and if he didn't entirely conquer - he came as close as
     anybody we are likely to see in the lifetime of this doomed generation.
The Edge... there is no honest way to explain it because the only people who
     really know where it is are the ones who have gone over.
The person who doesn't scatter the morning dew will not comb gray hairs.
For every moment of triumph, for every instance of beauty, many
     souls must be trampled.
Going to trial with a lawyer who considers your whole life-style a Crime in
     Progress is not a happy prospect.
I feel the same way about disco as I do about herpes.
I have a theory that the truth is never told during the nine-to-five hours.
I wouldn't recommend sex, drugs or insanity for everyone, but
     they've always worked for me.
If I'd written all the truth I knew for the past ten years, about 600 people -
     including me - would be rotting in prison cells from Rio to Seattle today.
     Absolute truth is a very rare and dangerous commodity in
     the context of professional journalism.
If you're going to be crazy, you have to get paid for it or else
     you're going to be locked
Buy the ticket, take the ride.

## HENRY DAVID THOREAU (Author, Naturalist, 1817-1862)

A man is rich in proportion to the number of things he can afford to let alone.

Any fool can make a rule, and any fool will mind it.

As if you could kill time without injuring eternity.

The squirrel that you kill in jest, dies in earnest.

Truths and roses have thorns about them.

Simplify, simplify.

Success usually comes to those who are too busy to be looking for it.

It is what a man thinks of himself that really determines his fate.

Men have become the tools of their tools.

Money is not required to buy one necessity of the soul.

Disobedience is the true foundation of liberty. The obedient must be slaves.

Go confidently in the direction of your dreams. Live the life you have imagined.

How vain it is to sit down to write when you have not stood up to live.

As you simplify your life, the laws of the universe will be simpler; solitude
       will not be solitude, poverty will not be poverty, nor weakness.

Every creature is better alive than dead, men and moose and pine trees, and
       he who understands it aright will rather preserve its life than destroy it.

Every people have gods to suit their circumstances

Be not simply good - be good for something.

Do not trouble yourself much to get new things, whether clothes or
       friends... Sell your clothes and keep your thoughts.

Be true to your work, your word, and your friend.

Books are the treasured wealth of the world and the fit inheritance
       of generations and nations.

Books are to be distinguished by the grandeur of their topics even more
       than by the manner in which they are treated.

Books can only reveal us to ourselves, and as often as they do us this service
       we lay them aside.

A man's interest in a single bluebird is worth more than a complete but dry
       list of the fauna and flora of a town.

A broad margin of leisure is as beautiful in a man's life as in a book. Haste makes
       waste, no less in life than in housekeeping. Keep the time, observe
       the hours of the universe, not of the cars.

A truly good book teaches me better than to read it. I must soon lay it
       down, and commence living on its hint. What I began by
       reading, I must finish by acting.

After the first blush of sin comes its indifference.

Aim above morality. Be not simply good, be good for something.

All endeavor calls for the ability to tramp the last mile, shape the last plan,
       endure the last hours toil. The fight to the finish spirit is the one...
       characteristic we must posses if we are to face the future as finishers.

All men are children, and of one family. The same tale sends them all to
       bed, and wakes them in the morning.

An early-morning walk is a blessing for the whole day.

As a single footstep will not make a path on the earth, so a single thought will
       not make a pathway in the mind. To make a deep physical path, we walk
       again and again. To make a deep mental path, we must think over and
       over the kind of thoughts we wish to dominate our lives.

As in geology, so in social institutions, we may discover the causes of
       all past changes in the present invariable order of society.

Faith keeps many doubts in her pay. If I could not doubt, I should not believe.
Faith never makes a confession.
Friends... they cherish one another's hopes. They are kind
      to one another's dreams.
Front yards are not made to walk in, but, at most,
      through, and you could go in the back way.
It is better to have your head in the clouds, and know where you
      are... than to breathe the clearer atmosphere below them,
      and think that you are in paradise.
It is never too late to give up our prejudices.
It is not desirable to cultivate a respect for the law, so much as for the right.
It is not enough to be busy. So are the ants. The question is: What
      are we busy about?
It is not part of a true culture to tame tigers, any more than it is
      to make sheep ferocious.
It is only when we forget all our learning that we begin to know.
It is remarkable how closely the history of the apple tree is
      connected with that of man.
It is the greatest of all advantages to enjoy no advantage at all.
It is usually the imagination that is wounded first, rather than the
      heart; it being much more sensitive.
The cost of a thing is the amount of what I will call life which is required to be
      exchanged for it, immediately or in the long run.
The fibers of all things have their tension and are strained like the
      strings of an instrument.
The finest workers in stone are not copper or steel tools, but the gentle touches
      of air and water working at their leisure with a liberal allowance of time.
The greatest compliment that was ever paid me was when one asked me what I
      thought, and attended to my answer.
The heart is forever inexperienced.
The language of excitement is at best picturesque merely. You must be
      calm before you can utter oracles.
The language of friendship is not words but meanings.
The law will never make a man free; it is men who have got to make the law free.
The lawyer's truth is not Truth, but consistency or a consistent expediency.
The light which puts out our eyes is darkness to us. Only that day dawns to which
      we are awake. There is more day to dawn. The sun is but a morning star.
The youth gets together his materials to build a bridge to the moon, or, perchance,
      a palace or temple on the earth, and, at length, the middle-aged man
      concludes to build a woodshed with them.
There are a thousand hacking at the branches of evil to one who
      is striking at the root.
There are certain pursuits which, if not wholly poetic and true, do at least
      suggest a nobler and finer relation to nature than we know. The
      keeping of bees, for instance.
There are moments when all anxiety and stated toil are becalmed in the infinite
      leisure and repose of nature.
There are old heads in the world who cannot help me by their example or advice
      to live worthily and satisfactorily to myself; but I believe that it is in my
      power to elevate myself this very hour above the common level of my life.
There is but one stage for the peasant and the actor.

There is more of good nature than of good sense at the bottom of most marriages.
There is no just and serene criticism as yet.
There is no more fatal blunderer than he who consumes the greater
part of his life getting his living.
There is no odor so bad as that which arises from goodness tainted.
There is no remedy for love but to love more.
There is no rule more invariable than that we are paid for our suspicions
by finding what we suspect.
There is no value in life except what you choose to place upon it and
no happiness in any place except what you bring to it yourself.
There is one consolation in being sick; and that is the possibility that you may
recover to a better state than you were ever in before.
There never was and is not likely soon to be a nation of philosophers, nor am I
certain it is desirable that there should be.
They can do without architecture who have no olives nor wines in the cellar.
Things do not change; we change.
The man who goes alone can start today; but he who travels with
another must wait till that other is ready.
The man who is dissatisfied with himself, what can he do?
The mass of men lead lives of quiet desperation.
The most I can do for my friend is simply be his friend.
The perception of beauty is a moral test.
The price of anything is the amount of life you exchange for it.
The rarest quality in an epitaph is truth.
The savage in man is never quite eradicated.
The smallest seed of faith is better than the largest fruit of happiness.
Through our own recovered innocence we discern the innocence of our neighbors.
Time is but the stream I go a-fishing in.
'Tis healthy to be sick sometimes.
To affect the quality of the day, that is the highest of arts.
To be admitted to Nature's hearth costs nothing. None is excluded, but
excludes himself. You have only to push aside the curtain.
To have done anything just for money is to have been truly idle.
True friendship can afford true knowledge. It does not depend on
darkness and ignorance.
Truth is always in harmony with herself, and is not concerned chiefly to
reveal the justice that may consist with wrong-doing.
Under a government which imprisons any unjustly, the true place
for a just man is also a prison.
We are always paid for our suspicion by finding what we suspect.
We are not what we are, nor do we treat or esteem each other for such,
but for what we are capable of being.
Wealth is the ability to fully experience life.
What is called genius is the abundance of life and health.
What is human warfare but just this; an effort to make the laws of God
and nature take sides with one party.
What is the use of a house if you haven't got a tolerable planet to put it on?
What lies behind us and what lies ahead of us are tiny matters
compared to what lives within us.
What old people say you cannot do, you try and find that you can. Old
deeds for old people, and new deeds for new.

What you get by achieving your goals is not as important as what you
        become by achieving your goals.
What is once well done is done forever.
When I hear music, I fear no danger. I am invulnerable. I see no foe. I am
        related to the earliest times, and to the latest.
Where there is an observatory and a telescope, we expect that any
        eyes will see new worlds at once.
While civilization has been improving our houses, it has not equally improved
        the men who are to inhabit them. It has created palaces, but it was
        not so easy to create noblemen and kings.
Why should we be in such desperate haste to succeed, and in such desperate
        enterprises? If a man does not keep pace with his companions,
        perhaps it is because he hears a different drummer.
You must live in the present, launch yourself on every wave,
        find your eternity in each moment.
We must learn to reawaken and keep ourselves awake, not by mechanical
        aid, but by an infinite expectation of the dawn.
We must walk consciously only part way toward our goal, and then
        leap in the dark to our success.
We shall see but a little way if we require to understand what we see.
Men are born to succeed, not to fail.
Men have a respect for scholarship and learning greatly out of proportion to
        the use they commonly serve.
Most men lead lives of quiet desperation and go to the grave with
        the song still in them.
Most of the luxuries and many of the so-called comforts of life are not only not
        indispensable, but positive hindrances to the elevation of mankind.
Nature and human life are as various as our several constitutions. Who
        shall say what prospect life offers to another?
Nature is full of genius, full of the divinity; so that not a snowflake
        escapes its fashioning hand.
Nature puts no question and answers none which we mortals ask.
        She has long ago taken her resolution.
Nature will bear the closest inspection. She invites us to lay our eye
        level with her smallest leaf, and take an insect view of its plain.
Nay, be a Columbus to whole new continents and worlds within you,
        opening new channels, not of trade, but of thought.
Never look back unless you are planning to go that way.
Night is certainly more novel and less profane than day.
No face which we can give to a matter will stead us so well at last as
        the truth. This alone wears well.
None are so old as those who have outlived enthusiasm.
Only he is successful in his business who makes that pursuit which affords
        him the highest pleasure sustain him.
Only that day dawns to which we are awake.
Our houses are such unwieldy property that we are often
        imprisoned rather than housed by them.
Our inventions are wont to be pretty toys, which distract our attention from
        serious things. They are but improved means to an unimproved end.
Our life is frittered away by detail... simplify, simplify.
Our truest life is when we are in dreams awake.

Our moments of inspiration are not lost though we have no particular poem
        to show for them; for those experiences have left an indelible
        impression, and we are ever and anon reminded of them.
Pursue some path, however narrow and crooked, in which you can
        walk with love and reverence.
Rather than love, than money, than fame, give me truth.
Read the best books first, or you may not have a chance to read them at all.
Shall I not have intelligence with the earth? Am I not partly
        leaves and vegetable mould myself.
Some are reputed sick and some are not. It often happens that the sicker
        man is the nurse to the sounder.
Thank God men cannot fly, and lay waste the sky as well as the earth.
That government is best which governs least.
That man is rich whose pleasures are the cheapest.
Thaw with her gentle persuasion is more powerful than Thor with his
        hammer. The one melts, the other breaks into pieces.
The Artist is he who detects and applies the law from observation of the works
        of Genius, whether of man or Nature. The Artisan is he who merely
        applies the rules which others have detected.
The bluebird carries the sky on his back
Not only must we be good, but we must also be good for something.
Not until we are lost do we begin to understand ourselves.
Nothing goes by luck in composition. It allows of no tricks. The best you
        can write will be the best you are.
Nothing makes the earth seem so spacious as to have friends at a
        distance; they make the latitudes and longitudes.
Live the life you've dreamed.
Live your beliefs and you can turn the world around.
Live your life, do your work, then take your hat.
Make the most of your regrets; never smother your sorrow, but tend and
        cherish it till it comes to have a separate and integral interest. To
        regret deeply is to live afresh.
Many men go fishing all of their lives without knowing
        that it is not fish they are after.
May we so love as never to have occasion to repent of our love!
Generally speaking, a howling wilderness does not howl: it is the
        imagination of the traveler that does the howling.
God reigns when we take a liberal view, when a liberal view is presented to us.
Goodness is the only investment that never fails.
Great men, unknown to their generation, have their fame among the great
        who have preceded them, and all true worldly fame subsides from
        their high estimate beyond the stars.
How could youths better learn to live than by at once trying
        the experiment of living?
How does it become a man to behave towards the American government
        today? I answer, that he cannot without disgrace be associated with it.
How many things there are concerning which we might well deliberate
        whether we had better know them.
How can any man be weak who dares to be at all?
I am sorry to think that you do not get a man's most effective criticism
        until you provoke him. Severe truth is expressed with some bitterness.

I did not wish to take a cabin passage, but rather to go before the mast and
　　on the deck of the world, for there I could best see the moonlight amid
　　the mountains. I do not wish to go below now.
Heaven is under our feet as well as over our heads.
I had three chairs in my house; one for solitude, two for friendship,
　　three for society.
I have a great deal of company in the house, especially in the
　　morning when nobody calls.
I have always been regretting that I was not as wise as the day I was born.
Before printing was discovered, a century was equal to a thousand years.
Being is the great explainer.
Beware of all enterprises that require a new set of clothes.
Could a greater miracle take place than for us to look through each
　　other's eyes for an instant?
Do not be too moral. You may cheat yourself out of much life so. Aim
　　above morality. Be not simply good; be good for something.
Do not hire a man who does your work for money, but him who
　　does it for love of it.
Do not worry if you have built your castles in the air. They are where
　　they should be. Now put the foundations under them.
Do what nobody else can do for you. Omit to do anything else.
Do what you love. Know your own bone; gnaw at it, bury it,
　　unearth it, and gnaw it still.
Dreams are the touchstones of our character.
Every generation laughs at the old fashions, but follows religiously the new.
Every man casts a shadow; not his body only, but his imperfectly mingled spirit.
　　This is his grief. Let him turn which way he will, it falls opposite to
　　the sun; short at noon, long at eve. Did you never see it?
Ignorance and bungling with love are better than wisdom and skill without.
I have been as sincere a worshiper of Aurora as the Greeks.
I have learned, that if one advances confidently in the direction of his dreams,
　　and endeavors to live the life he has imagined, he will meet with a
　　success unexpected in common hours.
I have never found a companion that was so companionable as solitude. We a
　　re for the most part more lonely when we go abroad among men than
　　when we stay in our chambers. A man thinking or working is always
　　alone, let him be where he will.
I have thought there was some advantage even in death, by which
　　we mingle with the herd of common men.
I know of no more encouraging fact than the unquestionable ability
　　of man to elevate his life by conscious endeavor.
I love to be alone. I never found the companion that was so
　　companionable as solitude.
I put a piece of paper under my pillow, and when I could not
　　sleep I wrote in the dark.
I say beware of all enterprises that require new clothes, and not
　　rather a new wearer of clothes.
If misery loves company, misery has company enough.
If one advances confidently in the direction of his dreams, and endeavors to
　　live the life which he has imagined, he will meet with success
　　unexpected in common hours.

If the machine of government is of such a nature that it requires you to be
the agent of injustice to another, then, I say, break the law.
I have seen how the foundations of the world are laid, and I have not
the least doubt that it will stand a good while.
If we will be quiet and ready enough, we shall find compensation I
n every disappointment.
If you can speak what you will never hear, if you can write what you will
never read, you have done rare things.
If you would convince a man that he does wrong, do right. Men will
believe what they see.
In human intercourse the tragedy begins, not when there is
misunderstanding about words, but when silence is not understood.
In the long run, men hit only what they aim at. Therefore, they had
better aim at something high.
In wilderness is the preservation of the world.
Instead of noblemen, let us have noble villages of men.
Is the babe young? When I behold it, it seems more venerable than the oldest man.
It appears to be a law that you cannot have a deep sympathy with
both man and nature.
It is a characteristic of wisdom not to do desperate things.
It is an interesting question how far men would retain their relative
rank if they were divested of their clothes.
It is best to avoid the beginnings of evil.
I was more independent than any farmer in Concord, for I was not
anchored to a house or farm, but could follow the bent of my genius,
which is a very crooked one, every moment.
I went to the woods because I wished to live deliberately, to front only the
essential facts of life, and see if I could not learn what it had to teach,
and not, when I came to die, discover that I had not lived.
I would rather sit on a pumpkin and have it all to myself, than be
crowded on a velvet cushion.
If a man constantly aspires is he not elevated?
If a man does not keep pace with his companions, perhaps it is because
he hears a different drummer. Let him step to the music which he
hears, however measured or far away.
If a man walks in the woods for love of them half of each day, he is in danger
of being regarded as a loafer. But if he spends his days as a speculator,
shearing off those woods and making the earth bald before her time,
he is deemed an industrious and enterprising citizen.
If I knew for a certainty that a man was coming to my house with the
conscious design of doing me good, I should run for my life.
If I seem to boast more than is becoming, my excuse is that I brag for
humanity rather than for myself.

## PETER TORK (Musician, 1942 - )

Pop music is aspirin and the blues are vitamins.
Every country has it trade offs.
Getting to play the blues has been transcendent for me. I can't say
if my finest hour is yet to come, you want to make a dent in
this world, well I do anyway.
You should be a hero to yourself. And if you`re not... check it out.

I don`t believe in `My country right or wrong`. My country wrong needs my help
Pop music, disco music, and heavy metal music is about shutting out the
      tensions of life, putting it away.
The blues brings you back into the fold. The blues isn't about the blues,
      it's about we have all had the blues and we are all in this together.
The Monkees was a straight sitcom, we used the same plots that were on
      the other situation comedies at the time. So the music wasn't
      threatening, we weren't threatening.
There hasn't been one show that we did, that I didn't enjoy to some extent.
The most significant thing about the Monkees as a pop phenomenon is that
      we were the only TV show about young adults that did not feature
      a wiser, older person.

## HARRY TRUMAN (President, 1884-1972)

A bureaucrat is a Democrat who holds some office that a Republican wants
A leader in the Democratic Party is a boss, in the Republican Party he is a leader.
A pessimist is one who makes difficulties of his opportunities and an
      optimist is one who makes opportunities of his difficulties.
A politician is a man who understands government. A statesman is a
      politician who's been dead for 15 years.
A President cannot always be popular.
A president either is constantly on top of events or, if he hesitates, events
      will soon be on top of him. I never felt that I could let up for a moment.
A President needs political understanding to run the government,
      but he may be elected without it.
Actions are the seed of fate deeds grow into destiny.
All my life, whenever it comes time to make a decision, I make
      it and forget about it.
All the president is, is a glorified public relations man who spends his time
      flattering, kissing, and kicking people to get them to do
      what they are supposed to do anyway.
Always be sincere, even if you don't mean it.
America was not built on fear. America was built on courage, on imagination
      and an unbeatable determination to do the job at hand.
Any man who has had the job I've had and didn't have a sense
      of humor wouldn't still be here.
Art is parasitic on life, just as criticism is parasitic on art.
Being too good is apt to be uninteresting.
Carry the battle to them. Don't let them bring it to you. Put them on
      the defensive and don't ever apologize for anything.
Experience has shown how deeply the seeds of war are planted by
      economic rivalry and social injustice.
I do not believe there is a problem in this country or the world today
      which could not be settled if approached through the teaching
      of the Sermon on the Mount.
I had faith in Israel before it was established, I have in it now. I believe
      it has a glorious future before it - not just another sovereign nation,
      but as an embodiment of the great ideals of our civilization.
I have found the best way to give advice to your children is to find out
      what they want and then advise them to do it.
I never did give anybody hell. I just told the truth and they thought it was hell.

I have no desire to crow over anybody or to see anybody eating crow,
      figuratively or otherwise. We should all get together and make a
      country in which everybody can eat turkey whenever he pleases.
I never gave anybody hell! I just told the truth and they thought it was hell.
I remember when I first came to Washington. For the first six months you
      wonder how the hell you ever got here. For the next six months you
      wonder how the hell the rest of them ever got here.
I would rather have peace in the world than be President.
I've said many a time that I think the Un-American Activities Committee in the
      House of Representatives was the most un-American thing in America!
If I hadn't been President of the United States, I probably would have
      ended up a piano player in a bawdy house.
If I'd known how much packing I'd have to do, I'd have run again.
If you can't convince them, confuse them.
If you can't stand the heat, get out of the kitchen.
In my opinion eight years as president is enough and sometimes too much
      for any man to serve in that capacity.
In reading the lives of great men, I found that the first victory they won
      was over themselves... self-discipline with all of them came first.
Intense feeling too often obscures the truth.
It is amazing what you can accomplish if you do not care who gets the credit.
It is understanding that gives us an ability to have peace. When we understand
      the other fellow's viewpoint, and he understands ours, then we can
      sit down and work out our differences.
It sure is hell to be president.
It's a recession when your neighbor loses his job; it's a depression
      when you lose yours.
It's plain hokum. If you can't convince 'em, confuse 'em. It's an
      old political trick. But this time it  won't work
Men make history and not the other way around. In periods where there is no
      leadership, society stands still. Progress occurs when courageous, skillful
      leaders seize the opportunity to change things for the better.
Most of the problems a President has to face have their roots in the past.
My choice early in life was either to be a piano-player in a whorehouse or a
      politician. And to tell the truth, there's hardly any difference.
My father was not a failure. After all, he was the father of a
      president of the United States.
Nixon is one of the few in the history of this country to run for high office talking
      out of both sides of his mouth at the same time and lying out of both sides.
Richard Nixon is a no good, lying bastard. He can lie out of both sides of his
      mouth at the same time, and if he ever caught himself telling the truth,
      he'd lie just to keep his hand in.
Study men, not historians.
The atom bomb was no "great decision." It was merely another powerful
      weapon in the arsenal of righteousness.
The buck stops here!
The best way to give advice to your children is to find out what
      they want and then advise them to do it.
The human animal cannot be trusted for anything good except en masse. The
      combined thought and action of the whole people of any race, creed or
      nationality, will always point in the right direction.

The Marine Corps is the Navy's police force and as long as I am President
    that is what it will remain. They have a propaganda machine that
    is almost equal to Stalin's.
The only things worth learning are the things you learn after you know it all.
The President is always abused. If he isn't, he isn't doing anything.
The reward of suffering is experience.
The United Nations is designed to make possible lasting freedom
    and independence for all its members.
The White House is the finest prison in the world.
There is nothing new in the world except the history you do not know.
This administration is going to be cussed and discussed for years to come.
Those who want the Government to regulate matters of the mind and spirit
    are like men who are so afraid of being murdered that they commit
    suicide to avoid assassination.
To hell with them. When history is written they will be the sons of bitches - not I.
Upon books the collective education of the race depends; they are the sole
    instruments of registering, perpetuating and transmitting thought.
Washington is a very easy city for you to forget where you came from and
    why you got there in the first place.
We shall never be able to remove suspicion and fear as potential causes of
    war until communication is permitted to flow, free and open,
    across international boundaries.
Well, I wouldn't say that I was in the great class, but I had a great
    time while I was trying to be great.
When even one American - who has done nothing wrong - is forced by fear to
    shut his mind and close his mouth - then all Americans are in peril.
When you get to be President, there are all those things, the honors, the
    twenty-one gun salutes, all those things. You have to remember it
    isn't for you. It's for the Presidency.
When you have an efficient government, you have a dictatorship.
Whenever a fellow tells me he's bipartisan, I know he's going to vote against me.
Whenever you put a man on the Supreme Court he ceases to be your friend.
You and I are stuck with the necessity of taking the worst of two evils or
    none at all. So-I'm taking the immature Democrat as the best of the
    two. Nixon is impossible.
You can always amend a big plan, but you can never expand a little one. I
    don't believe in little plans. I believe in plans big enough to meet a
    situation which we can't possibly foresee now.
You can never get all the facts from just one newspaper, and unless you have
    all the facts, you cannot make proper judgements about what is going on.
You know that being an American is more than a matter of where your parents
    came from. It is a belief that all men are created free and equal and that
    everyone deserves an even break.
You want a friend in Washington? Get a dog.

## MARK TWAIN (Humorist, Writer, Publisher, 1835-1910)
A man who carries a cat by the tail learns something he can learn in no other way.
Action speaks louder than words but not nearly as often.
All generalizations are false, including this one.
All right, then, I'll go to hell.
All you need is ignorance and confidence and the success is sure.

Always do right. This will gratify some people and astonish the rest.
Anger is an acid that can do more harm to the vessel in which it is stored
        than to anything on which it is poured.
As an example to others, and not that I care for moderation myself, it
        has always been my rule never to smoke when asleep, and never to
        refrain from smoking when awake.
Be careful about reading health books. You may die of a misprint
But who prays for Satan? Who, in eighteen centuries, has had the common
        humanity to pray for the one sinner that needed it most?
Buy land, they're not making it anymore.
By trying we can easily endure adversity. Another man's, I mean.
Civilization is the limitless multiplication of unnecessary necessities.
'Classic.' A book which people praise and don't read.
Climate is what we expect, weather is what we get.
Clothes make the man. Naked people have little or no influence on society.
Courage is resistance to fear, mastery of fear, not absence of fear.
Denial ain't just a river in Egypt.
Do the right thing. It will gratify some people and astonish the rest.
Do the thing you fear most  and the death of fear is certain.
Don't go around saying the world owes you a living. The world
        owes you nothing. It was here first.
Don't let schooling interfere with your education.
Don't part with your illusions. When they are gone, you may still
        exist, but you have ceased to live.
Don't say the old lady screamed. Bring her on and let her scream.
Don't tell fish stories where the people know you; but particularly, don't
        tell them where they know the fish.
Education consists mainly of what we have unlearned.
Everything has its limit - iron ore cannot be educated into gold.
Everything human is pathetic. The secret source of humor itself is not
        joy but sorrow. There is no humor in heaven.
Facts are stubborn, but statistics are more pliable.
Familiarity breeds contempt - and children.
Few things are harder to put up with than the annoyance of a good example.
Fiction is obliged to stick to possibilities. Truth isn't.
George Washington, as a boy, was ignorant of the commonest
        accomplishments of youth. He could not even lie.
Get your facts first, then you can distort them as you please.
Giving up smoking is the easiest thing in the world. I know
        because I've done it thousands of times.
Go to Heaven for the climate, Hell for the company.
God made the Idiot for practice, and then He made the School Board.
Golf  is a good walk spoiled.
Good breeding consists in concealing how much we think of ourselves
        and how little we think of the other person.
Good friends, good books and a sleepy conscience: this is the ideal life.
Grief can take care if itself, but to get the full value of a joy you
        must have somebody to divide it with.
He is now rising from affluence to poverty.
Honesty is the best policy - when there is money in it.
I don't give a damn for a man that can only spell a word one way.

I don't like to commit myself about heaven and hell - you see, I
have friends in both places.

I have been complimented many times and they always embarrass
me; I always feel that they have not said enough.

I have made it a rule never to smoke more that one cigar at a time.

It is just like man's vanity and impertinence to call an animal dumb
because it is dumb to his dull perceptions.

It is not best that we should all think alike; it is a difference of
opinion that makes horse races.

It usually takes me more than three weeks to prepare a good impromptu speech.

It was wonderful to find America, but it would have
been more wonderful to miss it.

It's good sportsmanship to not pick up lost golf balls while they are still rolling.

If you hold a cat by the tail you learn things you cannot learn any other way.

If you tell the truth, you don't have to remember anything.

In the first place, God made idiots. That was for practice. Then he
made school boards.

In the Spring, I have counted 136 different kinds of weather inside of 24 hours.

It ain't those parts of the Bible that I can't understand that bother me,
it is the parts that I do understand.

It ain't what you don't know that gets you into trouble. It's what
you know for sure that just ain't so.

It could probably be shown by facts and figures that there is no
distinctly native criminal class except Congress.

It is better to deserve honors and not have them than to have
them and not deserve them.

It is better to keep your mouth closed and let people think you are
a fool than to open it and remove all doubt.

It is better to take what does not belong to you than to let it
lie around neglected.

It is by the goodness of God that in our country we have those three
unspeakably precious things: freedom of speech, freedom of conscience,
and the prudence never to practice either of them.

It's good sportsmanship to not pick up lost golf balls while they are still rolling.

It's no wonder that truth is stranger than fiction. Fiction has to make sense.

It's not the size of the dog in the fight, it's the size of the fight in the dog.

Kindness is the language which the deaf can hear and the blind can see.

Laws control the lesser man... Right conduct controls the greater one.

Let us live so that when we come to die even the undertaker will be sorry.

Let us make a special effort to stop communicating with each other, so
we can have some conversation.

Let us not be too particular; it is better to have old secondhand
diamonds than none at all.

Life would be infinitely happier if we could only be born at the age
of eighty and gradually approach eighteen.

Lord save us all from a hope tree that has lost the faculty of putting out blossoms.

Loyalty to petrified opinion never yet broke a chain or freed a human soul.

Loyalty to the country always. Loyalty to the government when it deserves it.

Man - a creature made at the end of the week's work when God was tired.

Man is the only animal that blushes - or needs to.

Many a small thing has been made large by the right kind of advertising.

Martyrdom covers a multitude of sins.
My books are like water; those of the great geniuses are
        wine. (Fortunately) everybody drinks water.
Never put off till tomorrow what you can do the day after tomorrow.
Suppose you were an idiot, and suppose you were a member of
        Congress; but I repeat myself.
Repartee is something we think of twenty-four hours too late.
Soap and education are not as sudden as a massacre, but they
        are more deadly in the long run.
Sometimes too much to drink is barely enough.
Substitute "damn" every time you're inclined to write "very"; your editor
        will delete it and the writing will be just as it should be.
Only kings, presidents, editors, and people with tapeworms have
        the right to use the editorial "we."
Only one thing is impossible for God: To find any sense in any
        copyright law on the planet.
Part of the secret of a success in life is to eat what you like and
        let the food fight it out inside.
Patriot: the person who can holler the loudest without knowing
        what he is hollering about.
Patriotism is supporting your country all the time, and your
        government when it deserves it.
Principles have no real force except when one is well-fed.
The Christian's Bible is a drug store. Its contents remain the same,
        but the medical practice changes.
The difference between the right word and the almost right word is
        the difference between lightning and a lightning bug.
The fear of death follows from the fear of life. A man who lives
        fully is prepared to die at any time.
The first of April is the day we remember what we are the
        other 364 days of the year.
The human race has one really effective weapon, and that is laughter.
The human race is a race of cowards; and I am not only marching
        in that procession but carrying a banner.
The lack of money is the root of all evil.
The most interesting information comes from children, for they
        tell all they know and then stop.
The only way to keep your health is to eat what you don't want, drink
        what you don't like, and do what you'd rather not.
The public is the only critic whose opinion is worth anything at all.
The reports of my death have been greatly exaggerated.
The right word may be effective, but no word was ever as
        effective as a rightly timed pause.
The rule is perfect: in all matters of opinion our adversaries are insane.
The secret source of humor is not joy but sorrow; there is no humor in Heaven.
The trouble ain't that there is too many fools, but that the
        lightning ain't distributed right.
The very ink with which history is written is merely fluid prejudice.
The wit knows that his place is at the tail of a procession.
There are basically two types of people. People who accomplish things, and people
        who claim to have accomplished things. The first group is less crowded.

There are lies, damned lies and statistics.

There are several good protections against temptation, but the surest is cowardice.

There are times when one would like to hang the whole human
race, and finish the farce.

There is a charm about the forbidden that makes it unspeakably desirable.

There is no distinctly American criminal class - except Congress.

There is no sadder sight than a young pessimist.

Thousands of geniuses live and die undiscovered - either by themselves or by others.

Thunder is good, thunder is impressive; but it is lightning that does the work.

To be good is noble; but to show others how to be good is nobler and no trouble.

To refuse awards is another way of accepting them with more noise than is normal.

To succeed in life, you need two things: ignorance and confidence.

Truth is mighty and will prevail. There is nothing wrong with this,
except that it ain't so.

Truth is the most valuable thing we have. Let us economize it.

Under certain circumstances, profanity provides a relief denied even to prayer.

Water, taken in moderation, cannot hurt anybody.

We Americans... bear the ark of liberties of the world.

We are all alike, on the inside.

We have the best government that money can buy.

What a good thing Adam had. When he said a
good thing he knew nobody had said it before.

What a wee little part of a person's life are his acts and his words! His
real life is led in his head, and is known to none but himself.

What is the difference between a taxidermist and a tax
collector? The taxidermist takes only your skin.

What would men be without women? Scarce, sir, mighty scarce.

When angry, count to four; when very angry, swear.

When I was younger I could remember anything, whether it happened or not.

When in doubt tell the truth.

When people do not respect us we are sharply offended; yet in his private
heart no man much respects himself.

When red-haired people are above a certain social grade their hair is auburn.

When we remember we are all mad, the mysteries
disappear and life stands explained.

When you fish for love, bait with your heart, not your brain.

When your friends begin to flatter you on how young
you look, it's a sure sign you're getting old.

Whenever you find yourself on the side of the majority,
it is time to pause and reflect.

Why is it that we rejoice at a birth and grieve at a
funeral? It is because we are not the person involved.

Wit is the sudden marriage of ideas which before their
union were not perceived to have any relation.

Words are only painted fire; a look is the fire itself.

Work consists of whatever a body is obliged to do. Play consists of
whatever a body is not obliged to do.

Work is a necessary evil to be avoided.

Wrinkles should merely indicate where smiles have been.

You can't depend on your eyes when your imagination is out of focus.

## JOHN TYLER (President, 1790-1862)

I can never consent to being dictated to.

Let it be henceforth proclaimed to the world that man's conscience
was created free; that he is no longer accountable to his fellow
man for his religious opinions, being responsible therefore
only to his God.

Popularity, I have always thought, may aptly be compared to a coquette -
the more you woo her, the more apt is she to elude your embrace.

Wealth can only be accumulated by the earnings of industry and the
savings of frugality

## JOHN UPDIKE (Author, 1932-2009)

Writers may be disreputable, incorrigible, early to decay or
late to bloom but they dare to go it alone.

Now that I am sixty, I see why the idea of elder wisdom
has passed from currency.

Dreams come true; without that possibility,
nature would not incite us to have them.

Each morning my characters greet me with misty faces willing, though
chilled, to muster for another day's progress through the
dazzling quicksand the marsh of blank paper.

The essential support and encouragement comes from within,
arising out of the mad notion that your society needs to
know what only you can tell it.

A healthy male adult bore consumes each year one and a half times his
own weight in other people's patience.

Golf appeals to the idiot in us and the child. Just how childlike golf players
become is proven by their frequent inability to count past five.

Writing criticism is to writing fiction and poetry as hugging
the shore is to sailing in the open sea.

Most of American life consists of driving somewhere and then returning
home, wondering why the hell you went.

We do survive every moment, after all, except the last one.

America is a vast conspiracy to make you happy.

Every marriage tends to consist of an aristocrat and a peasant.  Of a
teacher and a learner.

Truth should not be forced; it should simply manifest itself, like a
woman who has in her privacy reflected and coolly decided to
bestow herself upon a certain man.

Until the 20th century it was generally assumed that a writer had said
what he had to say in his works.

We are most alive when we're in love.

We take our bearings, daily, from others. To be sane is,
to a great extent, to be sociable.

What art offers is space - a certain breathing room for the spirit.

When I write, I aim in my mind not toward New York but toward
a vague spot a little to the east of Kansas.

A leader is one who, out of madness or goodness, volunteers to take upon
himself the woe of the people. There are few men so foolish, hence
the erratic quality of leadership in the world.

I love my government not least for the extent to which it leaves me alone.

Government is either organized benevolence or organized madness;
 its peculiar magnitude permits no shading.
If men do not keep on speaking terms with children,
 they cease to be men, and become merely machines for eating
 and for earning money.
Inspiration arrives as a packet of material to be delivered.
Rain is grace; rain is the sky descending to the earth;
 without rain, there would be no life.
Religion enables us to ignore nothingness and get on with the jobs of life.
Sex is like money; only too much is enough.
That a marriage ends is less than ideal; but all things end under heaven, and if
 temporality is held to be invalidating, then nothing real succeeds.
The essential self is innocent, and when it tastes its own innocence
 knows that it lives for ever.
The first breath of adultery is the freest; after it, constraints aping marriage develop.
The Founding Fathers in their wisdom decided that children were an unnatural
 strain on parents. So they provided jails called schools, equipped with
 tortures called an education.
The inner spaces that a good story lets us enter are the old
 apartments of religion.
The refusal to rest content, the willingness to risk excess on behalf of
 one's obsessions, is what distinguishes artists from entertainers,
 and what makes some artists adventurers on behalf of us all.
There is no pleasing New Englanders, my dear, their soil
 is all rocks and their hearts are bloodless absolutes.
There's a crystallization that goes on in a poem which the young
 man can bring off, but which the middle-aged man can't.
A narrative is like a room on whose walls a number of false doors have been
 painted; while within the narrative, we have many apparent choices of
 exit, but when the author leads us to one particular door, we know it
 is the right one because it opens.
Americans have been conditioned to respect newness, whatever it costs them.
An affair wants to spill, to share its glory with the world. No act
 is so private it does not seek applause.
Any activity becomes creative when the doer cares
 about doing it right or better.
Art is like baby shoes. When you coat them with gold,
 they can no longer be worn.
Being naked approaches being revolutionary; going
 barefoot is mere populism.
But for a few phrases from his letters and an odd line or two of
 his verse, the poet walks gagged through his own biography.
By the time a partnership dissolves, it has dissolved.
 Customs and convictions change; respectable people are the last
 to know, or to admit, the change, and the ones most offended
 by fresh reflections of the facts in the mirror of art.
Existence itself does not feel horrible; it feels like an ecstasy, rather,
 which we have only to be still to experience.
For male and female alike, the bodies of the other sex are messages
 signaling what we must do, they are glowing signifiers of
 our own necessities.

Four years was enough of Harvard. I still had a lot to learn, but had
    been given the liberating notion that now I could teach myself.
From infancy on, we are all spies; the shame is not this but that the
    secrets to be discovered are so paltry and few.

## MARTIN VAN BUREN (President, 1782-1852)
The less government interferes with private pursuits, the
    better for general prosperity.
No evil can result from its inhibition more pernicious than
    its toleration.
The government should not be guided by Temporary Excitement,
    but by Sober Second Thought.
The national will is the supreme law of the Republic, and
    on all subjects within the limits of his constitutional
    powers should be faithfully obeyed by the public servant.
The people under our system, like the king in a monarchy,
    never dies.
There is a power in public opinion in this country - and I thank
    God for it: for it is the most honest and best of all powers -
    which will not tolerate an incompetent or unworthy man to
    hold in his weak or wicked hands the lives and fortunes of
    his fellow-citizens.
Those who have wrought great changes in the world never succeeded
    by gaining over chiefs; but always by exciting the multitude.
    The first is the resource of intrigue and produces only
    secondary results, the second is the resort of genius and
    transforms the universe.
As to the presidency, the two happiest days of my life were those
    of my entrance upon the office and my surrender of it.
If laws acting upon private interests can not always be avoided,
    they should be confined within the narrowest limits, and
    left wherever possible to the legislatures of the States.
In a government whose distinguishing characteristic should be a
    diffusion and equalization of its benefits and burdens the
    advantage of individuals will be augmented at the expense
    of the community at large.

## ROBERT VAUGHN (Actor, 1932 - )
My belief  in God is responsible for what I am... How can I refuse to talk about
    something which is so much a prt of my life both as a man and as a actor?
My childhood beliefs became so much a part of me that even today I find myself
    automatically living by a personal standard of conduct which can only be
    explained as resulting from my religious training.
My opposition to the Vietnam War. I was the first
    Hollywood actor to speak out against it.
The marvelous thing is that for thousands of years people have continued
    questioning and searching and ultimately concluding that reasons
    for certain occurrences are not given to man to know.
The world's philosophers and theologians searched for answers
    to the same mysteries.
By virtue of believing in a Supreme Being one embraces certain mysteries.

When you're a guest star on TV shows - particularly in the 1960s -
you're always the villain.
Why do people embrace God? In my opinion, belief in God and an
afterlife is a necessary extension of man's need to feel that this
life does not end with what we call death.
You see, some non-Catholic friends of mine have questioned the depth of
my faith because of the fact that I have a good education.
Audience response to The Man From U.N.C.L.E.  back in the '60s - well, I
was frankly  surprised by the show's success and the
attendant publicity for David and myself.
Finally, when the money was high enough, the script suddenly revealed
itself as being very clear to me.
All I did was basically play myself in the role of Napoleon Solo.
For example, I tend to personally reward myself for specific
acts of exceptional discipline.
I come from a long line of staunch Irish Catholics.
I have always been adventurous and rather daring.
I read Superman comics when I was a kid.
I sincerely believe I could have wound up in a lot of trouble if I had
not been taught as a boy to fear Hell, and to believe that certain
wicked acts could lead me to damnation.
I suppose you could sum up the religious aspects of my boyhood by saying
it was a time of life when I was taught the difference between right
and wrong as it specifically applied to Catholicism.
I was studying American politicians who were searching - allegedly - for
American communists because it would put them on the front pages
of the papers in their home towns.
I've been obsessed with clothes since I was a little boy.
Man has always needed to believe in some form of a continuity of achievement.
I can't allow myself to be caught up in chaos. It makes me crazy.

## JESSIE VENTURA (Athlete, Governor of Minnesota, 1952 - )

Organized religion is a sham and a crutch for weak-minded people who
need strength in numbers. It tells people to go out and stick their
noses in other people's business.
The Constitution guarantees us our rights to life, liberty, and the pursuit
of happiness. That's all. It doesn't guarantee our rights to charity.
There are a lot of good causes out there, but they can't possibly all be
served by government.
There is much more to being a patriot and a citizen than reciting the
pledge or raising a flag.
There's no question that we need tougher drunk-driving laws for repeat
offenders. We need to take a lesson from European countries where
driving isn't a right but a privilege.
We call our country home of the brave and land of the free, but it's not.
We give a false portrayal of freedom. We're not free - if we were,
we'd allow people their freedom.
Remember that government doesn't earn one single dollar it spends. In order
for you to get money from the government, that money must first be
taken from somebody else.
If I could be reincarnated as a fabric, I would come back as a 38 double-D bra.

I also believe that government has no business telling us how we should live our
lives. I think our lifestyle choices should be left up to us. What we do in
our private lives is none of the government's business. That position
rules out the Republican Party for me.
I speak my mind. If it offends some people, well, there's not much I can
do about that. But I'm going to be honest. I'm going to continue
to speak my mind, and that's who I am.
I believe patriotism comes from the heart. Patriotism is voluntary. It is a feeling
of loyalty and allegiance that is the result of knowledge and belief.
I decided to run for governor because I got mad... I want to make government
more directly accountable to the people.
All of us should have free choice when it comes to patriotic displays... a
government wisely acting within its bounds will earn loyalty and respect
from its citizens. A government dare not demand the same.
Congratulations, you have a sense of humor. And to those who didn't: Go
stick your head in the mud.
Government works less efficiently when it begins to grow out of control and
takes on more and more of the responsibilities that belong to the citizens.
Government's role should be only to keep the playing field level, and to work hand
in hand with business on issues such as employment. But beyond this, to
as great an extent as possible, it should get the hell out of the way.
I asked Dalai Lama the most important question that I think you could
ask - if he had ever seen Caddyshack.
I believe in the America people's ability to govern themselves. If government
would just get out of the way and allow them to lead their lives as they
choose, they will succeed.
I don't support abortion. I could never participate in one. But I think
it would be a mistake to make them illegal again.
I don't think I would want the responsibility for enforcing the death penalties.
There's always the inevitable question of whether someone you
gave the order to execute might truly have been innocent.
I don't want to spend the rest of my life in politics. When I'm finished with
my term as governor, I'm going back to the life that's waiting for me
In the private sector.
I'm against the draft. I believe we should have a professional
military; it might be smaller, but it would be more effective.

## MARGARET WALKER (Poet, 1915 - 1998)
When I was about eight, I decided that the most wonderful thing,
next to a human being, was a book.
The poetry of a people comes from the deep recesses of the unconscious,
the irrational and the collective body of our ancestral memories.
Let a new earth rise. Let another world be born. Let a bloody peace be
written in the sky. Let a second generation full of courage issue
forth; let a people loving freedom come to growth.
Friends and good manners will carry you where money won't go.
I want my careless song to strike no minor key; no fiend to stand between my body's
Southern song - the fusion of the South, my body's song and me.
Now when you hates you shrinks up inside and gets littler and you
squeezes your heart tight and you stays so mad with peoples
you feels sick all the time like you needs the doctor.

## GEORGE C. WALLACE (Politican, Governor of Alabama, 1919-1998)

I draw the line in the dust and toss the gauntlet before the
    feet of tyranny, and I say segregation now, segregation
    tomorrow, segregation forever.

I'm the lamest lame duck there could be.

I've seen many politicians paralyzed in the legs as myself,
    but I've seen more of them who were paralyzed in the head.

If any demonstrator ever lays down in front of my car, it'll be
    the last car he'll ever lay down in front of.

Look at all the buses now that want exact change, exact change.
    I figure if I give them exact change, they should
    take me exactly where I want to go.

Since my accident I am a little more mindful of the
    suffering of other people.

Sure, I look like a white man. But my heart is as
    black as anyone's here.

Why does the Air Force need expensive new bombers? Have the people
    we've been bombing over the years been complaining?

## HENRY A. WALLACE (Vice President, 1888-1965)

A liberal knows that the only certainty in this life is change but believes
    that the change can be directed toward a constructive end.

If we put our trust in the common sense of common men and 'with malice
    toward none and charity for all' go forward on the great adventure
    of making political, economic and social democracy a practical
    reality, we shall not fail.

The American fascist would prefer not to use violence. His method
    is to poison the channels of public information.

A fascist is one whose lust for money or power is combined with such an
    intensity of intolerance toward those of other races, parties, classes,
    religions, cultures, regions or nations as to make him ruthless in his
    use of deceit or violence to attain his ends.

Fascism is a worldwide disease. Its greatest threat to the United States will come
    after the war, either via Latin America or within the United States itself.

If we define an American fascist as one who in case of conflict puts money
    and power ahead of human beings, then there are undoubtedly
    several million fascists in the United States.

In an effort to eliminate the possibility of any rival growing up,
    some monopolists would sacrifice democracy itself.

It may be shocking to some people in this country to realize that, without
    meaning to do so, they hold views in common with Hitler when they
    preach discrimination against other religious, racial or economic groups.

Monopolists who fear competition and who distrust democracy because it
    stands for equal opportunity would like to secure their position
    against small and energetic enterprise.

The moral and spiritual aspects of both personal and international relationships
    have a practical bearing which so-called practical men deny.

The myth of fascist efficiency has deluded many people.

They are patriotic in time of war because it is to their interest to be
    so, but in time of peace they follow power and the dollar
    wherever they may lead.

This dullness of vision regarding the importance of the general welfare
      to the individual is the measure of the failure of our schools and
      churches to teach the spiritual significance of genuine democracy.
Until democracy in effective enthusiastic action fills the vacuum created
      by the power of modern inventions, we may expect the fascists
      to increase in power after the war both in the United States
      and in the world.
It is no coincidence that the growth of modern tyrants has in every
      case been heralded by the growth of prejudice.
We must not tolerate oppressive government or industrial oligarchy
      in the form of monopolies and cartels.
What we must understand is that the industries, processes, and
      inventions created by modern science can be used either to
      subjugate or liberate. The choice is up to us.

## BARBARA WALTERS (Journalist, 1931 - )

A great many people think that polysyllables are a sign of intelligence.
Deep breaths are very helpful at shallow parties.
Don't confuse being stimulating with being blunt.
If it's a woman, it's caustic; if it's a man, it's authoritative.
One may walk over the highest mountain one step at a time.
Parents of young children should realize that few people, and maybe no one,
      will find their children as enchanting as they do.
Show me someone who never gossips, and I will show you someone
      who is not interested in people.
Success can make you go one of two ways. It can make you a prima donna -
      or it can smooth the edges, take away the insecurities, let the
      nice things come out.
The sports page records people's accomplishments, the front page
      usually records nothing  but man's failures.
The world may be full of fourth-rate writers but it's also full of fourth-rate readers.
To feel valued, to know, even if only once in a while, that you can do a
      job well is an absolutely marvelous feeling.
It would be nice to feel that we are a better world, a world of more compassion
      and a world of more humanity, and to believe in the basic goodness of man.
A man cannot be made comfortable without his own approval.
All of the religions - with the exception of Tibetan Buddhism, which doesn't
      believe in a heaven - teach that heaven is a better place. At the end
      of the program, I say that heaven is a place where you are happy. All
      of the religions have that in common.
Although I myself don't go to church or synagogue, I do, whether it's
      superstition or whatever, pray every time I get on a plane. I just
      automatically do it. I say the same thing every time.
And I really do believe that the most important thing is the way you live
      your life on earth. But I think it's enormously comforting to believe
      that you're going to see your loved ones.
Wait for those unguarded moments. Relax the mood and, like the child
      dropping off to sleep, the subject often reveals his truest self.
Before we had airplanes and astronauts, we really thought that there was an
      actual place beyond the clouds, somewhere over the rainbow. There was
      an actual place, and we could go above the clouds and find it .there.

But for Muslims, everything that they don't have on earth is what they get
in heaven. They can drink, they can have sex. All of the forbidden
pleasures on earth, you can have in paradise.

First of all, the Jewish religion has a great deal in common with the Christian
religion because, as Rabbi Gillman points out in the show, Christianity
is based on Judaism. Christ was Jewish.

I also found that for myself, since I've had no religious education, it was so
interesting to see the different versions of heaven and what life on
earth means.

I can get a better grasp of what is going on in the world from one good
Washington dinner party than from all the background information
NBC piles on my desk.

I didn't have a very religious family.

I don't know about you, but I can never get enough David Letterman.

I found it interesting that as people become more technically oriented all over
the world, at the same time people are becoming increasingly spiritual.
The success of the Da Vinci code - even though it was a great yawn -
also showed people's interest in religion.

Most of us have trouble juggling. The woman who says she doesn't is
someone whom I admire but have never met.

## EARL WARREN (Chief Justice of the Supreme Court, 1891-1974)

All provisions of federal, state or local law requiring or permitting
discrimination in public education must yield.

Ben Franklin may have discovered electricity- but it is the man who
invented the meter who made the money.

Everything I did in my life that was worthwhile, I caught hell for.

I always turn to the sports pages first, which records people's
accomplishments. The front page has nothing but man's failures.

I feel that the greatest reward for doing is the opportunity to do more.

I hate banks. They do nothing positive for anybody except take care of themselves.
They're first in with their fees and first out when there's trouble.

If it is a mistake of the head and not the heart don't worry about it,
that's the way we learn.

If Nixon is not forced to turn over tapes of his conversations with the ring
of men who were conversing on their violations of the law, then
liberty will soon be dead in this nation.

In civilized life, law floats in a sea of ethics.

In these days, it is doubtful that any child may reasonably be expected to
succeed in life if he is denied the opportunity of an education.

It is the spirit and not the form of law that keeps justice alive.

Legislatures represent people, not acres or trees.

Liberty, not communism, is the most contagious force in the world.

Life and liberty can be as much endangered from illegal methods used to convict
those thought to be criminals as from the actual criminals themselves.

Many people consider the things government does for them to be social progress
but they regard the things government does for others as socialism.

Prior to any questioning, the person must be warned that he has a right to
remain silent, that any statement he does make may be used as
evidence against him and that he has a right to the presence of an
attorney, either retained or appointed.

Separate educational facilities are inherently unequal.

The censor's sword pierces deeply into the heart of free expression.

The most tragic paradox of our time is to be found in the failure of
nation-states to recognize the imperatives of internationalism.

The old Court you and I served so long will not be worthy of its traditions if Nixon
can twist, turn and fashion If Nixon gets away with that, then Nixon makes
the law as he goes along - not the Congress nor the courts.

The police must obey the law while enforcing the law.

To get what you want, STOP doing what isn't working.

To separate children from others of similar age and qualifications  solely
because of their race generates a feeling of inferiority  as to their
status in the community that may affect their hearts and minds
in a way unlikely ever to be undone.

You sit up there, and you see the whole gamut of human nature. Even if the
case being argued involves only a little fellow and $50, it involves
justice. That's what is important

## BOOKER T. WASHINGTON (Educator, 1856-1915)

We don't just borrow words; on occasion, English has pursued other
languages down alleyways to beat them unconscious and rifle
their pockets for new vocabulary.

There is no power on earth that can neutralize the influence of a high,
simple and useful life.

We do not want the men of another color for our brothers-in-law, but
we do want them for our brothers.

We must reinforce argument with results.

Associate yourself with people of good quality, for it is better to be alone
than in bad company.

Character is power.

Character, not circumstances, makes the man.

Dignify and glorify common labor. It is at the bottom of life that we
must begin, not at the top.

Excellence is to do a common thing in an uncommon way.

Few things can help an individual more than to place responsibility on
him, and to let him know that you trust him.

I have learned that success is to be measured not so much by the position
that one has reached in life as by the obstacles which he has had to
overcome while trying to succeed.

I shall allow no man to belittle my soul by making me hate him.

If you can't read, it's going to be hard to realize dreams.

If you want to lift yourself up, lift up someone else.

No greater injury can be done to any youth than to let him feel that
because he belongs to this or that race he will be advanced in life
regardless of his own merits or efforts.

No man, who continues to add something to the material, intellectual and moral
well-being of the place in which he lives, is left long without proper reward.

No race can prosper till it learns that there is as much dignity in tilling a field
as in writing a poem.

Nothing ever comes to one, that is worth having, except as a result of hard work.

One man cannot hold another man down in the ditch without remaining
down in the ditch with him.

Success in life is founded upon attention to the small things rather than to
the large things; to the every day things nearest to us rather than
to the things that are remote and uncommon.
Success is to be measured not so much by the position that one has
reached in life as by the obstacles which he has overcome.
The individual who can do something that the world wants done will, in
the end, make his way regardless of his race.
There are two ways of exerting one's strength: one is pushing down,
the other is pulling up.

## GEORGE WASHINGTON (President, 1732-1799)

It is better to offer no excuse than a bad one.
It is better to be alone than in bad company.
Laws made by common consent must not be trampled on by individuals.
Government is not reason; it is not eloquent; it is force.
Like fire, it is a dangerous servant and a fearful master.
Guard against the impostures of pretended patriotism.
Happiness and moral duty are inseparably connected.
Mankind, when left to themselves, are unfit for their own government.
My first wish is to see this plague of mankind, war, banished from the earth.
Few men have virtue to withstand the highest bidder.
The basis of our political system is the right of the people
to make and to alter their constitutions of government.
It will be found an unjust and unwise jealousy to deprive a man
of his natural liberty upon the supposition he may abuse it.
Truth will ultimately prevail where there is pains to bring it to light.
The foolish and wicked practice of profane cursing and swearing is a vice so mean
and low that every person of sense and character detests and despises it.
The marvel of all history is the patience with which men and women submit to
burdens unnecessarily laid upon them by their governments.
A slender acquaintance with the world must convince every man that actions,
not words, are the true criterion of the attachment of friends.
Arbitrary power is most easily established on the
ruins of liberty abused to licentiousness.
Some day, following the example of the United States of America,
there will be a United States of Europe.
The administration of justice is the firmest pillar of government.
The constitution vests the power of declaring war in Congress; therefore no
offensive expedition of importance can be undertaken until after they shall
have deliberated upon the subject and authorized such a measure.
The time is near at hand which must determine whether
Americans are to be free men or slaves.
The very atmosphere of firearms anywhere and everywhere restrains evil
interference - they deserve a place of honor with all that's good.
To be prepared for war is one of the most effective means of preserving peace.
True friendship is a plant of slow growth, and must undergo and withstand the
shocks of adversity, before it is entitled to the appellation.
War - An act of violence whose object is to constrain the enemy,
to accomplish our will.
We should not look back unless it is to derive useful lessons from past errors, and
for the purpose of profiting by dearly bought experience.

Worry is the interest paid by those who borrow trouble.

When we assumed the Soldier, we did not lay aside the Citizen.

Associate with men of good quality if you esteem your own
reputation; for it is better to be alone than in bad company.

It may be laid down as a primary position, and the basis of our system, that every
Citizen who enjoys the protection of a  Free Government, owes not only a
proportion of his property, but even of his personal services to its defense.

Labor to keep alive in your breast that little spark of celestial fire, called conscience.

Lenience will operate with greater force, in some instances  than rigor. It is
therefore my first wish to have all of my conduct distinguished by it.

Let us raise a standard to which the wise and honest can
repair; the rest is in the hands of God.

Let us with caution indulge the supposition that morality can be maintained without
religion. Reason and experience both forbid us to expect that national
morality can prevail in exclusion of religious principle.

Let your Discourse with Men of Business be Short and Comprehensive.

Let your heart feel for the afflictions and distress of everyone,
and let your hand give in proportion to your purse.

Liberty, when it begins to take root, is a plant of rapid growth.

My observation is that whenever one person is found adequate  to the discharge
of a duty... it is worse executed by two persons, and scarcely done at all if
three or more are employed therein.

Nothing can be more hurtful to the service, than the neglect of discipline; for that
discipline, more than numbers, gives one army the superiority over another.

Observe good faith and justice toward all nations. Cultivate
peace and harmony with all.

Over grown military establishments are under any form of
government inauspicious to liberty, and are to be
regarded as particularly hostile to republican liberty.

Be courteous to all, but intimate with few, and let those few
be well tried before you give them your confidence.

Discipline is the soul of an army. It makes small numbers formidable; procures
success to the weak, and esteem to all.

Experience teaches us that it is much easier to prevent an enemy from posting
themselves than it is to dislodge them after they have got possession.

Firearms are second only to the Constitution in importance;
they are the peoples' liberty's teeth.

Friendship is a plant of slow growth and must undergo  and withstand the shocks
of adversity before it is entitled to the appellation.

I have no other view than to promote the public good,   and am unambitious of
honors not founded in the approbation of my Country.

I hope I shall possess firmness and virtue enough to maintain what I consider
the most enviable of all titles, the character of an honest man.

I walk on untrodden ground. There is scarcely any part of my
conduct which may not hereafter be drawn into precedent.

If the freedom of speech is taken away then dumb and silent we
may be led, like sheep to the slaughter.

If we desire to avoid insult, we must be able to repel it; if we
desire to secure peace, one of the most powerful
instruments of our rising prosperity, it must be known,
that we are at all times ready for War.

## BILL WATTERSON (Cartoonist, 1958 - )

A real job is a job you hate.

Genius is never understood in its own time.

Weekends don't count unless you spend them doing something completely pointless.

When birds burp, it must taste like bugs.

Why waste time learning, when ignorance is instantaneous?

God put me on this earth to accomplish a certain number of things.
    Right now I am so far behind that I will never die.

Heck, what's a little extortion among friends?

I find my life is a lot easier the lower I keep everyone's expectations.

I know the world isn't fair, but why isn't it ever unfair in my favor?

I liked things better when I didn't understand them.

I'm not dumb. I just have a command of thoroughly useless information.

I've got to start listening to those quiet, nagging doubts.

If people sat outside and looked at the stars each night, I'll bet
    they'd live a lot differently.

It's not denial. I'm just selective about the reality I accept.

It's surprising how hard we'll work when the work is done just for ourselves.

Know what's weird? Day by day, nothing seems to change. But
    pretty soon, everything's different.

Letting your mind play is the best way to solve problems.

Nothing helps a bad mood like spreading it around.

Often it takes some calamity to make us live in the present. Then
    suddenly we wake up and see all the mistakes we have made.

Reality continues to ruin my life.

Shutting off the thought process is not rejuvenating; the mind is
    like a car battery - it recharges by running.

So, what's it like in the real world? Well, the food is better, but
    beyond that, don't recommend it.

Sometimes when I'm talking, my words can't keep up with my thoughts. I
    wonder why we think faster than we speak. Probably so we can think twice.

Talking with you is sort of the conversational equivalent
    of an out of body experience.

That's the whole problem with science. You've got a bunch of empiricists
    trying to describe things of unimaginable wonder.

The problem with the future is that it keeps turning into the present.

The purpose of writing is to inflate weak ideas, obscure pure reasoning, and
    inhibit clarity. With a little practice, writing can be an intimidating
    and impenetrable fog!

The world of a comic strip ought to be a special place with its own logic and life... I
    don't want the issue of Hobbes's reality settled by a doll manufacturer.

There is not enough time to do all the nothing we want to do.

Things are never quite as scary when you've got a best friend.

We all have different desires and needs, but if we don't discover what we want
    from ourselves and what we stand for, we will live passively and unfulfilled.

We don't devote enough scientific research to finding a cure for jerks.

## JOHN WAYNE (Actor, 1907-1979)

Courage is being scared to death... and saddling up anyway.

Get off your butt and join the Marines!

If everything isn't black and white, I say, 'Why the hell not?'

I don't feel we did wrong in taking this great country away from them. There
were great numbers of people who needed new land, and the Indians
were selfishly trying to keep it for themselves.
If you've got them by the balls their hearts and minds will follow
Life is tough, but it's tougher when you're stupid.
Talk low, talk slow and don't say too much.
Tomorrow hopes we have learned something from yesterday.
Tomorrow is the most important thing in life. Comes into us at midnight
very clean. It's perfect when it arrives and it puts itself in our hands.
It hopes we've learned something from yesterday

## DENNIS WEAVER (Actor, Environmentalist, 1924-2006)

Business has to change the way it does business, or we will make no
significant changes in the way we relate to the earth.
Business must be the solution, not the problem.
Changing mass consciousness is an individual responsibility.
I feel responsible; I feel I've got to do something that will leave the kids a place
where they can live healthy, safe, productive, creative and prosperous lives.
If we had a hydrogen economy worldwide, every nation on earth could create its
own energy source to support its economy, and the threat of war over
diminishing resources would just evaporate.
If we were driving pure hydrogen automobiles, that automobile would actually
help clean up the air because the air coming out of the exhaust would
be cleaner than the air going into the engine intake.
It's fun to be a little bit different in the world, to make a few new trails of your own.
It's not an if - we're going to have to change. Oil is simply going to be gone.
Practically every environmental problem we have can be traced to our
addiction to fossil fuels, primarily oil.
The earth is a tremendous gift. There is nothing else like it in the known
universe. I want to leave it the way I found it.
The people of the future will say, meat-eaters in disgust and regard us
in the same way that we regard cannibals and cannibalism.
The premise is simple: One economy and one environment, and
they're interdependent.
War is usually fought over diminishing resources, particularly those that
we perceive to be extremely valuable.
We don't have to sacrifice a strong economy for a healthy environment.
We should be able to support our own economy within our own borders.
We're the only species that have crapped up the planet and the only
species that can clean it up.
Whatever we'll be forced to do later, we should be doing now.
When I was a kid, we never heard of smog, ozone depletion, acid rain,
green house gasses.
When we realize we can make a buck cleaning up the environment, it will be done!

## DANIEL WEBSTER (Statesman, Lawyer, 1782-1852)

A country cannot subsist well without liberty, nor liberty without virtue.
A strong conviction that something must be done is the parent of
many bad measures.
An unlimited power to tax involves, necessarily, the power to destroy.
Failure is more frequently from want of energy than want of capital.

Every unpunished murder takes away something from the security of
         every man's life.
Falsehoods not only disagree with truths, but usually quarrel among themselves.
God grants liberty only to those who love it, and are always
         ready to guard and defend it.
How little do they see what really is, who frame their hasty
         judgment upon that which seems.
I mistrust the judgment of every man in a case in
         which his own wishes are concerned.
I was born an American; I will live an American; I shall die an American.
Inconsistencies of opinion, arising from changes of
         circumstances, are often justifiable.
It is my living sentiment, and by the blessing of God it shall be my dying
         sentiment, independence now and independence forever.
Justice, sir, is the great interest of man on earth. It is the ligament
         which holds civilized beings and civilized nations together.
Keep cool; anger is not an argument.
Let it be borne on the flag under which we rally in every exigency, that
         we have one country, one constitution, one destiny.
Let us not forget that the cultivation of the earth is the most important labor
         of man. When tillage begins, other arts will follow. The farmers,
         therefore, are the founders of civilization.
Liberty and Union, now and forever, one and inseparable.
Liberty exists in proportion to wholesome restraint.
Man is a special being, and if left to himself, in an isolated condition, would be one of
         the weakest creatures; but associated with his kind, he works wonders.
Mind is the great lever of all things; human thought is the process by
         which human ends are ultimately answered.
No man not inspired can make a good speech without preparation.
On the diffusion of education among the people rest the
         preservation and perpetuation of our free institutions.
One country, one constitution, one destiny.
The contest for ages has been to rescue liberty from the grasp of executive power.
The law: it has honored us; may we honor it.
The materials of wealth are in the earth, in the seas, and in their
         natural and unaided productions.
The most important thought that ever occupied my mind is that of my
         individual responsibility to God.
The people's government, made for the people, made by the people, and
         answerable to the people.
The right of an inventor to his invention is no monopoly - in any other
         sense than a man's house is a monopoly.
The world is governed more by appearance than realities so that it is fully as
         necessary to seem to know something as to know it.
There is always room at the top.
There is no refuge from confession but suicide; and suicide is confession.
There is nothing so powerful as truth, and often nothing so strange.
We are all agents of the same supreme power, the people.
We have been taught to regard a representative of the people as a
         sentinel on the watch-tower of liberty.
What a man does for others, not  what they do for him, gives him immortality.

Whatever government is not a government of laws, is a despotism, let it
be called what it may.
Whatever makes men good Christians, makes them good citizens
When tillage begins, other arts follow. The farmers, therefore, are the
founders of human civilization.
Wisdom begins at the end.

## RAQUEL WELCH (Actor, 1940 - )
Being a sex symbol was rather like being a convict.
I was not a classic mother. But my kids were never palmed off to boarding
school. So, I didn't bake cookies. You can buy cookies, but
you can't buy love.
Latinos are here to stay. As citizen Raquel, I'm proud to be Latina.
The mind can also be an erogenous zone.
Once you get rid of the idea that you must please other people before you
please yourself, and you begin to follow your own instincts - only then
can you be successful. You become more satisfied, and when you are,
other people will tend to be satisfied by what you do.
We all have a childhood dream that when there is love, everything goes
like silk, but the reality is that marriage requires a lot of compromise.
You can't fake listening. It shows.
Americans have always had sex symbols. It`a time-honored tradition and
I`m flattered to have been one. But it`s hard to have a long, fruitful
career once you`ve been stereotyped that way. That`s why I`m
proud to say I`ve endured.
If you have physical attractiveness you don`t have to act.

## ORSON WELLES (Actor, 1915-1985)
Criminals are never very amusing. It's because they're failures. Those who
make real money aren't counted as criminals. This is a class
distinction, not an ethical problem.
A film is never really good unless the camera is an eye in the head of a poet.
A good artist should be isolated. If he isn't isolated, something is wrong.
Did you ever stop to think why cops are always famous for being dumb?
Simple. Because they don't have to be anything else.
Every actor in his heart believes everything bad that's printed about him
Everybody denies I am a genius - but nobody ever called me one!
Ask not what you can do for your country. Ask what's for lunch.
At twenty-one, so many things appear solid, permanent, untenable.
Create your own visual style... let it be unique for yourself and yet
identifiable for others.

## MAE WEST (Actor, Comedian, 1893-1980)
Whenever I'm caught between two evils, I take the one I've never tried.
A dame that knows the ropes isn't likely to get tied up.
A hard man is good to find.
A man can be short and dumpy and getting bald but if he has fire,
women will like him.
A man has one hundred dollars and you leave him with two
dollars, that's subtraction.
A man in the house is worth two in the street.

A man's kiss is his signature.
A woman in love can't be reasonable - or she probably wouldn't be in love.
All discarded lovers should be given a second chance, but with somebody else.
An ounce of performance is worth pounds of promises.
Any time you got nothing to do - and lots of time to do it - come on up.
Any time you've got nothing to do and lots of time to do it come on up.
Anything worth doing is worth doing slowly.
Cultivate your curves - they may be dangerous but they won't be avoided.
Don't keep a man guessing too long - he's sure to find the answer somewhere else.
Don't marry a man to reform him - that's what reform schools are for.
Every man I meet wants to protect me. I can't figure out what from.
Give a man a free hand and he'll run it all over you.
He who hesitates is a damned fool.
He's the kind of man a woman would have to marry to get rid of.
His mother should have thrown him out and kept the stork.
I always say, keep a diary and someday it'll keep you
I believe in censorship. I made a fortune out of it.
I believe that it's better to be looked over than it is to be overlooked.
I didn't discover curves; I only uncovered them.
I enjoyed the courtroom as just another stage but not so amusing as Broadway.
I generally avoid temptation unless I can't resist it.
I like a man who's good, but not too good - for the good die young,
        and I hate a dead one.
I like restraint, if it doesn't go too far.
I never loved another person the way I loved myself.
I never worry about diets. The only carrots that interest me are the
        number you get in a diamond.
I only have 'yes' men around me. Who needs 'no' men?
I only like two kinds of men, domestic and imported.
I see you're a man with ideals. I better be going before you've still got them.
I speak two languages, Body and English.
I used to be Snow White, but I drifted.
I'd like to see Paris before I die. Philadelphia will do.
I'll try anything once, twice if I like it, three times to make sure.
I'm a woman of very few words, but lots of action.
I'm no model lady. A model's just an imitation of the real thing.
I've been in more laps than a napkin.
I've been things and seen places.
If I asked for a cup of coffee, someone would search for the double meaning.
It ain't no sin if you crack a few laws now and then, just so
        long as you don't break any.
It is better to be looked over than overlooked.
It isn't what I do, but how I do it. It isn't what I say, but how I say
        it, and how I look when I do it and say it.
It takes two to get one in trouble.
It's hard to be funny when you have to be clean.
It's not the men in my life that count, it's the life in my men.
Look your best - who said love is blind?
Love conquers all things except poverty and toothache.
Love isn't an emotion or an instinct - it's an art.
Marriage is a great institution, but I'm not ready for an institution.

Love thy neighbor - and if he happens to be tall, debonair and devastating,
    it will be that much easier.
One and one is two, and two and two is four, and five will get
    you ten if you know how to work it.
Opportunity knocks for every man, but you have to give a woman a ring.
Personality is the glitter that sends your little gleam across the footlights
    and the orchestra pit into that big black space where the audience is.
Personality is the most important thing to an actress's success.
Right now I think censorship is necessary; the things they're doing and
    saying in films right now just shouldn't be allowed. There's no dignity
    anymore and I think that's very important.
Save a boyfriend for a rainy day - and another, in case it doesn't rain.
Say what you want about long dresses, but they cover a multitude of shins.
Sex is emotion in motion.
She's the kind of girl who climbed the ladder of success wrong by wrong.
Ten men waiting for me at the door? Send one of them home, I'm tired.
The best way to hold a man is in your arms.
The score never interested me, only the game.
Those who are easily shocked should be shocked more often.
To err is human, but it feels divine.
Too much of a good thing can be taxing.
Too much of a good thing can be wonderful.
Virtue has its own reward, but no sale at the box office.
When I'm good, I'm very good. But when I'm bad I'm better.
When women go wrong, men go right after them.
You only live once, but if you do it right, once is enough.

## THEODORE WHITE (Journalist, 1915-1986)

A liberal is a person who believes that water can be made to run uphill. A
    conservative is someone who believes everybody should pay for
    his water. I'm somewhere in between: I believe water should be
    free, but that water flows downhill.
He who is created by television can be destroyed by television.
I class myself as a manual laborer.
I happen to think that American politics is one of the noblest arts of
    mankind; and I cannot do anything else but write about it.
I'd get into a room and disappear into the woodwork. Now the rooms are
    so crowded with reporters getting behind-the-scenes stories that
    nobody can get behind-the-scenes stories.
If you make a living, if you earn your own money, you're
    free - however free one can be on this planet.
Politics in America is the binding secular religion.
Power in America today is control of the means of communication.
Quality in a classical Greek sense is how to live with grace and
    intelligence, with bravery and mercy.
The best time to listen to a politician is when he's on a stump on a street
    corner in the rain late at night when he's exhausted. Then he doesn't lie.
The flood of money that gushes into politics today is a pollution of democracy.
There are two kinds of editors, those who correct your copy and
    those who say it's wonderful.
When a reporter sits down at the typewriter, he's nobody's friend.

There is no excitement anywhere in the world, short of war, to match
         the excitement of the American presidential campaign.
Those 40 or 50 national correspondents who had followed Kennedy since the
         beginning of his electoral exertions into the November days had become
         more than a press corps - they had become his friends and, some of
         them, his most devoted admirers.
With the end of the nominating process, American politics leaves logic behind.

## VANNA WHITE (Game Show Assistant, 1957 - )

I enjoy getting dressed as a Barbie doll.
I think people think of me as this elegant person because
         they always see me dressed up.
I will say I remember the best thing in terms of publicity was
         being on the cover of Newsweek.
It's not the most intellectual job in the world, but I do have to know the letters.
When I was having that alphabet soup, I never thought that it would pay off.

## WALT WHITMAN (Author, Poet, Naturalist, 1819-1892)

Be curious, not judgmental.
Whatever satisfies the soul is truth.
I am as bad as the worst, but, thank God, I am as good as the best.
Keep your face always toward the sunshine - and shadows will fall behind you.
Happiness, not in another place but this place...not for another hour, but this hour
I no doubt deserved my enemies, but I don't believe I deserved my friends.
I have learned that to be with those I like is enough
Do anything, but let it produce joy.
When I give, I give myself
Peace is always beautiful.
Battles are lost in the same spirit in which they are won.
Argue not concerning God,...re-examine all that you have been told at
         church or school or in any book, dismiss whatever insults your soul...
I believe a leaf of grass is no less than the journey-work of the stars.
The real war will never get in the books.
There is no God any more divine than Yourself.
I hear and behold God in every object, yet understand God not in the least.
A morning-glory at my window satisfies me more than the metaphysics of books.
After you have exhausted what there is in business, politics, conviviality, and
         so on - have found that none of these finally satisfy, or permanently
         wear - what remains? Nature remains.
All faults may be forgiven of him who has perfect candor.
Every moment of light and dark is a miracle.
Freedom - to walk free and own no superior.
Whatever satisfies the soul is truth.

## JOHN GREENLEAF WHITTIER (Poet, 1807-1892)

For all sad words of tongue and pen, The saddest are these, 'It might have been'.
One brave deed makes no hero.
All the windows of my heart I open to the day.
As a small businessperson, you have no greater leverage than the truth.
Beauty seen is never lost, God's colors all are fast.
Tradition wears a snowy beard, romance is always young.

From the death of the old the new proceeds, and the life of truth from
        the death of creeds.
Give fools their gold, and knaves their power; let fortune's bubbles rise and fall;
        who sows a field, or trains a flower, or plants a tree, is more than all.
I'll lift you and you lift me, and we'll both ascend together.
It is no use trying to sum people up. One must follow hints, not exactly
        what is said, nor yet entirely what is done.
The best of a book is not the thought which it contains, but the thought which it
        suggests; just as the charm of music dwells not in the tones but
        in the echoes of our hearts.
Peace  hath higher tests of manhood, than battle ever knew.
When faith is lost, when honor dies, the man is dead.
You don't always win your battles, but it's good to know you fought.

## NORBERT WIENER (Mathematician, 1894-1964)
Progress imposes not only new possibilities for the future but new restrictions.
The more we get out of the world the less we leave, and in the long run
        we shall have to pay our debts at a time that may be very
        inconvenient for our own survival.
To live effectively is to live with adequate information.
What most experimenters take for granted before they begin their
        experiments is infinitely more interesting than any results to
        which their experiments lead.

## GENE WILDER (Actor, 1933 - )
My idea of neurotic  is spending too much time trying to correct a
        wrong. When I feel that I'm doing that, then I snap out of it.
In 'Frisco Kid' and in 'The Woman in Red' I had to ride badly. Then
        you have to really ride well in order to ride badly.
A lot of comic actors derive their main force from childish behavior. Most great
        comics are doing such silly things; you'd say, 'That's what a child would do.'
Actors fall into this trap if they missed being loved for who they really were and not
        for what they could do - sing, dance, joke about - then they take that as love.
Great art direction is NOT the same thing as great film direction!
I don't mean to sound - I don't want it to come out funny, but I don't like show
        business. I  love - I love acting in films. I love it.
I never thought of it as God. I didn't know what to call it. I don't believe in devils,
        but demons I do because everyone at one time or another has some kind
        of a demon, even if you call it by another name, that drives them.
I write funny. If I can make my wife [Gilda Radner] laugh, I know I'm on the right
        track. But yes, I don't like to get Maudlin. And I have a tendency towards it.
I'm not so funny. Gilda [Radner] was funny. I'm funny on camera sometimes. In life,
        once in a while. Once in a while. But she was funny. She spent more time
        worrying about being liked than anything else.

## WENDELL L. WILKIE (Politician, Lawyer, 1892-1944)
Whenever we take away the liberties of those whom we hate we are
        opening the way to loss of liberty for those we love.
I would rather lose in a cause that I know some day will triumph than
        to triumph in a cause that I know some day will fail.
Be honorable yourself if you wish to associate with honorable people.

Education is the mother of leadership.

In no direction that we turn do we find ease or comfort. If we are honest
and if we have the will to win we find only danger, hard work and
iron resolution.

A good catchword can obscure analysis for fifty years.

It is from weakness that people reach for dictators and concentrated
government power. Only the strong can be free. And only the
productive can be strong.

The constitution does not provide for first and second class citizens.

## WOODROW WILSON (President, 1856-1924)

A conservative is a man who just sits and thinks, mostly sits.

Caution is the confidential agent of selfishness.

America is not anything if it consists of each of us. It is
something only if it consists of all of us.

I will not speak with disrespect of the Republican Party. I always
speak with respect of the past.

America lives in the heart of every man everywhere who
wishes to find a region where he will be free to work out
his destiny as he chooses.

America was established not to create wealth but to realize a vision,
to realize an ideal - to discover and maintain liberty among men.

Liberty has never come from Government. Liberty has always come
from the subjects of it. The history of liberty is a history of
limitations of governmental power, not the increase of it.

My dream of politics all my life has been that it is the common business,
that it is something we owe to each other to
understand and discuss with absolute frankness.

You cannot, in human experience, rush into the light. You have to go
through the twilight into the broadening day before the noon
comes and the full sun is upon the landscape.

There is little for the great part of the history of the world except the
bitter tears of pity and the hot tears of wrath.

The government, which was designed for the people, has got into the hands of
the bosses and their employers, the special  interests. An invisible empire
has been set up above the forms of democracy.

I would rather belong to a poor nation that was free than to a
rich nation that had ceased to be in love with liberty.

Democracy is not so much a form of government as a set of principles

A conservative is someone who makes no changes and
consults his grandmother when in doubt.

A little group of willful men, representing no opinion but their own,
have rendered the great government of the United
States helpless and contemptible.

If you think too much about being re-elected, it is very
difficult to be worth re-electing.

Never attempt to murder a man who is committing suicide.

If you want to make enemies, try to change something.

Absolute identity with one's cause is the first and great
condition of successful leadership.

I not only use all the brains that I have, but all that I can borrow.

If you want to make enemies, try to change something.
Absolute identity with one's cause is the first and great
        condition of successful leadership.
I not only use all the brains that I have, but all that I can borrow.
I would rather lose in a cause that will some day win, than
        win in a cause that will some day lose.
If a dog will not come to you after having looked you in the face,
        you should go home and examine your conscience.
If there are men in this country big enough to own the government
        of the United States, they are going to own it.
In the Lord's Prayer, the first petition is for daily bread. No one can
        worship God or love his neighbor on an empty stomach.
Interest does not tie nations together; it sometimes separates them.
        But sympathy and understanding does unite them.
Sometimes people call me an idealist. Well, that is the way I know I am an American.
        America is the only idealistic nation in the world.
It is like writing history with lightning and my only
        regret is that it is all so terribly true.
My own ideals for the university are those of a genuine democracy
        and serious scholarship. These two, indeed, seem to go together.
Neutrality is a negative word. It does not express what America ought
        to feel. We are not trying to keep out of trouble; we are trying to
        preserve the foundations on which peace may be rebuilt.
One cool judgment is worth a thousand hasty counsels. The thing to do is to
        supply light and not heat, ordered progress of society along the lines of
        greatest usefulness and convenience to itself.
Prosperity is necessarily the first theme of a political campaign.
So far as the colleges go, the sideshows are swallowing up the circus.
Tell me what is right and I will fight for it.
That a peasant may become king does not render the kingdom democratic.
The American Revolution was a beginning, not a consummation.
The ear of the leader must ring with the voices of the people.
The history of liberty is a history of resistance.
The man who is swimming against the stream knows the strength of it.
The method of political science is the interpretation of life; its instrument
        is insight, a nice understanding of subtle, unformulated conditions.
The only use of an obstacle is to be overcome. All that an obstacle does with
        brave men is, not to frighten them, but to challenge them.
The seed of revolution is repression.
The world is not looking for servants, there are plenty of these, but for
        masters, men who form their purposes and then carry them out,
        let the consequences be what they may.
The world must be made safe for democracy. Its peace must be planted
        upon the tested foundations of political liberty.
There are blessed intervals when I forget by one means or another
        that I am President of the United States.
We have not given science too big a place in our education,
        but we have made a perilous mistake in giving it too
        great a preponderance in method in every other branch of study.

What we seek is the reign of law, based upon the consent of the
governed and sustained by the organized opinion of mankind.
There is no higher religion than human service. To work for
the common good is the greatest creed.
When I give a man an office, I watch him carefully to see whether
he is swelling or growing.
You are not here merely to make a living. You are here in order to enable the world
to live more amply, with greater vision, to enrich the world, and you
impoverish yourself if you forget the errand.
There can be no equality or opportunity if men and women and children
be not of great industrial and social processes which they cannot
alter, control, or singly cope with.
Property as compared with humanity, as compared with the red blood in the American
people, must take second place, not first place.
At every crisis in one's life, it is absolute salvation to have some sympathetic friend
to whom you can think aloud without restraint or misgiving.
By 'radical,' I understand one who goes too far; by 'conservative,' one who does not
go far enough; by 'reactionary,' one who won't go at all.
Generally young men are regarded as radicals. This is a popular
misconception. The most conservative persons I ever met are
college undergraduates. The radicals are the men past middle life.
Golf is a game in which one endeavors to control a ball with
implements ill adapted for the purpose.
He is not a true man of the world who knows only the present fashions of it.
I am not sure that it is of the first importance that you should be happy. Many
an unhappy man has been of deep service to himself and to the world.
I have long enjoyed the friendship and companionship of Republicans because I
am by instinct a teacher, and I would like to teach them something.

## MALCOLM X (Black Activist, 1925-1965)
A man who stands for nothing will fall for anything.
Be peaceful, be courteous, obey the law, respect everyone; but if
someone puts his hand on you, send him to the cemetery.
Education is the passport to the future, for tomorrow belongs to those
who prepare for it today.
I believe in a religion that believes in freedom. Any time I have to accept a religion
that won't let me fight a battle for my people, I say to hell with that religion.
I believe in human beings, and that all human beings should be
respected as such, regardless of their color.
I don't even call it violence when it's in self defense; I call it intelligence.
I'm for truth, no matter who tells it. I'm for justice, no matter who it's for or against.
If you have no critics you'll likely have no success.
If you're not ready to die for it, put the word 'freedom' out of your vocabulary.
In all our deeds, the proper value and respect for time determines success or failure.
My Alma mater was books, a good library... I could spend the rest of my life
reading, just satisfying my curiosity.
Nobody can give you freedom. Nobody can give you equality or
justice or anything. If you're a man, you take it.
Nonviolence is fine as long as it works.

Without education, you are not going anywhere in this world.
You can't legislate good will - that comes through education.
You can't separate peace from freedom because no one can be at peace
      unless he has his freedom.
You don't have to be a man to fight for freedom. All you have to do is
      to be an intelligent human being.
You show me a capitalist, and I'll show you a bloodsucker.
You're not supposed to be so blind with patriotism that you can't
      face reality. Wrong is wrong, no matter who says it

## 'WEIRD' AL YANKOVIC (Musician, Comedian, 1959 - )

I don't really look at myself  as the kind  of person who craves attention,
      but I've never been to therapy so there's probably a lot of
      stuff about myself that I don't know.
I'm still a geek on the inside, that's the important thing.
What kind of morons do you have working at newspapers in Austin that
      would base an entire review of an artist's performance on whether
      or not they had a good seat?

## CHUCK YEAGER (Aviator, 1923 - )

Never wait for trouble.
Rules are made for people who aren't willing to make up their own.
You don't concentrate on risks. You concentrate on results. No risk is
      too great to prevent the necessary job from getting done.
There's no such thing as a natural-born pilot.
I was always afraid of dying. Always. It was my fear that made me  learn
      everything I could about my airplane and my emergency equipment, and
      kept me flying respectful of my machine and always alert in the cockpit.
If you want to grow old as a pilot, you've got to know when
      to push it, and when to back off.
Later, I realized that the mission had to end in a let-down because
      the real barrier wasn't in the sky but in our knowledge and
      experience of supersonic flight.
Most pilots learn, when they pin on their wings and go out and get in a
      fighter, especially, that one thing you don't do, you don't believe
      anything anybody tells you about an airplane.
You do what you can for as long as you can, and when you finally can't,
      you do the next best thing. You back up but you don't give up.

## YO-YO MA (Musician, 1955 - )

Music has always been transnational; people pick up whatever interests
      them, and certainly a lot of classical music has absorbed influences
      from all over the world.
After reaching 50, I began to wonder what the root of life is.
I learn something not because I have to, but because I really want to. That's
      the same view I have for performing. I'm performing because I really
      want to, not because I have to bring bread back home.
One is that you have to take time, lots of time, to let an idea grow from within.
      The second is that when you sign on to something, there will be issues
      of trust, deep trust, the way the members of a string quartet have to
      trust one another.

The role of the musician is to go from concept to full execution. Put another way, it's to go from understanding the content of something to really learning how to communicate it and make sure it's well-received and lives in somebody else.

Good things happen when you meet strangers.

The tango is really a combination of many cultures, though it eventually became the national music of Argentina.

Things can fall apart, or threaten to, for many reasons, and then there's got to be a leap of faith. Ultimately, when you're at the edge, you have to go forward or backward; if you go forward, you have to jump together.

When you learn something from people, or from a culture, you accept it as a gift, and it is your lifelong commitment to preserve it and build on it.

## JACK YOUNGBLOOD (Athlete, 1950 -)

Good luck is a residue of preparation.

I think we all want to be remembered for what we did.

I visualize things in my mind before I have to do them. It's like having a mental workshop.

You learn that, whatever you are doing in life, obstacles don't matter very much. Pain or other circumstances can be there, but if you want to do a job bad enough, you'll find a way to get it done.

## HENNY YOUNGMAN (Comedian, 1906-1998)

A self-taught man usually has a poor teacher and a worse student.

I once wanted to become an atheist, but I gave up - they have no holidays.

I've got all the money I'll ever need, if I die by four o'clock.

What's the use of happiness? It can't buy you money.

My wife dresses to kill. She cooks the same way.

A doctor gave a man six months to live. The man couldn't pay his bill, so he gave him another six months.

The secret of a happy marriage remains a secret.

A Jewish woman had two chickens. One got sick, so the woman made chicken soup out of the other one to help the sick one get well.

Do you know what it means to come home at night to a woman who'll give you a little love, a little affection, a little tenderness? It means you're in the wrong house, that's what it means.

How to drive a guy crazy: send him a telegram and on the top put 'page 2.'

I know a man who doesn't pay to have his trash taken out. How does he get rid of his trash? He gift wraps it, and puts in into an unlocked car.

I take my wife everywhere, but she keeps finding her way back.

I told the doctor I broke my leg in two places. He told me to quit going to those places.

I've been in love with the same woman for forty-one years. If my wife finds out, she'll kill me.

If you had your life to live over again, do it overseas.

If you're going to do something tonight that you'll be sorry for tomorrow morning, sleep late.

My brother was a lifeguard in a car wash.

My son complains about headaches. I tell him all the time, when you get out of bed, it's feet first!

Take my wife... Please!

That was the first time I saw a horse start from a kneeling position!
The horse I bet on was so slow, the jockey kept a diary of the trip.
This man used to go to school with his dog. Then they were
      separated. His dog graduated!
When God sneezed, I didn't know what to say.
When I read about the evils of drinking, I gave up reading.
When I told my doctor I couldn't afford an
      operation, he offered to touch-up my X-rays.
Why do Jewish divorces cost so much? They're worth it.
Why do Jewish men die before their wives? They want to.
Why don't Jews drink? It interferes with their suffering.
You can't buy love, but you can pay heavily for it.
You have a ready wit. Tell me when it's ready.
You look like a talent scout for a cemetery.

## EDWARD ZANDER (Businessman, 1947 - )

It's never as good as it feels, and it's never as bad as it seems.

## FRANK ZAPPA (Musician, 1940-1993)

There is more stupidity than hydrogen in the universe, and it
      has a longer shelf life.
Music is always a commentary on society.
The United States is a nation of laws: badly written and randomly enforced.
Without deviation progress is not possible.
It isn't necessary to imagine the world ending in fire or ice. There are
      two other possibilities: one is paperwork, and the other is nostalgia.
Without music to decorate it, time is just a bunch of boring production
      deadlines or dates by which bills must be paid.
You can't always write a chord ugly enough to say what you want to say,
      so sometimes you have to rely on a giraffe filled with whipped cream.
You can't be a real country unless you have a beer and an airline. It
      helps if  you have some kind of a football team, or some
      nuclear weapons, but at the very least you need a beer.
A composer is a guy who goes around forcing his will on unsuspecting air
      molecules, often with the assistance of unsuspecting musicians.
All the good music has already been written by people with wigs and stuff.
Art is making something out of nothing and selling it.
Communism doesn't work because people like to own stuff.
Everybody believes in something and everybody, by virtue of the
      fact that they believe in something, uses that something to
      support their own existence.
I searched for years I found no love. I'm sure that love will never
      be a product of plasticity.
If you want to get laid, go to college. If you want an education, go to the library.
Most people wouldn't know music if it came up and bit them on the ass.
Most rock journalism is people who can't write, interviewing people who
      can't talk, for people who can't read.
Music, in performance, is a type of sculpture. The air in the
      performance is sculpted into something.
No change in musical style will survive unless it is accompanied
      by a change in clothing style. Rock is to dress up to.

One of my favorite philosophical tenets is that people will agree with you only if
they already agree with you. You do not change people's minds.

I never set out to be weird. It was always other people who called me weird.

Politics is the entertainment branch of industry.

The computer can't tell you the emotional story. It can give you the exact
mathematical design, but what's missing is the eyebrows.

There are more love songs than anything else. If songs could make you do
something we'd all love one another.

## ZIG ZIGLAR (motivational speaker, author, 1926 - )

Money won't make you happy... but everybody wants to find out for themselves.

People often say that motivation doesn't last. Well, neither does
bathing - that's why we recommend it daily.

It was character that got us out of bed, commitment that moved us
into action, and discipline that enabled us to follow through.

It's not what you've got, it's what you use that makes a difference.

Little men with little minds and little imaginations go through life in little ruts,
smugly resisting all changes which would jar their little worlds.

Many marriages would be better if the husband and the wife clearly
understood that they are on the same side.

The way you see people is the way you treat them.

When you are tough on yourself, life is going to be infinitely easier on you.

You can have everything in life you want, if you will just help other
people get what they want.

People don't buy for logical reasons. They buy for emotional reasons.

People who have good relationships at home are more effective in the marketplace.

If you want to reach a goal, you must "see the reaching" in your own
mind before you actually arrive at your goal.

Money isn't the most important thing in life, but it's reasonably close
to oxygen on the "gotta have it" scale.

Positive thinking will let you do everything better than negative thinking will.

Remember that failure is an event, not a person.

Sometimes adversity is what you need to face in order to become successful.

Statistics suggest that when customers complain, business owners and
managers ought to get excited about it. The complaining customer
represents a huge opportunity for more business.

Success is dependent upon the glands - sweat glands.

Success is the maximum utilization of the ability that you have.

The foundation stones for a balanced success are honesty,
character, integrity, faith, love and loyalty.

You cannot climb the ladder of success dressed in the costume of failure.

You cannot perform in a manner inconsistent with the way you see yourself.

You cannot tailor-make the situations in life but you can tailor-make the
attitudes to fit those situations.

You do not pay the price of success, you enjoy the price of success.

You were born to win, but to be a winner, you must plan to win,
prepare to win, and expect to win.

Your attitude, not your aptitude, will determine your altitude

A goal properly set is halfway reached.

A lot of people quit looking for work as soon as they find a job.

Building a better you is the first step to building a better America.

Every choice you make has an end result.
Every obnoxious act is a cry for help.
Expect the best. Prepare for the worst. Capitalize on what comes.
Failure is a detour, not a dead-end street.
I believe that being successful means having a balance of success stories
across the many areas of your life. You can't truly be considered
successful in your business life if your home life is in shambles.
If God would have wanted us to live in a permissive society He would have
given us Ten Suggestions and not Ten Commandments.
If you can dream it, then you can achieve it. You will get all you want in
life if you help enough other people get what they want.
If you don't see yourself as a winner, then you cannot perform as a winner.
If you go looking for a friend, you're going to find they're very scarce. If
you go out to be a friend, you'll find them everywhere.
If you learn from defeat, you haven't really lost.
If you treat your wife like a thoroughbred, you'll never end up with a nag.

# SENECA-SECOR TITLES

To learn more about our book titles and other products, or to inquire about publishing with SENECA-SECOR BOOKS, please go to our website at www.seneca-secor.com.

# BOOKS BY JIM DURIGA

**DEVILS, DRAGONS, AND OTHER THINGS** - with J.A. Hayhurst and Michael Duriga (cover design by Robert Mortenson and James Duriga); released in 1972 by *Caleen Enterprises*; saddle stitched, 58pp; poetry, cartoons, artwork.

**UP ON BLACKHAWK HILL** - released in 1973 by *Caleen Enterprises*; perfect bound, 112pp; poetry, cartoons, artwork, photographs.

**OCTOBER WORDS** - released in 1975 by *Seneca-Secor Books*; perfect bound, 77pp; poetry, cartoons, artwork. Reviewed the same year by Ohioana Quaterly.

**TRAVELING AT WARP 7: IN SEARCH OF STAR TREK** - first edition released in 1979, second edition released in 1982, third edition released in 1998, fourth edition released in 1999, fifth edition released in 2005, 6th edition released in 2010;by *Seneca-Secor Books*; perfect bound, 282pp; personal views, interviews, & Star Trek information.

**SKETCHBOOK** - with M.A. Foote; released in 1980 by *Seneca-Secor Books*; saddle stitched, 54pp; poetry, artwork.

**TRAVELING ON THE EDGE OF TIME** - released in 1980 by *Seneca-Secor Books*; perfect bound, 53pp; poetry, artwork, photographs.

**THE UNICORN AND THE RAM** - released in 1980 by *Seneca-Secor Books*; perfect bound, 55pp; poetry, artwork, photographs.

**ELIPISON ERANDI: CONCORDIUM OF PLANETS** -released in 1980 by *Seneca-Secor Books*; perfect bound, 127pp; Science Fiction Stories

**THE HOLLYWOOD LEROY** - released in 1982 by *Seneca-Secor Books*; Saddle Stitched, 16pp; cartoons.

**SAGA OF THE LOST GENERATION** - released in 1982 by *Seneca-Secor Books*; saddle stitched, 22pp; poetry.

**THE CUSTER MANIFESTO** - original hardback version; released in 1987 by *Seneca-Secor Books*; hardback; 209pp; Alternate Universe Fiction.

**THEAMERIGAMERICA HANDBOOK** - book on using the commodore Amiga 500/2000 computer;released in 1990 by *Seneca-Secor Books*; comb bound; 152pp; Computer information and workarounds.

**THE LEROY COLLECTION** - released in 1992 by *Seneca-Secor Books*; perfect bound & comb bound versions; 60pp; cartoons.

**THE LAST POEM: AND OTHER FABLES** - released in 1993 by *Seneca-Secor Books*; perfect bound & comb bound versions; 60pp; poetry, artwork, photographs

**CENTERLINES AND OCTOBER WORDS** -released in 1995 by *Seneca-Secor Books*; perfect bound; 110 pp; Poetry, artwork

**THE PROVERBIAL LEROY** - released in 1995 by *Seneca-Secor Books*; perfect bound; 151 pp; cartoons.

**THE UNOFFICIAL KERN COUNTY GUIDE** - released in 1996 by *Seneca-Secor Books*; updated version with Ted Shine co-writing written in 1998; comb bound;186pp; Information about business and things to do in Kern County, California.

**THE KERN COUNTY TRIVIA BOOK** - released in 1998 by *Seneca-Secor Books*; perfect bound;110pp; Facts and trivia about Kern County,California.

**THE CUSTER MANIFESTO** - revised paperback version; released in 1999 by *Seneca-Secor Books*; perfect bound; 226pp; Alternate Universe Fiction.

**WOODSTOCK DAYDREAMS AND BAKERSFIELD SUNSETS** - released in 2000 by *Seneca-Secor Books*; (Prerelease in 1999 of 100 copies); perfect bound; 217pp; poetry, artwork.

**BEYOND THE CROSS** - released in 2002 by *Seneca-Secor Books*; perfect bound 268 pp; Analysis of Religion, Atheism, etc. One person's effort do answer questions about religion.

**A WALKING CONTRADICTION** - released in 2003 by *Seneca-Secor Books*; perfect bound; 75pp; poetry, photographs.

**TREKKIES, TREKKERS, AND RED SHIRTS; Fans, Dealers, and Supporting Actors in the World of Star Trek** (With Margaret Duriga and Laura Duriga) - released in 1992 by *Seneca-Secor Books*; perfect bound 60pp; Star Trek interviews.

**THE MONKEES - AN OUTSIDER'S RETROSPECTIVE** - released in 2010 by *Seneca-Secor Books*; perfect bound; 270pp; book about the 60s group *THE MONKEES*.(Originally planned for release in 2005 but withdrawn for updates and changes) Second edition released in 2012.

**THE GAS AND ENERGY SAVER'S HANDBOOK** - released in 2010 by *Seneca-Secor Books*; perfect bound; 60pp; tips and tricks for saving fuel and energy.

**NO GRACEFUL AGING** - released in 2010 by *Seneca-Secor Books*; perfect bound; 257pp; Poetry, photographs, cartoons, short stories, artwork

**JUST SAY U.N.C.L.E.** - released in 2010 by *Seneca-Secor Books*; perfect bound; 150 pp; A Look at **The Man From U.N.C.L.E.** a 1960s TV phenomenon.

**'WHAT IF" TELEVISION PARODIES** - released in 2010 by *Seneca-Secor Books*; perfect bound; 132 pp; A collection of TV parodies and 'what ifs.'

**TV EXPOSED** - released in 2010 by *Seneca-Secor Books*; perfect bound; 176 pp; TV Trivia about 33 great programs (*M*A*SH, All In The Family, Cheers, Seinfeld, Bonanza, WKRP, Taxi, Bewitched, I Dream of Jeannie, Gilligan's Island, Green Acres*, and more).

**THE GREAT AMERICAN QUOTE BOOK** - released in 2012 by *Seneca-Secor Books*; Perfect Bound, 312 pp; collection of quotes by over 300 famous Americans.

**LEFTOVERS** - released in 2012 by *Seneca-Secor Books*; Perfect Bound, 185pp; Poetry.

TELEVISION CROSSOVERS WE'VE NEVER SEEN - Released in 2012 by *Seneca-Secor Books*; Perfect Bound, 212 pp. (TV parodies).

# Anthologies which include Jim Duriga's work

**OF THEE I SING** - Poetry anthology released in 1975 by *New Dawn Publications*; perfect bound, 116pp; edited by Noel Alvin Gardner poetry, clipart. Includes one poem by Jim Duriga

**POETRY, COAST TO COAST** - Poetry anthology released in 1976 by *Manitou Publishing*, perfect bound, 116pp; edited by C.K. Luden poetry. Includes one poem by Jim Duriga

**SLATE GRAY POETRY** - Duriga edited and had one poem in this anthology released in 1993 by *Seneca-Secor Books*; perfectbound and comb bound versions; 28pp; Poetry.

**SANDSTONE AND STARSHINE - THE 1997 SENECA-SECOR POETRY ANTHOLOGY** - Duriga edited and had several poem in this collection; released in 1997 by *Seneca-Secor Books*; perfect bound; 114pp; Poetry, art.

**DOLPHINS AND TIN CANS - THE 1998 SENECA-SECOR POETRY ANTHOLOGY** - Duriga edited and had several poems in this collection; released in 1998 by *Seneca-Secor Books*; perfect bound; 105pp. Poetry, Art

**THE SENECA-SECOR SCI-FI ANTHOLOGY** - Originally released as **The Year 2000 Seneca-Secor Sci-fi Anthology**, but title changed in 2002 - Science Fiction articles by several writers; Duriga edited the collection and has some work within.

## Other Seneca-Secor Books

**Ginsing** by Jerry Czerbak; released in 1977 by *Seneca-Secor Books*; about the Ginsing herb.

**THE UNDECIDED 98%: The Research Community** by Margaret A. Foote - released in 1977 by *Panda Press Books*; perfect bound; 200pp. Book about the Research community.

**WORDS OF THE HEART** by Everett Alexander - released in 1982 by *Seneca-Secor Books*; perfect bound; 100pp. Poetry

**THE CHRISTIAN POET** by Ernest Trussell - released in 1997 by *Seneca-Secor Books*; perfect bound; poetry; 153pp.

**SOME MARRIAGES WERE MADE IN HEAVEN -SOME LIVED IN HELL** by Ruth Kelly - released in 1998 by *Seneca-Secor Books*; perfect bound; autobiography; 146pp.

**THE FLESH** by Gregary A. Moses - released in 1998 by *Seneca-Secor Books*; perfect bound; religious themes; 112pp.

**BIBLE FACTS** by Ted Shine - released in 1998 by *Seneca-Secor Books*; perfect bound; poetry; 108pp. Bible Trivia

**A FISHER OF MEN** by Ernest Trussell - released in 1999 by *Seneca-Secor Books*; perfect bound; poetry; 164pp.

**THE PATH I CHOSE** by Tina Morgan Cook - released in 1999 by *Seneca-Secor Books*; perfect bound; poetry; 139pp.

**FROM BELOW SEA LEVEL** by Marguerite Walks - released in 2000 by *Seneca-Secor Books*; perfect bound; poetry; 151 pp.Autobiography. (NOTE: MS. Walks - later issued an independent version of this book to give her more distribution control).

**THE DOOR OF SADNESS** by Harriet Berquist Kenniger - released in 2000 by *Seneca-Secor Books*; perfect bound; 43pp. Poetry

**MOTHER GOOSE GETS A MAKEOVER** by Harriet Berquist Kenniger - released in 2000 by *Seneca-Secor Books*; perfect bound; 36pp. Satire

**NON BURGERS - VEGETABLE SIDES** by Margaret Duriga - released in 2000 by *Seneca-Secor Books*; perfect bound; 92pp. Cookbook.

**NOTHING RHYMES WITH SOMETHING** by Walter Stormont - released in 2000 by *Seneca-Secor Books*; perfect bound; 108pp. Poetry

**HITLER HERE** by George Thomas Clark - released in 2003 by *Seneca-Secor Books*; perfect bound; Historical Novel; 500+ pp. (Later editions of this book were released by Mr. Thomas' own publishing firm).

**OUTLIVING FLYNN** by George Thomas Clark - released in 2003 by *Seneca-Secor Books*; perfect bound; short stories; 150 pp.(Later editions of this book were released by Mr. Thomas' own publishing firm).

**THE LIGHTER SIDE OF SCI-FI** by Tye Bourdony released in 2010 by *Seneca-Secor Books*; perfect bound; Sci-Fi Cartoons; 100pp.

**THE PUBLIC DOMAIN JOKE BOOK** by Judy Perkins released in 2010 by *Seneca-Secor Books*; perfect bound; Jokes and Cartoons; 70pp.